TV NOIR

DARK DRAMA ON
THE SMALL SCREEN

TV NOIR

DARK DRAMA ON THE SMALL SCREEN

Allen Glover

ABRAMS, NEW YORK

Cataloging-in-Publication Data is available from the Library of Congress

Book design and typeformatting by Bernard Schleifer
Printed in China

ISBN: 978-1-59020-167-1

10 9 8 7 6 5 4 3 2 1

Abrams books are available at special discounts when purchased in quantity for
premiums and promotions as well as fundraising or educational use.
Special editions can also be created to specification. For details, contact
specialsales@abramsbooks.com or the address below.

Abrams ® is a registered trademark of Harry N. Abrams, Inc.

ABRAMS The Art of Books
195 Broadway, New York, NY 10007
abramsbooks.com

For my parents

CONTENTS

INTRODUCTION:
Lights Out in the Wasteland

It is a not a fragrant world, but it is the world you live in, and certain writers with tough minds and a cool spirit of detachment can make very interesting and even amusing patterns out of it.

—Raymond Chandler

I

To label a work as noir is to acknowledge a delicate tension among its elements. Story and style, coupled with tone and theme, point us toward a distinct sensibility. Call it a worldliness, a sardonic gaze—a familiarity with the dark night of the soul. The narrative bias, if not the bleak core, of the prototypical noir story has its origins in the hardboiled literary tradition, specifically the detective fiction of Dashiell Hammett and Raymond Chandler. Both came up through the pulps. A colloquial sense of the underworld, a sort of urban coarseness, distinguishes their work. Its setting is the dark American city, a place of corruption and venality teeming with femmes fatales, rapacious gangsters, beleaguered policemen, perfidious husbands, deceitful wives, grasping losers, deviants, and thugs. Surviving such an unruly and ungodly realm requires cynical determination, a steely reserve, and a moral stance of some fluidity—the chief characteristics of Hammett's Continental Op (introduced in *Black Mask* in 1923) and Sam Spade (*The Maltese Falcon*, 1930). These are tough operators whose business is trouble. "This is my city and this is my game," Spade announces in *The Maltese Falcon*.

Chandler's detective stories, in contrast to Hammett's objective style and lapidary prose, follow a first-person narrative rich in melancholic metaphor. His Philip Marlowe is a knightly figure, honorable but disillusioned, adrift in a world in which "knights had no meaning," as Marlowe admits in Chandler's most famous work, *The Big Sleep* (1939). Knocked about and pushed around, lied to by nearly everyone, pressured by client and cop alike, Marlowe is tightly wound up in his investigations. To traverse this morally perilous terrain, he abides by a code of honor and resilience. "He is the hero, he is everything," Chandler explained. The same cannot be said of the lecherous, greedy lot that James M. Cain put into play in works like *Double Indemnity* (1936) and *The Postman Always Rings Twice* (1934), the sordid nature of which provoked scandal in prewar America. Cain's open-eyed chronicles of lust turned deadly illuminate the titillating aspect of noir—its signature conflation of desire and violence.

OPPOSITE PAGE: *Altered Carbon* (2017) with Joel Kinnaman.

Films made from the works of these writers were among the wave of Hollywood pictures released in Paris following World War II. The taxonomic tag applied to them by French cinéastes is appropriately stark: film noir, or black film. What Nino Frank and Jean-Pierre Chartier separately responded to in 1946, in pieces appearing in politically opposed journals, was a new attitude in American moviemaking marked by the "dynamism of violent death" (Frank) and streaked with a "pessimism and disgust toward humanity" (Chartier). Ever since film noir entered Anglo-American criticism in the late 1960s, the debate has raged as to whether it constitutes a genre, a movement, an attitude, or a style. Alfred Appel, writing in *Film Comment* in 1974, suggested that "what unites the seemingly disparate kinds of films noirs [is] their black vision of despair, loneliness, and dread—a vision that touches an audience most intimately because it assures them that their suppressed impulses and fears are shared human responses." Pushed into darkness, made aware of the world as a place of danger and death, the disoriented characters of noir seek a return to the light—a truth, a reckoning, some form of absolution.

Among the earliest writers to describe his own work as "noir" (well before it had a fancy name) was Cornell Woolrich, beginning with *The Bride Wore Black* (1940), first in his "black series." Woolrich's is a frightfully unstable universe in which the membrane between light and dark, safety and pitfall, is bound to burst at any time. Hammett, in *The Maltese Falcon*, hints at such volatility with his story-within-a-story of the falling beam that awakens the sleepwalking Flitcraft, who up till then had foolishly believed that life "was a clean orderly sane responsible affair," to the fact "that life was fundamentally none of those things." And Franz Kafka, earlier in the century, wrote of the sudden irreversible horrors that can befall the unsuspecting. But Woolrich shaped his entire oeuvre around a singularly dark and pessimistic worldview in which human existence is dominated by malevolent, impersonal forces. Immensely prolific, he provided the stories for more works of radio, film, and television noir than any other writer of the pulp school. His impact on noir, whether acknowledged or uncredited (his plots and tropes are regularly mimicked), is monumental, and his delineation of the asphalt nightscape endures.

Though the appeal of film noir is quite direct, its essence remains nebulous, particularly when one widens the parameters of its generally agreed-upon timeframe and takes into account the antecedents and the stragglers, as well as its transgeneric infiltration. The artistic and sociological developments that gradually fused into the so-called classic cycle of film noir (1940–1958) also coincided with the emergence of television as a mass medium—a vast arena for the telling of stories. Yet the reams of discourse on film noir have, for the most part, sidestepped any serious discussion of a noir ethos on television. Those works that do address it tend to position television noir as having evolved in the wake of, rather than concurrently with, film noir—a chase-the-tail approach perhaps shaped by the dearth of surviving programs from television's early live phase. The hundreds of live dramas staged on television during the 1940s and 1950s (the first full decades of commercial broadcasting) represent a key dimension of mid-century noir. Alongside adaptations of novels by Woolrich, Chandler, Hammett, David Goodis, W. R. Burnett, Dorothy B. Hughes, and others of the literary noir tradition, a generation of teleplay writers supplied the medium with original tales of American alienation and discontent reflective of an overall darkened cultural mood.

Another factor compounding the classification of television noir is that from the early 1950s, as it became apparent that the networks' model of a "living theatre of the air" was unsustainable, television increasingly became a conduit for filmed series, or telefilms, produced in Hollywood. A substantial portion of the programming within the mosaic of TV noir is but a parallel strain of *filmed* noir, produced and canned in much the same way as theatrical film noir. The noir telefilm has its origins in the "B" films, or lower-bill programmers, churned out by the studios' specialty divisions or along Poverty Row—wellsprings of what we now label film noir. (Comparatively few classic cycle titles could be considered "A" productions.) As "B" product began to fall out of favor with exhibitors, its writers, directors, actors, and cinematographers flooded the emerging telefilm market. By 1952, when *Variety* declared crime drama to be "the most attractive form of television presentations from the point of view of sponsors," more than half of the two dozen such series on the air were made in Hollywood, in many cases by the same filmmakers who had filled cinemas with film noir.

In this regard, the most apparent difference between film and television noir is the matter of delivery: cinema versus living room. Because each draws upon the same dramaturgical principles and visual vocabulary, one can discuss an episode of *Dragnet* (1951–1958) with the same approach to narrative, style, and tone with which one might appraise a "B" noir like *He Walked by Night* (1948). On the other hand, episodic television offers something the movies do not: the time and space to extend a noir premise into countless variations of the same dark tale, told and re-told in different ways. The construction of television noir further veers from that of film noir in that its sustaining format is of a hero whose continuing presence binds the series as whole. With each installment, the hero is expected to address and remedy whatever incident of chaos has disrupted the social order. The adversaries he encounters, colorfully depraved as they may be, begin and end the story on a doomed trajectory; in series television the hero is indeed

"On a Dark Night" (*Schlitz Playhouse of Stars*, 1956).

everything (at least until the 1980s). Outside of the anthology series (live and film) of the 1950s, which largely exempted themselves from this hero paradigm, one would be hard-pressed to find a television protagonist as aberrant or morally compromised as those in films noirs like *Double Indemnity* (1944), *Detour* (1945), *Ride the Pink Horse* (1947), *Gun Crazy* (1950), and *Kiss Me Deadly* (1955).

In their time, before "noir" entered the American lexicon, these films were regarded, by the industry and public alike, as strains of melodrama, with such qualifiers as "suspense-mystery" or "psychological whodunit" as the common shorthand for designating them of a darker nature. The genres most susceptible to the inflection of a noir sensibility—crime stories, police and detective adventures, gangster tales, westerns, works of horror and science fiction—all have their foundation in melodrama, and all can be said to share a heightened (or altered) state of reality, an intensification of human emotion, a preponderance of chance or coincidence in their plotting, and a predilection for violence, escalation, and action. Conflict is at the heart of the melodrama. Its protagonists struggle to overcome obstacles, solve mysteries, evade destruction. Evolving from Victorian-era theatre and literature into the first half of the twentieth century, the modern melodrama acquired, as Richard Schickel has phrased it, "an enlivening dose of the down and dirty—a note of devilishness." Across the narrative arts, such well-trod melodramatic devices as the deadly love triangle, the investigative quest, the journey into the unknown, and the entrapment of the hero began to exude a tenebrous aura, a sense of angst and foreboding, and an attendant smudging of the formerly clean line between good and evil.

In *A Panorama of American Film Noir* (1955), the first full-length study on film noir, Raymond Borde and Etienne Chaumeton attribute this disquieting black vision to a number of sociological influences, notably the grittiness of wartime newsreels, a rise in urban crime rates, and the dramaturgical appropriation of Freudian theory. Themes which had been presented just a few years prior with restraint, sometimes even levity, were now laced with sadism and a cynical regard for social institutions, and delivered to the public with an imprimatur of hard-edged realism. Others agreed: "Of late there has been a trend in Hollywood toward a wholesale production of lusty, hard-boiled, gut-and-gore crime stories, all fashioned on a theme with a combination of plausibly motivated murder and studded with high-powered Freudian implication," wrote Lloyd Shearer in the *New York Times* in 1945. "Hollywood says the moviegoer is getting this type of story because he likes it, and psychologists explain that he likes it because it serves as a violent escape in tune with the violence of the times, a cathartic for pent-up emotions." The development of a dramatic form for television in the 1940s went hand in hand with the larger cultural acceptance of these dark melodramas. In cinema, the assimilation of a noir sensibility marked a subversion of established forms of storytelling; in television, noir was there from the inception.

Indeed, there are seedlings of the emerging sensibility in the very first live staging of a drama for television, *The Queen's Messenger*, shown over W2XB, the experimental station of the General Electric Company, in Schenectady, New York, on September 11, 1928. Set in a lonely house on the outskirts of Berlin, this melodrama of intrigue and downfall tells of a British courier (Maurice Randall) seduced, drugged, and swindled by a vampish Russian spy (Izetta Jewel). *The Queen's Messenger* launched a new form of entertainment—"radio movies," as they were called for a time—yet a decade passed before the technical considerations of television were conducive to large-scale dramatic production. Anticipating the official unveiling of its television service at the 1939 World's Fair, New York–based radio giant NBC began beaming out live plays like *The Three Garridebs* (1937) and *The Mysterious Mummy Case* (1938). These and other three-camera productions staged prior to World War II, when the broadcasting activities of NBC and its rivals CBS and DuMont were put on hiatus, established a methodology for televisual storytelling that would remain in place until the telefilm invasion of the 1950s.

From the beginning, network story departments drew from the same cultural well of narrative properties as Hollywood. A key example is James Warwick's play *Blind Alley*, which pries into the criminal psyche as if it were a cadaver picked apart in the lecture hall of a medical school. *Blind Alley* began on Broadway in 1935, was made into a proto-noir picture in 1939 by Columbia, was presented live by NBC in 1941, was remade by Columbia as *The Dark Past*—by now showing all the markers of film noir—and finally was performed on CBS's *Studio One* in 1949.

The 1941 NBC production is unique in that it was the first drama to be telecast beyond New York, and the last drama to be presented before America's entry into World War II. The premise of *Blind Alley* is that prison escapee Hal Wilson (Charles Furcolowe) has commandeered the home of psychologist Dr. Shelby (Maurice Wells) and his startled family. What follows, as Shelby resolves to take his tormentor's "mind apart and let him see the pieces," is a withering psychological evisceration. Revealing that he was

On the set of *The Queen's Messenger* (1928) with Maurice Randall and Izetta Jewel.

On the set of *The Three Garridebs* (1937).

On the set of *This Gun for Hire* (1942) with W6XYZ chief Klaus Landsberg, Alan Ladd, and Veronica Lake.

ABOVE: *The Streets of New York or, Poverty Is No Crime* (1939).
BELOW: Lobby card for *Television Spy* (film, 1939).

abused as a youth by a criminal father, whose death at the hands of the police he facilitated (and over which he remains plagued with guilt), Wilson disavows his awful life, slinks into the next room, and turns his gat on himself.

Blind Alley's themes of psychosis and suicide, its depictions of brutality and the violation of home, make it a harbinger of the darkness that was to inundate the cinemas and television screens of America. Moreover, it illustrates how a story that begins with a burst of chaos—the intrusion of a villain bringing grim business and sudden death—can be twisted into a scenario of escalating suspense. As a melodramatic device, suspense is integral to the plotting of a noir story. This is how *Variety* described the step-up of events in the 1941 telecast: "After the first few minutes the script is a blend of mounting dread and consistently explosive dramatics, with not a single letdown on the wear and tear of the emotion permitted up to the final curtain." Suspense, at base level, involves giving the viewer a taste of something wicked, further details of which are parceled out selectively until the engorged balloon of tension is given a hearty "pop." In television noir, where the audience must be hooked from the onset lest they change the channel, this game of the tease is deployed mercilessly.

Aligning aberrant compulsions with long-buried trauma, the narrative of *Blind Alley* also anticipates the influx of psychologism into popular culture in the 1940s. The notions of repression and release that course through much of television and film noir are closely related to the theories of Sigmund Freud, disseminated, at least partially, to entertainment industry circles by the waves of German and Austrian émigrés fleeing Hitler. Upon the release of his mood-drenched film *Hangover Square* (1945), John Brahm remarked on how "psychological angles are responsible for the newly acquired dignity of what was once regarded as a rather lowly form of entertainment—the thriller. The skill and technique exercised in treating this type of motion picture have endowed it with heightened interest. Audiences are neither frightened nor awed at psychological stuff anymore." The legacy of Freudian psychoanalysis in noir is profound. Freudianism holds that the journey from infancy to adulthood produces inner wounds which are outwardly manifested in neurotic, obsessive, or deviant behavior. Absorbed into the noir narrative, this principle translates into the transgressive disturbance that incites the noir plot and, after much suspense, is ultimately brought to resolution. The sad path to self-destruction, the transference of a dark past into a present-day liability, the committing of a crime while in a fugue state, and other tropes make noir the most psychologically oriented form of storytelling.

II

Whodunits are a natural for surefire audience response as indicated by radio's Hooper ratings and it doesn't take a swami to foresee a rash of them breaking out on the videolanes.

FOLLOWING ITS ABORTED PREWAR START, TELEVISION RELAUNCHED ITSELF in late 1944. NBC set the standard with an ambitious four-part adaptation of Woolrich's *The Black Angel* (1945), a property selected as much for its dark, psychological tone as for the fact that its author was an exceptionally reliable fountain of stories for radio noir anthologies like *Suspense* (1942–1962) and *The Molle Mystery Theatre* (1943–1954). Early television molded itself on the programming formats that were most popular with a nation of radio listeners, in particular the mystery-suspense anthology, but also the police procedural, the private-eye show, the spy series, and the newspaper noir. Contingent to these generic forms, TV also took from radio its emphasis on mood and characterization, and, significantly, its reductive simplification of plot into easily ingestible (and commercially interruptible) segments. Radio, arriving on the scene around the same time as the talkies, is rarely mentioned among the host of factors that fostered a public demand for darker stories, yet its cultural pervasiveness was at least equal to that of the cinema for most of the 1930s and 1940s.

As a conduit for storytelling, radio had the distinct advantage of being a home appliance, inducing, as Aldous Huxley tartly put it, "a craving for daily or even hourly emotional enemas," an addictive quality later transferred to another household staple, the television set. Radio not only introduced a formulaic approach to narrative construction—timed to the split second to fill a quarter- or half-hour slot—but it filled America's airwaves with a veritable spectrum of lurid crime, psychoneurotic behavior, and horrific undoing. The disturbing and unseemly ambience of radio noir not only prepared American audiences for the noir fictions of film and television, but also inspired the techniques deployed to dramatize a noir story once it left the page. Billy Wilder, for one, admitted that in adapting *Double Indemnity* for the screen, he based the framing device of a voiceover—the dying confession Walter Neff narrates into a dictaphone—on the radio tactic of the interior monologue.

Double Indemnity (1944) with Barbara Stanwyck and Fred MacMurray.

The images conjured by radio noir are just as much the product of the listener's imagination as they are of the verbally doled-out exposition: "Out of the dark of the night, from the shadows of the senses, comes this—the fantasy of fear," intones Peter Lorre as the host of *Nightmare*, one of many noir-infused anthologies. Indeed, the most memorable radio noir hinges on a persuasive evocation of the unknown—darkness, nightfall, shadows, the void. These are stories of inner dread, the dark night of the soul, a milieu made clear in the catchphrases of the Shadow and the Whistler, two of the more popular radio heroes of the era. The Shadow's eerie come-on, "Who knows what evil lurks in the minds of men? The Shadow knows!" is echoed by that of the Whistler: "I am the Whistler and I know many things, for I walk by night. I know many strange tales hidden in the hearts of men and women who have stepped into the shadows." This is also the case with the eponymous narrator of *The Mysterious Traveler*, who arrives by midnight train to the cue of that loneliest of sounds, the wail of a locomotive, to relate the misfortunes of those detoured into a strange and terrifying night world.

Unfolding within a predetermined length, the narratives of radio noir abide by an inexorable fatalism in which death, doom, or some other unpleasantry is unavoidable. In Lucille Fletcher's "Sorry, Wrong Number," first presented by *Suspense* in 1942, Agnes Moorehead is a bedridden invalid who overhears, via crossed telephone wires, two men plotting to murder a woman within the next thirty minutes. Her efforts to alert the authorities, who dismiss her as a pest, prove fruitless. Frustration blossoms into hysteria as the appointed hour nears. Too late, she learns that the death being planned is her own (her husband has arranged it). The program ends with the memorable snap of a mortal coil: the resounding click of the phone receiver, the woman's lifeline, returned to its place by the arriving killers. By popular demand, "Sorry, Wrong Number" became a perennial on CBS radio, was translated into multiple languages, and was made into a film noir of the same name (1948).

In 1946, the television wing of CBS mounted a live video version of the story with Mildred Natwick in the lead. The reactions of the handful of television reviewers active at the time indicate not only an awareness of an emerging noir style, but the expectation that its expressionistic flourishes would be applied to specific types of stories. Judy Dupuy of *Televiser*, for instance, diagnosed a dilution of tension in the transfer of the story from radio to television, a condition she attributed to "in-

Publicity still for *The Shadow* (radio, 1937) with Orson Welles.

Sorry, Wrong Number (radio, 1943) with Agnes Moorehead.

adequate visual nuances in support of the woman's growing fears," namely a lack of "unusual camera angles." Along with her colleagues at *Variety* and *Billboard*, Dupuy was disappointed at how the famous ending was blocked, complaining that it "actually showed a man coming into the woman's bedroom instead of implying his entrance by showing the door opening and a shadow in the background." Industry journal *Telescreen*, on the other hand, critiqued the production not for its absence of symbolic imagery but rather for its intrusiveness in telling "a disturbing story which left a gruesome atmosphere hovering in the living room."

Another radio noir of significance is the anthology *Lights Out* (1934–1947), which thrived on placing its listeners inside the heads of the unbalanced and the fear-stricken. Wyllis Cooper, who created the series, and Arch Oboler, who later took over as head writer, pioneered a variety of expressionistic aural tactics (overlapping first-person voiceovers, booming voices from the dead) and complex narrative designs (extended flashbacks, dreams within dreams), all techniques later identified with film noir, to expose the tattered psyches of their characters. This "imagery" of sound yielded some truly unsettling set pieces, like a creeping mist that emerges from the night to turn people inside out, or a condemned murderer describing, in grave detail, the process of his own execution. *Lights Out* is testimony to the power of suggestion—the gripping dread of sitting alone in the dark—aided in no small part by the bond between the medium and the public. The radio listener, Oboler observed, "was as close to the performer as the microphone was to the performer."

In 1946, when NBC first brought *Lights Out* to television, this intimacy was translated into the video close-up, and the whisper into the ear of the rapt radio listener evolved into the piercing gaze of the video actor that greeted the transfixed viewer. "First Person Singular" (1946), the first *Lights Out* to air, was adapted by Cooper from one of his radio scripts and directed by Fred Coe. It takes us inside the head of a husband (Carl Frank) who strangles his nagging wife (Mary Wilsey) on a sweltering summer night when the whole town seems ready to blow. The wife-killer is never shown: what he sees and hears as he contemplates and carries out his crime, and is then hanged for it, is entirely conveyed through a first-person camera. This subjective mode, with its necessarily limited perspective, amplifies the air of claustrophobia and inescapable fate to offer a heightened reality crucial to the noir style. Six months after this broadcast, cinema-goers would marvel at the same use of subjective camera in *Lady in the Lake* (1947), a film noir directed by Robert Montgomery.

Publicity still for *Lights Outs* (radio, ca. 1938).

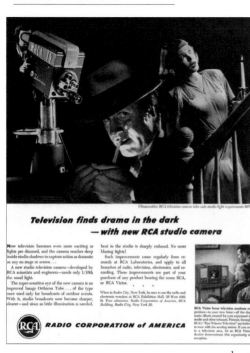

Advertisement for the Image-Orthicon, RCA (1946).

Many early television noirs utilized the subjective possibilities of the live video feed. In *Volume One* (ABC, 1949), a six-part series produced and written by Cooper, the camera is made an active participant in the plot. Its premiere installment, "No. 1," is an unsettling exercise in voyeurism in which the television frame doubles as the mirror over the bureau in a cheap hotel room. Floyd (Jack Lescoulie) and Georgia (Nancy Sheridan) have holed up there after robbing a bank. For the next thirty minutes, we're privy to what the mirror "sees"—and what is reflected back into it, and therefore onto our screen, is the psychological dissolution of this fugitive couple. Already on edge for having killed a guard to make their getaway, Floyd and Georgia become further unnerved when they discover that the door to their room is locked from the outside. Their gun goes missing, as does the loot they have stolen. Rather than the food, cigarettes, and matches they've requested, Milty (Frank Thomas, Jr.), the creepy bellhop, instead brings them a week-old newspaper and an incomplete deck of cards. A blaring siren, discordantly merged with loud bursts of Dixieland street music, further exacerbates their paranoia.

A great deal of "No. 1" is played directly to the viewer, such as when Georgia nervously fusses with her lipstick in stark concave close-up, as if to destabilize the viewing experience. Under mounting pressure, Floyd excitedly charges that he feels he's being spied upon and accusingly swings at the camera-mirror; thereafter, our screen is splintered. Everything has gone wrong for these criminals, and in the end they're simply swallowed by the camera-mirror itself, an indefinite conclusion that undoubtedly left viewers groping for a plausible explanation. At this juncture, with television on the verge of becoming a national enterprise, such narrative adventurousness was applauded. "This may be the program television has been waiting for to show those potentialities inherent in video which no other medium can duplicate," wrote *Billboard*. "A mood of tension and growing terror was unquestionably abetted by the stark set and the use of nearly shrill black and white light and shadow effects."

The chiaroscuro imagery of *Volume One* and other live video noirs was made possible by the introduction in 1946 of the Image-Orthicon, a television camera requiring a mere foot-candle of light for exposure. Scenes demanding expressive atmospherics could now, as its developer RCA proclaimed, successfully "be illuminated only by a match flame or a lit cigarette." Along with promoting a low-key style, the Orthicon, with its superior pictorial definition, changed the way television itself was perceived. The cinema may have had its broader canvas, its larger-than-life pictures, but the Orthicon delivered a lifelike experience. Coupled with high-fidelity FM sound, dramas staged before the hungry eye of the Orthicon were delivered to the viewer without any distortions, interferences, or interpretation. Moreover, the intimate scale and sense of simultaneity attendant to viewing a live production served to psychologically bind the audience to the actors and the story.

Noir tells its stories of confusion and anxiety through images that darken and disorient the narrative. The high-noir style, which has its roots in Germanic expressionism, amounts to a personified and exaggerated representation of reality. Lotte Eisner, the preeminent film critic of 1920s Berlin, defined this as "subjectivism driven to extreme"; expressionism, in its purest form as practiced in the art and cinema of prewar Europe, was generally correlated to conditions of madness, trauma, and deviance. The *Stimmung*, or mood, on display in *The Cabinet of Dr. Caligari* (1920), perhaps the most influential of German silent films, is directly calibrated to the perspective of a diseased, unstable mind. Leaping from the sound stages of Ufa to the factories of Hollywood, absorbed into a wealth of generic forms (crime, horror, gothic, gangster), the Caligari-esque touch gained distinct visual associations appropriate to scenarios of personal doom—a shorthand for conveying the bedeviling, infectious sting of the night world.

"Green Light" (*Breaking Bad*, 2010).

Style in noir works as a participatory element shaping characters' actions and our interpretations of them. In "Notes on Film Noir" (1971), Paul Schrader writes of how "light enters the dingy rooms of film noir in such odd shapes—jagged trapezoids, obtuse triangles, vertical slits—that one suspects the windows were cut with a pen knife. No character can speak authoritatively from a space which is continually cut into ribbons of light." Combined with environmental signifers (cityscapes, smoky rooms) and iconographic ones (mirrors, staircases) and mingled with the similarly evocative idioms of French poetic realism, this distinct visual lexicon welled into a repository of dark and fatalistic imagery from which, decades on, the makers of film and television noir continue to draw. The starkness of the expressionistic image, its ability to convey with precision the most ambiguous of conditions, made it ideal for the small screen, which remained monochromatic far past the point that the movies went to color. Of 1950s television noir, *Peter Gunn*

"Free For All" (*The Prisoner*, 1967).

(1958–1961), *Staccato* (1959–1960), and *The Twilight Zone* (1959–1964) in particular invoke this style to create a half-world of endless shadows, threatening shapes, and constant danger.

To tangle with the night is to put oneself at the mercy of its ecology. Menacing shadows (literal and figurative) are a constant presence for the scrambling heroes and lonely seekers of noir. "Sordid or strange, death always emerges at the end of a tortuous journey," Borde and Chaumeton write in *A Panorama of American Film Noir*. "Film noir is a film of death, in all senses of the word." Or consider this passage from *The Black Alibi* (1942) in which Woolrich likens the circadian rhythms of night and day to the cycle of chaos and order so central to the noir narrative:

> A breathless hush hung over everything, awaiting the arrival of the greatest killer of them all: night; remorselessly tracking down day and slaughtering it, every twenty-four hours, over and over again. The eternal murder, unpunished, unprevented.

The equation of death with darkness is ageless. From ancient times the night has held mystery, secrets, gloom; it is the great unknown, the well of human fear. Light is life, the day, a realm of clarity and comfort, while night, its enemy, is synonymous with the unavoidable end, the last reach of the spectrum. Noir pushes the struggle against death to the forefront, makes it palatable and urgent. The denizens of noir, even those who dispense the fatal ace of spades, strive mightily to avoid the final kiss-off, the black sack, the big sleep. The intrusion of darkness and chaos into the ordinary world sounds an alarm. Given a taste of death, the noir protagonist springs to action: the night journey begins.

LIVE
NOIR

LIVE NOIR I:
THE BLACK ANGEL (1945)
AND OTHER EARLY MELODRAMA

> Oh, it was so dark along this street. Just that hooded, half-dimmed
> light on the other side, too far behind me to do any good any more.
> —Cornell Woolrich, *The Black Angel*

T*HE BLACK ANGEL*, FOURTH IN CORNELL WOOLRICH'S "BLACK SERIES," IS
the basis for television's first serialized drama—a cornerstone of TV
noir. Like many of Woolrich's stories, it is both a clock-race mystery
and a chronicle of a heroine's passage through a heretofore unrevealed world.
Alberta Murray, played by Mary Patton, is twenty-two, a content newlywed until
the day her husband Kirk stops calling her by her pet name, "Angel Face." Fearing the worst, Alberta tracks down the "other woman," Mia Mercer, only to find
that she's been murdered. When Kirk is convicted of the crime and sentenced
to death, Alberta sets out to prove his innocence. Her clues in this endeavor,
surreptitiously lifted from the crime scene, are a matchbook monogrammed
"M" and the four corresponding "M" names (excepting her husband's) in Mia's
little black book: Marty, Mordaunt, Mason, and McKee. Through masquerade,
deceit, and manipulation, Alberta insinuates herself into the lives of each suspect until she finds the real killer.

Unfolding episodically, in self-contained vignettes that add up to a larger
whole, Woolrich's novel, published in 1943, is a marvel of structured suspense.
Each of the four men, Alberta discovers, had good reason to off Mia. In attach-
ing herself to them, Alberta in effect replaces her deceased rival, of whom a
policeman warns, "You're not her type; you wouldn't know how to handle these
people." Discarding the advice (as in most Woolrich stories, the police are dis-
pensable until needed), Alberta sets off through "a world of jungle violence
and of darkness, of strange hidden deeds in strange hidden places, of sharp-
clawed treachery and fanged gratitude." Having begun the story as a sheltered
innocent, she concludes her quest for marital restitution thoroughly de-
spoiled and with considerable carnage in her wake. Infected by the sordid,
corruptive world in which her husband became entangled, Alberta merely
spreads things around.

Presented over four Sundays in early 1945 by NBC's flagship station,
WNBT, *The Black Angel* marked the reactivation of the network's "live talent"
unit after a war-imposed hiatus. In seizing upon Woolrich's book, as of yet un-

OPPOSITE: On the set of *The Black Angel* (1945) with Mary Patton.

On the set of *The Black Angel* (1945) with Paul Conrad and Mary Patton.

discovered by Hollywood, the network sought to align its ambitious slate of forthcoming dramatic productions with a type of dark melodrama already proved popular on radio, and quickly gaining momentum in cinema. Ernest Colling, the NBC writer-director tasked with bringing the property to television, described it as "a natural for television production inasmuch as it is a psychological drama and therefore perfectly adaptable to the new medium." Colling's teleplay, unlike Universal's subsequent film version (*Black Angel*, 1946), is near-faithful to its source, with the novel's four central chapters comprising the four episodes of the television serial: "Heartbreak," "Dr. Death," "Playboy," and "The Last Name."

The first "M" is Marty Blair (Karl Swenson), Mia's abandoned, alcoholic husband. Alberta tracks him down in the Bowery, in a grimy tavern beneath the shadow of the El, still pining for the wife who crossed him out of her life. Apparently intent on drinking himself into oblivion, he's known as "Heartbreak" around skid row. "Dr. Death" finds Alberta taking over Mia's route as a heroin courier for the seedy Dr. Mordaunt (Vinton Hayworth), who dispatches her on an all-night mission through the lower depths of the city. Having determined that neither of these two is complicit in Mia's murder, Alberta moves on, in "Playboy," to the wealthy, charming bon vivant Ladd Mason (Philip Foster), who falls madly in love with her. Finally, in "The Last Name," Alberta uses her feminine wiles and cumulative experience to worm her way into the affairs of underworld kingpin Jerome McKee (Richard Keith). This last arrangement turns ugly when McKee, after presenting Alberta with an engagement ring, catches her in several lies and orders his goons, Skeeter (Paul Conrad) and Kittens (Don Grusso), to "handle her."

Escaping, Alberta arrives home to find Mason sulking in a dark corner, agitated and lovesick. In the row that ensues, Mason, the least despicable of the suspects (Woolrich was an ace at misdirection), reveals himself to be the true murderer, albeit one whose recollection of the killing remains hazy for neurasthenic reasons. Upon learning who Alberta really is, and that she's tricked him into a confession, Mason throws himself from a window. Colling ends his teleplay here, with Alberta now able to parlay Mason's death-scene revelation into exoneration for her husband. Woolrich continues the novel with a brief but disturbing coda entitled, as if to promote the cinematic quality of his writing, "Closing Scene": wrapped in her husband's embrace, Alberta longingly dreams of Mason, with whom she's secretly, perversely, fallen in love. "The door was all but closed now," she describes. "I could still see just the outline of his face slowly dimming behind it. My arms strained out in helpless appeal, while I kept calling after him, more loudly, more heartbrokenly with every breath, 'Don't leave me behind! Don't leave me behind!'"

The Black Angel is unique among Woolrich's "black series" in that it's told from the first-person perspective of his heroine, the effect of which, as his biographer, Francis M. Nevins, Jr., has pointed out, is that we are "trapped inside the narrator's warped soul, knowing everything she knows, feeling everything she feels, her terror and desperation and murderous obsession growing like a cancer within." "I was alone," Alberta admits, early in the novel, "a lost, frightened thing straying around, my whole world crumbling away all around me like the shell of an egg." We are also privy to the erosion of Alberta's innocence, her growing awareness of the world as no longer a place of light but of pitiless darkness. "This was it now," she relays as she scours the Bowery for Marty Blair. "The lowest depths of all, this side the grave. There was nothing beyond this, nothing further. Nothing came after it—only death, the river. These were not human beings any more. These were shadows." Having penetrated the noir world, Alberta continues on, undeterred in her determination "to make contact and fasten myself onto them."

Colling, when adapting *The Black Angel* for television, retained the singularity of this perspective by supplying Alberta with a voiceover, most of it taken verbatim from Woolrich's text. While subjective narration was common in radio drama of the 1930s and early 1940s (e.g. *Lights Out*), it was all but unheard of in television, and still relatively new to cinema, with *Double Indemnity* (1944) and *Murder, My Sweet* (1944) being notable exceptions. In these films noirs, the voiceovers of Walter Neff (Fred MacMurray) and Philip Marlowe (Dick Powell) operate in tandem with a confessional framing structure wherein the bulk of the story plays out in flashback. Neff, for instance, begins his narration of *Double Indemnity* by wondering, "How could I have known that murder would smell like honeysuckle?"—situating his tale as one of posthumous appraisal. Alberta's voiceover, in contrast, is correlated to a bewildering succession of events unfolding in the narrative present, an approach perfectly suited to the immediacy of live television.

The Black Angel aired a few years before kinescoping, the process of filming (and thus preserving) a live broadcast from the studio monitor, was put into practice. Aside from a handful of production stills, and Colling's personal script, it survives only in the form of Alberta's voiceover, as cut to vinyl by Mary Patton prior to each broadcast and played back, with what must have required impeccable coordination, in concert with the spoken dialogue of the live performance. (These recordings, uncovered among the uncatalogued holdings of the Library of Congress in the course of preparing this book, are the earliest artifacts of a made-for-television noir.) Narratively, there's little need for Alberta's near-continuous voiceover—the story could just as well have been told without it, through perhaps not as interestingly. And so it becomes a stylistic choice, a means of urging the viewer to occupy the same anxious, paranoid state from which Alberta herself cannot escape. In his teleplay, Colling takes pains to de-marcate Alberta's exposition-oriented narration ("Alberta's Voice") from her interior monologue ("The Mind")—with instructions to record the latter with a filter effect as if to suggest its hazy origins in the subconscious.

For those viewers unaccustomed to filmic narration outside of, say, a newsreel's "voice of God," or as the explanatory soundtrack to a flashback, Colling's double layering of voiceover induced some confusion. The *Billboard* television critic, for one, grumbled: "The impact would have been far greater if the girl in the action had been doing just what the narration said she was." Of course, as the 1940s went on, the counterpointing of subjective voiceover to on-screen events would become a hallmark of film noir. The relative novelty of a noir style is also apparent in how issue was taken with the low-key atmospherics that Colling, over the protestations of his technicians, devised for the production. Noting how the lack of back- and cross-lighting failed to fill in the settings, one critic wondered whether "the viewer will think the tube's pooped out." Colling's eschewal of torpid, over-illuminated settings—his annotated script is riddled with directives like "darker" and "face in shadow"—did much to align live television drama with the developing idioms of Hollywood-made film noir.

Light, and the absence of it, are central to Woolrich's delineation of the cityscape, most vividly in Alberta's interlude with Dr. Mordaunt, for whom she spends a tense night delivering packets of heroin to dodgy clients around the city. "It never closed," she tells us of a decrepit movie house off the Deuce. "Continually, throughout the night and throughout the day and around to the night again, lines of hissing, spitting, bluish motes given off by the livid screen ran downward in the darkness like rain, and cracked, mechanical voices, sounding just like voices talking outside in a rain, echoed hollowly through it." To recreate Woolrich's careful mapping of Alberta's psychological state onto the menacing city she traverses, Colling draws upon a mise-en-scène already indelibly graphed in the book. In "Dr. Death," as Alberta approaches Mordaunt's house, she reacts as if she's made her way to the very abyss of the noir world:

ALBERTA'S VOICE: I was creeping down the side street toward that darkened, waiting house. Frightened and helpless and alone, yet moving forward, nearer, nearer, all the time nearer. It was so dark along that grubby street, and when I came to the house, its black windows and grinning steps seemed to say, "I knew you'd come; I knew I'd get you."

Poster for *Black Angel* (film, 1946).

Startled to find Mordaunt concealed in the darkness of the foyer, Alberta allows herself to be prodded down a lightless corridor and into a dim subterranean room where she fully expects to be killed:

ALBERTA'S MIND: Whatever was to happen to me was to happen down here, back from the street, in the dark of the basement floor.

Later, after she's delivered the drugs for Mordaunt and made her way back to his dreaded low-wattage space, she relays her apprehension in oneiric terms:

ALBERTA'S VOICE: I traveled blindly along the tunnel-like basement bore like someone pacing in a dream. A dream whose foreknown outcome is doom, yet which must unfold itself without reprieve to its appointed climax.

For this return to Mordaunt's, Alberta's fear of death is intensified by her having fouled up one of the drug transactions; Mordaunt now believes her to be working with the police. It's here that Colling, in his only significant change from Woolrich's plot (but one well in tune with the heedless nature of Alberta's scheme) pulls a surprising reversal. In the novel, just as Mordaunt is about to stick Alberta with a lethal hypodermic, the police burst in—the sort of deus ex machina at which Woolrich excelled. Colling, however, climaxes the struggle with Alberta snatching up a gun and shooting Mordaunt. "His head dropped to the table. He was dead," she tells us. "He just looked—inert, like an old packing case. Worn out—used up." Alberta's apathetic reaction points us toward the fraudulent (some would say psychotic) essence of a quest based on betraying and then discarding four names from a phone diary.

The "domino effect," sparked by the transgression of one and relayed accordingly, held a particular fascination for Woolrich. Alberta's life has been upturned by her husband's infidelity, and so it goes that she herself irrevocably alters the lives of others. From the outset, despite her veneer of naiveté, she proves herself to be rather calculating, if not disingenuous and pitiless. "The really clever woman is all things to all men. Like the chameleon, she takes her coloring from his ideal of her," Woolrich writes of his vigilante-heroine Julie Killeen in *The Bride Wore Black* (1940)—a description equally applicable to Alberta. With each name, she puts on the face of the woman who fills the void of the man she hopes will replace her husband on death row. Mason, a former beau of Mia's, finds in Alberta the girl of his dreams, a perception Alberta encourages, albeit with increasingly confused feelings, and to ultimately dire results. "You crawled into my blood, into my brain! But I was just a name on your list!" Mason rails before taking his life.

"He thought he was the pursuer," Alberta muses of McKee in "The Last Name," "but he didn't know how relentlessly I had been following on his tail, how every move I had made was leading up to this one thing, the chance to get into his place, to get into his private life." And Marty, in his inebriated state, ini-

THE HARDBOILED BASIS OF EARLY LIVE TELEVISION. *Works are listed by their on-screen titles, series, and date.*

The Black Angel (1945).

"Edge of Panic" (*Suspense*, 1945).

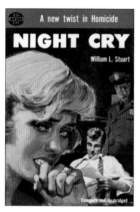

"Night Cry" (*Kraft Mystery Theatre*, 1958).

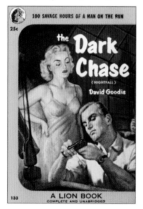

"Nightfall" (*Sure as Fate*, 1950; *Studio One*, 1951).

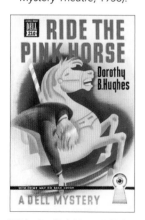

"Ride the Pink Horse" (*Robert Montgomery Presents*, 1950).

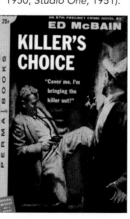

"Killer's Choice" (*Kraft Mystery Theatre*, 1958).

tially thinks Alberta to be the resurrection of his beloved Mia, a delusion Alberta takes her time correcting while she baits him into revealing his (presumed) guilt. By making Marty confront the reality of Mia's death, something he's managed to skirt by drowning himself in "smoke," and then planting in him the idea that he might actually be a murderer, Alberta drives Marty toward an apparent suicide, a fact to which she remains blithely indifferent. "Did I kill him, by what I did tonight?" "Alberta's Mind" wonders. "No, I was kind to him. I gave him something to die for. It's better to die for something than to live for nothing." While Alberta succeeds in saving her husband from wrongful execution, she finishes her story with three strangers dead and a fourth thoroughly shattered. The advertisements described it as "the story of a woman who was 'Angel Face' to her husband but to four other men the angel of destruction."

As NBC's most ambitious offering since it began service in 1937, *The Black Angel* set the standard for the "live talent" presentations to follow. Indeed, the network used the occasion to measure, for the first time, public response to a dramatic production. Along with mailing surveys out to the five thousand or so television-equipped households in New York City circa January 1945, it concluded each episode with an open invitation for viewers to write in with their comments. Thereafter, dark tales of murder and mystery proliferated. Many of them, including Woolrich's own *The Black Alibi*, which NBC presented over two nights in 1946, followed the open-ended whodunit scenario of *The Black Angel*, a form thought to be instrumental in retaining viewership. "We won back the same audience every Sunday night, plus new ones," explained Mary Patton. "The tele-audience had to wait weeks to find the answer and the suspense was too much for them!"

For the most part, however, the noir-infused one-offs aired by NBC and, competitively, by CBS and DuMont in the second half of the 1940s, as the networks sussed out what types of programming audiences might most want to see, were of the "red meat" variety popularized by James M. Cain. That the sensibility of these productions was in tune with what Cain liked to describe as "blood melodrama" is best summarized in *Billboard*'s sighing complaint: "NBC tonight presented another in its studies of husband-killing wives." The sordid *Dark Hammock* (NBC, 1946), from a teleplay by Mary Orr and Reginald Denham, is an especially ripe example. Orr, fresh off writing the source story for what would become *All About Eve* (1950), plays Coral, a dance-hall floozy who marries wealthy rancher Marvin Platt (Robert Lynn) for his fortune and quickly begins scheming to kill him—while also seducing Marvin's adopted son, Carlos (James Gannon), with "a kiss no married woman ought to be giving to another man."

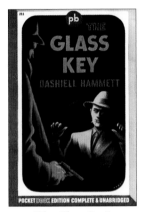
"The Glass Key" (*Studio One*, 1949).

"The Black Path of Fear" (*Suspense*, 1949).

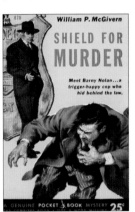
"Shield for Murder" (*Studio One*, 1951).

"Run from the Sun" (*Sure as Fate*, 1950).

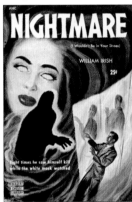
"Nightmare" (*Sure as Fate*, 1950; *Studio One*, 1951).

"Little Men, Big World" (*Studio One*, 1953).

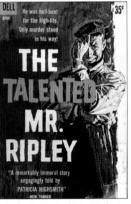
"The Talented Mr. Ripley" (*Playhouse 90*, 1958).

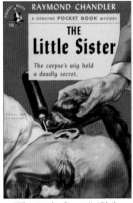
"The Little Sister" (*Philco Television Playhouse*, 1949).

"Journey Into Fear" (*Climax!*, 1956).

"The Long Goodbye" (*Climax!*, 1954).

"Rendezvous in Black" (*Playhouse 90*, 1956).

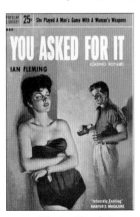
"Casino Royale" (*Climax!*, 1954).

Dark Hammock (1946).

Yet Coral's aim in murdering Marvin isn't to run away with Carlos, whom she soon discards, but to win back the affections of Henry, her former boyfriend and pimp.

Like many femmes fatales, Coral is a misguided protagonist, conniving and murderous, but also masochistic and vulnerable. "Frustrated and guilty, half man-eater, half man-eaten, blasé and cornered, she falls victim to her own wiles," Borde and Chaumeton write of the archetype in *A Panorama of American Film Noir*. A fixture in stories dealing with illicit sex and premeditated murder, the femme fatale rarely escapes punishment for her transgressions. *Dark Hammock* ends with Coral inadvertently ingesting a fatal dose of the poison she's been feeding her husband, and pleading for a second chance: "Don't you understand, I'm sick!" she cries. The psychopathic bride of *Bedelia* (NBC, 1945), directed by Fred Coe from the novel by Vera Caspary (of *Laura* fame) says much the same when confronted with her crime. Bedelia (Fay Ball), as her aggrieved husband, Charlie (Thomas Hume), comes to learn in the weeks after their wedding, is a serial widower known for her handiness with herbal poisons: she's been the death of all her husbands. "You wouldn't let them take me away, would you? I'm your wife, you know, and I'm sick. I'm a very sick woman, your wife," Bedelia implores upon learning that the tenacious detective (Walter Coy) combing the country for her has finally arrived at the door.

Despite being set at the turn of the century, *Bedelia* is as wicked as any pulp contrivance: the stock characters of femme fatale, duped male, and investigator are simply recast from their lurid dime-novel origins into a stuffier but no less menacing environment. Plot-wise, it's a flip-flop of the Victorian gothic thriller, of which *Angel Street* (NBC, 1946), from the hit Broadway play by Patrick Hamilton (also the author of *Hangover Square*), is the exemplar. Young bride Bella (Judith Evelyn) is gradually awakened to the possibility that her husband Jack (Henry Daniel), who has a habit of unexplained nocturnal excursions, may be the nefarious murderer stalking London. Already in a fog, Bella is pushed further toward instability when no one will believe her theories. As with most "gaslight noir," the suspenseful extrapolation of such a premise hinges on the heroine's susceptibility to outward suggestions of inner madness, a mental state Ernest Colling, the director, conveys through imaginative mirror compositions and skewed first-person shots of Bella's hostile, stifling surroundings. Only the last-minute intervention of a detective (Cecil Humphrey) saves Bella from a complete breakdown.

Where NBC focused on literary or theatrical adaptations, CBS drew its blood melodramas from a hefty catalog of radio serials like *Suspense, Crime*

Photographer, and *The Whistler*. The latter yielded *Brief Pause for Murder* (CBS, 1946), which tells of a radio newscaster (David Manners) obsessed with killing his two-timing wife (Mary Patton) in the "perfect crime"—the pipe dream of noir. After prerecording his audio duties, the announcer sets out to do the deed, but is tripped up by fate when the tape defaults on air, thus ruining his alibi of having been behind a microphone at the moment his wife was being chopped to pieces. Another *Whistler* play brought over from radio, *Delivery Guaranteed* (CBS, 1947), treads the same line of noir irony: husband (Robert Bolder) strangles wife (Anne Burr) in a fit of temper when she threatens him with Reno, packs her up in a trunk for disposal in the country, and becomes hysterical when he's pulled over by the police for a minor traffic violation.

On the set of *Angel Street* (1945) with Henry Daniel and Judith Evelyn.

Stories like these, with their undercurrents of marital discord, murderous fixation, and corrosive guilt, point toward the influence of Cain's *Double Indemnity*, which finally made it to cinemas in 1944 after a near-decade of Hays Office suppression. But it also highlights the increasing acceptability of such themes as suitable for television. Given that the purpose of presentations like *The Black Angel* and *Bedelia* was to popularize television for the postwar masses, the dark mystery-melodrama clearly served as an integral part of network strategy from the beginning of commercial television. "Crime plays are now enjoying unprecedented popularity on stage, screen, and on the air," *Televiser* reported in 1946, citing the trend toward stories with "psychological and psychopathological complications" as especially appealing. "Through its continually moving spatial cameras, television is able to show in defocused shots, close-ups, angle shots, and surprising dollies how the world appears to the neurotic, the criminal and the insane. Unlike the theatre it can create a subjective reality and effect subconscious identification of the viewer with the criminal who invades his living room." The invasion, having proved to be a welcome one, continued ferociously as the new medium developed.

On the set of *Bedelia* (1946) with Fay Ball and Thomas Hume.

LIVE NOIR II:
THE ANTHOLOGIES

Television is at its best when it offers us faces, reactions, explorations of emotions registered by human beings.

—Horace Newcomb

IN HIS ESSAY "Un nouveau genre 'policier': L'Aventure criminelle" (1946), Nino Frank, the French critic who defined film noir, identified his grouping of dark narratives as being fixated with "the faces, the behavior, the thoughts—consequently, the trueness to life of the characters." This attentiveness to the messy, hard truths of modern living is equally fervent in the live dramatic anthologies that flourished on American television from the late 1940s to the early 1960s. Beginning with *Kraft Television Theatre* (1947–1958), the presentation of a weekly play brought to the masses through corporate largesse proved to be a necessary boon to the economic and creative development of the medium. As the number of television households swelled—from less than two hundred thousand in 1947 to twelve million in 1951—industrial titans like Westinghouse, Philco, Goodyear, Ford, Lux, Lucky Strike, Armstrong, and

U.S. Steel readily signed on. Buy our pre-sliced cheese and tomorrow-world appliances, our miracle tires and electric shavers, went the reasoning, and we'll keep that box in your living room flickering with drama— one week the tragedy of a sociopathic policeman, the next a downbeat chronicle of a self-loathing butcher.

The live anthologies favor the flawed, fraying hero, a man under the wheel; their predominant conflicts are those of personal crisis—the moral dilemmas brought on by unsatisfied urges and overreaching aims; the quagmires exposed by sudden shifts in the currents of fate. Their protagonists tend to suffer and struggle, sometimes even bleed. Things rarely end well in these plays. In much the same way that the classic cycle of film noir, despite accounting for a mere slice of 1940s Hollywood output, has come to embody the zeitgeist of its era, it's the mordantly toned, angst-driven productions that graph the ethos of "golden age" live television— plays like "Patterns" and "Crime in the Streets" and "A

On the set of "The Petrified Forest" (*Producer's Showcase*, 1955). *Left to right*, Jack Klugman, Richard Jaeckel, Humphrey Bogart, and Paul Hartman emerge from the desert night.

Man is Ten Feet Tall," to name three from 1955, a peak year for the anthologies. These and other live noirs put forth a critical vision of mid-century America that both complements and overlaps the one purveyed by film noir, only they do so in brazen juxtaposition to the optimistically jingled sales pitches that paid for their broadcast.

Where the earlier wave of live drama (e.g. *The Black Angel*) was presented commercial-free, and allowed to run at odd lengths, the introduction of advertising altered the rules of how a drama was to be constructed for television: the development of exposition and character, the ratcheting of suspense and tension, the placement of revelation and resolution were now at the service of "a word from our sponsor." This restrictive model, with its specific act breaks, each building to a critical point, swelled a vibe that was already heady. The anthologies began staking space on network schedules at a time when dramatic standards were evolving. The element of life-born trueness that Frank singled out when describing his concept of film noir was gaining traction across all arts, from the street photography of Weegee and Robert Frank to the Method acting taking root in the New York theatre scene. This realist, psychologically oriented approach found a particularly receptive arena in live television. In 1952, Edward Barry Roberts, the script editor for *Armstrong Circle Theatre* (1950–1963), wrote of how "the unique quality of television is its revelation of character in quick, intense touches. . . . Television, with its immediacy, gets to the heart of the matter, to the essence of the character, to the depicting of the human being who is there, as if under a microscope."

A story unfolding in the "now" only enhanced the existential aspect so vital to the noir style. Sweltering, claustrophobic sets, stark black-and-white imagery, roving, probing camerawork, and close-up after close-up of sweaty, anxious faces coalesced to create a personalized atmosphere of disquietude and imminent chaos. "If this technique of penetrating the mind is a familiar one in the films," wrote *New York Times* critic Jack Gould in 1949, "it is a new experience when it comes in the stillness of one's own living room." Gould was particularly taken with how the medium had turned its supposed limitations of scale and size to a singular advantage, beginning with a three-camera system that allowed for uninterrupted performance—a fluidity not possible in film. In favoring actuality over montage, live drama

TOP: "Patterns" (*Kraft Television Theatre*, 1955) with Richard Kiley and Ed Begley. CENTER: "Crime in the Streets" (*Elgin Hour*, 1954) with John Cassavetes and Robert Preston. BOTTOM: "A Man Is Ten Feet Tall" (*Philco TV Playhouse*, 1955) with Don Murray and Sidney Poitier.

TOP TO BOTTOM: "Julius Caesar" (*Studio One*, 1949); "The Glass Key" (*Studio One*, 1949); "The Long Goodbye" (*Climax!*, 1954) with Dick Powell and Theresa Wright; "The Little Sister" (*Philco TV Playhouse*, 1949) with John Marley (center) and William Esty (right).

revised the vocabulary of moving-image storytelling. And what it lacked in panorama it made up for in depth: its scope went inward rather than outward. The wide-angle lens, a necessity because of the close quarters (converted radio studios) in which the early anthologies were made, became the go-to looking glass, resulting in a deep-focus perspective well-suited to narratives centered on inner distress.

Even a moldy fig like *Julius Caesar*, as presented by *Studio One* in 1949, gained fresh psychological shading when brought to television. Worthington Miner, who oversaw the series, recast the action to a dark, contemporary city, a setting of visceral impact. His conniving senators—fedoras pulled low, collars turned up, faces slitted in shadow—huddle like gangland minions arranging the disposal of their kingpin. Halfway through, when Caesar (William Post, Jr.) is studded with knives, a camera hurtles across the set to find the troubled eyes of his betrayer, Brutus (Robert Keith), whose guilt-ridden reaction is conveyed not in the traditional soliloquy but as a noir-style voiceover. Throughout, the low-key designs of lighting director George Stoetzel moderate the Shakespearean gloom and doom. "Using hardly a fraction of the candlepower which so often washes out the image," Gould reported, Stoetzel "achieved a symphony in delicate shadings that . . . sustained the mood of tragic inevitability." Some Sundays later, by popular demand, Miner restaged the play (a television first), which he followed the next week with another story of politics and treachery: Dashiell Hammett's *The Glass Key*. That Hammett's streetwise poetry is the linguistic polar to Shakespeare's iambic pentameter is a secondary distinction, for the two productions occupy the same corruptive, hard-edged milieu—one in which double-crossers like Brutus are themselves double-crossed, and then spitefully rolled over dead in the gutter.

Hammett is among a host of hardboiled writers whose work was sourced for the anthologies: others include Raymond Chandler ("The Long Goodbye," *Climax!*, 1954; "The Little Sister," *Philco TV Playhouse*, 1949), David Goodis ("Nightfall," *Sure as Fate*, 1950; again for *Studio One*, 1951), David Dodge ("Angel's Ransom," *Kaiser Aluminum Hour*, 1956), John Hawkins and Ward Hawkins ("Burden of Guilt," *Studio One*, 1952; "A Matter of Life and Death," *Climax!*, 1957), and Cornell Woolrich ("Rendezvous in Black," *Playhouse 90*, 1956, among dozens). Because preserving these one-time-only broadcasts was of little priority, live noirs like "The Long Goodbye," with Dick Powell recreating his Marlowe from *Murder, My Sweet* (1944), or another first-time Chandler adaptation, "The King in Yellow" (*Studio One*, 1951), are no longer with us. Also vanished are Robert Montgomery's live remake of "Ride the Pink Horse" (*Your Lucky Strike Theatre*, 1950), and his presentations of Woolrich's "Phantom Lady" (*Lucky Strike*, 1950) and "Three O'Clock" (*Lucky Strike*, 1951). Patricia Highsmith's "The Talented Mr. Ripley" (*Studio One*, 1956), which predates *Plein*

Soleil (1960), can be added to this list, as can her unpublished story "To Scream at Midnight" (*Climax!*, 1956). These and other productions join the unfortunate ranks of live noirs believed lost; those that survive as kinescopes are a resilient and revelatory bunch.

New York City, with its nervous, glimmering twilight, imbues the anthologies with a gritty melancholia. A blast of fanfare, the crisp declaration of "Tonight, *live* . . .", and the scene would fade in on a sad-looking Everyman alone in a room. The home viewer, planted before a twenty-inch screen from which a pair of wounded eyes stared back, may as well have been looking through a mirror. More than the theatre, with its proscenium arch, or the cinema, with its CinemaScope-sized canvas, live television diminished the distance between spectator and drama, resulting in a "realness" that was relatable yet intensified. In "Marty" (*Philco*, 1953), one of the more celebrated productions of its day, Paddy Chayefsky chronicles with documentary-like precision the drab existence of an unhappy butcher in the Bronx. "Whatever it is that women like, I ain't got it. I'm a fat little man, a fat ugly man," Marty (Rod Steiger) says to his mother. "I had enough pain." Chayefsky came upon the idea one afternoon while wandering through a dance hall off Times Square; the queues of wallflowers, with their faces of pained longing, struck him as the quintessential tableau of modern alienation. "I tried to write the dialogue as if it had been wire-tapped," he said.

There are no back-alley stabbings in "Marty," no conspiracies of murder and money. Yet the city it inhabits is the same naked one as displayed in countless films noirs—in the sorrowful paintings of Hopper and the tabloid snapshots of Weegee. The plaintive, inarticulate delivery of Steiger, the latest Actor's Studio memory mumbler to wander up from Broadway onto the bustling stages of NBC's Rockefeller studios, only adds to the grimy naturalism, as do the touches of the cityscape outside—the fluorescent cafeterias, cage-like phone booths, and falling-apart ballrooms of an estranging urban geography.

Off in another corner of New York, in an all-night hash joint, the sort of place where the coffee tastes like the neon circulating through the window, Joe Harris (James Dean) spends the first night of his parole chewing on the collar of his jacket the way an angry dog tears at its leash: he's just learned that his wife left him while he was in the clink. Bemoaning the rotten city, "this sewer of phonies" that turned life against him, he cries out to Poppa (Rudolf Weiss), the counterman: "Prison I can take—but this!" The entrance of Lt. Case (Robert Simon), the bull who sent Joe up, heightens the pitch. Joe's hand curls to a fist as Case appraises him as a "no-good punk—he'll wipe his eyes with one hand and slit your throat with the other!" Poppa rushes Case out the door, but it's already too late. His fuse at an end, Joe turns his rage to Poppa. Once a thief, now a murderer, he flees into the night.

BELOW: On the set of "Ride the Pink Horse" (*Robert Montgomery Presents*, 1950). BOTTOM: "Marty" (*Philco TV Playhouse*, 1954) with Rod Steiger.

"A Long Time Till Dawn" *(Kraft Television Theatre*, 1953) with James Dean.

So begins "A Long Time Till Dawn" (*Kraft*, 1953) by Rod Serling. For the remainder of an hour neatly sliced in thirds, during which there's much ado about "cheese made the old way," the improbability of Joe claiming some kind of redemption is made clear. For all his nostalgic yearnings, his efforts to gain a foothold in the time before he went astray, he arrives at an epiphany that matters very little. The obstacle he faces isn't the unclaimed past, or the rotten city, or even the pursuing police, but, as Poppa points out right before Joe kills him, an insurmountable something within: "Nobody was against you. You were against yourself, like a fish flashing around in a net." This emphasis on inner torment, on how the cracks of self-division can only lead to self-destruction, is perhaps the salient, unifying characteristic of live noir. For Joe, there's no route back or forward, only a steady sideways slide further from the light. Holed up inside his father's suburban house, where he's gone to hide, and where he'll finish the play dead on the lawn, he howls out his epitaph: "This is not the way I want it at all!" The dire ending is hardly an anomaly: the signature kiss-off of the live noir, when not death, is the sting of disappointment, compromise, shame—as far away from triumph as the circumstances permit. NBC's print ads run for the broadcast aptly summarized the chilling dissonance at play: "Tonight, a tense psychological drama of a strangely likable and violent man— and you'll also enjoy the ideas for good eating the Kraft Kitchen offers!"

"A Long Time Till Dawn" elevated Serling, then toiling in Cincinnati radio, to a rising breed of original teleplay writers. "Patterns" (*Kraft*, 1955), his blistering take on big business and the modern organization man, and the first play he wrote upon relocating to New York, made him a household name. Through acts one and two, he establishes the bustling midtown headquarters of Ramsey & Co. as an exemplar of thriving American commerce, and as a viper's nest of infighting and mistrust; it's a place in which the supremacy of growth and profit is fearsomely defended by the cold prick of a CEO, Walter Ramsey (Everett Sloane). Our entry to this fractious arena is junior executive Fred Staples (Richard Kiley), recently recruited to the firm. Act three, in which Staples's mentor, the earnest, conscientious Andy Sloane (Ed Begley), is driven to a fatal heart attack by the humiliations and abuse heaped on him by Ramsey, steers "Patterns" toward tragedy. Indignantly, Staples marches into Ramsey's suite, determined to assert himself as a heroic martyr; he exits, blinders removed, and several rungs higher on the corporate ladder, with a lucrative promotion to Sloane's vacancy.

While exposing fissures in postwar capitalism—the scornfulness toward ethical values; the pressures imposed by the few at the top upon the many at the bottom—that resonate today, Serling stops short of condemning American enterprise as irretrievably corrupted. True, the wheel turns on pitiless self-interest and greed, but it functions so by necessity, or so Ramsey declares in dismissing Sloane's death as a matter of natural selection. To prevail in this world, he argues, requires not only resolve and drive, but a flexible grip on one's ideals and principles. What makes "Patterns" so startlingly dark is the ambivalence with which Serling's ostensible hero absorbs this troubling lesson. While suspecting from the get-go that he's been hired to replace the aging Sloane, Staples allows the actual mechanics of such a turnover to be lost to the naiveté of his heartland upbringing. Leave it to Mrs. Staples (June Dayton), whom Serling, in his teleplay, describes as a "hungering kind of woman whose appetite is that of the competitive American wife," to point out the impracticality of sentimentalism. Only upon Sloane's demise does Staples allow himself to swallow the bitter pill lodged in his throat: for him to move up, someone above needed to fall.

Serling liked to describe "Patterns" as "a story of ambition and the price tag that hangs on success." Resituating this theme to other environments of power and force—politics, the military, organized labor, show business, sport—he turned out a succession of searing plays about the compromises a man must make to ensure his personal or professional survival. In "Requiem for a Heavyweight" (*Playhouse 90*, 1956), the arena is the sordid, iconographically noir world of prizefighting. Mountain McClintock (Jack Palance), Serling's knocked-about boxer, is a perennial contender, once ranked as high as no. 5, now arriving at the terminus of his career. Washed up at thirty-two, "a battered hulk covered with the un-healing scars that are the legacy of his trade," he has little idea what to do with himself. Maish (Keenan Wynn), his manager, wants to set him up in the sideshow of wrestling. Maish even has a persona drummed up, "The Mountaineer," complete with buckskin jacket and coonskin cap. Mountain, who prides himself on having never taken a dive, hesitates—a step too low, he says. Maish persists, cajoling, insulting, manipulating. Gradually, Mountain pieces together just how far up the river he's been sold: his beloved Maish lost every nickel betting against him and owes a towering stack of markers to the mob.

Serling's teleplay, brilliantly rendered by director Ralph Nelson, sends Mountain through a noir city papered with fading fight posters—reminders of the glory he reached for and missed. The central set is a seedy tavern, otherwise known as "the graveyard," chock-a-block with other almost-champions drunkenly reminiscing about past turns in the ring. Wherever Mountain goes, death rears its head. He casts the lonely,

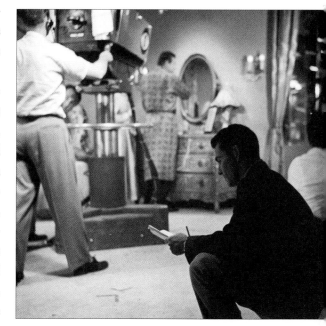

On the set of "Portrait in Celluloid" (*Climax*, 1955) with Rod Serling (foreground) and Jack Carson (mirror).

"Requiem for a Heavyweight" (*Playhouse 90*, 1956) with Kim Hunter, Jack Palance, and Keenan Wynn.

ghostly shadow of a returning soldier divested of his place in the world. Throughout "Requiem," as well as in his script for the feature-film remake (1962), an underheralded late-cycle noir, also directed by Nelson, Serling draws parallels to the archetype of the disillusioned veteran. "A guy goes along fourteen years," Mountain says to Grace (Kim Hunter), the employment counselor his dedicated cut man, Army (Ed Wynn), encourages him to visit. "All he does is fight. Once a week, twice a week, prelims, semifinals, finals. He don't know nothin' but that. All he can do is fight. Then they tell him no more. And what's he do? What's he supposed to do? What's he supposed to know how to do besides fight?" Serling paints a scrambling, top-down system in which exploitation paves the way to societal ejection. Groomed, weighed, and monetized since youth, but now having exhausted his usefulness, Mountain is simply spit out of the wheel to fend for himself.

The idea of an American Dream attainable by some but not others fascinated Serling. "The Velvet Alley," (*Playhouse 90*, 1959), one of his last live plays, and certainly his most personal, introduces Ernie Pandish (Art Carney), a hungry playwright who, at forty-two, is ready to throw in the towel; overnight, his longtime agent (Jack Klugman) delivers the dream—a Hollywood contract. Summoned out to "the land of mink swimming pools," where fame and fortune await, Pandish takes a meeting with one of the town's hardened survivors, an alcoholic producer (Leslie Nielsen) who offers a lesson on how things really work:

> You know how they do it, Ernie? They give you a thousand dollars a week. And they keep on giving you a thousand dollars a week until that's what you need to live on. And then after that, you live every day afraid they'll take it away from you. It's all very scientific. It's based on the psychological fact that man is a grubbing, hungry little sleaze who adapts like a chameleon.

Undeterred, Pandish plows ahead, changing his colors as it befits his pursuit of success. Through three acts, each punctuated with a chirpy demonstration of how "new Kleenex tissues tear evenly, every time, and come in white or pretty pastel colors," "The Velvet Alley" offers a grim tour of a luxuriously vacant nightmare. Serling, by then ensconced in a Beverly Hills estate, where he took to dictating his scripts poolside, issues a dark, guilt-ridden lament. He ends the play with Pandish in a snow heap outside his old New York tenement, wailing for all that's been lost. "Were I to write a next chapter," Serling explained, "Ernie would be jacking out scripts for some TV film factory."

As Serling saw it, personal integrity (including his own, he worried) had become just another commodity, something to be traded in on the way up. An equally jaundiced portrait of how discontent eats the soul is to be found in Budd Schulberg's "What Makes Sammy Run?" (*Sunday Showcase*, 1959). Adapting, with his brother, Stuart, his own notoriously unadaptable (by Hollywood) novel, Schulberg gives us Sammy Glick (Larry Blyden), exemplar of the crass, class-jumping show business hustler. Glick tramples his way from mailroom to studio chiefdom with

"The Velvet Alley" (*Playhouse 90*, 1959) with Art Carney.

the sort of behavior that causes friends and enemies alike to reach for the Kleenex. He, too, completes his climb scooped out from the inside. Humiliated but not exactly satiated, he vows to continue running "with death as the only finish line." The striving madness of the Glicks and the Pandishes, joined to all the other pathologies on evidence in these live noirs, would seem symptomatic of a malady for which the sponsor mascots prancing about on the tube held no easy fix. Dour and existentialist, peopled with the dissatisfied and dispossessed, the sponsored anthology drama, as Erik Barnouw famously put it, "made the commercial seem fraudulent."

The landscape of cultural paradox in which live television arose demanded excavation. On the sunny side, there was unprecedented prosperity—the post-war boom. In the shadowy part, beyond the billboards of the Dream, beyond the Cadillacs and the tract homes, beyond commercial television and its sixty-second promises of the "good life," lay some sobering realities: higher crime, more divorce, spikes in social, racial, and economic injustice—all of it made more dire by unrelenting forecasts of nuclear rain. The incongruities yielded not only stories of personal dissatisfaction, but evidence of a society tearing at itself from within. Though doing so brought them into a tug-of-war with skittish sponsors, writers like Rod Serling, Reginald Rose, and Robert Alan Aurthur steadily pushed the live drama toward headline-based significance, producing plays themed on persecution ("A Town Has Turned to Dust," *Playhouse 90*, 1958), prejudice ("Thunder on Sycamore Street," *Studio One*, 1954), and political paranoia ("The Spy Next Door," *Armstrong Circle Theatre*, 1961), all heavily steeped in a noir ethos. "The Rag Jungle" (*Kaiser Aluminum Hour*, 1956), Steve Gethers's exposé of graft and gangsterism in the garment industry, is typical of the politicized tone. So is Aurthur's "A Man Is Ten Feet Tall" (*Philco*, 1955), a story of crime and bigotry along the New York waterfront.

Aurthur's antihero, longshoreman Axel Nordmann (Don Murray), is an Army deserter in hiding. Because he faces prison if caught, he sticks to himself, anxious and self-hating, until he's taken under the wing of another outsider, Tommy Tyler (Sidney Poitier). "A man's gotta make a choice," Tyler explains. "There are the men and there are the lower forms. You go with the men and you're ten feet tall. You go with the lower forms and you are down in the slime." When Charlie Malick (Martin Balsam), the foreman, uncovers Nordmann's identity and blackmails him, Tyler intervenes, and is killed for it. Robert Mulligan directs the scene as a *pas de deux* of combat with baling hooks. During the police inquest, Nordmann, intimidated by Malick, keeps his lips zipped. But his cowardice eats away at his conscience. A morality play about "doing the right thing" becomes a reflection on the consequences of naming names, a potent subject in this time of blacklists and HUAC hearings. The dilemma Aurthur contrives for Nordmann neatly flip-flops the quandary imposed on those called before the "Red Baiters": remain silent, and doom himself to "the slime"; expose Malick, and risk discovery by the authorities. The Deciding Moment, caught in a mono-chromatic tight shot on a twenty-inch Philco, made for compelling television.

This constant tension between the instinct for self-preservation and the fear of going through life with the taste of ashes in one's mouth gets to the heart of the inner conflict so often faced by the noir protagonist. In "Fearful Decision" (*U.S. Steel Hour*, 1954), Ralph Bellamy plays a headstrong millionaire who gains the enmity of his wife (Meg Mundy) and much of the community when, on prin-ciple, he refuses to fork over the ransom demanded by his son's kidnappers. Re-peated close-ups of Bellamy's agonized expression achieve, as *Variety* noted, "a perfect picture of a lonely, broken man who wonders whether he's done the right thing." Ever attuned to success in rival mediums, Hollywood took notice: "Fearful Decision" became *Ransom!* (1956), a film noir starring Glenn Ford. Indeed, the studios snapped up scores of live teleplays, along with the directors and actors who made them. "A Man Is Ten Feet Tall" was turned into *Edge of the City* (1957), a gritty "B" noir directed by Martin Ritt, who came straight from television. Adrian Spies's "A Case of Identity" (*Robert Montgomery Presents*, 1954), the true-life account of a musician (Robert Ellenstein) falsely accused of robbery, yielded Alfred Hitchcock's *The Wrong Man* (1956). "Crime in the Streets" (*Elgin Hour*, 1955), Rose's acclaimed treatment of juvenile delinquency, was brought to film by Don Siegel (1956), with John Cassavetes reprising his role as a Hell's Kitchen hooligan.

In the original, which Sidney Lumet directed, Cassavetes plays his Frankie Dane as a haughty cutthroat, tough but emotionally unstable. He rules his domain from a rickety fire escape a few notches up from the "guttuh." It's there that he riles his sidekicks (Mark Rydell and Ivan Curry) into icing the fink he thinks slighted him. Lumet and Rose aim Frankie's path of vengeance through a tene-ment maze of blind alleys and windowless flats ringed by a cacophony of tugboat horns and clattering trains. Frankie's tic, the manifestation of his entrapment, is that he abhors being touched. When his aged-beyond-her-years mother (Glenda Farrell) tries to get through to him, and accidentally grazes his face, Frankie reacts with such fury that his kid brother Richie (Van Dyke Parks) runs screaming. As the hour of murder nears (indicated, of course, by inserts of an Elgin wristwatch), Frankie remains resolute. Only at the last second, when Richie darts between the knife and the would-be victim, does Frankie gives pause to his bloodlust. Yet the question of whether he's been redeemed is left open. The towering dark-ness, the encircling city sounds, suggest a long climb up before he sees the light.

Cassavetes, like Dean, was part of a television-trained generation who came of age when the j.d. drama was all the rage. He plays another budding gangster in "Judge Contain's Hotel" (*Kraft*, 1955): a sneering numbers-running sharpie at

odds with his father (Charles Dingle), an iron-fisted judge whose career he nearly destroys. This go-round, with leafy suburbs replacing the asphalt jungle, there's no conditional excuse for the youth's criminal proclivities. He's simply a bad seed. Juvenile delinquent stories emanate from an unsettling corner of noir, for they imply a deep-rooted deviance that begins young and only grows with adulthood. The mouthy kid with the chip on his shoulder and a switchblade in his pocket graduates to any number of noir archetypes—quick-tempered sidekick, sullen hitman, smarmy racketeer. But the likelier outcome is that of a noir perennial, the on-the-lam loser, like the one Paul Newman plays in "One for the Road" (*The Web*, 1953). Newman's Mickey, an ex-G.I., is introduced on a train bound for the Big House. "It's a fine setup," he grumbles to his police escort, Gant (Wally Brown). "Two years in Korea. You get out, you get a job, and then this." His alibi for the murder he says he didn't commit is a buddy still missing on the front. "If you hadn't been a vet, you'd have gotten the chair," Gant offers.

"One for the Road" (*The Web*, 1953) with Paul Newman and Betty Bartley.

Hearing it like this, Mickey overpowers Gant and takes a powder. He winds up in a saloon on the wharf, the sort of hell pit where trouble arrives in a tight dress. Her name is Bernice (Betty Bartley), and it isn't long before Mickey is drawn into a brawl with her pimp, whom he leaves crumpled under a pile of broken bar furniture. Hiding out in a nearby dance hall, he meets Ellie (Grace Raynor), a fresh-faced blind girl. "You smell good, like a bar of soap, not like stale beer and cheap perfume," he tells her. Mickey's moments with Grace suggest a glimmer of hope, a new start; for one, she'd never recognize him from a wanted poster. But his dream is promptly squelched when Bernice, authorities in tow, appears on the scene. "Boy, everything I've ever done, or tried to do, has gotten fouled up along the line some place—I can't win," Mickey grumbles as he's tossed back in the clink to await the next prison train. The *why-me?* fatalism Newman exudes as Mickey continues in "Knife in the Dark" (*Danger*, 1954). Jeff, his loser-hero, is already in jail, counting out the three months left on his sentence. Trouble finds him anyway when he inadvertently witnesses prison bully Willie (James Gregory) stab another inmate to death.

Jeff keeps his trap shut, despite a lashing from the warden, only to lose his cool once Willie starts boasting about the "cute" corpse he left on the shower floor. After Jeff spouts off to the lug, Peaches (Walter Burke), his bunkmate, warns: "I'll bet it felt good coming out, but he's got a knife, and now he's going to have to use it." The remarkable nightmare sequence that follows must have taxed every technician under the command of first-time director John Frankenheimer. Where most live directors had their hands full keeping the cameras from crashing into one another, Frankenheimer unhinges his: they dart about like mongooses on benzedrine, clambering, poking, peering. Relishing all the gee-whiz gimmickry suddenly at his fingertips after years as a studio floor manager, Frankenheimer visualizes Jeff's turmoil through a whirl of superimpositions, macro shots, spinning frames, and subjective effects, with Peaches' words looping endlessly on the soundtrack. At one point the camera drops down from the ceiling to capture Jeff in clenching close-up before abruptly cutting to a kaleidoscopic view of Willie advancing from some mist; where there was one Willie, there are now six Willies, six knives. Equally impressive is Frankenheimer's setting of the climactic, knife-or-life brawl amidst the jail's contrasting shafts of light and shadow.

> We deal exclusively with crime melodrama, involving recognizable people.
>
> —MARTIN MANULIS, producer, *Suspense*

On the set of "Padlocks" (*Danger*, 1953) with James Dean and Mildred Dunnock.

Danger, The Web,* and *Suspense (1949–1954) formed a troika of half-hour "specialty" anthologies on CBS known as "The Three Weird Sisters." Like *Lights Out* (1949–1952) and *The Clock* (1949–1952) on NBC, or *Hands of Murder* (1949–1951) on DuMont, their domain was that of the psychological mystery-melodrama; such hour-longs as *The Trap* (a/k/a *Sure as Fate*, 1949–1951) and *Moment of Fear* (1960) belong here as well. In contrast to the "prestige" anthologies, with their alternating-genre format, the specialties thrived on generic consistency. While each week brought a turnover in plot and characters, the overriding architecture remained bound to the thematic determinant promised in the title. Viewers tuning in to *The Clock* could expect a mystery involving "the inevitable penalties of time." On *The Web*, CBS's standing requirements for the writers stipulated "a sympathetic central character caught in a web of fate or dangerous circumstances of crime."

The concept of fate, as practiced in noir fiction, is integral to the specialty anthologies. To varying degrees, each plies the notion that some ineffable force—chance, destiny, dumb luck—is silently at work, steering human ants down blind alleys. The prototypical specialty plot functions as a fable. A dreadful act is committed and concealed, only to be exposed through an ironic twist; the wrong-doer, brought to unanticipated comeuppance (confession, handcuffs, disgrace), is left to decry the intrusion of "fate" in an otherwise surefire scheme.

One early episode of *The Clock* tells of a clerk, already up to his neck in adultery and blackmail, who strangles his employer, cleans out the office vault, fakes his death, and hires a plastic surgeon to carve him a new face. Transformed from a sneaky, miserable menace into an anonymous, wealthy one, he flits guilelessly about until the day he's swept up in a random police dragnet. Unwilling to disclose his whereabouts on the night of his surgery, he finds himself charged with murder—his own. In these and other stories, a quantum of presumed guilt, an original sin, is a foundational necessity. That no indiscretion stays hidden for long is, of course, axiomatic to noir. But running parallel to the trope of a past that's never far behind is the equally trenchant one of a future that's all used up. Free will, the capacity to choose x or y, is merely the instrument with which to paint a fatal target on one's back.

In *Lights Out*, a speculative-fiction anthology whose DNA lingers on in noir hybrids like *The Twilight Zone* and *The X-Files*, fate is synonymous with the supernatural—the inexplicable. The freaky, nightmarish circumstances that derail its characters have little rational basis, an air of unreality the series reinforces with an eerie theremin score and a habit of isolating the faces of those brushed with death and doom against sparse, inked-out backgrounds. The narrator's cackling introduction of "Lights out, everybody!" serves to awaken all to the horrors that lurk in the shadows. Other series begin with fate having already cast its net. *The Web*, quite literally: it opens each episode with the image of a figure squirming beneath a superimposed graphic of the eponymous construction. The story to follow is one of attempted self-extraction, nearly always futile. Fate, in this strain of noir, particularly among the "Weird Sisters," works in tandem with the human tendency toward self-destruction.

"Revenge" (*Suspense*, 1949), from Woolrich's 1943 novel *The Black Path of Fear*, begins with a happy-seeming man and woman stepping off a boat in Havana. No sooner have they taken in their first nightclub when she is fatally stabbed and he, to his surprise, is left holding the bloodied knife. Off he dashes, our hero, Scott (Eddie Albert), blamed for something he can't even begin to comprehend. Woolrich starts here, with the stamp of guilt, the flight through dark, unfriendly streets, before rewinding several months to explain how Scott, penniless and adrift, came to be the chauffeur of a Miami gangster. Smitten with the boss's wife, he ran away with her; their first night alone, clinging to one another in the hot Cuban air, was also their last. Abridging a narrative as dense and fractured as this for a half-hour teleplay involved distilling the story to its situational essence while also molding it to accommodate the obligatory commercial, a formula CBS's guidelines for the "Weird Sisters" outlined as "a two-act structure with a cliff-hanger middle-break." "Revenge" hits this point with Scott, blood on his hands and the hollering police at his heels, rounding a corner and reaching a dead end. Woolrich writes: "Two doorways in a darkened alley; one spelled life and one spelled death." Only via the "correct" door does Scott extend his adventure long enough to find someone with the wits to extract him from this mess.

A system of gateways and passages is important to a noir story: the prevalent iconography of winding stairwells and lonely streets goes lock-and-key with the labyrinthine plots. No other storytelling mechanism places such stress on causality, on the consequences of crossing literal and figurative thresholds. Even the most insignificant of actions can spell catastrophe; conversely, in turning one knob but not the other, hapless night-dashers like Scott can temporarily sidestep their inevitable reckoning. Woolrich's confused and lost fool is typical of noir's loser-heroes in that he retains complicity in misfortune. For these types, acting out, indulging desires or convictions, is an invitation for fate to sling its arrow. (Conformity, in this era, was a virtue on par with patriotism, regular church attendance, and a solid corporate job.) Were Scott to have kept his lust in check, he'd be safely back in Miami, scrubbing the boss's cars. Had the clerk in *The Clock* resisted the temptation to violate the vault, he might have avoided the conundrum of having to confess to one crime to prove his innocence in another.

The moral promoted by these fables is as conservative as it is cardinal: to err from the straight and narrow is to steer oneself headlong into the nightmare. Hence the title sequence of portending doom with which each *Danger* begins: a careening POV shot of a threatening highway at night in which the program title whizzes by as an unheeded sign. Noir fatalists like Woolrich and David Goodis built their canons describing the pitfalls awaiting those who travel dark roads with false impunity. Goodis, in his novel *Cassidy's Girl* (1951), paints his luckless protagonist's struggle to avoid the abyss in language familiar to any viewer of *Danger*: "Keeping his eye on the road and his mind on the wheel was a protective fence holding him back from internal as well as external catastrophe." In programs like *The Web* or *The Clock*, the barrier has likely already been hedged; in others, especially *Hands of Murder*, it's usually a pushing influence, a mitigating circumstance, which drives the protagonist over. What distinguishes one from the other is simply at what chapter in the downfall of a man (very rarely a woman) the story initiates.

Each *Hands of Murder* begins with a pair of disembodied hands mimicking the act of strangulation. "Hands commit murder," an off-screen voice explains. "But these hands merely obey the mind of the murderer. Hands are the vehicle through which the depths of human passion are funneled into one final act of violence." The murdering hands invariably belong to some poor sod prodded down an avenue of narrowing options. In "Street Gang" (1949), it's a weary ex-G.I. (Jack Palance) who can't seem to get a break. Tired of living on scraps, he pulls together a stick-up crew involving other embittered veterans from the neighborhood; when it comes time to split the loot, knives and guns get drawn. None of the would-be gangsters survive the fade-out. Other episodes linger on the moment at which an otherwise decent citizen reaches the breaking point. "A Room Full of Water" (1949), which takes place in a dystopian future of water rationing, tells of a desperate father (Henry Jones) who, after much frustration and haggling, kills a bootlegger of the precious fluid. Despondent with guilt, and not knowing how to explain his sin to his sickly son, he cries out, "It's all pounding in on me in waves!" Torn between criminality and responsibility, the noir antihero drowns in a sea of compunction and conflicted emotion.

Fixated as it is on the trauma of being pushed into a dark corner, *Hands of Murder* favors an atmosphere of subjective disquietude. Eschewing full-scale sets, creator-director Lawrence Menkin and his cameraman, Frank Bunetta, a video wizard he hired over from the DuMont assembly line, developed an expressionistic, at times abstract, schema of painted shadows, disproportionally sized props, and abnormal framings. One script called for an overhead shot of a character experiencing an anxiety dream; working around the limited verticality of the studio cameras, they brought the composition about by upending a bed and pinning linens around the actor, who then stood in his "sleep." For "A Room Full of Water," Menkin wanted the effect of the outer world closing in, so Bunetta devised an umbrella-like ceiling flat that curved inward on cue. Such trickery had to be performed seamlessly, and to the second, within the paces of what was already a nerve-racking endeavor. Where a program like *Suspense* would consist of a half-dozen scenes, or dramatic beats, *Hands of Murder* integrated more than thirty into a synchronized whole. "For here, at last," enthused *Billboard*, "is a half-hour show which leaves the audience as satisfied and emotionally exhausted as a ninety-minute movie. Isn't that what television has been groping for?"

For all its innovative stretching of a budget thin even by early television standards—DuMont, unlike its radio-buoyed rivals, floated in red ink—*Hands of Murder* drew considerable controversy for flaunting a premise by which violence became the situational recourse to life's vexing problems. After *Life*, in a 1949 feature article titled "TV Mayhem," chided the program for "a close-up of [a] victim's hand with blood slowly dribbling down over the fingers," DuMont hastily changed the title to *Hands of Destiny* (and, later, to *Hands of Mystery*.) Getting the audience invested in the murderous louses and losers paraded forth by the specialties was an ongoing challenge. Writers for *The Web*, mandated to drum up a "central sympathetic figure," frequently took to confining the action to a twenty-four-hour stretch—the idea being that an accordion-style narrative in which the hero is squeezed from both ends might appeal to a universal fear of engulfment.

In "The Line of Duty" (*The Web*, 1953), the entangled one is Tom (Richard Kiley), a homicide detective; the entity that has him in its grip is Rose (Ann Summers), a woman he's been seeing on the side. Even before Tom gets his first close-up, Rose is shown stretched out in a cheap-rent flat, smirking to herself as Tom frantically buzzes her door. Already we know the power dynamic of this coupling. Tom, when finally let in, declares their affair over—his wife suspects, he fears. Rose laughs in his face, promising to set things straight. From there, as they tear at each other with animalistic fervor, fighting for control of

"Incident in an Alley" (*U.S. Steel*, 1955) with Farley Granger.

"87th Precinct" (*Kraft*, 1958).

the telephone, and Rose slips the gun from Tom's holster, the veil between savagery and lust dissolves. When it's all over, Rose, her limbs twisted this way and that, is left silent on the floor. Tom, in a panic, gathers up his gun and his hat and runs. Arriving home to his wife, Joan (Norma Crane), and yet another cold supper, he tensely endures some rote inquiries about his day. The charade continues at the office, where Tom and his partner, Sal (Lou Polan), are assigned a homicide—Rose's. "What's the matter?" Sal wonders. "You look a little green."

By now it's clear that Tom is hardly heroic, or even redeemable. Yet his point of view dominates. Shots in which he isn't fore and center nevertheless treat him as the focal point, as in how he lingers in the background, nervously chain-smoking, while Sal interviews Rose's hulking husband, Laramie (Jack Warden). Onward from the main-title depiction of Tom imbedded in a web, we're asked to identity with his predicament. We watch him with morbid curiosity, his status that of a specimen squeezed into a biological slide. At the midway cliffhanger, a tight shot of Tom trying to avoid eye contact with the widower sums up the lingering question: when, and how thoroughly, will this SOB be taken apart? The second act responds with a whirl of revelations and reversals. Sal and Joan already know about the affair, as does Laramie. Rose, turns out, regained consciousness after the brawl with Tom long enough to find herself being throttled to death by her irate husband, who now aims to blackmail Tom into exonerating him. Tom's been had—toyed with by everyone. "You know, it's a funny thing," he says, handing over his shield and his gun. "Every time we made an arrest, I used to ask myself, 'How can a human being go so wrong?' I still don't know. I'm still asking."

The downfall of a cop is a recurrent theme of 1950s anthology drama. Exempted from the heroic consistency required of episodic fare, the anthologies position their police heroes as a conflicted, unreliable lot—if not weak and disgraced (as in "The Line of Duty"), then besieged and nearly undone, like Nick Vallejo (Dane Clark) of "Mad Bomber" (*Climax!*, 1957). The only Latino detective in his Spanish Harlem precinct, Vallejo is already a defensive, tightly wound wreck before his name begins appearing in the crayon-scrawled manifestos of an anonymous terrorist. "I will have my vengeance," the madman warns. "Anyone connected with Vallejo must share his punishment." Clueless as to why he's been singled out, but feeling responsible for the escalating mayhem, Vallejo struggles to untangle a vendetta that's morphed into a threat against the community at large. The resolution of such plots often hinges on whether the cop will catch the psycho-villain before he himself goes toppling over the edge. While Vallejo proves his competency as a detective by apprehending the bomber (a very creepy Theodore Bikel), the strain induces a nervous breakdown. A closing shot of the hero-cop on his knees, reduced to a whimper, is a startling one in a decade that had, by this point, also birthed the supercops of *Dragnet* and *M Squad*.

"Mad Bomber" (*Climax!, 1957*) with Dane Clark.

The dark energies percolating through the noir city have a way of swallowing even the most stalwart. Operating on a nocturnal clock, alienated from normative rituals, our detectives become neurotically fixated with the doings of the night. Ed Brooks (Richard Boone), the plainclothesman of "To Walk the Night" (*Climax!*, 1957), is so obsessed with trapping a masked rapist known as the "holiday prowler" that he spends Christmas Eve cajoling the fiend's previous victims into recounting the horrors of their assaults. Deluged with lawlessness, the noir enforcer becomes frazzled, incapable of judgment, like the beat cop (Farley Granger) in "Incident in an Alley" (*U.S. Steel*, 1955) who rashly guns down a boy he sees fleeing the scene of a crime. Other cops armor themselves with a defensive layer of callousness—a self-enforced cynicism. In "87th Precinct" (*Kraft*, 1958), from the novel by Evan Hunter, a shrill recluse phones Steve Carella (Robert Bray) to report a prowler for the umpteenth time that month, but the jaded detective brushes her off. Later, when the old lady is found dead, he goes into a tailspin, his guilt and self-loathing given symbolic transference in the oppressive heat wave that's gripped the city.

"The Man Who Killed Hitler" (*Hands of Murder*, 1949).

"87th Precinct" was adapted for television by Larry Cohen, an NBC page at the time. For his second script, also staged for *Kraft*, he turned to a paperback original by William L. Stuart about a cold, hard brute of a cop. "Night Cry" (1958) begins with Mark Deglin (Jack Klugman) staring scornfully into the camera as he learns that he's once again been passed over for promotion. "The way you operate, the boys downtown are scared to trust you," his captain (Ray Poole) explains. When the call comes in that there's been a stabbing at a gambling club, and that the suspect, Kendall Paine (Harry Millard), is a war hero whose prowess with a knife got him through Korea, Deglin jumps at the chance to bring him in. "You got medals for carving up people, don't you, hero?" he hisses as he darkens the doorway of Paine's rented room. But the "hero" is hardly that; drunk and sour, a bloodied patch over his eye, Paine is no match for Deglin. He tells the cop to kiss off. Deglin's fists go up. His punches are merciless. When Paine stops moving, Deglin steps back, his face in close-up, as the realization of what he's done takes hold. "The barriers that had held his emotions broke and thoughts came flooding at him, released," writes Stuart. "They had escaped and now they would burrow and work, reappearing briefly and scuttlingly, like rats in an alley."

"In the Line of Duty" (*The Web*, 1953) with Richard Kiley.

Having brought himself to the abyss, Deglin becomes a plaything of fate, beginning with the twist, as he learns upon phoning in to headquarters, that the dead man at his feet is no longer a police suspect. Told to bring him in anyway, Deglin makes up some business about Paine appearing to have skipped town, a fiction he elongates by impersonating his victim and pretending to catch a train in haste. Thereafter, he finds himself in room after room with someone who threatens to expose his lie, from the captain who puts him in charge of the "missing-person" investigation, to the speculating lowlife (Peter Falk) who tries to extort him, and whom he bullies into silence, to the neighborhood chatterbox

"To Walk the Night" (*Climax!*, 1957)
with Richard Boone.

who comes forward to finger Deglin as the shady character she saw dragging a rolled-up carpet toward the waterfront. Deglin silences her as well. The grumble of scuttling feet persists. It's with plays like "Night Cry" that the live noir fully exploits the hermetic nature of its production conditions. Set in New York and broadcast from there, yet prevented from bringing its tethered cameras outside, "Night Cry" is left to occupy a landscape with no visible means of escape. Deglin's is a journey through airless, close-ended spaces—an oppressive realm in which fate and a self-destructive impulse are bound to intersect.

Stuart's novel, published in 1948, was also the basis for the Otto Preminger film *Where the Sidewalk Ends* (1950). There, the Deglin character, renamed Dixon and played by Dana Andrews, is what he is because of his father, a notorious criminal: "I've worked all my life to be different from him," he says. Deglin, in the *Kraft* play, is given little motivation for his pugnacity beyond the attritive effects of his environment. Years of policing "the punks and the hoods and the fast-buck boys and girls" have stoked him with the steely violence of the city, a condition made evident in the hopeless relationship he begins with Paine's socialite girlfriend, Morgan (Diana Van der Vlis). Mistaking the cop's anguished state for a vulnerable nature, Morgan clings to Deglin as a substitute for her disappeared lover. Paine, she reveals, returned from the war with a metal plate in his head (hence the potency of Deglin's punches); depressed and angry, he took to picking fights. "He gets irrational and aggressive, almost brutal," she volunteers during one of Deglin's farcical inquiries. "He becomes frightening. He becomes a man who absolutely must smash somebody else to relieve himself of some terrible tension." Hearing it like this, present-tense references and all, Deglin seems ready to crawl out of his skin. This mirroring of fallen cop and fallen veteran, each a bruised/bruising figure maladjusted to society, epitomizes the "dark other" trope central to noir.

In the Preminger film, the cop pins his crime on a mobster against whom he has a long-standing grudge, a man guilty of *something*. Deglin, in contrast, misdirects the investigation by framing an innocent, Paine's friend Pete (Mark Roberts), an altogether more cynical choice. Once Morgan, whom Pete had secretly been wooing, is implicated, Deglin, engorged with shame, implodes. In Stuart's novel, Dixon/Deglin extricates himself by scramming town, leaving Morgan and Pete to fry. Preminger finishes his film with the fanciful promise of romance between Dixon and Morgan. Cohen's ending for *Kraft* is bleaker, more in keeping with live noir's emphasis on personal accountability. Owing up to his sins, Deglin turns in his shield and is left standing before a wall map of the city, his head hung low. The camera, having completed its examination of this troubled soul, slowly retreats. "Night Cry" was one of the last live dramas presented by *Kraft*. By then, in hopes of competing with the genre-based telefilms being churned out by Hollywood, it had retitled itself *Kraft Mystery Theatre*. It left the air in 1958, as did *Studio One* and *Climax!*, thus sounding the death rattle of the live anthology drama.

LIVE NOIR III:
THE DETECTIVES

The story of the honest detective who thinks faster than the police and is maneuvered into impossible situations only to wiggle out just in time is a standard pattern in the movies and on the radio. Now the same theme is proving just as trustworthy on TV.

—*Newsweek*, 1949

A SWIRLING CLOUD OF SMOKE IS AS UBIQUITOUS IN NOIR AS A CREEPING shadow: both add to the dim and nihilistic atmosphere of a world burning from the inside. The nightclubs and salons of noir are filled with smoke, as are its precinct houses (discount cigarettes) and gangsters' lairs (imported cigars). Marlowe smoked, as did Spade; both were brought to the screen by Humphrey Bogart—hence the dangling "bogey" synonymous with the public image of the detective. It was because of associations like these that Big Tobacco, keen on appealing to the demographic that devoured crime fiction in its many forms (movies, radio, pulps, and paperbacks), became the primary sponsor of such early episodic noir as *Man Against Crime* (CBS, 1949–1953; NBC/DuMont, 1953–1954), *Martin Kane, Private Eye* (NBC, 1949–1954), and *The Plainclothes Man* (DuMont, 1949–1953). The detective genre, with its rote

Publicity still for *Martin Kane, Private Eye* with William Gargan (1949).

cycle of a case assumed, investigated, and solved, offered the ideal platform for the repetitive hawking of a product that was meant to be ignited, inhaled, and extinguished. Smoking represented ritual, and the ritual was parlayed into formula: a weekly whodunit.

The U.S. Tobacco Company, in assuming sponsorship of *Martin Kane, Private Eye*, felt strongly that its detective should be a pipe smoker and saw to it that a tobacco shop be written into the show, lest Kane ever find himself in a spot without a pouch of Old Briar, that "master mixture of rare flavor and aroma." Though a cigarette smoker offscreen, William Gargan, who originated the role, proved himself adept at the courtly art of pipe stuffing; Lloyd Nolan and Lee Tracy, the actors who succeeded him, less so. Mark Stevens, the fourth and

TOP: Title Sequence (*Man Against Crime*, 1951).

CENTER: *The Plainclothes Man* (1953).

BOTTOM: Publicity still for *Detective Story* (stage, 1949) with Ralph Bellamy.

final Martin Kane, insisted his fix be wrapped in paper, like Joe Friday, a Chesterfield man. Over on *Man Against Crime*, a private-eye show bankrolled by R.J. Reynolds, Mike Barnett filled his ashtray with the butts of Camels; Ralph Bellamy, who played him, made a point of angling the pack on his desk for maximum camera exposure. Given that these shows were put on the air live, under excruciating pressure, the actors probably welcomed the license to smoke while working.

Debuting a few weeks apart, *Martin Kane, Man Against Crime,* and *The Plainclothes Man* successfully introduced the episodic crime series, with its continuing hero, a solver of crimes, to television audiences. Their prototype is the Hammett-Chandler hardboiled mystery, ironed out to fit a half-hour slot, and then bisected with a commercial—a two-act paradigm already proven successful on radio. As the peddlers of tobacco saw it, an immediate splash of chaos was essential in retaining viewer interest through the first act and into the obligatory break. In a memorandum to the writers of *Man Against Crime*, the William Esty Agency, which produced the series for Reynolds, outlined the formula: "It has been found that we retain audience interest best when our story is concerned with murder. Therefore, although other crimes may be introduced, somebody must be murdered, preferably early, with the threat of more violence to come." The detective-hero, though battered about, was to conclude his adventure triumphant and unscathed, his fingers, despite the beatings administered or endured, in reasonable enough working order to operate a Zippo for the closing plug.

Attendant to its dramaturgical advice, the Esty Agency issued strict guidelines for the proper alignment of nicotine intake with heroic stature: "Do not have the heavy or any disreputable person smoking a cigarette. Do not associate the smoking of cigarettes with undesirable scenes or situations plot-wise." Only Barnett, "defender of the oppressed and a fearless fighter for common justice," was to enjoy the extra mildness, extra coolness, and extra flavor of a filterless Camel, preferably one after another. Likewise on *Martin Kane* smoking was a privilege reserved for the discerning professional: only Kane and the police smoke. Rather than stop the action for the sponsor's message, the J. Walter Thompson Agency, which oversaw the show, simply integrated it into the plot. Halfway through each investigation, regardless of how muddled a puzzle he faces, Kane drops by Happy McMann's tobacco emporium. "Boy, this one really is a humdinger," Happy (Walter Kinsella), a retired detective himself, will say as he chats up Kane. Commercials had quietly been a part of television since 1946; by 1949 they were overt: glad you're enjoying the story, now how about reconsidering your purchasing habits?

Happy's is also where Kane interacts with the police; depending on the Kane, this can be a fruitful encounter or a very unpleasant one. Often, Kane and the cops will move to the foreground to hammer out a theory between puffs, while Happy, back at his counter, can be heard extolling the virtues of his wares to a customer, resulting in a soundtrack that's part expository patter and part smooth salesmanship. Because the timing of every *Kane* had to be accurate to the second, the writers allotted a search scene in the second act: if the show was over schedule, the actor would find the clue instantly; if it was running slow, he could rummage more carelessly. *Man Against Crime* deployed the same tactic. A live telecast introduced other perils: forgotten dialogue, "walking corpses," wandering stagehands, visible microphones, electrical shortages, and so forth. In *Martin Kane*, when Lloyd Nolan slugs a fellow with his right hand while boasting of his "left hook," we take it not as a line flub, but as the utterance of a man caught in the thrall of an uninterrupted performance. As Nolan's successor, Lee Tracy, put it: "The good old adrenalin glands start working, and you're operating on a rarefied plane."

Each episode of *Kane* and *Crime* opens with someone stabbed, shot, or swindled (sometimes all three). The police, baffled, step aside to make way for the private eye. From there, Borde and Chaumeton's generic outline of the investigator-hero plot fills in: "He's tailed, hit over the head, arrested. Let him ask for information, and he finds himself tied up, bleeding, in some deep cellar. Various men, questioned at night, shoot and then run off. There is, in this incoherent brutality, something dreamlike . . ." In both series, this oneiric quality is further developed by the dreamy buzz of a story told live. The claustrophobic arrangement of the detective's milieu; his breathless dashing about from set to set, fight to chase, inquisition to confession; the illogical piling up of strange clues, wrong impressions, doors that open to bursts of gunfire—all conspire with a gloomy (to modern ears) organ score to create a private-eye adventure of considerable lucidity. Moreover, the economy of production, coupled with the imperative to evoke and sustain an aura of mystery, gives rise to a creative use of light and shadow that's at one with the noir style, particularly on *Martin Kane*.

Telecast from NBC headquarters in Rockefeller Center, *Kane* was the first crime series to straddle two mediums. U.S. Tobacco, eager to reach any potential smoker not within range of a television signal, launched

Trade Advertisement for *Martin Kane, Private Eye* with Lloyd Nolan (1951).

LLOYD NOLAN

as Martin Kane, Private Eye

Television – N B C • T V
Thursdays...61 Stations
10 TO 10:30 P.M. – *E. D. T.*

Radio – N B C
Sundays...167 Stations
4:30 TO 5:00 P.M. – *E. D. T.*

Sponsor
U. S. TOBACCO CO.

Kudner Agency, Jnc.

PERSONAL MANAGEMENT
Lester Linsk

PUBLIC RELATIONS
Rogers & Cowan

ABOVE: *Mike Barnett: Man Against Crime* (Fawcett, 1952).

RIGHT: On the set of *Man Against Crime* (1950) with Ralph Bellamy.

an alternate version on radio—same Kane, different scripts. "On radio I usually pack a gun, and my relation with the cops is snarling and antagonistic," Tracy explained. "On television, to get a gun, I usually have to take it away by force from some crook, and I'm such a pal of the cops I play pinochle with them." A few blocks away, Ralph Bellamy ran his own juggling act: he spent his first year as Mike Barnett pulling double duty as the lead in the Broadway production of *Detective Story*. "I finished *Man Against Crime* at about two minutes to nine every Friday night," he writes in his autobiography, "and was then rushed to a waiting elevator that took me down to a waiting squad car." Siren wailing, Bellamy would scram across midtown to make his second curtain.

Man Against Crime originated in a tiny studio on the top floor of Grand Central Station, until it went to film (and left CBS) in its fourth season, when it was produced at the old Edison complex in the Bronx. The filmed episodes of *Man Against Crime*, syndicated as *Follow That Man* (and appearing on both NBC and DuMont), engage the five boroughs of New York City as an extended backlot. While gaining some travelogue appeal, the telefilm incarnation of the series forfeits the manic, anything-goes vibe of its live period. In his crusade against crime, the live Barnett gets in more tight spots than a shoehorn. Lawrence Klee, the former radio noir writer (*The Fat Man*; *Mr. Keen, Tracer of Lost Persons*) who created the character, conceived of him as an average fellow, neither too bright nor too dumb, tough yet gallant. While Barnett doesn't carry a gun ("My tailor objects," he quips), he's quite adept at obtaining them, particularly from opponents with wrists of straw. His signature move goes like this: twist the villain's arm into a pretzel, kick out his feet, disarm him, and pocket the gun. "At the end of one show," Bellamy noted, "I ended up with five pistols, none of them mine originally."

Meticulous about appearances and especially his name ("that's Barnett with two t's"), Barnett is quick to notice details. "No man's wife would sew a button on a blue suit with tan thread," he points out to a thug who tries to pass himself off as the husband of an acquaintance. Barnett is highly prone to derring-do. In one episode from 1951 (none of the live shows were given titles), he barges into a physician's office, sweeps aside the receptionist, yanks a stethoscope from a cabinet, and slaps it to the wall—the clinic, it goes, adjoins the office of the criminal he's after. Unable to make sense of the mumbles, Barnett marches over to the window. "That's a drop of five stories," a nurse warns. "It's all right," Barnett says as he climbs out on the ledge. "I've got rubber heels." Barnett's inexhaustible pursuit of villainy, coupled with his ability to absorb and deliver all kinds of bodily harm, made *Man Against Crime* a national sensation. In 1954, when Albert L. Patterson ran for Attorney General of Alabama on a pledge to clean up the notoriously lawless honky-tonk district of Phenix City (an endeavor chronicled to its tragic end in Phil Karlson's 1955 docu-noir *The Phenix City Story*), he billed himself as "A Man Against Crime" in a clear ode to Barnett.

Publicity still for *Man Against Crime* (1953) with Ralph Bellamy and Gloria McGhee.

In another 1951 segment, Barnett, seeking a break from big-city crime, goes on a fishing holiday in Vermont, where he's enlisted by an anxious beauty (Carole Matthews) to find out why her father, a traveling salesman, was found floating facedown in a nearby lake. Several scuffles later, Barnett gets to the root of a nefarious scheme whereby gold bullion is being smuggled across the border in the vehicles of unsuspecting commuters. His discovery, arrived at during his second-act search, that the chief smuggler (Parker Fennelly) is not only the chief of police, but is also in league with a gang of communists (the gold is for destabilizing the economy), fits in well with noir's cynical regard for power structures. But it's Barnett's wisecracking persona, hardboiled to the point of near-parody ("Nickels and dimes don't add up to murder, but that rifle does—that's the sound grand larceny makes!"), that situates *Man Against Crime* as the cupped hand at the end of a pipeline of pulp snaking from the penny-a-word prose of

TOP: *Martin Kane, Private Eye* (1952) with Lloyd Nolan.

CENTER: *Man Against Crime* (1952).

BOTTOM: *Martin Kane, Private Eye* (1952) with Lloyd Nolan and Walter Matthau.

Black Mask through a decade's worth of film and radio detective mysteries. With its audacious plotting, its paneling of action, its bubbling of dialogue, it's about as close to a cartoon as a live-action work of noir can get.

Martin Kane, on the other hand, is a comparatively intricate and textured work, a construction likely owed to the workings of paperback novelist Henry Kane, its head writer for three seasons. *Martin Kane*'s installments unfold hastily, often deliriously, as if there were too much story for too few minutes. More so than in *Man Against Crime*, the emphasis is on presenting a seemingly unsolvable whodunit: the denser the narrative, the more red herrings and false leads tossed at the detective, the more likely the viewer will remained glued through the integrated commercials. Typical of its multi-layered plotting is "The District Attorney Killer" (1951), from a teleplay by Kane, in which murder, infidelity, and revenge are wrapped around the noir cores of the dark past, the wrong man, and the transference of guilt. The story opens with a sudden act of violence in a Manhattan courtroom. Convicted killer Thomas Randall (Frank de Kova), mere days away from his execution at Sing Sing, has volunteered to deliver testimony that will exonerate Harry Wright (Mason Curry), his presumed accomplice in a robbery-homicide. No sooner is he sworn in when Randall whips out a pistol and assassinates the district attorney, Harrison (John Boruff), responsible for his conviction. "I'm gonna fry anyway!" he hollers in tight close-up.

When the judge demands to know how a gun entered the courtroom, Randall points an accusing finger at his defense counsel, Jeffrey O'Donnell (Vinton Hayworth), who reacts with bewilderment. Enter Martin Kane (played here by Gargan), brought on to the case by O'Donnell's legal assistant, John Blake (Will Hare). In narrated flashback, Blake describes how Randall and an accomplice with a cross-flag tattoo on his arm barged into a mom-and-pop grocery store, guns ablaze. Director Frank Burns begins the flashback from the first-person perspective of the unseen accomplice—a disorienting, opaque way of visualizing the events, but one that becomes clear by the story's end. After the criminals flee, the camera remains, its subjective stance now assuming a stable, objective one. As the camera moves down the length of the store to where the grocer cradles his dead wife, the frame widens to show a policeman dragging in Wright, whom the grocer then positively identifies. For a live production, it's a tricky bit of blocking. In a film, such exposition would be conveyed via montage; here, the stick-up, the murder and its aftermath, and the arrest of the wrong man are all compressed into a single uninterrupted dolly shot.

Blake goes on to explain to Kane how O'Donnell always presumed Wright to be innocent, but given the amount of circumstantial evidence—a prior spell in reform school; his squirrelly behavior outside the store ("He got panicky and ran—right into the arms of a cop"); and, notably, his having a cross-flag tattoo—Wright was convicted alongside Randall. Kane, in assuming the case, is tasked with unraveling a series of puzzles: establishing Wright's innocence; determining the true identity of Randall's tattooed accomplice; ascertaining how Randall came to possess O'Donnell's personal handgun; and, ultimately, clearing O'Donnell of involvement in the death of the district attorney (a matter complicated by the revelation that O'Donnell's wife had been running around with Harrison). The interrelation of each underscores the complexity of the noir private eye's work. No case ever follows a straight line, and, more often than not, several smaller puzzles must be solved before the larger enigma can be clearly assessed, let alone successfully unraveled.

In 1951, U.S. Tobacco, tiring of Gargan as their pitchman, brought in Nolan, a breezier Kane—a real cocky bastard. In one episode, after his arm has been nearly snapped in half, he says to the camera, "Don't worry about this, I heal fast." Nolan was in turn replaced, after one season, by Tracy; his Kane, a tough cynic with a thick streak of sentimentality, was not unlike his Hildy Johnson in the original stage run of *The Front Page*. "Martin Kane is getting to be one of those roles like Hamlet," wrote *New York Herald-Tribune* critic John Crosby. "You compare the present actor to all those who proceed him, generally to his disadvantage, the others being beclouded by time." The fourth Kane, Mark

Publicity still for *Martin Kane, Private Eye* (1951) with Lloyd Nolan.

Stevens, a generation younger than his forebears, fancied himself the next Jack Webb. He sought to reinvent the character as the private-eye incarnation of Joe Friday, an ambition shared by U.S. Tobacco, which was incensed that its rival Fatimo had scored big with *Dragnet* (1951–1959). "The legendary private eye is a myth, sometimes a laughable one," Stevens complained. "That business about the slick 'eye' solving the case himself, then handing over the crooks wrapped in cellophane paper to the dim-witted police is nonsense."

While *Dragnet* is often cited as the first police program, it was preceded on the air by *The Plainclothes Man*, a live subjective-camera series for DuMont. As with *Man Against Crime* and *Martin Kane*, it borrows heavily from the Hammett-Chandler milieu: there are gangsters and gunsels, femmes fatales, sexual deviants, double- and triple-crossers, and more. Ken Lynch, who plays the titular Lieutenant, is never seen; rather, we see what he sees. His off-screen voice, occasional gestures, and near-constant stream of pipe smoke

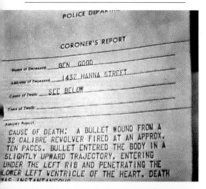

The Plainclothes Man (1949).

(Edgeworth Tobacco sponsored the show) guide us through each investigation. The primary camera, the one standing in for the Lieutenant, is set at eye level: when a body is splayed out on the floor, our view tilts down to reveal its twisted form. When the forensic boys hand over a coroner's report, we read along, absorbing the grisly, typed-up facts—time of death, number of wounds, likely weapon. When the clues coalesce, and the Lieutenant finally corners his culprit, we're confronted with a mean-looking mug glaring back, poised for confrontation or a hasty denial. Should someone take a swipe at the Lieutenant, a fairly common occurrence, a huge fist smashes into the lens.

In lieu of a visible leading man, the Lieutenant's second banana, Sgt. Brady (Jack Orrison), is the most familiar face. His gruff patter, delivered directly to the camera, reinforces the notion that we're a central participant in the investigation at hand. But where a film noir like *Lady in the Lake* (1947) purveys an exclusively singular viewpoint, *The Plainclothes Man* lets in a little air. This isn't completely "our" story: when the Lieutenant interrogates a criminal or takes a statement from a witness, the action cuts back in time to reveal, from a traditionally neutral perspective, the events being discussed. Through flashback, the bits and pieces of the ancillary narratives that add up to the crime being solved are put forth to be dissected and analyzed. The result of such deft weaving of past and present, third- and first-person, is that we're along for the juicier parts of the ride, as in one episode from 1953, when a trigger-happy punk (Bob Readich) and his moll (Sally Gracie) tear a swath of chaos through the underworld, robbing and killing one high-level racketeer after another, until "we" finally put them down—case closed.

Series director William Marceau mounts it all with convincing style and a gritty tempo, from an extreme close-up of a nervous hand loading a revolver to a startling match cut between the Lieutenant's shoes up on his desk and a pair of tagged feet on a morgue slab. Along with the innately intimate quality of live television, the mostly first-person viewpoint of the series encourages the hero identification so critical to the investigative story. As Marceau explained, "the format is built directly around the fact that there is in all lovers of the detective story the subconscious desire to be a detective and actively share in the unraveling of clues." Given that the Lieutenant makes full use of his pre-Miranda authority, we're also made complicit in any funny business that occurs. One viewer, writing in to *TV Guide*, complained, "He goes through everybody's personal property without warrant and talks to all people as though they were no good." From this early stage, television's investigator-hero was entrusted to be a tough but fair custodian of justice. In due order, he'd become an altogether different creation—morose, obsessive, driven to the extreme. The ritual of a mystery sparked, experienced, and finished would endure.

A
CLASSIC
CYCLE

HOLLYWOOD NOIR: THE RISE OF THE TELEFILM

Morning, noon and night the channels are cluttered with eye-wearying monstrosities called films for TV—half-hour aberrations that in story and acting would make an erstwhile Hollywood producer of 'B' pictures shake his head in dismay.

—JACK GOULD, 1952

L IVE DRAMA MAY HAVE PROVIDED A CULTURAL CACHET, AN AIR OF PRESTIGE, but it was the Hollywood-made telefilm, or filmed series, that supplied the hungry medium with its sustenance—its filler. While the studios argued internally about how, and for how much, they might get involved in television, the "eye-wearying monstrosities" that would finally unite and thoroughly transform both industries were already breeding along a stretch of Sunset Boulevard known as Poverty Row. Home to high-volume, low-cost stables like Monogram, Republic, and Eagle-Lion, and scores of fly-by-night hucksters, it was here that the telefilm was invented, with the "B" (or lower) crime melodrama being the preferred template. And it was in this vein that independent producer Jerry Fairbanks created "The Case of the Missing Bullet," television's first pilot. A whodunit about a slain policeman, filmed in the voguish style of subjective camera, it ends with a public prosecutor pointing his finger to the camera-eye and naming "You!" as the killer. Seventeen-minute reel in hand, Fairbanks marched into NBC's New York headquarters in August of 1947 to make the pitch for "freeing television from the shackles of the live stage." Returned to Hollywood with some seed money, he hired prolific "B" movie director Lew Landers to film a rash of additional episodes, all the while refining the technical kinks of his pioneering method of emulating, on film, the three-camera system of live drama. While the resulting series, *Public Prosecutor*, was ultimately rejected by NBC (to be picked up some years later by DuMont), Fairbanks's initiative inspired other entrepreneurs.

As a speculative endeavor, the production of films for television held all the promise of a gold rush. Stanley Rubin was an out-of-work screenwriter with a pair of film noir "quickies," *Decoy* (1946) and *Violence* (1947), to his name when he decided to go into television. Unwilling to remain idle during the Hollywood slump of 1947–1948, he talked his co-writer on *Violence*, Lewis Lantz, into helping him adapt Guy de Maupassant's short story "The Necklace" into a short film—the first entry in a series to be known as *Your Show Time*. Anthologies like the recently launched *Kraft TV Theatre*, Rubin surmised, were likely to become the mainstay of prime time—why not make one on celluloid? While nei-

OPPOSITE PAGE: *China Smith* with Dan Duryea (1953).

"The Man Who Had Nothing to Lose" (*Bigelow Theatre,* 1951) with Neville Brand.

ther scribe knew much about television, they had the foresight, along with their producer Marshall Grant (*Moonrise,* 1947), to lease the series directly to a powerhouse sponsor, U.S. Tobacco, which in turn exercised its muscle in finding a berth for it in NBC's 1949 lineup. Television's first filmed series debuted just as the coaxial cable linking New York to Chicago brought the networks one time zone closer to becoming a fully national enterprise. With twelve stations in operation, and hundreds more awaiting licensing, it was clear that an alternative was needed to live programming. But where the appetite for ready-to-play material was bottomless, the means of settling the bill required some ironing out.

Fireside Theatre (1949–1958) was the first to settle on a viable formula. To keep costs in line with what Procter & Gamble paid in commercial fees, it farmed production out to director-producers well versed in bare-bones practices, like John Reinhardt, who made *The Guilty* and *For You I Die* (both 1947) and Jack Bernhard, who put Stanley Rubin's words into pictures in *Decoy* and *Violence.* Reinhardt's segments mostly deal with corruptive individuals: a cop blackmails a judge ("Epilogue," 1949); a hoodlum frames his partner ("Double Jeopardy," 1950). Bernhard's tend to rely on noir's ironic twists of fate. "Reprieve" (1950) tells of a woman who contracts her own murder after learning that she has a fatal disease; only too late does she learn that she's been misdiagnosed—the hitman offers no refund. Frank Wisbar, whose career traced back to Weimar cinema, oversaw the early seasons of *Fireside.* With fellow émigrés Curt Siodmak and Arnold Phillips on his writing staff, he turned out one telenoir after another on an average budget of $17,000. Many, like "The Green Convertible" (1950), in which an unfaithful spouse is besieged with paranoid visions of a mysterious stalker, or "The Hot Spot" (1951), about a wife who shoots her gangster of a husband and escapes to the desert, where she quickly loses her way, deal with persecution and entrapment, themes familiar to those who fled Hitler. Others introduce an element of the absurd—an awareness of how quickly life can turn upside down. "Back to Zero" (1951) follows a girl chased by the police for reasons she's unable to fathom. "Torture" (1951) features Vincent Price as a hitman hiding out in a labyrinthine tenement building from which there seems to be no exit.

Wisbar suffuses these stories with a heady dose of noir atmospherics. "Marked for Death" (1955), a thriller about a former POW hunting the Gestapo agent who tortured him, unwinds against morbid Day of the Dead festivities.

Variety described it as a "stark drama of smoldering hatred and revenge that has the cutting edge of cold steel and grips like a vise." *TV Guide* may have decried that *Fireside Theatre* "makes no attempt at artiness, profundity, or significance," but by the end of its first season it was the second-most-watched program on the air (topped only by Mr. Television himself, Milton Berle). No other anthology of the 1950s, live or filmed, matched its popularity. The success of *Fireside* spurred many of the anthologies that began live, like *Ford Theatre* (1948–1957) and *Schlitz Playhouse of Stars* (1951–1958), to relocate westward, to where telefilms were made. At the same time, episodic series like *Dragnet* (1951–1959), *China Smith* (1952–1955), and *I Led 3 Lives* (1953–1956) eschewed the live route altogether by originating directly on film. By 1952, the production of films for television eclipsed the output of movies made for cinemas. Signs began appearing in film labs: "Unless otherwise specified, all film will be processed for TV." From the Big Five (20th Century-Fox, MGM, Paramount, RKO, Warner Bros.) to the Little Three (Columbia, United Artists, Universal-International), the studios began renting out, or outright selling, their backlots to telefilm producers, or producing their own fare for television. The telefilm was here to stay. Hollywood, nearly wiped out in the late 1940s, became a boomtown.

"The Unlighted Road" (*Schlitz Playhouse of Stars*, 1955) with James Dean and Patricia Hardy.

"The Untouchables" (*Westinghouse Desilu Playhouse*, 1959) with Keenan Wynn and Robert Stack.

As demand for canned content exploded, those "B" veterans adept at crafting fast-moving stories on limited means became, for budget-conscious packagers, the directors of choice: Robert Florey, Felix Feist, Phil Karlson, John Brahm, William Beaudine, John Meredyth Lucas. By 1956, for the telefilm anthologies alone, there were nearly two thousand stand-alone titles in circulation—television's equivalent of the salacious paperbacks filling the racks in drugstores and bus stations. Recyclable rather than disposable, they could be repeated, endlessly, without the degradation of picture quality characteristic of kinescopes; once a series finished its run, its segments were bundled with other telefilms and re-aired with new sponsorship for local markets, ad infinitum, thus disproving concerns that audiences wouldn't watch the same story more than once. Those who viewed live drama as a singular cultural experience regarded the trend with dismay. In reviewing one early tele-noir, "Satan's Waitin'"(*Colgate Theatre*, 1951), a product of Jerry Fairbanks's Sunset workshop, Jack Gould sniffed, "No doubt the television boys know their own business, but more than one viewer must be wondering why a new medium, with all its technical magic, persists in turning back the clock and uses celluloid when the electron is more satisfactory."

Leonard Goldenson, chief of ABC, was indeed a boy who knew his business. His network was a perennial flounderer until, in 1955, he entered into an exclusive telefilm pact with Warner Bros. Goldenson made no excuses for his programming strategy; eyeballs, not accolades, sold ad spots: "ABC believes that the 'B' picture is the correct television show, as once it was the correct show in the neighborhood movie house." Jim Kitses, in his monograph on *Gun Crazy* (1950), writes of how "the classic position of the 'B' movie on the lower half of the program defined it as a bonus, a gift, a freebie [and] made excusable the frequently shoddy quality of the production, and its often shameless catering to the audience's baser instincts." While criticized for catering to popular tastes, the filmed series that steadily gained dominance over the live ones grew directly out of the aesthetic (visceral, compelling) and economic (cheap, quick) imperatives of Hollywood's second-tier factories. The "B" movie never died; it simply moved to television, an exodus encouraged not only by the glaring conundrum of too much airtime and too little product to fill it, but by a surge in the number of television-equipped households. No longer the high-luxury totem it had been in the immediate postwar years, television by the early 1950s was a staple in the homes of many blue-collar and middle-class families—the target audience of the genre fare down at the local bijou. Spun out in mass-produced frenzy for a nation of *TV Guide* subscribers, the tropes and iconography of "B" movies, and in particular "B" noir, became an integral facet of how stories were told for television.

TOP: "Man Without Fear" (*Ford Theatre*, 1956) with Raymond Burr.

BOTTOM: "Catch at Straws" *Ford Theatre*, 1956) with Kerwin Matthews and Carol Corby.

When Columbia's Screen Gems took over production of *Ford Theatre* in 1952, it marked the first entry into the telefilm market by a Hollywood heavyweight. Trade announcements leading up to the relaunch touted its acquisition of Richard Deming's pulp saga of a syndicate hit man, *Edge of the Law*, as well as its hiring of film writers like Karen De Wolfe (*Bury Me Dead*, 1947), Steve Fisher (*I Wake Up Screaming*, 1941), and Charles Bennett (*Where Danger Lives*, 1950). Like other branded anthologies, *Ford* followed a round-robin format in which the noir melodrama occupied a prime spot. The subversions of law and order on display in, for example, "Margin for Fear" (1953), about a detective arrested on a brutality charge, and "The Night Visitor" (1954), which deals with a zealous cop accused of taking a bribe, attest to a complex treatment of police-heroes rarely seen outside live noir. Vigilantism, as interwoven with stories of men returning from war or a stint in prison, was another popular theme. "Catch at Straws" (1956) opens with the near-fatal beating of a veteran (Kerwin Matthews) accused of having "gone commie" during his captivity in Korea. "I've had my fill of running," he mutters to his sweetheart as the high-key beam of an automobile fatalistically pins them against a fence. In De Wolfe's "Man Without

Fear" (1956), Raymond Burr is an escaped convict intent on snuffing out the shifty business partner (Joseph Cotten) who framed him for embezzlement and took up with his wife. Typical of half-hour tele-noir, it picks up just before the climax of a longer, unseen story, with Burr's would-be murderer huddling in the rain outside his target's home, scowling and determined, before charging inside for a confrontation.

Where the live anthologies focused on internal conflict, crises of the soul, monologues, self-analysis, the telefilm anthologies dealt in external conflict—chases, stand-offs, running-gun battles. Free to shoot all over Los Angeles, so long as the show was in the can in two days, they played out their clashes on sets already sketched. *Rebound* (a/k/a *Counterpoint*; 1952–1953), from MCA's Revue Studios, was among the first to make use of extensive location filming. As overseen by Bernard Girard, author of "B" noirs like *Waterfront at Midnight* (1948) and *This Woman Is Danger* (1952), and lensed by ace cameraman Lucien Andriot, the series gives conspicuous attention to noir geography. Relying more on movement and motive than dialogue or superfluous plotting, its installments strive for a naturalistic ambience and a low-simmering tension. The central set piece of "The Witness" (1952) isn't the heist upon which the first act turns—a shot of a plundered vault and the stiff feet of a guard fill in the blanks—but the immediate aftermath, a long-take exterior scene in which everything goes awry. Master thief Talley (Edwin Max), cursing his spell of bad luck, has vowed to skip town with his moll, Annie (Vera Marshe). But first, so they have some scratch to live on, he has one last score to pull down: a jewelry store. Vaguely cognizant that unseen forces are shaping his life—his muttered line, "I tell you, this town is a jinx," opens the film—Talley nevertheless boasts enough confidence in his expertise as a safecracker to convince himself that he can sidestep fate. "Don't worry, this is duck soup," he tells Annie as he leaves for the job.

Post-heist, as Talley slips out the back of the store, a languid camera movement takes him across a vacant lot, eventually revealing a funny-looking figure idling by the stage entrance of a burlesque theatre. Talley pauses, transfixed by what appears to be a clown. But something seems off about its grotesquely grinning face and oddly swaying limbs. Crook and clown face off for a beat, and then each goes their own way. Rattled, Talley hurries toward a more populated street, yielding a terrific sequence in which the everyday flow of pedestrian traffic is contrasted with his nervous, hastening gait. At this point, a police antagonist, Sgt. Kronne (Lee Marvin), is introduced, but his scenes are perfunctory and brief. The focus remains on the dissolution of Talley's professional composure by the greater foe of an urban geography literally fixed in stone. Returning to the theatre to kill the clown, Talley stealthily makes his way to the subterranean dressing rooms by dodging in and out of shadows, columns,

TOP: "Thunder in the Night" (*Westinghouse Desilu Playhouse*, 1960) with Desi Arnaz.

BOTTOM: "The Witness" (*Rebound*, 1952) with Edwin Max.

and other shelters. He commits the kill with meticulous precision, only to be once more undone by an unforeseen collusion of space and time. One of Kronne's team has stuck around the wings to ogle the half-naked dancers; Talley, rewinding his way through the theatre, nearly collides with the cad. Exit blocked, he's easily cornered and gunned down.

When Annie is brought in to identify Talley, she does so with an indifferent shrug. But the sight of the dead clown, flipped over to reveal the two-faced mask he wore as part of his act, sparks a different reaction. "How do you like that?" she cracks. "His back was to him the whole time." With its birds-eye-view shots, hidden-camera sequences of Talley navigating the city, and flat, murmured dia-

TOP: "Long Count" (*Four Star Playhouse*, 1954) with Paul Picerni, Audrey Totter, and Frank Lovejoy.

BOTTOM: "Boiling Point" (*Schlitz Playhouse of Stars*, 1956) with Dane Clark and Carolyn Jones.

logue (the actors sound like voices on a wiretap), "The Witness" achieves a documentary-like neutrality at perfect pitch with the dark irony it purveys. Girard, one of the more sought-after directors of telefilms, would go on to shape the noir style of programs like *M Squad* (1957–1960) and *Staccato* (1959–1960). With *Rebound*, as suggested by his preference for unelaborated episode titles ("The Cheat," "The Wreck"), he favored a lean, sober approach in which the futile actions of hustlers, grifters, and thieves are depicted with unblinking causality. Reassurances are made, blueprints double-checked, but always some inelegant element interferes. "The Henchmen" (1952) opens with cleanly detailed scenes of five robbers casing a bank. Come the day of the knock-over, four creep inside, leaving behind their nervous wheelman—who, the instant things turns sour, screeches away. The ensuing game of robber vs. robber, played out to nihilistic end amongst the sun-baked canyons of downtown LA—as if the crew of *Heat* (1995) had suddenly turned their automatic rifles on each other—prompted *Variety* to note: "There seems to be a sadistic satisfaction on the part of a number of telepix producers in assembling an unsavory assortment of characters in a story, then eradicating all of them in the twenty-seven minutes allotted."

Seasoned cinematographers like Andriot, who got his start working for Jean Renoir, and George Diskant, one of the key cameramen of film noir, were instrumental in raising the artistry of the telefilm. Diskant capped a brilliant career as the director of photography on pictures like *They Live By Night* (1948) and *The Narrow Margin* (1952) by joining up with actor-producer Dick Powell's Four Star Productions, among the largest tele-film outfits in town. Through his collaborations with Robert Aldrich, Blake Edwards, and Robert Florey, he infused an *echt* noir look into countless hours of television. A Diskant specialty was the "woman in jeopardy" scenario: he was a master at correlating inner terrors to outer dangers. "End of the Line" (*Stage 7*, 1955) opens with a startled young woman being forced into a car by two goons and taken on a scary drive. Allotted but a small, V-shaped slice of the view outside, Madge (Maria Riva) hangs on in terror. Diskant's close-ups heighten Madge's isolation from the everyday by irising out everything but her eyes. The ride ends on the edge of town, at the hideout of Sharpy (Don Haggerty), a hoodlum Madge once dated. Sharpy, it seems, has accidentally killed a female companion: he wants Madge to give him an alibi, or else he'll have his boys "handle" her. Diskant frames Madge's frantic escape through the surrounding industrial neighborhood as if every structure, every shadow, were part of an intricate, deadly maze. Even when she manages to flag a public bus, Madge remains in a heightened state of agitation, her fear of death amplified as much by the ambiguous expressions of the other passengers as by her own terrified image reflected in the bus window.

Meanwhile, Sharpy sends word out to the underworld: Madge is to be killed on sight. Convinced that she's been followed, Madge removes a cosmetic mirror from her purse to spy on the man behind her; the malicious, penetrating eyes that fill the glass in her hand send her scrambling for another seat, closer to the front. Her new companion is an elderly woman (Ellen Corby), the matronly sort who peppers her chat with "dear" and "honey." Madge relaxes, slinking out of frame. Diskant pushes his camera into the old lady, shifting his key light to illuminate her from below so that her seemingly kind face gains a sinister aspect: the old lady is part of Sharpy's world. Madge has delivered herself for slaughter.

Such perilous circumstances stem from a gothic tradition in which a trusting heroine is awakened to the unpleasantries of the world. In "Sound Off, My Love" (*Four Star Playhouse*, 1955), another Diskant-Florey pairing, Merle Oberon plays Martha, a loving housewife too proud to admit that she's nearly deaf; she fakes her way through each day by reading lips. When Bill (Gordon Oliver), her unctuous husband, mumbles behind his paper that he "won't be home for dinner," Martha smiles and nods and pretends to understand. Depressed and socially withdrawn, she finally allows herself to be fixed up with a hearing aid. "Don't be ashamed of it, it's given you back the precious gift of sound," the doctor says, encouraging her to "go out into the wide world and find out what it sounds like."

Martha arrives at a party where her friends and neighbors, oblivious to her re-tuning, speak freely and cruelly. After years of silence, the truth comes flood-

TOP: "End of the Line" (*Stage 7*, 1955).

BOTTOM: "Sound Off, My Love" (*Four Star Playhouse*, 1955) with Merle Oberon.

ing into her ears—a cacophony of two-faced vileness. Worst is the revelation, delivered as an aside to a crack about her being "deaf as a post—and dumb too," that her husband is in the next room canoodling with his girlfriend. Martha hastily exits. That night, as she lays in bed, describing in voiceover how her world has collapsed, Diskant sends a lattice of shadows creeping over her face. When Bill stumbles home and makes a phone call, Martha silently listens in. "Of course she can't hear me," Bill brays, going on to apologize to his paramour for dashing out on her at the party. "Darling, please, be patient," he pleads. "I'll get rid of her, I promise you. But it's got to look like an accident." Martha slowly sinks, as if underwater, her eyes registering the loss of stability. Next morning, she tells her best friend, Betty (Barbara Billingsley), about the dark turn her marriage has taken. Offered Betty's weekend home as a place to get her bearings, Martha arrives just after dusk. No sooner has she taken her suitcase out of the trunk when Bill materializes from the shadows, his hands out like pincers: "That's right. It's been Betty and I all along." In most stories of this sort, the certainty of death for the heroine is curtailed with a deus ex machina—in this case, a shotgun-toting caretaker—which leaves intact the gothic finale of a wife made a widow by her husband's black heart. Noir sees to it that the innocents of the world suffer before they learn the way things really are.

The most prominent telefilm-maker of the 1950s was Alfred Hitchcock. He, too, had a thing for putting women in harm's way. In "Revenge" (1955), the opening segment of his eponymous anthology (1955–1965), he sets pretty, fragile Elsa (Vera Miles) afloat in a beach chair outside a mobile home while her husband, Carl (Ralph Meeker), trots off to his factory job. Carl returns home to find Elsa in a nearly catatonic state, the apparent victim of a sexual assault. "You think you'd recognize him if you saw him again?" Carl asks. "Oh, yes," she promises. Days go by. The police have no leads. Elsa remains listless, so Carl takes her for a drive into town. Elsa suddenly points to a man on the sidewalk. "There he is— that's him," she says, definitively. Carl's face darkens. He parks, collects a wrench from under the seat, and follows the man into a hotel. Hitchcock stages the killing obliquely, his camera peeking around a door frame as Carl's creeping shadow does the business. Feeling vindicated, Carl replaces the soiled weapon beneath his seat and motors on. Husband and wife stare straight ahead, silent in their complicity. Blocks go by. Elsa perks up, jabbing her finger at another pedestrian. "There he is," she insists. "That's him." Just out of the gate and Hitchcock had trampled all over the newly instituted Television Code: "sex crimes and abnormalities are generally unacceptable as program material" and "the presentation of murder, or revenge as a motive for murder, shall not be presented as justifiable." To remedy such transgressions (of which there were many), he served as emcee—a portly silhouette prone to sardonic observation. "Well, they were a pathetic couple," he sighs at the end of "Revenge." "We had intended on calling that one 'Death of a Salesman,' but there were protests from certain quarters. Naturally, Elsa's husband was caught, indicted, tried, convicted, sentenced, and paid his debt to society for taking the law into his own hands. You see, crime does not pay, not even on television: you must have a sponsor."

Hitchcock's is a calamitous worldview, albeit one rendered with bursts of wicked drollness, like the doppelgänger who smugly inserts himself into the rigorously organized existence of a successful attorney in "The Case of Mr. Pelham" (1955). To his psychiatrist, Pelham (Tom Ewell) complains, "I have the feeling that he's trying to move into my life, to crowd closer and closer to me so that one day he is where I was, standing in my shoes, my clothes, my life, and I—I am gone, vanished." Urged to break from his routine, Pelham purchases a garish tie, something he would never wear; having acted out of the ordinary, he's now regarded as the impostor. "Why, why did this have to happen?" he cries out when the police arrive to evict him from his home. "No reason," smirks the double, comfortably ensconced in Pelham's robe and slippers. "It just did." Threats of immobility, alienation, and madness hang over the Hitchcockian heroes, inching them further toward catastrophe. "Four O'Clock" (1957), which Hitch directed from a story by Cornell Woolrich for another of his anthologies, *Suspicion* (1957–1958), casts E.G. Marshall as a watchmaker who hopes to kill his wife and her presumed lover with a homemade bomb. His plan goes awry when some burglars break in and tie him up in the basement, a few feet away from his ticking contraption. As his minutes wind down, he watches the world go by outside a small window— the gas man reading the meter, a neighborhood child chasing a bug, mundane events elevated to an altered state. Woolrich writes:

"An Out for Oscar" (*Alfred Hitchcock Hour,* 1963) with Linda Christian.

> He couldn't feel any more, terror or hope or anything else. A sort of numbness had set in, with a core of gleaming awareness remaining that was his mind. That would be all that the detonation would be able to blot out by the time it came. It was like having a tooth extracted with the aid of novocaine. There remained of him now only this single pulsing nerve of premonition; the tissue around it was frozen. So protracted foreknowledge of death was in itself its own anesthetic.

Hitchcock concludes with a canonical close-up of a face frozen in a death-mask stare, one of many ticks linking his television work to his film work. By his own admission, the telefilms he directed were "purer and with fewer concessions" than the features he made. "It is paradoxical, of course," he said, "but

"One More Mile to Go" (*Alfred Hitchcock Presents*, 1957) with David Wayne (top) and *Psycho* (1960) with Janet Leigh (bottom).

the movie people hedge you in with all sorts of artistic restrictions; whereas in television I can quite literally get away with murder." With "One More Mile to Go" (1957), Hitch puts us directly in the mind frame of a murderer. He opens with a jerky handheld shot of a rural home and the sounds of a man and a woman in vicious disagreement. The effect is voyeuristic, as if we've pulled over on a dark highway and crept through some trees to spy on the lives of the country folk. A jump cut brings us to the window just in time to see the husband swing a fire iron at his wife; the next edit takes us inside as he steps back to survey, with uneasy satisfaction, her crumpled corpse.

For the rest of "One More Mile to Go," as Sam Jacoby (David Wayne), cleans up his tracks, neatly wraps the body in a tarp, and drives off to dispose of it, we're given a step-by-step rehearsal for the sequence of Norman Bates tidying up "mother's" dispatching of Marion Crane in *Psycho* (1960). There are other moments of overlap as well, like the interrogation by a brutish, meddlesome cop which both Crane and Jacoby are made to endure. Hitchcock made *Psycho* cheaply and quickly, forsaking his usual crew for the one from *Alfred Hitchcock Presents*. His little black-and-white crowd pleaser, with its lurid subject matter, ironic sensibility, and stark visuals (framed at a television-like 1.37:1 aspect ratio), asserts itself as a stretch-out of the half-hour playlets he presented each week on television—a venue he seriously considered during its troubled journey toward theatrical release. (His television earnings, after all, had paid for it: no studio would bankroll the film.) *Psycho* confused the distinction between "A" and "B" product, high and low art, spectacle and small-scale, in much the same way the first wave of telefilm series encouraged viewers to accept filmed television as but a differently delivered form of moving-image storytelling. While an admirer of live television—see, for instance, his *Rope* (1948)—Hitchcock unwittingly became the lead pallbearer at its funeral. His very involvement in telefilms, the pedigree he lent the form, the polish he insisted upon, provided the final, necessary push toward a level of respectability and mass acceptance. The dramatic television we enjoy today owes its lineage to the 1950s telefilm.

DRAGNET
NBC 1951–1959

This is the city. Los Angeles, California. I work here. I'm a cop.

—JOE FRIDAY

THROUGHOUT THE 1950S, THE UNSMILING, JUG-EARED MUG OF JACK WEBB was the emblem of American justice. Each week, as Sgt. Joe Friday, he plodded through Los Angeles, coaxed its murderers and petty thieves from filthy rented rooms and sad corner taverns, and made them face their crimes. It was a never-ending cycle of transgression and banishment—a circular lesson in how society's miscreants are identified, captured, and convicted. Friday rarely used his gun; words, sparsely uttered but always to the point, were his weapon of choice. In crafting *Dragnet* for radio (1949–1955), and then transferring it to television, Webb took inspiration from the bulging files of the LAPD, with whom he worked closely in recreating the tedious, methodical routine of police procedure. Eschewing pulpy melodrama for prosaic authenticity, he made the real City of Angels, in all its blistering sin, an integral part of the proceedings. Its inhabitants, collated by degrees of culpability, formed a human mosaic of crime in the big city. Los Angeles emerged as a place of eternal chaos contained, but only barely, by the quiet, grinding persistence of Joe Friday.

Each *Dragnet* launches with a proclamation of authority: an image of Friday's sergeant's shield (no. 714) accompanied by Walter Schumann's emphatic four-note motto ("dum-de-dum-dum"), an introduction equally foreboding and reassuring. The police, personified by Friday, are good. The criminals are bad, if often compelling. It's all, we're told, true: "Only the names have been changed to protect the innocent." Thusly framed, the story is handed over to Friday, through whom we learn how police evidence is accrued. "We use the old-fashioned, plain way of reporting, where you don't know any more than the cops do," Webb explained. "It makes you a cop and you unwind the story." Through false leads, dead ends, detours to the morgue, the hall of records, the crime lab, Friday, who narrates as if reading from a police blotter, takes us through a

Actor-director-producer Jack Webb in the *Dragnet* production office (ca. 1954).

case. Some are solved in hours; others drag on for months. With each Friday exposes another rotten fact-piece of the city and its people.

John Crosby, a prominent television critic at the time, wrote of *Dragnet*: "An investigation of crime, if it is as pitilessly honest as this program, is frequently an investigation into man's deeper motives, crime simply being the more violent aberration of the urges we all possess." *Dragnet*'s stories climax not with a triumphant hail of gunfire, or even with the obligatory slapping on of handcuffs, but with a peeling back of lies and bluster to get to the ugly truths at the heart of the chaos, so that the appropriate punishment may be meted. The specifics are then relayed over an image of the culprit glumly posing for a mug shot as a sentencing is spelled out: Lester Zachary Wylie, child molester, "now serving his term in the State Penitentiary, San Quentin, California" ("The Big Crime"). Or Henry Elsworth Ross, serial killer, "executed in the lethal gas chamber" ("The Big Cast"). After this, a pair of hands bearing a chisel and a hammer bang out the logo for Mark VII, Webb's production company, sealing the case with a clang of finality.

Given the moral stridency inherent in such a formula, *Dragnet* would appear to reject a noir sensibility. Yet its portrait of Los Angeles as infested with deviance and teeming with alienated, grasping souls suggests otherwise. Because *Dragnet*'s stories are drawn from closed files, many of them dating back decades, the city on display is much like the one written about by Raymond Chandler and Horace McCoy, and even more like the one in which Webb himself came of age, sickly and fatherless, during the Depression. Growing up in Bunker Hill, a neighborhood of "epic dereliction . . . the rot in the heart of the expanding metropolis," as social historian Mike Davis has described this since-razed patch of downtown, Webb shared a single-room flat with his mother and his grandmother. Public relief put food on the table and shirts on his back. The squalid conditions of his upbringing are reflected throughout a vision of Los Angeles as an environment of hardship and desperation.

"The bums, priests, con men, whining housewives, burglars, waitresses, children, and bewildered ordinary citizens who people *Dragnet* seem as sorrowfully genuine as old pistols in a hockshop window," said *Time* magazine in a 1954 cover piece. "By using them to dramatize real cases from the Los Angeles police files—and by viewing them with a compassion totally absent in most fictional tales of private eyes—Webb has been able to utilize many a difficult theme (dope addiction, sex perversion) with scarcely a murmur of protest from his huge public." Though *Dragnet*'s hustlers and smut peddlers, its smack fiends and killers, are invariably rounded up and put away, the dispensing of justice is hardly conclusive. Week after week, like Sisyphus, Friday returns to roll yet another suspect up the steps of City Hall. This pervasive sense of futility, coupled with the obsessive endeavor to defy it, affirms *Dragnet* as dire a work of noir as any.

Webb's centering of *Dragnet* around a "real" detective marked a departure from the hardboiled gumshoes he played on his way up through radio. From his professional breakthrough, *Pat Novak, for Hire* (ABC, 1946–1947; 1949), and continuing through *Johnny Madero, Pier 23* (Mutual, 1947) and *Jeff Regan, Investigator* (CBS, 1948–1950), Webb gave voice to what contemporary audiences expected of a crime solver: the tough-as-nails shamus at odds with the police and quite deadly with a wisecrack. In between voice-work gigs, Webb picked up small movie roles, including that of a crime lab specialist in *He Walked by Night* (1948), one of the first films to be produced with the cooperation of the LAPD. A sombre chronicle of an all-out hunt for a cop killer, *He Walked by Night* was among the wave of semidocumentary thrillers like *The House on 92nd Street* (1945) and *The Naked City* (1948) to merge the factual reenacting of Louis de Rochemont's *March of Time* newsreels with the vérité aspirations of the neorealist movement.

On the set of *Dragnet* (1954).

The emphasis in these location-shot, government-stamped policiers is on investigative technique: the methodology of forensics, identification, lineups, interrogations, stakeouts, surveillance, all helpfully delineated with stentorian authority. "Police work is not all glamour and excitement and glory," *He Walked by Night*'s narrator (Reed Hadley) explains. "There are days and days of routine, of tedious probing, of tireless searching." Notwithstanding their veneer of authenticity, many of the docu-noirs are in fact hybridizations, their nonfiction sobriety tempered with passages of expressionistic stylization. Most enact a bifurcated narrative in which criminal action and police reaction are suspensefully intertwined. *He Walked by Night* splits itself equally between the mechanical police and their enigmatic quarry, the killer-fugitive Ray Morgan—who, as he scrambles about evading their "dragnet," emerges as the most complex and compelling presence in the picture. Though Webb would borrow much from semidocumentary noir, he pointedly avoided its reliance on melodramatic construction by limiting the narrative scope to what Friday himself see, hears, and learns.

He Walked By Night (1948).

It was on the set of *He Walked by Night* that *Dragnet* was germinated. When Sgt. Marty Wynn, the LAPD detective assigned as technical advisor, learned that Webb starred on radio as a private eye, he chastised the actor for contributing to the cultural misconceptions of how crimes are solved in the everyday world. "It rankles every damn cop in the country when they hear those farfetched stories," Wynn said. "Why don't you do a real story about policemen?" Webb toyed with the idea for several months before taking on the challenge. He rode along on calls with Wynn and his partner, Det. Vance Brasher; studied how the detectives talked, dressed, and behaved; pored through hundreds of closed case files; attended police academy classes; asked endless questions about how to bust down a door, interrogate a suspect, query a witness—all the while soaking up the minutiae of the city's fabled criminal history, much of which would make its way into his 1958 book *The Badge*, an anthology of cases too scandalous for *Dragnet*.

The yield of Webb's immersion in the workings of the LAPD was a radio detective story unlike any that had come before. CBS rejected it outright on the grounds that Joe Friday "wasn't enough like Sam Spade." NBC was equally unimpressed—where were the scenes of outlaw derring-do, the bank robberies and running gun battles? In privileging the perspective of the police over that of the villain, Webb thumbed his nose at all the vicarious pleasures that made *Gang Busters* and other "ripped-from-the-files" radio serials so popular with audiences. "Our idea," Webb explained, "is to let the listener eavesdrop on the police detective as he goes through his daily routine and to hear him as he is— an average workingman with an above average amount of patience." Ultimately, it was this promise of exclusivity—along with the vacancies in their schedule resulting from CBS's poaching of their programming—that convinced NBC to give *Dragnet* a trial radio run in the summer of 1949.

Realism, from the outset, was the marketing pitch for the show: "For here is sleuthing as it is in real life—unromanticized, painstaking, relentless!" From *He Walked by Night* Webb and his head writer James E. Moser took not only its blending of noir atmosphere with procedural legitimacy, but its use of un-explicated police jargon. "We realize that the man in Duluth may not understand the first time he hears it that an 'APB' means an All-Points Bulletin," Webb said, "but we think he'll prefer the true ring of the dialogue to some pointed-up, stilted translation." While most radio shows employed one or two sound-effects personnel, Webb demanded five: he wanted the squawk of an actual police radio, the shuffling of real police documents, the precise number of footsteps it took to get from one floor of City Hall to another.

The early radio *Dragnet*s open with a teaser encouraging the listener to actively participate in the solving of the case. "You're a detective sergeant," the narrator (Hal Gibney) will say. "You're assigned to homicide detail." From there, the premise is outlined: "*Dragnet*, the documented drama of an actual crime. For the next thirty minutes, in cooperation with the Los Angeles Police Department, you will travel step by step on the side of the law through an actual case transcribed from official police files. From beginning to end, from crime to punishment, *Dragnet* is the story of your police force in action." A burst of "dum-de-dum-dum," and then Friday takes over: "It was Wednesday, October 6. It was sultry in Los Angeles. We were working the day watch out of homicide." Thereafter, Friday's understated personage holds sway over the story. It's through his point of view that *Dragnet* moves beyond the objective "voice of God" stance of semidocumentary noir toward a more personal and unique experience.

Webb transferred *Dragnet* to television nearly intact. For the first several seasons, he simply filmed the radio scripts; when those ran out, he commissioned new ones. His primary adjustment to the format was an expanded prologue meant to intensify the bond between story and setting: most of the television installments open with a brief, narrated tour of Friday's domain. From "The Big Casing," as Webb's camera scans the Los Angeles sprawl:

> FRIDAY: This is the city. This is the way it looks from downtown. Steel and stone and two million people. They produce everything by the millions. They use it up by the millions. And they waste it the same way. Every month they throw away thousands of dollars' worth of everything. Some of them waste food and water. Some of them waste time and money. And some of them just waste themselves. When they do, I pick up the pieces. I'm a cop.

Publicity still for *Dragnet* with Jack Webb and Ben Alexander.

Through such linking of cop to beat, story to city, Webb locks the ensuing events to a real-life stage, dissolving the border between dramatization and documentary.

Webb resisted much pressure to produce the show live. As many saw it, the telefilm, still in its infancy, was an affront to the uniqueness of video—a déclassé product. Determined to avoid the billowing walls and miscued dialogue of a live staging, Webb wanted the reliability of film. Given that his experiences with visual storytelling up to this point were in the Hollywood productions that sporadically employed him as an actor, we can assume he gravitated toward what he knew. But another factor emerges when one takes account of the nature of live television—the real-time rhythms that make it near-impossible for an actor to appear in contiguous scenes from start to finish. It's for this reason that crime dramas like *The Plainclothes Man* were flexibly structured to allot periodic lapses in the detective-hero's point of view. A direct staging of a *Dragnet* radio script for live television, with Friday's unique perspective intact, would have proved unsustainable. By putting *Dragnet* to celluloid, Webb preserved his hero's primacy to the story, the very factor that made it special in the first place.

Webb's subjective treatment of crime and punishment is further personalized by the control he wielded over every aspect of the production. On the Disney lot in Burbank, he constructed a full-scale replica of the LAPD's headquarters at City Hall, accurate to the locks and doorknobs (cast from plaster molds of the originals), the dents in the walls and the stains on the floors, and the extension numbers pasted on every departmental telephone. Photographers were dispatched around Bunker Hill to document the interiors of hotels, boarding houses, low-rent apartments, bars, diners—locations Webb either used outright or faithfully recreated on a sound stage. Episodes were put in the can hastily, sometimes three a week. Ben Alexander, who played Frank Smith, Friday's faithful sidekick, for most of the series, described the process: "Hurriedly, he reads the first page of the script and says, 'We'll do a long shot here, another long shot there and everything else in close-up.' We start shooting immediately. The show is never rehearsed."

To further move things along, while retaining the flat, monotone style of performance that distinguished *Dragnet* on radio, Webb brought in a TelePrompTer, a new device at the time. Lines were to be recited rather than memorized. "When I come across a corpse I report it with about as much emotion as a man finding a penny on the sidewalk, and with the same amount of preparation," he said. "It seems to work better than the big musical build-up followed by a shriek that you hear on some of the private-eye shows." The more dramatic the situation, the more it was played against the moment. Rounding out his regular players with non-professionals, he directed his cast to "act" without inflection or nuance. Costumes were what the actors arrived wearing; make-up was strictly forbidden. In interviews, Webb described his aim as "naturalism pitched in a low key." Because words not action pushed his plots forward, he shot mostly in close-up—the unwashed faces that go with the dirty secrets that move each case to its resolution.

Dragnet owes much of its celebrated televisual style to its radio origins. Dialogue, crafted for the speed of radio, is volleyed with briskness; through montage, Webb maintains the aural cadences of a story intended to be heard first, seen second. Now and then he'll interrupt the back-and-forth to direct our attention to a seemingly gratuitous detail—a matchbook, a coffee cup, a half-eaten apple. Other times he'll break away for an intriguingly layered composition, like that from "The Big Counterfeit" of a suspect framed through the spinning reel of a tape deck. His "look-ma" flourish is the extreme overhead shot. When things quiet down, and there's little left to say, he pulls the camera up high to situate his characters in their environment, resulting in some wonderfully evocative, high-noir compositions, like the diagonally fixed angle of Friday and Smith under a neon sign at night ("The Big Frank"); or the birds-eye view of the detectives in the middle of a deserted nocturnal boulevard as a colleague, smoke trailing from his cigarette, joins them from the bottom of the frame ("The Big .22 Rifle for Christmas").

Much of what happens in *Dragnet* is conversational, a dialectic between policeman and perpetrator rounded out with testimony from victims, witnesses, bystanders—a whirl of clipped excuses, half-finished thoughts, and endless questions. While Friday never utters the "Just the facts, ma'am" adage roundly attributed to him (for that, we can thank Stan Freberg's 1953 parody record, *St. George and the Dragonet*), it's an apt summation of his method of policing: he's a relentless seeker of facts. His pursuit of them rivets our attention to the very mechanism of police efficiency, to how facts are gathered, analyzed, shaped into next steps. Everything leads to the Big Fact: the suspect's account of how and why a crime was committed. *Dragnet*'s criminals are never shown outside the presence of Friday. Nor are they given any of the contextual bearings afforded them by other cops-and-robbers programs. There are no flashbacks to the scene of the crime in *Dragnet*, no cutaways to criminals running rampant, no expository scenes of sad criminal childhoods. What we learn about each crime and the person who committed it is determined by Friday's hold over the narrative, which is singular and unyielding.

The telefilm version of "The Big Cast" opens with Friday and his partner du jour, Ed Jacobs (Barney Phillips), entering a dimly lighted flophouse. In voiceover, Friday describes Henry Elsworth Ross, the homicide suspect they've come to collect, as "a heavy drinker and a man with a violent temper." The detail proves accurate when Ross (Lee Marvin) answers the knock at his door with raised fists. "I didn't know you were cops," he mumbles, repeatedly, as he's subdued and cuffed; in his world someone's "always looking for trouble." Friday outlines for Ross why he's been picked up: "According to his wife, Paul Davis left Los Angeles by auto a little over four months ago. He was driving up to Oakdale, never got there." Dropped in the hot seat down at City Hall, Ross denies culpability. But he's eager to share his theories on why detective magazines and movies are bunk. Murder, he argues, doesn't mean a thing. "Some people kill, that's all," he offers. As the interrogation stretches on, fruitlessly, Webb supplants facial close-ups with tighter close-ups of eyes, ears, mouths, as if to reduce an already frustrating exercise to the fundamentals of see, hear, speak—the admission of evil required to close the case.

When Ross suggests they conclude the interview at Helga's Health Shop, Friday and Jacobs indulge him with a last supper. Over a meal of salad, molasses bread, yogurt, a vegetable burger, and some grape juice, Ross finally delivers the goods:

"The Big Cast" (1952) with Lee Marvin, Jack Webb, and Barney Phillips.

> ROSS: You don't need any big reason to kill somebody. Davis had eighteen bucks. Suppose I told that to a writer—somebody killing a guy for eighteen bucks? Wouldn't make much sense, huh? I tell you, it would never sell. You need a million dollars, beautiful woman, good motive.

FRIDAY: Where'd you kill him, Henry?

ROSS: Outside of Bakersfield, a little canyon there. I picked up a fifth of sherry in Bakersfield and I got Davis to drink some on the way. Say, would you pass the salt again? Lettuce is no good without a lot of salt.

Dragnet's ultimate noir statement is its de-sensationalization of crime, its overlapping of the horrific with the mundane. A citizen disappears one night; some time later, the perpetrator casually, anticlimactically, fills in what happened. The grand motive, as Ross himself points out, is a melodramatic device. In the real world, people die because of other people—just like that. "I don't know why I killed her," a maintenance worker (Tom McKee) says of his girlfriend in "The Big Hands." "Sounds funny, doesn't it? No reason at all. I just killed her." Even with crimes less final than murder, *Dragnet* situates the transgression in the most elemental of terms: "Yeah, I'm ashamed," an aging pornographer admits in "The Big Producer." "Who wouldn't be? I had to eat. It was the only way. I had to live." As each of Friday's investigations builds up to a revelation, a crime exposed, another filament in the populace's capacity to resist evil goes pop.

Because each *Dragnet* begins with a crime already committed before working backward to uncover the who and the how, the victims, especially the murdered ones, remain ciphers—their histories to be reconstituted posthumously. We discover them, as Friday does, through the words of others. In "The Big Trunk," Friday and Smith are called to a decrepit boarding house where a resident has

"The Big Trunk" (1954) with Jack Webb and Ben Alexander.

been tied to a chair and beaten to death with a lead pipe. "There's no reason for it at all," the landlady (Lillian Palmer) says. "She's wasn't too old or too young or very pretty. She wasn't worth anything. She didn't even have a decent coat to go out in." The victim, Thelma, was a fading vaudeville star, as well as an alcoholic. Figuring that she may have met her executioner(s) in a bar, Friday and Smith make the rounds until they turn up a trio of ruffians arguing about the fortune in mining stock (worthless, it turns out) Thelma was purported to have squirreled away in her trunk.

Sequestering the gang in pairs in hopes one will entrap the other, Friday and Smith listen in via hidden microphone. So as not to relinquish Friday's perspective, Webb stages the scene as a rapid-fire montage of inserts—knobs and earphones, grave expressions, a hand nervously picking apart a comb—soundtracked to the piped-in squabbling of the suspects. Once the guilty one, John Parkson (Richard Garland), is given up by his mates, he's brought back into the picture. Tightly framed, he gushes: "She wasn't supposed to be in her room. It wouldn't have happened if she wasn't there. I just wanted to see what was in that trunk. She was going to scream. So I hit her. With a pipe. She was suffering. So I killed her. I didn't want her to suffer." Up to this confession, all we knew of Thelma is that she died horribly; now, with her murderer's face in jarring close-up, we learn that she was killed in a panic, and for nothing, which seems worse.

In lieu of crimes depicted, *Dragnet* supplies the very face of criminality—venal, murderous, indignant; but also sorrowful, ashamed, glum. Once cornered, the criminal turns irate and morose, like Lester Wylie (Jack Kruschen), the pudgy child molester of "The Big Crime." As Friday and Smith sternly question him about an incident involving a pair of eight-year-old girls, Wylie slugs back cup after cup of wine. Having drained the bottle, he swings it at Smith, but is quickly brought to his knees and handcuffed by Friday. "Get out!" Wylie wails. "Get out of my house!" Pitifully, he tries to make sense of it all: "I didn't mean it, that's all. I didn't mean it. It's just that once in a while something goes wrong with me. I like kids. I like them too much, I guess. I didn't mean to hurt them." Lest we feel sympathy for this fiend, Webb's camera lingers on after Wylie is escorted off-screen, and then pans down to the floor where we see a pocketknife Wylie had earlier referenced—the one he was glad to have misplaced because "I was going to kill them."

SCENES FROM: "The Big .22 Rifle for Christmas" (1952) with Herb Ellis, Jack Webb, and Sammy Ogg.

Involving children in scenarios of danger was one of many taboos *Dragnet* broke in its fidelity to realism. The most sobering example, in that it unfolds with grim causality, is the holiday perennial "The Big .22 Rifle for Christmas." Two youngsters, Stanley Johnstone and Steve Martin, are missing, as is the gun Stanley's parents were planning to give him on Christmas. Withholding their discovery of some blood and a spent shell casing in Stanley's backyard, Friday and Smith (played here by Herb Ellis), enact their search with an unspoken sense of dread. "I feel there's more to this thing, something you're not telling me," Mrs. Martin (Virginia Christine) says to them. Some hours later, when Stanley (Sammy Ogg) reappears, alone, he's sullen and afraid. "I killed him," he offers. "I killed Steve. With the twenty-two. We were only playing. But I killed him . . . The gun went off. We forgot we put bullets in there. . . . I hid him. I was scared. I didn't want anybody to find him. I don't want to go to jail."

A monologue like this from the mouth of a nine-year-old demonstrates Webb's adherence to the confession paradigm so central to his formula. While no crime has been perpetrated—Steve tripped and accidentally set off the gun—he makes a point of showing us the face of the victim: a close-up of Friday's hand brushing away some leaves to reveal an angelic-looking child. Nearby, Stanley cries and explains how after burying his friend he spent the day "praying

"The Big .22 Rifle for Christmas" (1952).

for God to make him alive again." One would be stretched to find another television program from the era in which a child (let alone an adult) is saddled with such anguish and guilt. A subsequent scene of Steve's bereaved father addressing the body of his son in a darkened room is staged without a hint of mawkishness. Despite its pretext of objectivity, Webb's is hardly a worldview of documentary indifference—not when death, grief, and an empty chair at the family Christmas dinner are put forth as the consequences of child's play. The closing slate informing us that Stanley was "absolved of any legal responsibility for his friend's death" is hardly a comforting one.

In denying until the end a full illustration of the corpus delicti, the grisly bits and pieces, *Dragnet* pushes toward a darkly unsettling conclusion. With rare exception, the worst is verbalized rather than visualized, and nearly always withheld until a moment of maximum impact. By turning the conventions of the whodunit around, by making the audience sit through soliloquies of criminals coming clean, Webb seems to be insisting that we understand the impulses behind each transgression. As such we're made witness to what amounts to a pre-sentencing humiliation of the criminal, a ritualistic cleansing of conscience brought on by a steady tightening of the screws. In "The Big Phone Call," Ernest Garvey (Vic Perrin), a diamond merchant, stands accused of robbing a rival jeweler. Plunked in a chair in Friday's office, he glowers as the results of a five-month police investigation—reams of surveillance documents and audio recordings—are spelled out:

> FRIDAY: You engineered that hold-up. We know who you got to do it. We know how it was carried out. We know how you planned on disposing of the diamonds. We know who your fence was. We know what the split was. We know what you did with part of the money and we know how much you got left.

The more evidence piled on, the more Garvey lashes back with threats, bribes, denials—until finally his weaselly recrimination withers away to rambling admission, not so much of his guilt, but of how Mrs. Garvey drove him out of his head:

> GARVEY: She kept riding me day in and day out. I wasn't making enough money. She didn't have any clothes. The kids ought to go to a better school. We ought to have a new house. On and on and on. I had to go into business for myself. Make money, lots of money, same thing, all the time, talk talk talk, there's only so much you can take . . . Private school for the children, wall to wall carpets in the house, new dishwasher, new coat, new car, everything. She just had to have them. You want to take me, book me in? I don't care.

Other times, Friday's presentation of the gathered facts to his targeted suspect elicits an admission that's essentially therapeutic. "The Big Shoplift" begins with Virginia Sterling (Peggy Webber), the wife of a doctor, proudly refusing to admit what the police already know: she's been pilfering the finer boutiques along Wilshire Blvd. for months. After a few go-arounds of outraged denial, Mrs. Sterling allows herself the first smatterings of confession. Friday, eager to hurry the session along, cuts through it in voiceover:

> FRIDAY: She told us her kleptomania, her urge to steal things, had started as far back as her junior high school years. She admitted as a girl she stole books, tablets, pencils, pieces of chalk, and as she grew older, it seemed to get more serious with her. It carried over to her college years and that's when her stealing first got her into trouble.

Virginia is again allowed her place on the soundtrack: "I just couldn't help it. It always means so much to me. Taking things. Not being caught. Getting away." The close-ups get tighter as she gets to the brunt of her discontented state, to the marriage that's left her unfulfilled:

> VIRGINIA: We both wanted children. We wanted them very much. There weren't any. Bruce began to spend more time away from home. It was just like before. I wasn't important. I was all alone again. There wasn't anybody . . . There isn't anything worse than being alone. There has to be an answer someplace.

"There is," Friday frowns, "but you won't find it in jail." This arc of an individual driven to crime out of inner disquietude rather than greed or malevolence is repeated throughout *Dragnet*. One of the more salient, in that it, too, deals with the pathology of a troubled woman, is "The Big Show." The case begins with Friday and Smith called down to the bus depot, where Marjorie Lewis (Virginia Gregg) has found an abandoned infant. Her elaborate description of the discovery is framed with some odd business in the foreground: a funny-looking fellow primping in a twenty-five-cent photo booth. Compositions such as these contextualize the drama on hand within the wider diaspora of Los Angeles: this is but one story in millions. The detectives' efforts to reunite mother and child take a roundabout route when all evidence of maternal origin points back to Mrs. Lewis; her military husband, they learn, has just returned from a two-year tour overseas. "Do you want to tell us about it?" Friday prompts. So begins another wrenching confession:

ABOVE: "The Big Shoplift" (1954).
BELOW: "The Big Crime" (1954).

> MARJORIE: Having him away all the time, I knew there was going to be trouble. I started going out, having dates. I had to get out. I started going to parties. Different people. I guess I drank too much. I didn't want to be alone. I guess I always drank too much . . . There was one party. I don't even remember who I went with. I guess I was drinking. I don't know. When I left, I don't even remember who I was with. It didn't have to be this way. It didn't have to happen like this.

Through portraits—confessions—like this, of ordinary people pushed to dark ends by life's turns, we arrive at the melancholy nadir of the noir world, the stage where longing and loneliness give way to desperation and transgressive guilt.

Jack Webb in the series pilot: "The Human Bomb" (*Chesterfield Sound-Off Time,* 1951).

The assertion of Friday as a modest hero, hardworking and morally strident, is critical to *Dragnet*'s docu-noir aesthetic, particularly its credibility as a "true" story. Every now and then someone will throw a chair at the detective, or make a fast break for the nearest exit, but overall the show is determinedly free of action. One of the few times we see Friday sweat is in "The Human Bomb," the series pilot, when he's called upon to stop a madman from blowing up City Hall. Dashing out of the building with the bomb in a pail of water, he stumbles and drops the contraption—it fails to detonate. "The Big Thief" proceeds along calmly with little expectation of violence until Friday and Smith, on the trail of a Bonnie and Clyde–like couple, barge into a hotel room and are met with a blaze of gunfire. Friday steadies his aim and knocks off a single, fatal shot. "You shot him in cold blood," the dead robber's companion (Gloria Saunders) accuses. "You didn't have to kill him . . . I hope you're real proud of yourself, cop."

Thusly chastised, Friday is too distressed to fill out the obligatory paperwork. Through Anne Baxter (Dorothy Abbott), his sometime girlfriend from the records department, we learn that Friday draws an extra six dollars a month for having scored highly on a marksmanship exam—a skill he'd yet to deploy in the line of duty. "First time I ever killed a man," he quietly admits. "Not a good thing, Anne. You kind of wonder if maybe there wasn't some other way." Friday's subdued heroism can be attributed to Webb's desire, at the urging of his patrons at City Hall, to make his cop a wholly committed organization man. Friday has no identity beyond his job: no past, no politics, no religion, no supper waiting for him in a tract home. Aside from a few references to a "Ma Friday," and his chaste, noncommittal romancing of Ms. Baxter, who disappears soon enough, he seems to have no significant human attachments other than his partner. What we know of him and his place in the world can be summed up in his perfunctory openings: "I work here. I'm a cop."

In the lineage of noir flatfoots, Friday is a saint. So far as television policemen go, he's both prototype and rare exception. Free of disillusionment, fallibility, scandal, not at all conflicted about his role as a civil servant, he remains an anomaly: a stoic model of policemanship steadily tainted over the ensuing decades. If one is to go by the measuring stick of self-parody, the sullying began in the late 1960s when Universal induced Webb to revive his character for a new cycle of *Dragnet* installments, in color no less. By the Age of Aquarius, Friday's means of policing had become anachronistic, if not farcical. Conceived in a climate of postwar optimism and American superiority, he was now adrift in a nation increasingly defined by the mores of the counterculture. "The total disregard today for Constitutional authority is appalling," Webb stated by way of explaining the resurrection of Joe Friday. The best-known episode of the nouveau-*Dragnet* is "The LSD Story," in which Friday and his partner Bill Gannon (Henry Morgan) deal with a strange-behaving acid-head known as Blue Boy—who, when the cops first encounter him, has his head buried underground. The irony is not lost.

I LED 3 LIVES
SYNDICATED 1953–1956

Wouldn't it be a fine thing, I often thought, if the evil I was trying to fight consumed me instead?

—HERBERT A. PHILBRICK

Publicity stills for *I Led 3 Lives* (1953): Herbert A. Philbrick with Richard Carlson BELOW: Richard Carlson as Herbert Philbrick.

I LED 3 LIVES IS DOCUDRAMA AS PROPAGANDA AS NOIR. ITS BASIS IS THE PUBLISHED memoir of Herbert A. Philbrick, a Boston advertising executive, who "for nine frightening years did lead three lives—average citizen, high-level member of the communist party, and counterspy for the Federal Bureau of Investigation." Philbrick, a father, husband, and devoted Baptist, met his first communist at the age of twenty-six. It was 1940 and Philbrick, who chaired a local youth council, was perturbed to discover that some communists had quietly taken over his organization. Rather than resign, he went to the FBI, who suggested that he stay on, at least temporarily, to discover the intentions of these interlopers. What ensued was a fascinating and hazardously layered triple life: during the day, Philbrick supported his growing family; by night, he wound his way through the cellular structure of the Communist Party of America; in the gray hours of the morning, he retired to a hidden room in his house and typed out everything he had seen, heard, and done, which he then passed on to his FBI handlers.

In his book, Philbrick describes his years as a counterspy as "manufactured schizophrenia," and writes of how his interactions with communists "rendered me susceptible to their infectious poison." The performative nature of his decade-long masquerade, and the psychic toll it claimed, is made clear:

> I was sinking so deep that it was no longer possible for me to "play" the role of a spy. I could no longer simply make believe that I was a Marxist. Like an experienced actor, who must sublimate himself to his part and immerse himself in the playwright's creation, whenever I walked into the stage setting of a cell meeting, I had to be a young Communist. The costume alone was not enough. No disguise would have been adequate.

"Secret Call" (1953).

In the passage from print to telefilm, this sense of apprehensiveness and fracture is severely amplified: the television Philbrick, played by Richard Carlson, is a jittery, jumbled mess. He sees everything as a conspiracy—a "red menace" that threatens to swallow him whole. In this, the series aligns itself with the prevalent McCarthyism of the era.

In 1940, as the real Philbrick began his infiltration of America's communist apparatus, the U.S. and the Soviet Union were allies, albeit uneasy ones, in the fight against Nazi Germany. Fascism, rather than communism, was the greater enemy. By the time *I Led 3 Lives* arrived on television in 1953, the fear of a commie lurking behind every bush had become grist for popular culture, especially postwar film noir. When Sen. Joseph McCarthy appeared on *See It Now* in 1954 and likened the "worldwide communist conspiracy" to a "trail of deceit, lies, terror, murder, treason, blackmail," he might as well have been outlining the ingredients of a crime melodrama. Among the more notorious examples of the pulp fictions and cheap thrillers that sprang up in response to the Red Scare is *The Red Menace* (1949), which tells of a disgruntled war veteran (Robert Rockwell) lured to his near-doom by debauched communist agents. Gravely narrated by Los Angeles City Councilman Lloyd G. Douglas, who frames the story as something of an instructional manual for anticommunist vigilance, it's a work of alarmist fervor, complete with an opening graphic of a giant red octopus devouring the free world.

The Philbrick of *I Led 3 Lives* speaks to himself in second person. "Watch yourself, Philbrick," he'll say as he scurries down a dark street. In its entry on "Paranoid Conditions and Paranoia," the *American Handbook of Psychiatry* (1959) states that "the paranoid engages in solitary observation, searches for hidden meanings, asks leading questions, pondering over the answers like a detective, and listens attentively for clues in others' conversations to help him understand." Forever looking over his shoulder or misreading the gaze of another, Philbrick exists in a paranoiac hothouse in which the ordinary chaos of the outside world has been internalized. His is the only narrative line to which we're made privy. Coupled with his dissociative voiceover, such subjectivity yields an unsettling sense of claustrophobia in which the viewer is meant to share in his state of edginess and panic—a not-surprising aim given the cultural and political climate in which the series was made.

To the television Philbrick, everyday objects, places, words, and situations assume an air of menace. "Don't go straight to the phone booth, Philbrick," he warns himself. "Remember: a straight line is the shortest distance to danger." Philbrick's reality is ambiguous and shifting, open to moment-by-moment interpretation. Pregnant stares, lingering poses, and innocuous questions are all harbingers of potential doom. Living dangerously and unnaturally as three rather than one has altered his conditional responses. The ring of a phone makes him jump. His attempts at an "objective" voiceover become the means of ordering a world over which he has no control. Philbrick is incessantly being made to enact the bidding of both the communists and the FBI. He has little time for work and, anyway, his office is regularly infiltrated by communist agents, whether it be the new girl in the secretarial pool or a prospective client who wheedles through the door. "They never give up," he reminds himself. "As long as there are two communists left in the world, one of them will be spying on the other one."

For the real Philbrick, the masquerade ended in April 1949 when he was summoned to New York to serve as the government's witness at the trial of eleven communist leaders. Afterwards, he took a leave of absence from his job as sales-promotion manager for the Maintain Store Engineering Service and

"Secret Call" (1953). Forever on the alert for danger around the next bend, Philbrick moves through the city in a paranoiac haze.

"The Spy Next Door" (*Armstrong Circle Theatre*, 1961) with Wesley Addy and William Daniels.

joined the *New York Herald-Tribune* as a columnist. His experiences as a counterspy were collected and published in 1952. "Mr. Philbrick's chronicle of his difficult years is written mainly in a muted and factual manner, and his sensational disclosures are made with practically no cloak-and-dagger nonsense," *The New Yorker* said in its review. His memoir a best seller, Philbrick quit his job in advertising and became a fixture on the lecture circuit, where he delivered speeches on topics like "Christianity vs. Communism"; the need for a vigilant citizenry in building a stronger, safer America; and, of course, the years he spent splitting his personality three ways for J. Edgar Hoover.

Philbrick wasn't the only citizen-spy recruited during World War II. In 1941, informed that he was two inches too short for military service, Matt Cvetic of Pittsburgh was asked to join his local branch of the Communist Party instead. Throughout the war, and for several years thereafter, he dutifully supplied the government with some twenty thousand typewritten pages of everything he learned about communist plans, communist policies, and communist personnel. Cvetic, who testified at the same 1949 trial of the Red Eleven as Philbrick, and was an integral figure at the hearings of the House Un-American Activities Committee, was a diligent informant; to his family and friends, whom he left in the dark, he was something of an enigma, if not a fink. When his arrangement with the FBI ended, Cvetic gathered up his experiences as a counterspy and sold them to *The Saturday Evening Post*, which serialized the lot under the title "I Posed As a Communist for the FBI . . . as told to Peter Martin."

Warner Bros. snapped up the film rights, cast Frank Lovejoy as Cvetic, and in 1951 released *I Was a Communist for the FBI*. Directed by Gordon Douglas from a screenplay by Crane Wilbur, who specialized in crafting spectacular plots from page-one headlines, the picture cannily manipulates the conventions of the crime melodrama in the service of a "true-life" exposé of communist menace. "I know a hundred secrets," read its tagline, "and each one is worth my life." Incredibly, the film was nominated for an Academy Award for best *documentary* of the year. One person who saw further potential in this mash-up of nonfiction and noir was Frederick W. Ziv, one of the founding fathers of first-run syndication. In 1952 he acquired the radio rights to Cvetic's articles and began syndicating a popular serial in which Dana Andrews, as Cvetic, faced a weekly onslaught of red-hued racketeers.

Hoping to replicate this success for television, Ziv was met with resistance from Warner Bros., which had the telefilm rights—but no telefilm department as of yet—and so he turned to another, similar property: Philbrick's book. "We do not have the job of dreaming up impossible situations," Philbrick, who signed on as a consultant, wrote to the show's producers. "We already have 'impossible' situations and facts, and the big job for us will be to make them believable to the television audience." Following the Ziv mantra of "cheap—not inexpensively—cheap," each episode was put to film in two days or less. Studio sets were eschewed, as were makeup and hair departments, all of which not only cost money, but detracted from the documentary flavor that Ziv sought. "They may not be arty," Carlson conceded, "but the exteriors are real, all shot on location, and the stories are one hundred percent factual."

The real Philbrick's experiences inside the Communist Party were varied. Along with attending endless meetings and handing out pamphlets extolling the communist way, he reorganized a party cell in a Boston suburb, subverted the campaign of an anti-communist candidate for Congress, taught revolutionary tactics to the offspring of communists, organized a communist-controlled union's infiltration of an insurance company, and rewrote a speech for Henry Wallace, the Progressive Party presidential candidate of 1948. The television Philbrick faces off against, and is very much a part of, a vast criminal enterprise. The communists of *I Led 3 Lives* commit sabotage, dismantle unions, defraud churches, kidnap children, operate gambling dens—all of it financed by their sidelines in narcotics, prostitution, and gun-running. "How much do you know about the communist dope traffic locally?" Philbrick is asked in "Dope Photographic" before being sent to learn all he can about the "nearly two hundred tons of uncut heroin" the comrades have stockpiled, apparently in hopes of putting a giant monkey on America's back.

While contemporaneous series like *Foreign Intrigue* (1951–1955) and *China Smith* (1952–1955) regularly featured commies, pinkos, radicals, fifth columnists, and fellow travelers as heavies, never before on television—or even, excepting *The Red Menace*, in cinema—had communist characters been depicted as such a consistent and virulent scourge. "The contrast between the peaceful, productive, democratic way of life in America and the hate-filled activities of communists determined to smash what America stands for is the story of Herbert Philbrick and *I Led 3 Lives*," went the press release. Released for syndication in September

Promotional flyer for *I Led 3 Lives* (ca. 1953).

1953, the show proved a windfall. Ziv Inc. successfully placed the show in 137 cities, a record for an off-network offering, with eighty-five sponsors (Phillips Petroleum, with fifty markets, was the largest) footing the bill. By comparison, *I Love Lucy*, which went out over the CBS network, was seen on seventy-nine stations that fall.

In its sales pitches and trade ads, Ziv positioned *I Led 3 Lives* as timely, educational entertainment: "Tense because it's factual! Gripping because it's real! Frightening because it's true!" Implicit in this promise of authentic-

ity was the suggestion that electing to sponsor *I Led 3 Lives* amounted to a fulfillment of patriotic duty. "Since the Red conspiracy thrives on public ignorance of its existence and methods," one brochure explained, "Ziv Television Programs, Inc., is proud of the opportunity of bringing a message so vital and necessary to our nation's security to the television audience." Newcomers to television—the oil and steel concerns, banks, car dealerships, and utilities that picked up the series for local sponsorship—readily aligned their identity with the one propagated by the show. The Cleveland Electric Illuminating Company was the first sponsor to sign on. Its broadcasts began with an announcer intoning "The Illuminating Company! Supplying low-cost electricity to business, industry, hospitals, schools, and homes throughout the Cleveland-Northeast Ohio area!" as corresponding images of a power station, a skyscraper, a factory, and so forth, flashed on screen. To swelling music, these bastions of American might/potential communist targets gave way to a close-up of Philbrick's book as the announcer affirmed the link between public utility and public service: "The Illuminating Company presents *I Led 3 Lives*."

While Ziv maintained that *I Led 3 Lives* had no polemic ambitions—"Our chief purpose is to find good story properties, turn them into good films, and sell them" went the official line—its salesmen mounted a grassroots publicity strategy. "When you've seen the first installment, you will be able to judge for yourself why America's Reds are so violently opposed to the televising of Mr. Philbrick's story," read a form letter sent out to the leading citizens of the greater Cleveland area by the vice president of the Cleveland Electric Illuminating Company. *The Daily Worker*, preferred reading material of America's leading communists, held a different view of Philbrick: "The truth is—he is a man without a conscience who lived a shameless lie for nine years. By his own admission Philbrick made friends only to betray them and the ideals of the American working class."

Many of the "friends" Philbrick makes as a spy are women. Following its source material, *I Led 3 Lives* not only criminalizes communism, it feminizes it (with the implication of this being unnatural and unsettling). "She was bossy, and could tell men what to do as well as she could tell her own sex," Philbrick writes of one "squat, stocky, square-jawed functionary" in his book. Time and again, the television Philbrick encounters powerful communist women, their faces severe, their demeanors unyielding, who command a clan of ineffective, subservient male comrades. As the real Philbrick noted in his comments on one script: "Here again, be sure not to paint Comrade Mary as too soft a type. She would not be a person such as you would find working at Republican or even Socialist Party headquarters." Nor would she be like Philbrick's patient, everloving wife, Eva (played by Virginia Stefan in the series), whom Hoover personally praised for her devotion to her husband's patriotism. Throughout *I Led 3 Lives*, Philbrick's role as father, husband, and breadwinner is aligned with the righteousness exhibited by the patriarchal FBI; together they constitute his day world. His night world, on the other hand, is mostly stocked by matriarchal figures—strong, terse, domineering spider women.

The communist females of *I Led 3 Lives*, because they represent all that is forbidden and dark, hold an unusual sway over Philbrick. In his book, Philbrick hints at this attraction-repulsion conundrum when he describes "a demonstration of Party fervor" which carried "an attractive young girl" to great "heights of ardor" that "unnerved me to the extent that when I reached home that night, I could not sleep." In this context, communism assumes the archetype of the femme fatale: an imposing yet alluring force that interferes with Philbrick's duties as family man and citizen. It's the secret call he answers in the night—the one that sends him slinking through the shadows for an illicit rendezvous. In film noir the femme fatale incarnates the perceived threat of female sexuality; she's the alluring siren who beckons a man to doom by inciting and then undermining his masculinity. As in *I Was a Communist for the FBI*, where pretty school teacher Eve Merrick (Dorothy Hart) is sent to confuse the widowed and lonely Matt Cvetic (Frank Lovejoy), beautiful Mata Hari–type commie agents are regularly dispatched Philbrick's way in *I Led 3 Lives*.

I Was a Communist for the F.B.I. (film, 1951) with Frank Lovejoy as Matt Cvetic.

"Deportation" finds Philbrick in a lingerie store entangling with an Eastern European diplomat—"the comrades' number-one pinup girl," he gushingly tells us. Well aware that Philbrick has followed her, the woman suggestively invites him up to her room. "The things a man has to put up with leading a triple life," Philbrick muses as he steps into the elevator. "The things that can happen to a nice domesticated counterspy with a pretty wife and five small kids." Philbrick, in doing his duty for God and country, has made himself into something of a sap. He lives with shame and guilt, and in a constant state of anxiety, trapped in the spell of one femme fatale after another. "They can't all be communists," he reassures himself. "They can't all be dangerous—they can't all be watching me." It's these agents of Mother Russia—the ones he fears will "liquidate" him if his cover is blown—who cause Philbrick to glance furtively over his shoulder or to launch into a paranoiac jumble of vocalized thoughts, as if the thrall of a dark and mysterious force has brought him to the height of self-awareness. That Philbrick is caught between these two worlds, day and night, FBI and femme fatale, birthes all of his tension and paranoia. In leading three lives, he's invalidated the one he once enjoyed.

M SQUAD
NBC 1957–1960

> Ballinger is my kind of man. His own guy. No broads, no mother, no sleep, no eat, just a dumb, fair cop.
>
> —LEE MARVIN

WHETHER CAST AS COP OR CROOK, LEE MARVIN RADIATED VIOLENCE. His malevolent screen presence, avidly exploited in scores of films noirs, is brought to no less a menacing simmer in *M Squad*, in which he plays Frank Ballinger, a lieutenant with the Chicago police. Ballinger is a workaday cop, hard-nosed and uncomplicated. The crimes he tackles are of the pulp-noir breed: dope peddling, hijacking, bank robbing, kidnapping, swindling, forgery, and innumerable instances of foul play. At his desk, Ballinger is restless; his frame does not fit in his chair and his feet instinctively point toward the door that leads out to the street where the criminals run free. Even in the field, his lithe torso, gangly limbs, and oversized piscine head conspire to create an orchestration of ominous intent. When Ballinger springs to action, the release of pent-up rage is fierce. Jack Webb may have established the archetype of the television cop with his diligent automaton Joe Friday, but it was Marvin's Ballinger who shaped him into a ferocious and virile bull—a proactive defender of urban sanctity.

Pushed along by a driving jazz score from Count Basie and Stanley Wilson, each *M Squad* comes to its point quickly, underlines the conflict between criminal chaos and societal order, and then follows Ballinger as he races through the noir city to the moment at which guns are drawn and bad men fall. The sparse expository style of *Dragnet* is recalled, only here it serves to cut corners of time and space by moving the often convoluted story swiftly along to an ear-splitting conclusion. Where Webb, intent on presenting Friday as the emblem of police efficiency, sought verisimilitude, Marvin (who also produced the show) was after something else: the cocky aura of a Chicago cop. The ease with weapons, the gallows humor, the way of handling a snide suspect or a sobbing victim—he winnows all the behavioral patterns of a seasoned policeman into his "busi-

Publicity still for *M Squad* with Lee Marvin as Lt. Frank Ballinger.

ness," as he was known to call his method of shaping a character. In "The Specialists," his Ballinger puts it plainly: "I'm not a nice guy."

For Marvin, the role of Ballinger marked a breach in a run of alarmingly mean bullies. The dark proclivities that once led Bosley Crowther to describe him as "the number one sadist of the screen" are vividly demonstrated in his earliest studio picture, *The Big Heat* (1953). Leering and loose-jointed as the gangster Vince Stone, Marvin induces queasiness from the moment he steps into frame. Halfway through, when he throws a pitcher of scalding coffee at Gloria Grahame's face, it's a supreme act of finality startling in its viciousness but not at all surprising in context. The scene introduced a new threshold for screen violence, one which Marvin would persist in toeing throughout the 1950s, whether as the psychopathic leader of a motorcycle gang in *The Wild One* (1953), the sinister head of a communist spy ring in *Shack Out on 101* (1955), or the benzedrine-snorting thief in *Violent Saturday* (1955). Of Marvin's small-town lout in *Bad Day at Black Rock* (1955), John O'Hara, the film critic for *Colliers*, wrote, "By the time he gets his head bashed in you hate him so much that you could supply a supererogatory kick in the face."

Marvin's film noir heavies tend to live in the moment, displaying both an urgent predatory need and the crude means of satisfying it. "That kisser in itself—it's a great face," explained Don Weiss, who directed Marvin through multiple installments of *M Squad*. "But the rest is entirely physical. He's got a system. The way he walks, the way he talks, the way he slings a gun—it's all in the crotch with Lee." A troubled kid from a wealthy family, drummed out of every boarding school in the East, Marvin ran away to join the Marines while still in his teens—two years before the attack on Pearl Harbor. As a scout sniper in the Pacific campaign, he survived two dozen island landings until "some Jap bastard on Saipan" nailed him just below the spine. He spent thirteen months learning how to move again. "When I got out, all my values had changed," he explained. "Up to that time I was playing it tough, but then I knew you have to be tough to survive. The most useless word in the world is 'help!'" As Ballinger, Marvin is hardly fallible: it's the criminals, squirming beneath his withering presence, whose actions strike us as futile.

M Squad's title sequence, parodied with great hilarity in the *Naked Gun* and *Police Squad* comedies, begins with the flashing lights of a squad car roaring down a dismal avenue; in this noir city, a police response is a not-infrequent occurrence. "They don't help too much," Marvin said of the Chicago police. "According to some officials, there's no crime in Chicago. Well, here's an example: When we'd roll the camera out to do a scene in the street, a bunch of kids would usually run up and ask, 'Who got killed?'" *M Squad* distills each vari-

TOP: "The Executioner" (1958).
CENTER: "Trade School" (1959).
BOTTOM: "The Long Ride" (1958).

TOP: "The Big Kill" (1958).
CENTER: "The Cover-Up" (1958).
BOTTOM: "Contraband" (1958).

ant of the noir plot to its primal exigencies—the hard, brutal, messy elements of tabloid-ready human behavior. "How do you tell a guy that his wife's been using his name, his job, his reputation, for cheap grifting?" Ballinger ponders in "The Matinee Trade," a nasty tale about a woman (Natalie Norwick) who sells ersatz protection to a racketeer by insinuating that her cop-husband (Barry Atwater) is ripe for corruption. When the cop uncovers the fix (his wife had done the same thing to her previous spouse, also a policeman), he becomes crazed and sets his mind to murder, as the only "logical" solution to his conundrum. On this dark stage, there are but so many ways such elements coalesce.

Often, a simple line, early on, cues us to the direction of the drama. In "Pete Loves Mary," a brash hood (Mike Connors), freshly paroled, flashes a bundle of cash to his younger brother, who wants to know where he got it. "From the guys who had it," he snarls. Already we know that whatever lessons this ex-convict failed to learn the first time around are soon to be hammered down his throat by a certain Chicago flatfoot. Ballinger, we're assured, will right all wrongs. His disdain for criminality is palpable. In "The Specialist," summoned to attend a courtroom proceeding, he pivots away from the spectacle of a lawyer adamantly defending a trio of lowlifes and stares down at the floor, disgusted with such folly. Though saddled with a superior, Capt. Grey (Paul Newlan), Ballinger, as an elite detective on special detail, not only relishes his independent status, but seems to regard the other branches with skepticism, as if their intrusion will force him back into the office. "May as well take the day off, now that the science-fiction boys got it all wrapped up," he mutters when a forensic team arrives at his crime scene.

Whereas Friday's aptitude as an investigator resides in his ears and mouth, in the rigorous question-and-answer sessions by which he brings crook to book, Ballinger's method of policing entails a far more physical game involving a sturdy pair of rubber-soled shoes, a familiarity with the city's malfeasant geography, and an unholstered Smith & Wesson. The rule of Ballinger's gun is absolute; free of anguish or neurosis, this lawman always prevails. Naturally, he's the go-to guy for undercover work. "It cost the taxpayers forty bucks to get that black mermaid tattoo taken off my arm," he tells us after one such endeavor. In "The Hard Case," Ballinger gets himself sentenced to prison to ferret out the location of some hidden swag; other masquerades include cop-hating thief ("Diamond Hard"); outlaw biker ("The Phantom Raiders"); and illicit diamond merchant ("The Man With the Ice"). In "Frank's Double," when he learns that he looks a lot like a hitman from Detroit, he passes himself off as exactly that.

The emphasis on Ballinger as a lone wolf marks a noticeable shift away from the teamwork on display in procedurals like *Dragnet* and *The Lineup* (1954–1960). Some critics even took to calling it "Marvin Squad." "The M doesn't stand for anything," Marvin asserted. "It's any dirty job. Let's face it, we're the storm troopers.

LEFT: Publicity still for *M Squad*.

And I play Ballinger any way I feel like. Sometimes it's me, sometimes it's acting. Who knows the difference? I don't, not always. It's just unrest." In certain circles it was known that the actor, when suitably liquored up, had the tendency to discharge firearms (he had a vast collection) with reckless abandon in his front yard; these trigger-happy bouts occurred with increasing frequency during the production of *M Squad*. Betty, his wife at the time, later recalled: "Two things frightened me most of all—Lee's powerful capacity for violence, and his obsession with guns." For most of his career, Marvin would invariably be called upon to address the persona he'd honed. "Violence is ingrained in every drop of blood that I have because I came from the caveman, baby, like everybody else," he offered.

For its era, the violence in *M Squad* is astounding. Nowhere in the lineage of cops-and-robbers fare had the act of killing been shown in such unambiguously visceral terms. Tradition held that murder be visualized via montage: a shot of the shooter cuts to a shot of the victim clutching his gut. *M Squad* frequently supplies the middle—the moment of impact—yet manages to conform to the Television Code of the time by avoiding the depiction of blood (not to mention brains and bones). "It's theatrical," Marvin explained. "If someone rates a beating in the script, he gets one." Ballinger is said to have been based on the legendary Chicago police detective Frank Pape, who, in his four decades on the force, sent some three hundred criminals to jail, nine to the morgue, and another five to the electric chair. Pape's zeal for engaging the gangsters of his city in running gun battles was well chronicled in the true-crime rags that filled newsstands of the postwar era. The same lurid melding of no-nonsense policing and unrepentant bloodletting is the hook on which the plots of *M Squad* are hung. Breezy and audacious, this is pulp television at its most lurid, and without apology.

Many a crime investigated by Ballinger revolves around noir's deadly female. Ora Kane (Ruta Lee), the baby-faced blonde whose wiles supply the title of "More Deadly," certainly earns her billing. The disruption to masculinity she represents is cued directly upon the fade-in when, over an establishing shot of a check-cashing operation, a male voice can be heard complaining, "Ora, I just can't cover up for you anymore. I'm in this thing way too deep already." Inside, we're greeted with the sight of Ora clinging to her boss, Jim Landry (Paul Maxwell). "Oh, honey, please, my bookie's getting anxious," she pleads. Jim, in exchange for certain favors, has been helping Ora embezzle company funds to cover a gambling habit—only now he's gone and thrown a wet blanket on their arrangement. When a customer arrives, disrupting their squabble, and Jim scurries away to handle the transaction, the camera stays with Ora. She chews her lip for a moment, pulls one gun from her pocketbook, a second from a desk drawer, marches over to the cashier's window, raises both barrels, and—bang, bang, bang.

ABOVE: Chicago police detective Frank Pape, right (ca. 1955).

BELOW: *The Music from M Squad* (RCA-Victor, 1959).

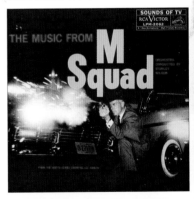

RIGHT: Advertisement for *M Squad* (ca. 1958).

ABOVE: Promotional still for *M Squad* (1959).

BELOW: "Blue Indigo" (1958).

BOTTOM: "The Terror on Dark Street" (1959).

The two men dead at her feet, Ora shuffles things around so it looks like a hold-up gone sour, puts her hands to her pretty head, and screams for help. Ballinger, confronted with this crime-within-a-crime, sifts through the evidence, separating fact from untruth. Nearly half the story goes by before he succeeds in clearing "the names of two good men," and then steers his investigation toward the vamp who buried them. From there, he sets a trap by making a romantic play for Ora, who's all too happy to have the detective responsible for solving her crime squire her around town. ("Be careful," Ballinger's captain helpfully warns.) The date goes reasonably well until Ballinger slyly lets slip his knowledge of Ora's misdeed, at which point Ora again whips out her purse-gun and—click, click, click. Realizing that she's fired off several rounds of police-issue blanks, Ora throws a fit. "Ora Kane had killed two men to hide a fifteen-hundred-dollar theft," Ballinger says in his closing voiceover. "To hide murder, she had tried to kill me. And for all her efforts, she ended up in the death house at Statesville prison."

In television noir of this era, the femme fatale rarely gets the upper hand on the policeman (or, for that matter, the private-eye). His asceticism, his sense of duty (for the private-eye, his adherence to a code), and his single-mindedness on the case at hand enable him to regard the charms of this deadliest of creatures with commensurate suspicion. Ballinger, savvy to the murderous urge, remains immune. The crime presented him in "More Deadly," driven as it is by base desires—girl needs money; steals and kills to get it—is relatively uncomplicated. All the clues he needs are at the scene. But to prevail over Ora, or any of the other depraved, conniving criminals he faces, Ballinger must supplement the ratiocinative tactics expected of him as a detective. In the hardboiled tradition, which *M Squad* draws from as readily as it does the police procedural, Ballinger must operate from a cynical perspective—a sociological awareness about the nature of society and the sinfulness of its people.

In "Blue Indigo," Ballinger investigates a string of dance-hall-girl murders in which the killer leaves behind broken vinyl records—remnants of the music he plays while he strangles. Settling upon Henry Edam (Nico Minardos), effete scion of an upper-crust family, as his primary suspect, Ballinger is escorted into a parlor and made to sit on a sofa, a porcelain cup precariously balanced in his lap, as the boy's mother decries the method of policing that has brought this blue-collar cop into her home. "I won't have this, these accusations and suspicions," Mrs. Edam (Lillian Buyeff) rails. "Just because my son was in trouble once, he is not mentally disturbed." Ballinger's officious reply, "Mrs. Edam, everyone is capable of becoming mentally disturbed," while likely straight from the department's primer on criminal pathology, aptly summarizes the one-way departure from reason that's known to hold many a noir deviant in its grip.

John Brahm, who directed "Blue Indigo" and many other *M Squad*s, was among those veterans of 1940s film noir who transitioned to telefilms. His "Dolly's Bar," from a script by Lewis Reed, brims with the unsettling stench of the noir underworld. The action centers around a massive safe wherein a vicious gossip columnist, Marty Collins (Michael Bachus), has secured all the dirty secrets he's gathered over the years. Diagnosed with a terminal illness, Collins entrusts this Pandora's box to Dolly Mundy (Clare Carleton), madam of a burlesque club, and then euthanizes himself by hiring someone to put a bullet in his head. Collins's death baffles the police, but it's also something of a last laugh in that it casts a wide net of guilt over the innumerable citizens he's blackmailed during his career. As Ballinger stakes a vigil to see who among the populace will converge upon the vault to retrieve evidence of their past sins, Dolly becomes increasingly agitated.

Publicity still for *M Squad* (1957).

> DOLLY: Frank, I'm scared stiff. Somebody's gonna blast you and shoot up my place.
> BALLINGER: Well, that'll be something, huh? Beats waiting. I expected dozens of Marty's victims to show up on flap of what he had on them.
> DOLLY: I kept strictly out of that part of his business.
> BALLINGER: You've said that too many times, Dolly.
> DOLLY: So help me, it's the truth.
> BALLINGER: You know, Dolly, I can hear you ticking. Just like an old tin clock. I can hear the works.
> DOLLY: It's only my joints.

The charade continues. The longer Ballinger lingers on (he has, by this time, called in a safecracker), the more tense Dolly becomes—it's her own secret, in the safe among the others, that has led her to obfuscate the investigation.

BELOW: "The Executioner" (1958).

BOTTOM: "Dolly's Bar" (1958).

> DOLLY: What will you do with what's in there?
> BALLINGER: Impound it. Check for any criminal evidence, burn the usual things, the compromising letters that break no laws.
> DOLLY: You'd have to read them to know which is which.
> BALLINGER: That's right.
> DOLLY: There's one letter there with my name on it. You read it, so help me God, I will kill you.

Brahm composes "Dolly's Bar" with the same expressive splitting of frame and motion he exhibited in films like *The Lodger* (1944) and *Hangover Square* (1945): a plate-glass wall (a one-way mirror) in Dolly's office through which the ongoing burlesque revue can be seen becomes the backdrop to the tense drama in the foreground. Given the theme of a dark, shared past that refuses to withdraw from the present, it's a highly appropriate flourish, while also underscoring, in stark visual terms, the sleaze and sin with which the noir investigator must sully his hands.

RICHARD DIAMOND
CBS 1957–1959
NBC 1959–1960
PETER GUNN
NBC 1958–1960
ABC 1960–1961

Publicity still for *Richard Diamond, Private Eye* (radio, 1950) with Dick Powell.

> Down these mean streets a man must go who himself is not mean, who is neither tarnished nor afraid.
>
> —RAYMOND CHANDLER, "The Simple Art of Murder"

AT THE TIME OF HIS DEATH IN 1959, THE MOST CONSPICUOUS EVIDENCE of Chandler's considerable legacy was that television, a medium in perennial need of heroes, had fully absorbed and endlessly mimeographed his iconic detective. The snappiest of the Philip Marlowe knock-offs rampaging through America's living rooms that year were Richard Diamond and Peter Gunn. Both were devised by Blake Edwards, the former initially for radio (1949–1952), the latter expressly for television. Bridging the two is a telefilm iteration of Diamond produced by Dick Powell, who voiced the character on radio. The route from Marlowe to Gunn by way of two Diamonds underlines not only the elasticity of the prototype but the sustainability of the pervasively corrupt and nihilistic milieu Chandler outlined for his hero. While mostly stripped of the original's melancholic world-weariness, the atomic-age clones share his disenchantment with the state of things, his need to rectify the ills of "a world gone wrong, a world in which, long before the atom bomb, civilization had created the machinery for its own destruction and was learning to use it with all the moronic delight of a gangster trying out his first machine gun," as Chandler writes in his 1950 anthology *Trouble Is My Business.*

The radio Diamond is a singing detective. Powell plays him as an arch cynic, albeit one who celebrates the conclusion of a case by belting out a song or two from the hit parade. By 1949, Marlowe's tenth year in books and the movies made from them, Chandler's prototype had proved durable enough to be toyed with and riffed upon. Powell himself had contributed to the building of the myth as the screen's first (official) Marlowe in *Murder, My Sweet* (1944), from Chandler's 1940 novel *Farewell, My Lovely.* Visually, Edward Dymtryk's film noir coalesced

Still from "Soft Touch" (*Diamond*, 1958) with David Janssen.

much of what is now celebrated as the noir style; narratively, it reinvented the detective film by presenting its protagonist as the interpreter of the action. Marlowe is introduced in a cellar where he's been sequestered by the police. Blindfolded, he's made to talk, and it's through his lucid, sardonic narration, the filmic iteration of Chandler's first-person prose, that the story emerges. Edwards, in developing *Diamond* for radio, drew heavily on this paradigm of the detective-hero as the appraiser of his own adventure. By connecting and commenting upon the progress of his convoluted investigation, Powell's Diamond immeasurably colors the listener's experience of the story.

Murder, My Sweet (film, 1944) with a blindfolded Dick Powell.

"The Merry-Go-Round Case" (1952; radio), from a script by Richard Carr, opens with Diamond on the telephone in his office, flirting with his girlfriend Helen (Virginia Gregg), when he learns that his mentor from his days with the NYPD has been gunned down. Grimly, Diamond agrees to assist the police in the manhunt for the shooter, Smiley Brill (Paul Richards), but vows, "If I find him, I won't guarantee that you'll get him in one piece." Driving down to the Bowery, where Smiley is said to be hiding, Diamond seethes:

> DIAMOND: I kept seeing two faces in front of me. One, a white-haired policeman ready for retirement, lying in a hospital fighting for his life. And the other, a weasel-faced punk with a slimy smile. You don't often get mad in my business; it doesn't pay off. But there are times when it can't be helped.

Through the underworld Diamond combs, bribing and strong-arming his way to Birdy Morgan (Howard McNear), Smiley's former cellmate. "Birdy Morgan was a little man with a nose that resembled a parrot's beak," he tells us. "He had beady, bird-like eyes that stared straight at you and never seemed to blink." And a mouth that refuses to cooperate. So Diamond knocks Birdy around until he learns that Smiley has gone into hiding at a downtown amusement park; arriving there, Diamond is promptly knocked cold. "He must have hit me with an old piece of pipe," he reckons. "But whatever it was, it caused the blood to rush past my eyes and a million rockets to go off in my head." Regaining his wits, Diamonds tells us that "standing over me was the man I'd spent all day trying to find." A fight ensues; Smiley, escaping, takes refuge in a carousel, which is where Diamond's vengeful bullets finally find their mark.

> DIAMOND: He staggered, then fell against the big control lever in the center of the machine. The machine started going around and the painted animals moved up and down as they circled Smiley's still body. I stood there and watched. Funny, but I didn't even feel sorry for Smiley. After all, how many cop-killers have music at their funerals?

The fading sound of the calliope cues a shift in locale to Helen's penthouse, where Diamond ends his case with a ballad: "I get a warm feeling when you're by my side," he sings. "The kind of warm feeling that my kiss can't hide." Notwithstanding its musical codas, *Diamond* was resoundingly violent radio. "In less than a year on the air," reported *Parade*, "Powell has been slugged, shot, strangled, poisoned, knifed, heaved overboard, gassed and doped, crowned with crockery, and caressed with brass knuckles." As many critics saw it, the hazard-laden Hammett-Chandler formula had already peaked by the end of the 1940s. *Billboard* opened its review by declaring that the "appeal of the hardboiled gumshoe type of whodunit, by now, is wearing thin, except to die-hard fans." Few could have predicted the enduring, escalating popularity of the urban detective, not only in cinema and radio, but especially on television, where the private-eye would soon rival the western gunslinger as the medium's preeminent hero.

TOP: "The Kill" (*Peter Gunn*, 1958) with Craig Stevens and Lola Albright.

BOTTOM: Network Interstitial (*Peter Gunn*, 1958).

Peter Gunn

Stretching out into producing, Powell was among the first in Hollywood to get in on the telefilm market; his Four Star Productions was a leading supplier of filmed series in the 1950s, particularly anthologies. Eager to bring Diamond over from radio, but deeming himself unfit ("I can't hold my stomach in for thirty-nine weeks"), he knighted the relatively unknown David Janssen. *Richard Diamond, Private Detective* debuted on CBS in 1957 as a thirteen-week summer replacement series. Janssen's Diamond is a tough loner, capable yet frequently overwhelmed—a junior Marlowe. A former New York City cop who's gone into business for himself, he's also a slightly threadbare operative, hungry and lean, at least for the initial go-around. Edwards, meanwhile, having parted company with Powell, set to work on *Peter Gunn*, which arrived on NBC the following year. Gunn, played by Craig Stevens, and introduced with a walking bass and blaring trumpet that would make Henry Mancini a household name, is sleek and cocksure—a visceral man of action. "Gunn is a present-day soldier of fortune who has found himself a gimmick that pays him a very comfortable living," Edwards explained. "The gimmick is trouble."

Like many screenwriters of his generation, Edwards idolized Chandler—"my hero," he liked to say. That trouble is the gimmick, or business, of the private-eye is, of course, a very Chandlerian view. Marlowe doesn't want trouble, and certainly doesn't initiate it, but once it arrives at his door or sits in his lap he isn't left with much choice: his code dictates that he do what needs to be done to make it disappear. He exists to absolve others of the pickles that seem to accompany urban life. Take any *Diamond* (in either medium) or *Gunn*, and it becomes apparent how thoroughly ingrained Chandler's design had become in the telling of detective stories from the 1940s on. Which isn't to say that they're uninspired or repetitive, but that they succeed in isolating the sublime within the derivative. Clichés and tropes persist because we expect them to be where they ought to be and function as they should, in the same way one automatically reaches for the light switch in a darkened room. Familiarity, in television, breeds not complacency, but reassurance. So long as the hero behaves heroically, so long as wrongs are corrected and the pitch remains the same, all is right in the world—even if our own day in the world was one for the dogs.

Recording Session for *Peter Gunn* with Lola Albright and Henry Mancini (1959).

So it goes that each episode of *Diamond* and *Gunn* adheres to a formula as stringently obvious as the jingles that paid for their broadcast: a crime is committed, investigated, and resolved. Along the way, the detective interviews victims and witnesses; makes the rounds of lowlifes and likely suspects; is followed, bullied, thrashed, all the while enduring (and ignoring) repeated warnings not to poke around in other people's affairs; arrives at a semi-resolution, sometimes in concert with the police, most often not; is promptly knocked out or otherwise incapacitated; comes to with renewed clarity; finds his way through the murky business at hand; and finally, violently, wraps everything up in a way that keeps the boys down at the morgue busy for the next week. Throughout this pattern of action and reaction, Diamond and Gunn, despite the preening presence of their counterparts in uniform, serve as the arbiters of justice: the rectifiers of the chaos that has ruffled the status quo.

ABOVE: Title sequence, *Richard Diamond, Private Eye.*

BELOW: "The Kill" (*Gunn, 1958*).

Deviating from the radio template, both shows introduced an element soon to become standard practice in episodic television: a pre-credit set piece, or teaser, in which the instigating crime is played out. More so than in the movies, where some allowance is made for the audience's patience, television, particularly 1950s half-hour television, functions at restless expediency; the teaser, by establishing in concise terms the puzzle at hand, prevents the channel from being changed. Yet it also marks an anomaly in private-eye tradition by placing the audience one step ahead of the detective. This is quite different from the plotting of a Chandler novel, or the films made from them, in which we remain in the dark as long as Marlowe does. Television's revelation of the crime (and very often the perpetrator) up front predicates the ensuing story on the detective's ability to decipher and correct an initial act of violence. Though the case may constitute a mystery for the detective, it's one of escalating suspense for the rest of us.

Many of the television Diamond's cases (and a few of Gunn's) have their origins in the *Diamond* radio series. "The Merry-Go-Round Case," for example, was revisited in 1957 by the same writer, Carr, but given an altogether darker, more complex treatment. This time around, the culprit is an old friend of Diamond's, someone he served with in Korea. In the teaser, director Roy Del Ruth, best known for his early talkie version of *The Maltese Falcon* (1931), wastes little time in establishing the unredeemable nature of Jack Milhoan (James Best), who in the course of robbing a filling station takes several lives, and then dashes off, leaving behind his critically wounded accomplice. From this vignette of lawlessness and criminal dishonor we cut to a main title sequence designed to situate Diamond within a Chandlerian "down these mean streets" mythos. A swooping crane shot begins with the image of a solitary figure on a deserted city block at night and ends with a close-up of Janssen illuminating his clean, boyish features with the snap of a cigarette lighter. Diamond is next shown in his office, the shadow-pattern of a venetian blind falling on his desk, where he's called upon by Milhoan's distraught sister, Marilyn (Nancy Marshall). "It doesn't make sense," Diamond says when told why Milhoan is wanted by the police. Like Marlowe in *The Long Goodbye*, his illusions about his friend are to be shattered in due course.

Even after his police contact, Lt. McGough (Regis Toomey), fills in the details, Diamond remains skeptical: "You got a friend, a guy you share a foxhole with, a guy you joke with, a guy you talk seriously with, and this guy turns out to be a killer?" From McGough, Diamond learns that Milhoan had been seeing a singer, Eve Miller (Lugene Sanders), whom the police are unable to locate. Diamond hits the streets, describing in voiceover how one of his informants has pointed him toward a lounge where Eve once worked. There he meets a taxi dancer, Jane Thomas (Gloria Winters), whose cooperation he gains by passing himself off as a Texan oilman intent on courting Eve: "I figured the best way to get Ms. Thomas to open up was to fill the air with the sound of wedding bells and the sweet smell of orange blossoms," he tells us. Diamond's preying upon the girl's matrimonial fantasies (she even offers herself as a more suitable mate) is a ruse common to the noir eye, who draws readily from an arsenal of questionable practices (lies, payoffs, masquerade) to advance his investigation. To bend society back into place, the detective has to be willing to stretch small truths.

The imperative that underlies Diamond's investigation is made clear through repeated references to "change," from Jane's observation that "Eve's changed a lot" to Marilyn's appraisal of Milhoan: "But he's changed . . . said he wanted to make some big money." As Milhoan angrily puts it, when Diamond tracks him down to the motel where he's been hiding with Eve: "You're darn right I've changed. I got tired of slaving under the hood of a car for sixty bucks a week. I like clothes like this, a dame like that." Milhoan's urge for change,

Diamond points out, will require sustaining acts of aberrancy: expensive tastes and an impatient girlfriend hardly pay for themselves. At this midpoint, unaware that Eve has crept up behind him, Diamond is knocked unconscious. The blacking out of the hero—a clobber to the head, an injection of drugs, a shove down some stairs—is a ritualistic aspect of private-eye noir. "I caught the blackjack right behind my ear," Marlowe tells us in *Murder, My Sweet*. "A black pool opened up at my feet. I dived in. It had no bottom." Or, as the radio Diamond says in "The Barton Case" (1949): "I felt like I was lying in the middle of a crowded sink and someone had piled all the dishes on my head. They turned on the faucet and I floated up with the dirty coffee cups and took a look around." The television Diamond, when struck, usually says nothing; rather, the story cuts to a commercial.

"The George Dale Case" (*Richard Diamond*, 1958).

In most private-eye noir, the incapacitation of the hero divides the inciting section of the mystery from its resolution. Regaining consciousness, the detective finds himself in the company of the police, with whom, because of his vulnerable state, he'll now be forced to cooperate, as happens in "The Merry-Go-Round Case." In both the radio and TV versions, Diamond's case culminates in the noir setting of a deserted amusement park, only what was staged for radio as a triumphant felling of a cop killer is on television given ambivalent shading by the hero's promise (to his client, and the police) of a bloodless outcome. Del Ruth begins the sequence with Diamond, on stakeout with McGough and some jacked-up cops, again being reminded of Milhoan's changed nature. "He's no good, Rick," McGough declares when Diamond expresses regret at having to trap his friend this way. When Milhoan slinks into view, guns go off, despite McGough's orders to the contrary. Wounded in the crossfire, the lieutenant passes his pistol over to Diamond, a symbolic transference of authority—the titular hero will resolve the crisis.

"The Merry-Go-Round Case" (*Richard Diamond*, 1957).

Diamond yells out to Milhoan, who's hidden himself in a carousel, to surrender. "Let 'em take me," Milhoan yells back as his fingers put more bullets in his gun. "They'll pay! For me they're gonna pay!" His nihilistic bluster, with its implicit submission to public execution, speaks to the absolute law of the desperate hour: he's hit the end, and he'll take down as many coppers with him as he can. Diamond, a moral hero, seeks to negotiate a cleaner solution. Moving toward the carousel, he remains surprised by his friend's bloodlust. "You think I won't shoot, but I will!" Milhoan shouts. "I'll kill you, Rick, I will!" Diamond marches on. Del Ruth frames his progress with tight, low-angled compositions. A shot rings out, the immediate impact of which is withheld in favor of a succession of close-ups—from the excitable, trigger-happy cops to the grinning

"The Sport" (*Richard Diamond*, 1959).

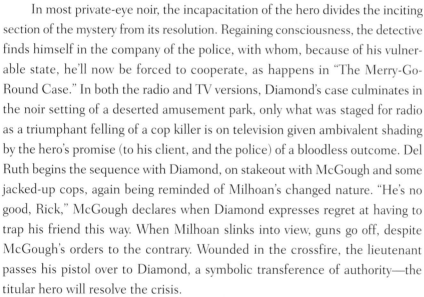

On the set of "The Sport" (*Richard Diamond*, 1959).

"Edie Finds a Corpse" (*Peter Gunn*, 1959) with Craig Stevens, Lola Albright, and Herschel Bernardi.

carousel horses to Diamond, isolated and no longer given a heroic framing. From the silence, the sounds of the calliope strike up as the merry-go-round is set in motion. The final image of Milhoan, slumped over the carousel's gears, bobbing ridiculously, going nowhere, sums up the absurd claim of the detective. Diamond stands confronted with a diorama of his own failure.

Revived for a second round of summer airings, *Diamond* did well enough that it was given a full series commission in early 1959. By then the ranks of television's detectives had swelled to a proportion *Time* magazine deemed cover-worthy. The slickest of the eyes—the new archetype, in that it slayed from the start—was the tough yet debonair Peter Gunn. "We tailored him in high style," Edwards explained of Gunn's impact. "Gunn is intelligent, dresses well, and is as much at home with hoodlums as high society." Over at Four Star, Diamond was honed accordingly. Shifted to Los Angeles, given sprawling quarters, a flashy wardrobe, and an open-topped Cadillac with a car phone, he became an affluent member of the professional class. Chandler's mandate of "a relatively poor man, or he would not be a detective at all" was seemingly no longer a signifier of virtue. Rather, an aura of success and virility positioned Gunn and the new sparkly Diamond (not to mention the playboy sleuths over on 77 *Sunset Strip*) as heroes to be lived through vicariously.

Edwards made Gunn equal parts quester (a seeker of truths) and catalyst (a fixer of messes), skills for which the detective expects to be well remunerated. "A thousand dollars for a night's work?" a client asks. "I didn't think the job was that hard." "Not hard," says Gunn, "dirty." Gunn's domain is a nameless and desolate city illuminated almost solely by neon. There are shadows everywhere—creeping around corners, climbing up walls, nipping at the heels of citizens scurrying to get behind locked doors. Mother's, the waterfront jazz den where Gunn's girlfriend, Edie Hart (Lola Albright), is a torch singer, is the liveliest, though far from safest, place around. "The show has the right kind of smell to it," wrote *Los Angeles Times* critic Cecil Smith. "It's a smoky, ginny odor that is quite proper in the dark corners where murder lurks." Edwards, who directed most of the first season, imprints *Gunn* with a mise-en-scène of canted angles and chiaroscuro lighting straight from *Murder, My Sweet.*

After hours, when the band has broken down and the chairs are stacked on the tables, Gunn and Edie slink off to the patio behind Mother's for some nuzzling. Their backdrop for these fleeting moments of tenderness is an inky canal through which many a corpse has been known to float—it might as well be the River Styx. Death and claustrophobia define the geography of this city. Even the cemetery feels like it has a roof on it. Gunn visits it in "The Kill," the series premiere, when he attends the funeral of legendary mobster Al Fusary (Sam Scar), whose passing he views with nostalgia. "He was unique," Gunn tells us in voiceover, "the last of a rare breed who crawled out of a bathtub of bootleg gin, grabbed a submachine gun, and made the twenties roar." Fusary's assassination on a nighttime highway, where his limousine is ambushed by younger, meaner gangsters disguised as policemen, makes for a vivid teaser. The mobster's final, confused words ("What is this?") as a "cop" sticks a gun to his head bespeak a new order of corruption; comfortably part of the established order, the old-timer thought himself immune to police intervention, let alone a double-cross by his own kind.

Fusary, Gunn discovers, was rubbed out by George Fallon (Gavin MacLeod), "a little man with a big appetite." Gunn's distaste for such usurpers drives him to counter the threat of nouveau gangsterism. He, alone, will do the legwork that brings about a restoration of moral order. Throughout *Peter Gunn*, as in *Richard Diamond*, the law is a nebulous presence. Gunn will find his police contact, Lt. Jacoby (Bernard Jacobi), asleep in his chair or idly strumming a guitar. Diamond, in his move to Los Angeles, faces off against a hostile, ineffectual counterpart in the LAPD. Both detectives are more suited than the police to deal with the assorted oddities and social outcasts that pave the path to the criminal's lair. The freaky subterraneans Gunn encounters on his night-journeys, like Babby (Billy Barty), the diminutive pool shark who sells him information, or Wilbur (Herb Ellis), the beatnik artiste who keeps him apprised of doings on the bohemian side of town, are the gatekeepers of an intricate urban maze.

Gunn's unflappability, his knowledge of how to handle tight situations, is complemented by a Marlowe-derived chivalric code. "Lynn's Blues" finds him coming to the aid of a suicidal chanteuse. Lynn Martel (Linda Lawson) is the unhappily kept mistress of gangster Nat Kruger (Guy Prescott): "He owns me," she tells Gunn with the plaintive resignation of one who's bartered her taste for luxury for a form of sexual servitude. Desperate for a healthier kind of love, Lynn had begun seeing another man, Roger Dwyer (William Masters), whom Kruger promptly had killed. The murder, the episode's teaser, is committed with

Publicity still for *Peter Gunn* with Craig Stevens.

Advertisement for a *Peter Gunn* soundtrack (Contemporary Records, 1959).

acrobatic precision: Kruger's henchman Santano (David Tomack) jimmies the elevator in Lynn's building, climbs down the shaft, pries open the carriage, and shoots Dwyer from above. The no-way-out staging of the hit aptly visualizes the cruel power Kruger wields over others, especially Lynn.

After Dwyer is killed, and with Kruger accounting for her every move, Lynn can barely bring herself to finish the sad songs ("Blue is the color of the sea / Till my love left me") she sings for a living. "You drink enough, you finally drink yourself sober, and then you see how really hopeless everything is," she tells Gunn. This trapped woman is as common to noir as her opposite, the vicious and predatory femme fatale. Incapable of destruction (except of herself) she nonetheless serves as a magnet for violence. Gunn, in endeavoring to free Lynn from Kruger, incurs a litany of threats and discouragement—from Santano ("Pretend you don't know her"), Jacoby ("Pete, don't fool with Kruger"), even Lynn herself ("Do yourself a favor, you might get hurt")—to which he responds with wry indifference. Soon enough, he's hauled before Kruger, thrown to the floor, and harassed with a knife, a humiliation he takes in stride. The pressures exerted on Gunn only strengthen his resolve; by persisting, he asserts himself as a man who's not to be trifled with, an important aspect of our identification with him as a hero.

The warnings Gunn endures in "Lynn's Blues" are commensurate with the mission at hand—a professional hazard when dealing with gangsters. In other instances, the intimidation he faces rings false in its severity, alerting him to the possibility that his quest may have been compromised from the start. In

ABOVE: "Lynn's Blues" (*Gunn*, 1958).

"Skin Deep," Gunn's search for a missing heiress leads him to a muscled-up, self-styled Casanova, Ramón (Eduardo Noriega), whom he dismisses, after a fruitless Q&A, as "too stupid" to be a suspect—a dead end. Leaving Ramón's, he's promptly ambushed by some strange men, dragged around a dark corner, and given a thorough beating: "You got a big nose, chump, and we're going to cut it down to size." Since he's uncovered little up to this point that might merit such treatment, the battering strikes him as incongruous. Now riled, and with his bespoke-tailored suit in shreds, Gunn retraces his steps and resumes his interrogation of Ramón, this time with his fists, until he learns what he needs to get back on the right path—one that will return him to a murderous client who's been less than forthcoming.

The setting of the assault in "Skin Deep" is an iconic one: a dark alley illuminated by a single source of light that casts the combatants in oblique silhouette. Incidents in

On the set of "Skin Deep" (*Gunn*, 1959). Stunt coordinator Dick Crockett rehearses a fight scene between Craig Stevens and Eduardo Noriega.

blind alleys highlight the precariousness and unpredictability of the noir city—around every bend lies catastrophe. One can be obliviously skipping along a well-lighted main drag one moment, and be facedown, lifeblood oozing away, in some obscure passageway the next. As metaphor, such settings also express the dark currents that run through troubled souls. In "The Comic," the deserted, grimy space behind a nightclub is where Danny Holland, a stand-up comedian played by a real-life one, Shelley Berman, goes to address his pre-show jitters: this is where he murders a vagrant. The deed done, he stares at the camera with glazed eyes; for now, his proclivity will be our secret, something to be kept from Gunn.

ABOVE AND BELOW:
"The Comic" (*Gunn*, 1959).

It's with a blank slate that Gunn arrives at the club the next morning to meet with Holland, who fills his ear with a long, messy, paranoid rant. Though such displays make his lip curl, Gunn perks up when Holland begins to outline how he thinks his wife, Ann, is plotting to kill him: he wants Gunn's protection. In what would appear to be a refutation of his client's claim, Gunn confronts Ann (Patricia Donahue) with the accusation: "Your husband thinks you want him dead." Only Ann is fearful for her own life. She declares her husband to be delusional, driven mad by the rigors of his profession. Faced with contradictory testimonies, and having yet to learn of Holland's dirty business with the vagrant, or of Jacoby's investigation into it, Gunn remains ambivalent. That night, hoping to re-interview Ann, he's struck over the head by an unseen assailant; regaining consciousness, he finds Jacoby poking around Holland's dressing room. Their cases having converged, detective and cop follow a trail of blood out into the alley where, inside an old trunk, they discover Ann, dead.

Holland, meanwhile, has taken the stage for his nightly performance. Sweaty and tense, he stares out at the sea of expectant faces—and freezes. His inner turmoil is conveyed expressionistically by close-ups of eyes and mouths and the thunder of whispers that suddenly fill the room—distractions he blocks out by clasping his hands over his ears. Fidgeting with the microphone, he elicits a few unexpected chuckles. "You see, a classic example of the condition of the American people—you're brainwashed," he offers. More laughter. His composure regained, he launches into a bravura piece culled from Berman's own repertoire as a so-called "sick comic," a phrase coined by *Time* in 1959 in an effort to collect stand-up monologuists like Berman, Lenny Bruce, Mort Sahl, Tom Lehrer, Jonathan Winters, et al., under a single label: "What the sickniks dispense is partly social criticism liberally laced with cyanide, partly a Charles Addams kind of jolly ghoulishness, and partly a personal and highly disturbing hostility toward all the world." Distinctly urban, syncopated to the rhythm of jazz (and benzedrine), obsessed with sex and death and the surreal contradictions of human nature, the satire of sick comedy drew from the same palette as noir.

To the sickniks, it was society itself that was sick—neurotic, laden with anomie, and given to the mindless pursuit of self-interest. One of Berman's signature bits from this period concerns an increasingly hysterical hotel guest who finds himself stuck in a room with no windows or doors. Another deals with a man who imagines that he's slowly bleeding to death from a paper cut; frantic, he calls everyone he knows, but no one will listen. In "The Comic," just as Gunn and the police pour into the nightclub, Holland goes into a sage bit about the ebb and flow of photosynthesis—a routine intended, perhaps, to remind his "brainwashed" audience of their rightful place. When humans exhale, he explains, they release "a big poisonous bubble of carbon dioxide" that is then absorbed by plants who return the favor by breathing out oxygen," which we're all waiting around for like vultures." Nervous laughter. "And so," he concludes, "it all boils down to this: No matter how mean or rotten or sinful you have been throughout this day, every time you breath out you make a little flower happy." The audience erupts with applause; Holland lowers his head in shame. He's acutely aware how the world, as Chandler foretold, is "dark with something more than night."

77 SUNSET STRIP
ABC 1958–1963

Our philosophy is that you should work hard and play hard, and strive to get into the sophisticated upper crust.

—HUGH HEFNER

ROY HUGGINS, THE CREATOR OF *77 SUNSET STRIP*, LIKED TO SAY THAT HE taught himself how to write by copying, in longhand, the prose of Raymond Chandler. Even without this admission, the inspiration for his debut novel, *The Double Take* (1946), a febrile adventure equal parts *Farewell, My Lovely* and *Lady in the Lake*, is about as inconspicuous as a tarantula on a slice of angel food cake: the simile-laden, first-person narration that steers his private eye hero, Stuart Bailey, around Los Angeles would seem to be the origin of that oft-tossed around qualifier "Chandler-esque." Huggins's immediate sequels, the novelettes *Now You See It* and *Appointment with Fear,* both published in *The Saturday Evening Post* in 1946, follow the same template. The literary Bailey, broke, alcoholic, sarcastic, at odds with the police, misled by his clients, never quite in the clear, is an unabashed mimeograph of Philip Marlowe. One can imagine them warily eyeballing each other at a stoplight at four in the morning.

"I don't know Roy Huggins and have never laid eyes on him," Chandler wrote in a 1948 letter to his friend Cleve Adams. "He sent me an autographed copy of his book with his apologies and the dedication he says the publishers would not let him put in. In writing to thank him I said his apologies were either unnecessary or inadequate and that I could name three or four writers who had gone as far as he had, without his frankness about it." That same year, Huggins made the jump from novelist to screenwriter with Columbia's adaptation of *The Double Take.* Released as *I Love Trouble* (a retitling Huggins loathed), the film follows the basic plot of its source, only Bailey (Franchot Tone), working out of a suite of offices, is already a little further up the social scale than his literary predecessor(s). It was with *77 Sunset Strip,* and the two pilots that preceded it, that Bailey was further pushed out from Marlowe's long and lonely shadow. His sardonic defenses replaced with an easygoing, man-about-Los-Angeles-air, the Bailey of television is as unflappable as he is upwardly mobile.

Before becoming a playboy private eye, the Bailey of *Sunset* is said to have run with the OSS, "the cloak-and-dagger boys," during the war, and then dabbled in academia, earning a PhD in Indo-European languages along the way. Erudite and worldly, fond of bespoke tailoring and open-topped cars, and never at a loss

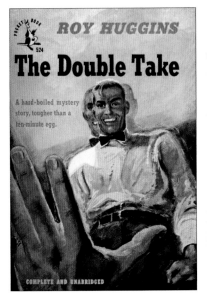

The Double Take by Roy Huggins (Pocket Books, 1946).

One-sheet for *I Love Trouble* (Columbia, 1947).

for female company, he moves through the rapacious underworld of Los Angeles with determined breeziness. Where the literary Bailey scratches the walls of a one-room flat with a pull-down bed, the television Bailey, as the show's weekly jingle tells us, operates out of swank, expansive digs on "the street that wears the fancy label/that's glorified in song and fable." Therein lies the essence of 77 *Sunset Strip*: there's no such shingle as seventy-seven along Sunset Blvd., nor are we meant to believe (or care) that there ever could be. Just as its titular address, chosen for reasons of cadence, is half real and half not, the series itself is a melodic hybrid—rooted in dark noir soil but brightened by the clear Californian sky.

77 *Sunset Strip* owes much of its appeal to this melding of sunshine and seediness, a reflection of a setting the dichotomous nature of which has long fascinated. "The ultimate world-historical significance—and oddity—of Los Angeles is that it has come to play the double role of utopia and dystopia for advanced capitalism," Mike Davis writes in *City of Quartz*. "The same place, as Brecht noted, symbolized both heaven and hell." 77 *Sunset Strip* straddles both poles of this urban dialectic to present a mythic Los Angeles that's part promised land and part Hades. But LA is also a place wherein reality and image collide on a daily basis, something Huggins hints at toward the end of *The Double Take* when Bailey describes a certain Mrs. Cabrillo, a gold digger who fled a sordid past by marrying up, way up, into a long-standing California family, as "still the most beautiful thing I'd ever seen this side of the big gate at Warner Bros." Huggins's reference to the studio's legacy of image-making, its knack for crafting tailor-made fantasies, gives way, a decade later, to the brushing off and smoothing over of his Marlowe-Bailey pastiche into an eminently likable and staggeringly successful television hero.

Publicity still for *77 Sunset Strip* (1958) with Efrem Zimbalist, Jr. as Stuart Bailey.

Warners was the first of the Hollywood majors to commit to television when, in 1955, it entered into a production pact with ABC, a network desperate for the high-gloss programming that might enable it to compete with NBC and CBS. Huggins, meanwhile, had bounced around town as the writer of "B" noirs like *Too Late for Tears* (1949), *Woman in Hiding* (1950), and *Pushover* (1954). Hired on to Warners as a writer-producer, he was given the task of salvaging the studio's inauspicious entry into the telefilm market. Huggins set about retooling *Cheyenne*, the most promising of the segments on the revolving anthology *Warner Bros. Presents*, into the freestanding saga of an honorable, drifting loner—an elastic, self-perpetuating format which would prove to be a television mainstay. Encouraged to replicate *Cheyenne* (1955–1963), Huggins responded with *Maverick* (1957–1962), a seriocomic western centered on the maxim "He who fights and runs away lives to fight another day." Together these shows not only legitimized Warners' involvement in television, but helped save ABC from the fate of DuMont, R.I.P. 1956.

With Warner Bros. now a player in telefilms, William T. Orr, son-in-law of Jack Warner and head of the studio's television department, engaged Huggins to do for the private eye genre what he had done for the western. Having already sold off the rights to *Now You See It* and *Appointment with Fear* (each adapted, inexplicably, into a screwball comedy), Huggins turned to his fourth and final Bailey novelette, *Death and the Skylark* (*Esquire*, 1952), which became the basis for an hour-long pilot film, "Anything for Money" (*Conflict*, 1956). As the re-titling suggests, Bailey, played by Efrem Zimbalist, Jr., and introduced in a crummy office idly flipping cards into a hat, is positioned as the not-so-picky, down-and-out type. For a retainer well above his regular forty dollars a day, Bailey agrees to accompany cuckolded tycoon Callister (Barton MacLane) on a cruise to Hawaii during which Callister suspects that his wife and the first mate of his yacht will try to murder him.

The cruise is an unpleasant one—James M. Cain on a boat. There's the predatory, sourly alcoholic Mrs. Callister (Maggie Hayes), the guitar-strumming first mate, Madden (Richard Webb), and Callister's daughter (Joanna Barnes) by a previous marriage, brought along, as Warners would have it, to nourish our hero's knack for flirtatious one-liners. Once Bailey finds his client flat on the deck—shot to the head—the story becomes a classic "closed room" mystery, wavering finger of suspicion and all. "I kept feeding Madden drinks and asking him questions," he says in voiceover. "He accepted the drinks and avoided the questions." His inquiries leading nowhere, Bailey sets out to prove, with a length of yarn, that Callister rigged the gun to fire upon himself, ensuring guilt all around. In *Death and the Skylark*, the old geezer is wrapped in a blanket and tossed over the gunwale; in "Anything for Money," he survives to be reunited with his spider-wife. Per the newly updated TV Code, the suicide of an "innocent" (e.g. someone who hasn't already committed murder) was strictly forbidden.

Warners followed up "Anything for Money" with another pilot, "Girl on the Run," scripted by Marion Hargrove from a story by Huggins. This time around, death is pushed to the forefront. The story begins in a Northwestern city with assassinations spurred by an investigation into what Bailey describes as "graft and corruption in high places," i.e. labor racketeering. A housewife in curlers watches from a kitchen window as her husband expires in a car explosion; across town, a labor leader is gunned down outside a nightclub in view of the resident chanteuse. Director Richard L. Bare, a Warners "B" unit veteran, frames each murder in such a way that the female on-looker has nowhere to gaze but toward the carnage; in the corrupt noir city, sudden death is an inescapable fact. Because Kathy Allen (Erin O'Brien), witness to the club-land murder, is able to identify the shooter, she's placed in protective custody, only to face an attempt on her life. Fleeing to Los Angeles, she changes her name (Karen Shay) and hair color (blonde to brunette), resumes her

Publicity still for "Girl on the Run" (1958)
with Erin O'Brien and Efrem Zimbalist, Jr.

"Girl on the Run" (1958).

Wire photo of Edd Byrnes greeting his fans at a junket in Chicago (1959).

Edd "Kookie" Byrnes, stars on "77 Sunset Strip" a Warner Brothers TV production.

BRYLCREEM

FOR SMART HAIR GROOMING

BRYLCREEM

PUTS LIFE IN YOUR DRY HAIR— AND FUN BACK INTO YOUR LIFE!

Advertisement for Brylcreem (ca. 1960).

singing career, and begins dating a polite, well-dressed professional: Stuart Bailey. Once she learns that Bailey's been hired to find her, she runs again.

Given its layering of ambiguity atop duplicity—everyone here, including the hero, misrepresents themselves—"Girl on the Run" exudes an unrelenting tension, particularly when James McCullough (Shepperd Strudwick), the crooked district attorney behind the mayhem, hires baby-faced hitman Kevin Smiley (Edward Byrnes) to square things up. As the "Mr. Big" of the story, McCullough effectively controls the plot by surreptitiously aligning the paths of Bailey and Smiley toward a confrontation. Yet it's Smiley, played with unnerving j.d. charisma by Byrnes, who steals the show with a single swipe of a ten-cent pocket comb through his greasy hair. Huggins, in crafting the story, had envisioned Smiley as a middle-aged Murder Inc. type, but Hargrove, his writing partner, "had seen the younger generation developing people who were probably very close to being sociopathic, probably because they were raised on a 'do anything you want' theory." In the film, no explanation is provided for Smiley's destructive appetites: this is a kid who kills because "it's a ball once you get with it."

Equally unsettling is that Smiley is given his own underscore, a raucous, jazzy theme that effectively mitigates the menace he represents. At the finale, when Smiley is summoned to identify McCullough, the personalized cue anticipates his smirking entrance and continues until he's sauntered to his mark at center-frame—the "ginchiest" of sociopaths. The effect wasn't lost on Huggins, particularly when, after a sneak preview of "Girl on the Run," it was Byrnes, not Zimbalist, who was mobbed by the young audience. "We got the shock of our lives," Huggins recalled. "But it was also a message that there was something here that we had not realized." Warners, determined to provide ABC a product with appeal to the Pepsi Generation, an elusive but highly coveted demographic, ordered a place be found for Byrnes in the series. In the interim, the studio booked "Girl on the Run" for a fortnight in a West Indies cinema, a remarkably disingenuous ploy whereby it could now claim copyright on Huggins's concept and avoiding paying him any royalties. From there on, guided by Orr and a band of lot producers, Huggins's creation became a Warner Bros. construction.

More so than any TV Noir that preceded it, 77 *Sunset Strip* was tailored for mass market consumption. Central to this was the building of a workplace "family" around Bailey, beginning with the recasting of Byrnes as Gerald Lloyd Kookson III, a/k/a Kookie, carhop, aspiring detective, and post-Beat motor-mouth, and continuing with what the finger-snapping theme song describes as "the starlet and the pony tipster"—or, rather, the sister and the wacky uncle: receptionist Suzanne (Jacqueline Beer) and gopher Roscoe (Louis Quinn). To prevent anyone's salary demands from halting production, as had happened on *Cheyenne*, Warners saw to it that *Sunset* follow a dual-lead format. For a private-eye show, this was a first: Mike Barnett, Martin Kane, Richard Diamond, et al., worked alone, Marlowe-style. Because *Sunset* was an hour-long program requiring six days of production, having not one but two detectives enabled the studio to film several installments at once, while at the same time lending greater flexibility to the structure of each. So, in a decisive break from private-eye mythos, Bailey was joined by a partner, Jeff Spencer (Roger Smith, cast at the urging of his mentor, James Cagney), a former government agent with a degree in law and a black belt in judo.

The double paradigm was such that Zimbalist and Smith alternated leads each week or split duties between the "A" and "B" plots of a single episode, with Byrnes as the fulcrum between the two. The intertwining storylines of "Pasadena Caper," from a teleplay by N.B. Stone, demonstrate how the series correlated this arrangement to its blanc-noir ethos. It begins with a shot (snipped from Warners' *The Big Sleep*) of a sedan being fished out of the harbor off Long Beach. The dead fellow inside is identified as Peter Baker, who happens to be the missing person Bailey has just been hired to find. Suspecting that his client, Baker's mother (Hallene Hill), might be running an insurance scam in concert with her housekeeper (Elizabeth Patterson), whose own son, Harry Diamond, has disappeared, Bailey feigns a back injury so that he can hole up in their Gothic mansion and snoop around. Bailey's interactions with the two spinsters, who finish each other's acrid bon mots with the giddiest of smiles, and try more than once to poison the detective, are played strictly for guffaws, as are Bailey's fabricated infirmity, furthered by Kookie's turn as a clueless medical orderly, and, especially, the "haunted" house itself—a warren of cobwebs, secret passages, and paintings with moving eyes.

"The Kookie Caper" (1959).

Spencer, meanwhile, in trying to figure out which of the old ladies' spectral sons is truly dead, steers the story into darker, more sobering territory. "He threatened to fix my face so no man would ever look at me twice—as if they ever look at my face," Diamond's depressive ex-wife, Kim (Carol Kelly), tells Spencer. Her marriage reduced to a jumble of traumatic memories, Kim is a shell of a woman. Spencer's inquest unfolds in sharp contrast to Bailey's misadventures in the ghost house. Throughout "Pasadena Caper," and other A-B episodes, the detectives operate in tandem, each advancing the other's investigation. Spencer's upturning of Diamond's alimony payments, postmarked "Mexico" and dug out of Kim's trash, prompts Bailey's discovery of similarly stamped

"The Pasadena Caper" (1959).

"A Check Will Do Nicely" (1959).

letters addressed to Mrs. Baker from her son. From this implicit linking of Diamond and Baker, who, as Spencer discovers, "shared the same clothes and gals" (much like the detectives themselves), the story's parallel investigations coalesce. Spencer, in back-tracing the letters to a south-of-the-border cantina, is able to identify Baker (Murvyn Vye) because he displays the same loathsome traits as Diamond in his treatment of women, namely his girlfriend, Erin, whom he forces to perform for the gathered drunks.

Montgomery Pittman, who directed "Pasadena Caper," stages the cantina sequence with a flair for the grotesque: the lopsided toupee that Baker sports to pass himself off as Diamond; the out-of-tune guitar that accompanies Erin's mangling of a number from the Warner Bros. music catalog; and, finally, the lurid grin that crosses Erin's face when she catches Spencer winking at her from across the cantina. From this, an abrupt cut returns us stateside, where Spencer, having spirited Erin away, uses her as bait to lure Baker into a climactic confrontation with Bailey. A coda in which Bailey, cup of undrinkable tea in hand, patiently listens to the biddies' jovial outline of how Diamond's "accidental" death sparked their criminal scheme supplies the requisite, restorative measure of blanc. The sum effect of "Pasadena Caper" is a strange but effective merging of farce and melodrama, as if Warners' *Arsenic and Old Lace* had been fused with any number of its slickly made films noirs. Yet buried within its overtures to as wide an audience as possible is a strikingly dark characterization of victimhood: Kim Diamond.

Spencer first tracks Kim down in a seedy tavern ("troublesville," as Kookie calls it) where she struggles to make ends meet as a cigarette girl enduring regular abuse from a nasty, scar-faced employer. Rightly figuring Kim for an alcoholic, Spencer gains entrance to her apartment with a bottle of rye. After several drinks, Kim steps away to fix herself another, and Spencer, nosing around, opens a closed door to find a sad-looking crib and a pile of unused toys. Behind him, some ice jingles. "I had a baby, a boy," Kim begins, as if looking into a void. "He died at the age of one month, four days, fourteen hours, and six minutes. That's when I divorced Harry." With her husband declared officially dead by the end of the episode, it can be presumed that the monthly checks sent Kim's way to maintain the ruse of his being alive will now cease; Kim's horizon remains one of degradation, if not destitution. How the series manages to reconcile as bleak a portrait as this with Bailey's pratfalls and winces, the spinsters' jokes of "and here we had a perfectly good body going waste," is either a marvel of bait-and-switch, or, more likely, a shrewd commodification of noir for an audience desiring its whodunits and its sitcoms in the same serving.

Kim Diamond is but one of the wandering dead who pass through *77 Sunset Strip*. In "The Girl Who Couldn't Remember," an amnesiac (Nancy Gates) finds herself on Hollywood Blvd. having no idea how she got there or why her purse is stuffed with cash. "It's like having a horrible nightmare and I can't seem to wake up—please, you've got to help me," she says to Spencer and Kookie. A viewer groomed on 1940s film noir might expect to find a hidden motive behind the woman's plea, but her fear is genuine: through no fault of her own, strange men want to kill her. The truly duplicitous, scheming femme fatale is hard to find in *77 Sunset Strip*; the more likely characterization is of a petrified, disoriented creature caught up in a nightmare not of her making. Indeed, the series offers a surprising array of threats made to the integrity of the female face: "You know you got a nice voice. Could make the big time. Got a pretty face, too, but you'll never get to be a girl singer if somebody goes to work on it—for keeps." ("The Bouncing Chip"); or "This time it's water; the next time it'll be acid." ("Dark Vengeance"). The latter warning is issued to Margo Harris (Adele Mara), the assistant of Bailey's friend Cosgrove (Jerome Thor), an investigative journalist. Cosgrove's beat is organized crime, only his on-air tirades have raised the ire of Vincent Barrett (Barry Kelley), kingpin of the narcotics trade. Knowing that Margo once flirted with heroin, Barrett reintroduces her to the needle, gets her good and hooked, and then forces her to betray her boss and Bailey.

The sight of Margo, once beautiful, now haggard, feverishly scratching her arms and agonizing over whether to go through with the double-cross sums up the bewildering, contradictory circumstances in which the female of *Sunset* typically finds herself. But it also points to how the series is rife with those marked for extinction. One of the more pitiful, in that he's utterly helpless in thwarting his damnation, is the safecracker of "The Double Death of Benny Markham." Hired to steal a seemingly innocuous canister, Markham (Walter Burke) soon learns that what he's lifted is a radioactive isotope, a bounty poisonous enough to impart a slow and agonizing death to those who handle it. The clock ticking, Markham, with Spencer's assistance, sets out to learn who contracted the theft, only to be gunned down before he can enact his vengeance. Notions of retribution, in noir, are nearly always given a final, ironic twist of futility: whatever satisfaction one may expect to gain is rendered naught in the end. As Thomas C. Renzi points out in his study of Cornell Woolrich, who wrote frequently on this theme, "the character who resorts to revenge often reveals a dark side of human nature, the suppressed wicked vindictiveness that lies within all of us and has the potential to surface and take possession of our actions and our attitudes."

In "Two and Two Make Six," Spencer tries to find the common factor linking several seemingly unrelated murders. What he eventually discerns is that the victims all crossed paths for a single day in Korea, during which, in the heat of battle, they left behind a wounded comrade. The abandoned soldier, Coletti (Barney Phillips), after surviving a brutal spell in an enemy prison, returned home burning with bloodlust. Frank Gruber's teleplay cleverly situates Coletti, years on, as an elevator operator, a little, limping man disregarded by nearly everyone: he carries on only to carry out his agenda of revenge killings. When Spencer finally corners him, Coletti explains himself as driven by "a hatred for five men—five men that I swore I'd kill if it was the last act of my miserable life." That Coletti is inadvertently extinguished by one of his own hand grenades is testament to the cruel end the noir story holds for those who march to the drum of hateful resolve. In episodes like this, *Sunset*'s fluency with comedy is at a loss.

For a series so tonally representative of Los Angeles's signature blend of sunshine and grime, the urban landscape on view is brazenly indeterminate—it could just as well be Any Big City, USA. Conspicuously free of bloodstains or broken bottles, it's a place that exists only on the Warner Bros. backlot, in the pictures made there. This fake Los Angeles, an older, mostly Beaux Arts version, is simultaneously expansive and claustrophobic: a grid of dead-end streets, cul-de-sacs, and roundabouts adaptable into any multitude of configurations, none of which really go anywhere. The real Los Angeles of the late 1950s, the one outside the studio gate, was simply too unwieldy, too chockfull of sprawling Googie neon, to be corralled for the benefit of the telefilm frame. Stripped of its natural rhythms, its atomic-age modernism, the Los Angeles of *77 Sunset Strip* is incongruous, yet crucial to the fantasy being peddled. Next door to the studio-lot offices of Bailey & Spencer is a re-creation of a real-life nightspot, Dino's Lodge, owned by Dean Martin; adjoining the two is perhaps the show's real center of action. The parking lot manned by Kookie, who "stables the horses" (parks the cars) with the snapping, squeezing, popping, braking zeal of a clean-cut, un-drugged Dean Moriarty, is where the series indulges its one concession to the actual Los Angeles—its defining car culture.

Warner Bros., in seeking to clone *77 Sunset Strip*, a windfall begun before the first season was half finished, capitalized mightily upon the centrality of location to premise. The formula was simple enough: a sunny locale; a pair of swinging-bachelor investigators; a Kookie-like sidekick; and a hanger-on or two, all glossed over with blanc and dipped in noir. From this, they yielded an intercontinental network of private-eyes: *Bourbon Street Beat* (1959–1960), *Hawaiian Eye* (1959–1963); and *Surfside Six* (1960–1962). A fourth attempt, to be set in Bermuda, got tossed when it dawned on the studio just how few actors of color there were in Hollywood. By then it hardly mattered: the studio's stable of private-eyes and cowboys already filled out a good portion of ABC's prime-time schedule.

To keep the assembly line at full capacity, Warners encouraged an exchanging of scripts among the shows, and regularly raided its own vault for material; with a little tinkering, *Woman in the Window* (1944), *White Heat* (1949), and *Strangers on a Train* (1951) all became episodes of *77 Sunset Strip*.

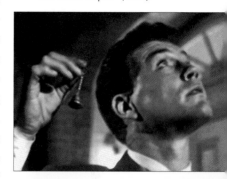

The crime jazz soundtrack, courtesy of Warren Barker and His Orchestra, that proves a fit accompaniment to this palm-lined dreamland of fabulous danger reaches culmination in "The Silent Caper," an entirely dialogue-free episode written by Roger Smith. From its opening in the deserted nocturnal fake-scape of Los Angeles to the closing scroll of generic character names (The Man, The Hood, etc.), this is one of the richest examples of purely expressive storytelling in television noir. Spencer, bored one night, goes for an aimless drive, and soon finds himself on the hunt for a missing stripper, Jingle Bells (Ann Duncan), so named for the one item remaining at the climax of her performance. At once sadistic and sexy, yet adhering to the show's blanc aesthetic with its "no words" gimmick, "The Silent Caper" unfolds as an intensely exciting chain of clues (a lost earring, a cigarette with lipstick) and complications (a getaway car stuck in the sand, a witness too doped-up to testify) driven forward by Barker's burlesque-flavored score. At one point, Spencer, tracing Jingle Bells to a ranch in the desert, is abducted and locked in a shed, from which he watches, through a peephole, a grave being dug—evidently his own. Escaping only to be cornered in a cavern, in which he's nearly burned alive, he frees himself by luring his tormentor close enough so that he can garrote him with his belt; even then, he must navigate his way past a flesh-hungry guard dog, and outwit yet another murderous hoodlum, before finally, successfully, rescuing the girl.

The milieu of the detective, as John Paterson describes in his essay "A Cosmic View of the private-eye" (*The Saturday Review*, 1953), is one "where things happen and people act, and where the things that happen and the people that act are not predictable. It is the place of violent and irrational human behavior, a region where law and formula do not apply." Huggins, in *The Double Take*, has Bailey describe facing "a disjointed pattern of blind alleys, of contradictions and irrelevancies, that left me staring into the sudden darkness, a blank uneasy feeling crawling slowly over me." In the stronger of *Sunset*'s installments, the detectives are made to face this abyss—to feel at a loss before triumphing. Oftentimes the puzzle they confront is indecipherable, if not meaningless. "I don't like working on cases where the client keeps secrets from me," Bailey says in "The Secret of Adam Cain" when it becomes apparent that the "missing vase" job for which he's been hired is far murkier and more perilous than he imagined. Hoping to follow a suspect to South America, he gets a blackjack to the head and wakes up in North Africa, the other side of the world, instead.

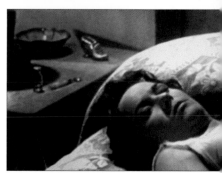

Bailey faces similarly confounding circumstances in "Downbeat," one of

"The Paper Chase" (1963).

"Eighty-Eight Bars" (1963).

several installments to address the Cold War, when he's unjustly accused of treason and stripped of his license. For the first half of the story, as he grows a beard and goes on a wicked bender, bouncing from one saloon to the next, Bailey is anything but heroic. When he's finally plucked out of the gutter by some unsmiling commies, we're inclined to applaud the regime of sobriety they force upon him, even if it entails our hero becoming their courier. Lest we think Bailey has become an unreliable figure, a fink of a hero, the story reverses course to reveal that his fall from grace was a dodge: he's been working for Uncle Sam all along. It's an affirmation of American moral supremacy that would make Joe Friday blush. So it goes that Friday himself, Jack Webb, was brought on to revitalize the show for its sixth and final season. He began by firing the entire cast save Zimbalist. Alongside his stated intention of presenting an "old-fashioned, hard-hitting private-eye," Webb sought to reshape Bailey in the mold of his most famous creation. As Zimbalist explained it: "I became Friday. I even had his suit—his grey sport coat—and I didn't realize it at the time."

Bailey, again a lone operative, was relocated from the Strip to that downtown noir landmark, the Bradbury Building, a stone's throw from the literary Bailey's haunt, the Pacific Electric Building. Webb's *Sunset* is darker, less jaunty than the seasons before it, seemingly predicated on resurrecting the hardboiled sprit of Huggins's stories through a florid use of sardonic voiceover ("Come to think of it, show me a happy loser and I'll show you an idiot without money") and a renewal of the traditional running conflict between private-eye and police. In "5," the multipart arc that opened the season, Bailey is given a thorough dressing down by a police lieutenant (Richard Conte): "You're high-priced thieves, all you guys. You set your fees without conscience." Yet as Harry Essex, a writer of many 1940s noirs, outlines in his teleplay, Bailey is not only flat broke, but treading deep waters—befuddled in a way he's never been. Late in the season, in "Eighty-Eight Bars," during a conference with his client (Cloris Leachman), the third-richest woman in the world, Bailey gives voice to a surprising sense of disillusionment:

BAILEY: You hire a man, you tell him everything; you don't hold back just because some of the mud may spatter in the wrong places. I've been beating my brains out, scratching for openings you could have dropped in my lap from the very beginning. And all I've got to show for it is a cop who wants to lift my ticket. It just isn't worth the price of admission.

Bailey's dialogue, as tuned by Webb, gained directions like "DRYLY" and "FLAT," resulting in a character of "Bogartian insolence," as *TV Guide* put it. In regressing Bailey to an amalgam of 1940s private eye and 1950s police flat-foot, Webb and his producer-director, William Conrad, effectively stripped the character of its trademark modernization—the high-verve, carefree, semi-boiled playboy-ness that had made Bailey such a popular television hero to begin with. The anachronism that Bailey became is vividly encapsulated in a lecture delivered to him in "Eighty-Eight Bars" by a disarmingly lucid gangster: "You'd better get out of that LA smog, Bailey. It's fuzzing up your thinking," the hood (Barry Kelley) scoffs. "What I mean: you're standing still while the rest of the world progresses. You're making noises like a man in a trench coat, like a 'B' movie. Next you'll be talking about cement overcoats and fellows getting hit." Such an epitaph aside, the signature blanc-noir tone of *Sunset*'s first five seasons, pushed through decades of detective fare, remains its primary legacy.

STACCATO
NBC 1959–1960

First of all, I don't play a private eye. I'm a jazz pianist—that's a hell of a lot of difference, pal.

—JOHN CASSAVETES

JOHN CASSAVETES WAS NEARING THIRTY WHEN HE RECEIVED THE OFFER TO play Johnny Staccato, jazz pianist and sometime private eye. After a successful decade in live television and a handful of "B" movies, the leap to leading man seemed overdue. Yet the actor, who really wanted to be a director, had largely removed himself from industry call sheets to concentrate on the making of a self-financed, sixteen-millimeter film spun out of the acting workshop he ran on the side. Hustled together on the streets of New York with an amateur cast and crew, *Shadows* (1959) was a raw, strangely beatific, jazz-scored fuck-all to mainstream moviemaking. As it has since ascended to the pantheon of American independent cinema, the lingering consensus, particularly among those who view film as art and television as industry, is that Cassavetes took on *Staccato* purely for the paycheck. Why else, goes the reasoning, would the young rebel behind such a kinetic debut sully himself with a telefilm contract?

When the call came from Revue, the television wing of agency powerhouse MCA, Cassavetes was indeed broke from shooting and re-shooting *Shadows*; also, he and wife Gena Rowlands were expecting their first child. Yet an editorial Cassavetes wrote for *Film Culture* around that time suggests that his motivation for accepting the role went beyond financial security. In his piece, titled, with characteristic insolence, "What's Wrong with Hollywood," he urges the town's writers, directors, and actors to seize control of their art. "Without individual creative expression, we are left with a medium of irrelevant fantasies that can add nothing but

"The Naked Truth" (1959) with John Cassavetes as Johnny Staccato.

slim diversion to an already diversified world," he writes. "The answer cannot be left in the hands of the money men . . . the answer must come from the artist himself." The appeal a weekly prime-time slot would have held for as ambitious and shrewd an iconoclast as Cassavetes can't easily be dismissed. *Shadows*, as its director was the first to concede, had limited commercial prospects. *Staccato*, on the other hand, offered the chance to work the system from the inside.

In his negotiations, Cassavetes made all the demands actors weren't supposed to make. He wanted creative input, he wanted to name his own producer (Everett Chambers), and, most importantly, he wanted to direct—and he simply tore up every contract presented to him until he got his way. The show he joined had been in development for several years: its high-concept premise came out of a 1956 meeting between MCA chief Lew Wasserman, his lieutenant Jennings Lang, and the composer Elmer Bernstein, who was keen on scoring something for television. Though a pilot script, commissioned from Dick Berg, already existed, Cassavetes set to work reshaping his jazz detective into an artist-seeker whose innate humanism serves as his compass through a precarious noir landscape. Together with Chambers, Cassavetes rewrote nearly all of *Staccato*'s teleplays. Special attention was given to the dialogue, to the naturalistic cadences of how people on the margins, where niceties turn to dissonance, clarity to evasiveness, really articulate themselves.

Cassavetes also sought to fill in the spaces of Staccato's world, of which a boisterously sordid nightlife is an integral part. The noir city of *Staccato* bustles with sound—jazz, classical, rockabilly, even polka. Beginning with Bernstein's jolting title theme, music pours from doorways and windows, cafes and nightclubs, tuning the viewer to the acoustics of a concentrated metropolis. The result is a milieu that neatly overlaps that of *Shadows*, and fully anticipates the setting of *Too Late for Blues* (1961), Cassavetes's sophomore feature. Nearly all of the cases Staccato takes on revolve around those for whom life (and very often death) is music: a strung-out horn man ("The Wild Reed"); a blackmailed bandleader ("Collector's Item"); a psychopathic composer ("Murder for Credit"); a scandal-tainted singer ("The Naked Truth"); a mob-connected chanteuse ("Murder in Hi-Fi"). To these can be added: a pianist who seeks political asylum ("Singing Longhair"); a troubled accordionist who turns to crime ("An Angry Young Man"); a trumpeter accused of being a derelict father ("Man in the Pit").

Aside from asserting his vision of New York after dark, Cassavetes saw to it that *Staccato* tackled the sorts of hefty themes—payola, dope addiction, McCarthyism—that generally made advertisers squeamish. But it was his radical notion of downplaying the heroic qualities of his ambivalent private eye that would really raise the ire of the money men. The series, as Cassavetes would later explain, was doomed from the beginning by his urge to upend genre

Johnny Staccato by Frank Boyd (Gold Medal, 1960).

convention. "They felt that a show would have to be a detective show, strictly and absolutely with a hero," he said. "I felt that my style is a human style. I'm a human being and I want to make mistakes just as well as solve the crimes; I want to *not* solve some crimes too." On that last bit, there was much hair-pulling among the money men.

When *Staccato* appeared in the fall of 1959 as part of a great flood of private-eye programs, it was roundly dismissed as the latest in a line of knock-offs. "Each Eye is an unabashed copy of the last," went *Time* magazine's take on the trend. "Characters who ought to be able to trace their lineage all the way back to Edgar Allan Poe have been changed by their packagers until each one looks and sounds like the spawn of a supercilious contemporary named Peter Gunn." While *Staccato* shares, if not intensifies, *Gunn*'s highly charged mise-en-scène, it veers from the formula via Cassavetes's insistence that his pianist-detective be deeply invested in the lives of the troubled souls he assists. "True, I get mixed up in a little intrigue, but it's like a sideline with me," he said, in pointed contradiction to NBC's own press releases. "I don't do it just for the fun of it, or strictly for cash, or hire." Most of those who seek out Staccato are friends or associates in need of third-party intervention—a smoother-over of trouble.

Like a musician fluent in every key, every jump between the notes, Staccato is supremely well connected. He knows the lowlifes and the freaks, the hustlers and the Beats; he's also on terms with the city's elite, the political movers, the penthouse gangsters, the big-money mouthpieces. Though he frequently buys or bribes his way through the night world, he's never shown pocketing a fin for himself. His humanism, as James Ursini has pointed out ("Angst at Sixty Fields per

BELOW:
"The Nature of the Night" (1959).

BOTTOM:
"The Naked Truth" (1959) with Eduardo Ciannelli, Chick Chandler, and Cassavetes.

Second," 1995), places him "emotional light years away from Gunn's detached stoicism." Far from a tougher-than-nails gunman, or a laconic, easygoing eye, Staccato is vulnerable and anxious. Violence, guns, and death vex him. At the end of "The Naked Truth," after taking one life to save another, he tells us, "Fear is often a delayed reaction. So is guilt. Twenty-four hours later I was still getting over the fact that I had to kill a man. The kind of man he was makes it no easier. That's why I need Waldo's." To purge his professional woes, Staccato retreats to his art.

Waldo's is Staccato's haven—the nexus of his world. It's here, in a subterranean jazz

mecca on MacDougal Street, under the paternal eye of Gus (Eduardo Ciannelli), that his cases typically originate and conclude. Waldo's is where trouble finds Staccato. In "Tempted," she goes by the name of Fay, a society girl (Elizabeth Montgomery). The instant Fay saunters down the stairs, pausing to let the detective's eyes wrap around her shapely figure as she softly purrs, "Hello, Johnny," Staccato's mood drops an octave. Fay's been naughty: she's stolen a priceless necklace and wants Staccato to help her outwit the insurance investigator on her heels. Her gloved fingers toying with Staccato's hair, Fay promises to split the spoils of her gains. Were she less sure of her seductive abilities, she might realize that "Johnny" abides by a code. Several double-crosses later, "Tempted" concludes where it started, with Fay slinking into Waldo's for what she expects to be a payoff secured on her behalf by Staccato. Only this time, our detective, immune to temptation of any sort, has the law waiting in the wings.

The devious female is perhaps *Staccato*'s most trenchant concession to a noir archetype. Many of its episodes deal with men driven to the brink by the sort of women who leave a sting. In "The Nature of the Night" the source of anxiety for Waldo's new barkeep Dave (Dean Stockwell) is the wife who ran out on him to find her fortune in the movies. "I cried and cried and cried," he says to Staccato. "And then, when I woke up, I was in the hospital. They gave me shock treatments. I ached, I really ached." Dave's lovesickness manifests itself in misogynistic rage. He takes to sneaking about the night slashing the pretty faces of every blonde he meets. "A scar, what if it makes a scar?" one victim cries to the cops. Faces are important in *Staccato*. The conspicuously expressive, artfully composed close-ups on display, particularly those arranged by Cassavetes, who came up through live television, where the human face held much value, deliver far more than a matching up of words to a moving mouth.

"The Mask of Jason" finds Staccato hired to protect a beauty queen, Bonnie (Mary Tyler Moore), from a horribly disfigured stalker. Staccato tracks him to a seedy hotel only to learn that he's Bonnie's ex-husband, Jason (Bert Remsen), and that he earned the brutal scars on his face while saving her from a fire. "Day the bandages came off was the last time I saw her," Jason tells Staccato, whose own face immediately registers disgust and a complete evaporation of loyalty to his client. Unlike the defeated, emasculated Dave, Jason isn't seeking vengeance: he simply, inexplicably, wants to win back Bonnie's love. "She's kind and gentle, a warm person," he reminisces. "She's good, really good, and I know she'll come back if I just get a chance to talk to her." Against his better judgment, Staccato arranges a reunion between the two, but it goes awry when Bonnie, wielding a purse-pistol, viciously shreds what remains of Jason's dignity. "I don't want you to touch me or to be near me," she bellows. "I don't love you! I never loved you! I would have left you anyway!" Director Paul Henreid frames

"Tempted" (1959) with Cassavetes and Elizabeth Montgomery.

"Viva, Paco!" (1959) with Cassavetes and Miriam Colon.

"The Mask of Jason" (1960) with Mary Tyler Moore.

Bonnie from a low angle in which a harsh, unflattering key light thoroughly illuminates the ugliness beneath the mask.

In keeping with the terms he'd wrested, Cassavetes directed five episodes, endeavoring, he said, "to do each one differently" in an effort to "develop some kind of style and technique." The ambition is evident, as are the influences, from the lyrical realism of Vittorio De Sica and Roberto Rossellini to the baroque expressionism of Orson Welles. Working with a professional crew for the first time, he demonstrates an uncanny grasp of noir idioms. His masterful "Night of Jeopardy," in particular, displays a keen visual unity as well as an awareness of how geography and chaos bind the characters and plot of a noir story. It opens with a gang of counterfeiters frantically incinerating piles of currency in advance of an imminent police raid. "Burn it!" shouts the boss, Eddie Wayneright (Frank de Kova), who, right before scramming, hands his valued printing plates over to a sidekick, Roman (Mario Gallo), for sakekeeping. Cassavetes captures the pandemonium with an overhead tracking shot that culminates with the screen itself bursting into flame.

Some blocks away, Staccato, in one of those intersections deployed to get the half-hour tele-noir off to a roaring start, happens upon Roman shooting it out with a policeman from within a gutted tenement. Staccato draws his gun and tips the fight accordingly. Roman, crouched in the shadows, stashes the plates before expiring in tight close-up. When the officials arrive, they refuse to tell Staccato what it's all about. "Go home," Sgt. Thomas (Jimmy Joyce) advises. No sooner is Staccato through his door when Wayneright and his torpedoes burst in, demanding that Staccato hand over their unspecified property. Staccato is mystified. Already, he's knee-deep in a situation he doesn't fully understand. Strong arms hold him in place as Wayneright, cigarette dangling from toothless mouth, moves in, fist raised. Cassavetes shoots this subjectively: the camera takes the beating. Elmer Bernstein's raucous cues fill the room.

"Night of Jeopardy" (1960).

Regaining consciousness, Staccato goes to the morgue and confronts Thomas and a treasury agent, Martin (William A. Forester). They're hostile, annoyed with Staccato. "If you're smart, kiddo, you'll get lost," Martin snarls. Thomas pipes in: "That means no police cooperation. The word is to blow, Johnny, so that's what you gotta do." Staccato slinks off to Waldo's only to find that Wayneright has taken over the joint. Unless Staccato produces the package, Waldo, the bar man (Dennis Sallas), and the hat check girl (Jane Burgess) are toast. From here on, it's both a clock-race and a hunt for the unknown. "I had two hours. Two desperate hours to find the package," Staccato tells us in a voiceover that brings him to the site of an orgiastic party at the loft of his informant,

Shad (Frank London). The jazzed-up crowd is so tightly packed that Shad, a sweaty little rat with bulging eyes, has to crawl through legs to get to Staccato. He seems confused that Staccato isn't in the mood for some reefer or a broad. "Man, you're, like, throwing professional questions at me," Shad complains. "This comes for bread. Loot!" Terms arranged, Shad places a call to "a guy upstairs" who "deals in who, what, where, when."

In saunters an even less trustworthy cat, Lazarus, with soda-bottle glasses and a dainty scarf. More money changes hands. With lurid grin, Lazarus sends Staccato up to Harlem to see Bobo, a handyman of sorts for the mob. A taxi ride brings Staccato to a long, dark stairwell. Bernstein's cue is a tense, low rumble. When Staccato gets to the top landing, he's grabbed from behind and disarmed: Bobo (Morris Buchanan) loathes visitors. Staccato talks himself out of a strangling and is pushed into Bobo's room—or is it a storage closet? There's junk everywhere—car parts, an upturned bed, old clocks, birdcages. And Bobo's several clouds higher than any of the beatniks downtown. He has little interest in assisting Staccato in his quest to find the mysterious package. Staccato persists. Cassavetes frames their fruitless exchange through the bric-a-brac:

"Night of Jeopardy" (1960).

STACCATO: Look, I need your help.

BOBO: How much?

STACCATO: Everything I got.

BOBO: How much that?

STACCATO: Well, there's ten bucks and some change.

BOBO: Buy nothing.

STACCATO: What's in the package?

BOBO: Buy nothing! No talk. Talk for loot. You dig? What do you think I am, some two-bit dealing square? . . . You stupid, man. Real stupid. Got yourself into a barrel. You'll find your way out. Now get out of here. And don't ask no questions to men who know the score, 'cause that costs money, square. You dig?

STACCATO: What about the gun?

BOBO: No gun. You travels alone tonight, daddy.

Staccato leaves with less than he arrived with. Downstairs, Wayneright and his boys pour in; Staccato hides in the shadows. Cassavetes's camera detaches from the detective's perspective to go behind Bobo's closed door. The dynamic of the restricted space is now reversed: Bobo, for all his bluster, is no match for the determined quartet who back him into the corner. Whatever affiliation he may have had with their racket is severed with the quick stab of an ice pick. Deed done, killers gone, Staccato removes himself from the shadows and tends to Bobo, who's got just enough breath left to tell the detective what all the huff is about: "plates so good they say Uncle Sam could've used them for the real thing." Staccato's voiceover returns us downtown to "the beginning and the burnt-out building" where he shot down Roman. His discovery of the package coincides with the arrival of the gangsters, who have followed him, as well as his realization that Thomas and the T-Men are already there, waiting in the dark with fingers on triggers.

When the gunfire dies down, Staccato tears open the package. Empty. He's been a patsy all along—the bait in a trap. "Night of Jeopardy," from a teleplay credited to Richard Carr and Everett Chambers, propels Staccato through a nihilistic, me-first world. At its core is the inherently noir notion that nothing is beyond commodification. Money itself is disposable, as evidenced by Wayneright's exhortation to his gang to destroy it all. The ability to actually produce money trumps everything, including life. "They'll have to kill me to get it," Roman vows when he takes possession of the plates. To recover them, Wayneright lines up three innocents for execution, and seems prepared to add a fourth. "Now, if you want us to kill you, we'll gladly oblige," he says to Staccato, who snaps back, "Everybody dies." But here Staccato is playing it tough; he really has only one option, as Cassavetes indicates by intercutting Staccato's aggrieved expression with sustained close-ups of each of the anxious hostages.

Not only Wayneright but the police bank on Staccato's inability to allow Waldo and company to die. Staccato, they know, will do what needs to be done to prevent any bloodshed. Meanwhile, Shad and Lazarus, despite their drugged state, are cognizant enough to interpret his desperation as an opportunity for financial gain, never mind that lives are at stake. Same with Bobo, who holds steadfast: "Money, now." The all-around hardness of these characters is solidified by the mirroring aspects of the story, not only in how Staccato is squeezed by both the police and the gangsters, but in how Cassavetes stages the two middle set pieces. Just as the throng of people at Shad's party gives way to the maze of junk in Bobo's attic hideaway, Shad's comment to Staccato, "Everybody talks. Nobody listens," is echoed by Bobo's curt instruction, "Talk fast. What do you want?" Amidst the distractions of modern living, words lose their value—round numbers are what matter. Only Staccato, the knight errant, is willing to push through the babble.

The impossibility of meaningful human contact in the cluttered noir city is further explored in Cassavetes's "A Piece of Paradise," in which Staccato investigates the murder of a taxi dancer. "Stella Taylor was dead," he tells us as the camera glides through a tableau of girls with bored faces listlessly draped on the shoulders of lonely men. But these pairings are fleeting; when the lights come on, the girls simply move on to the next paying customer. It's a rote cycle of coupling and uncoupling, interaction and alienation. The taxi-dance hall, a ubiquitous feature of urban America until the 1960s, features prominently in the noir landscape, from Stanley Kubrick's *Killer's Kiss* (1955), with its central setting of Pleasure Land, a Times Square landmark, to the stories of Cornell

"A Piece of Paradise" (1959).

Woolrich, who wrote vividly of how such places symbolize the isolating aspect of big city living. In *The Black Angel* (1943), Alberta, upon entering the Mimi Club, relays her impression of the dime-a-dance couplings as "a publicly performed ritual to mortality, and I found it grimly melancholy over and above the grim melancholy of my own errand. A bacchanalia at fixed prices. The never-ending, never-succeeding attempt to hold pain, despair, death at bay for a little while. A little while longer."

"A Piece of Paradise" (1959).

Staccato's impression of the Paradise Dance Hall is similarly evocative: "The pink lights, the shimmering stars, the sultry music, combined to create the Paradise Dance Hall," he narrates. "Here, everybody reaching out for a piece of paradise. Here, ten cents a dance. One minute of paradise and, suddenly, it's honky-tonk. And here I am trying to solve a murder and save a friend." The friend in question is Mack (Walter Burke), a once-great but now-crippled jockey who drank himself out of the saddle. When Staccato's police nemesis, Sgt. Joe Gillen (Bert Freed), drops into Waldo's looking for Mack, his chief suspect in Stella's murder, Staccato refuses to cooperate: he'll launch his own inquiry. Interviewing the dime dancers, he learns that Stella had been dating a cop, "a big fat fuzz," who became jealous upon learning that her rent was being paid by a secret admirer. Staccato assumes the obvious—Gillen killed Stella—but he's proved wrong on this count: the bull has an alibi for the night of the murder. So it must be Mack—but how? "It just happened," the jockey admits. Curled up in a dim stable, his face a permanent scowl of defeat, this broken little man quietly reveals how, after months of showering Stella with gifts, he finally raised the courage to show up at her door with an engagement ring.

> MACK: She couldn't stop laughing. She started making fun of me. She told me I could hold her hand, but it would cost me ten cents a minute like down at the Paradise. And, Johnny, I started doing it, paying her ten cents . . . She thought it was real kicks.

The revelation that his friend humiliated himself for a moment of human contact deeply troubles Staccato. Cassavetes frames the scene in alternating close-ups. As Mack's self-flagellation builds on itself, Cassavetes homes in on the distraught reaction of Staccato, whose face he obscures in crisscrossing shadows. Mack's expression, meanwhile, becomes lighter and less burdened. Visually, it suggests a transference of guilt. Taking on the sins of his friends, and very often his enemies, is what distinguishes Staccato from all the other private eyes on the scene.

Even when he isn't calling the shots, Cassavetes seems hyper-aware of the camera, of how its proximity might best exploit his wolfish intensity. Having played irascible, knife-wielding "juvies" for much of his career, he imbues his detective with a similar sense of volatility. He delivers his lines with a cutting emphasis to

"The Nature of the Night" (1959).

match his character's name, and even those three syllables he stretches out with unmistakable petulance. Oddly, this side of the eye—his razor-like edginess, his surly unpredictability—works in tandem with his altruistic nature. In "Nature of the Night," when Dave, the slasher, clambers to a rooftop and threatens to end his life, Staccato goads him on. "Oh, man, you make me sick," he brays as he tosses Dave's suicide note to the air. "You've been grandstanding here for half an hour now. Look down there, whaddaya got, seven or eight people watching you? What are you waiting for, a full house? Go, on! Jump!" Dumbfounded by such abrasiveness, Dave is easily plucked off the ledge by the waiting police.

At Variety Arts, the acting workshop he ran in the 1950s, Cassavetes was notorious for pushing his students to unexpected revelations. He does the same in "Solomon" within a minimalist setting and the sketchiest of setups. Solomon (Elisha Cook), "the world's greatest defense attorney," hires Staccato to test the alibi of his client Jessica Winthrop (Cloris Leachman), a renowned pacifist accused of stabbing her husband nine times. In a barren holding cell, Jessica placidly explains that while her husband regularly abused her, she herself is incapable of violence: "I turned the other cheek," she maintains. Staccato spends the good part of a day running Jessica through a mock cross-examination. His berating is merciless; at one point he even questions whether the troubles in the Winthrops' marriage might not have been the result of her "frigidity"—or was it, perhaps, that her husband didn't like women? Jessica remains unruffled. Staccato punctuates the interrogation with a fierce slap across her face; while she glares back with silent rage, her hands remain folded in her lap. Seemingly satisfied that his vitriol has failed to elicit a response, Staccato turns away. Solomon registers relief: he'll win this case after all. Behind them, Jessica reaches for the murder weapon, deliberately left nearby, and lunges at Staccato. "It was pitiful," Staccato tells us in voiceover, "a woman revealed right to her core."

The series' updating of 1940s film noir tropes is amply illustrated in its preoccupation with the legacy of war, specifically the conflict in Korea, of which Staccato is a veteran, as are many of his clients. In "The Return," shell-shocked soldier Eddie Dasko (Tom Allen, one of many *Shadows* alumni), confined to the psych ward at Bellevue, is convinced that his wife has been unfaithful while he's been away. An elliptical exchange with the hospital shrink (Ben Hammer) reveals both the uncertainty behind his fears and the only plausible resolution, in his view, to such a dilemma:

EDDIE: I know.
DOCTOR: You know what, Eddie?
EDDIE: I know what's going on.

DOCTOR: What is going on, Eddie?

EDDIE: She's deceitful, doc. She's cunning. Like all women. She thinks I can't see through all that sweet talk. She doesn't fool me.

DOCTOR: Did you ever stop to think that maybe she isn't trying to fool you?

EDDIE: You don't know women like we do, doc.

DOCTOR: We?

EDDIE: Us guys in Korea, freezing in the mud, snow up to our necks. And then the "Dear Johns" and the lies! They're all the same, doc. And Jeanie's no different.

"Double Feature" (1960).

Asked what he would do if he were released, Eddie says, "I'd kill her." Hours later, Eddie escapes and sets out to fulfill his vow, something Staccato spends a frantic night trying to prevent.

Another war-related trope, common to Cold War-era noir, is that of the returning POW suspected of turning "red" during captivity. This is the scenario of "A Nice Little Town," the most overtly political installment of *Staccato*. When a soldier back from Korea less than a week is ripped from his home by some masked marauders and lynched in his front yard, the victim's sister, Royal (Christine White), a retired jazz singer, sends for Staccato. Arriving upstate, Staccato finds a town mired in corruption, its authorities and citizens openly hostile. "Somebody in this town killed a man and nobody seems to be doing anything about it," he barks to the mayor and his coterie. "Now that strikes me as pretty un-American." Neither the authorities nor any of the townsfolk will assist in solving the case. As they see it, the interloper with the foreign surname is just as subversive as the could-be commie they allowed to be murdered.

"A Nice Little Town" climaxes with a fiercely delivered monologue. After Royal herself is killed by the mob, the mayor and his ilk again refuse to intervene, Staccato, bloodied and torn from the beatings he's endured, gathers up the body and pushes his way through the townspeople to deliver a blistering lecture on the evils of moral inertia. Proclaiming that he, not they, will bury Royal, Staccato effectively assumes their collective guilt. The burdens this sometime detective bears on behalf of others are pushed to the limit in "The Wild Reed," the episode that got the series canceled. Upon learning that his old friend Franky Aspen (Harry Gaurdino), a once-celebrated saxophonist, is now fielding catcalls in a seedy Lower East Side dive, Staccato pays him a visit. Almost immediately, our detective breaks into an embarrassed wince: Franky has forsaken the mellow sounds that made him famous for the free-associative form of bebop. "How could a guy who was so good a few years ago be so lousy now?" Staccato ponders in voiceover. "There had to be an answer, and that's what I wanted to know now. Just an answer."

"There's one thing I won't do— play with a female who knows more than I do!"

JOHN CASSAVETES as "JOHNNY STACCATO"
tonight 8:30 NBC CH 4
Presented by Salem Cigarettes and Bristol-Myers Company

Advert for *Staccato* (1959).

TOP: "Double Feature" (1960).

MIDDLE: "Solomon" (1960) with Elisha Cook Jr., Cassavetes, and Cloris Leachman.

BOTTOM: "A Piece of Paradise" (1959) with Cassavetes and Bert Freed.

The answer that Franky offers—that the travails of fame led to a nervous breakdown and a stint in Bellevue—fails to satisfy Staccato, who fears that his friend's sweaty, manic disposition betrays a vicious heroin addiction. "He's sick," Staccato says to Franky's new gal, Sally (Olive Deering). "He plays sick and he talks sick." When Sally responds with apathy, Staccato senses, instinctively, that something is amiss. But it's already too late: Sally, a dope fiend herself, has drugged his drink. Hours later, Staccato wakes up in a jail cell, stupefied and disoriented, and surrounded by junkies whose emaciated fingers grope through his pockets. "Just you wait, just you wait until you get the shakes," one of them warns. Eventually, a cop friend, Lou (J. Pat O'Malley), bails Staccato out. "Patrolman found you," Lou explains, sternly. "You had a high-point in your hand, a needle mark on your arm—you'd had a fix." It's the ultimate noir nightmare: the unwilling surrender to forces dark and inexplicable.

And still Staccato pushes. Retracing his steps, he makes his way from Sally to the gang of dope peddlers who have Franky under their thumb. Once again, they try to stuff Staccato with junk. This will be his final dose, the gang boss (Joseph Sargent) promises, the one that kicks his habit. Now we see the flip side of Staccato's humanism: his all-or-nothingness. To save a friend, he'll traverse any path. Grinning like a lunatic, Staccato rolls up his sleeve, slaps a vein, and snaps out a tempo with his fingers. "I'm playing it cool, man," he announces. "No law says a man's got to die with a frown on his face. C'mon, lay it on!" When the executives at NBC and sponsor Procter & Gamble saw this scene— their hero begging for heroin—they pulled "The Wild Reed" from its scheduled broadcast and summoned Cassavetes to New York.

Tired of clashing with the brass over the direction of the show, as well as their insistence in softening its title to *Johnny Staccato* (à la *Peter Gunn*), Cassavetes took his dissatisfaction to the press, a maneuver as frowned upon at the time as an actor demanding a place behind the camera. "It is virtually impossible to get approval on a script that has substance," he complained to the *New York Herald-Tribune*. "There is no limit on violence; you can get approval on a story in which a woman is slaughtered, but an honest story about a dope addict is rejected because it would be injurious to the sponsor's product—an underarm deodorant." *Staccato*, which had always been hammered by its bucolic time-slot competitor *The Real McCoys*, was taken out of production after twenty-seven episodes—twelve short of Cassavetes's fiercely wrought but short-lived Hollywood deal.

THE TWILIGHT ZONE
CBS 1959–1964

> As Gregor Samsa awoke one morning from uneasy dreams he found himself transformed in his bed into a gigantic insect-like creature.
> —FRANZ KAFKA, *The Metamorphosis*

HALF A CENTURY ON, THE VERY TITLE OF *THE TWILIGHT ZONE* REMAINS IN the public lexicon as a signifier of eerie ambiguity. As with much postwar film noir, particularly those strains developed beneath the shadow of the Bomb, it posits a universe in which the chasm between security and annihilation looms open-mouthed. Dispatched by fate to "a fifth dimension beyond that which is known to man"—as Rod Serling, who created the show, and narrates each of its episodes, explains over the main titles—its characters all find themselves neck-deep in a noir nightmare that's been turned inside out and stretched to its full otherworldly potential. Serling arrived at this speculative realm by way of a prolific decade as one of the leading dramatists of the live anthologies. When it was announced that he was doing a telefilm series, and a genre-based one at that, many assumed, as Mike Wallace indelicately put it during an on-air interview, that he'd "given up writing anything important for television." Far from it. Through metaphor, irony, and paradox, the socially conscious themes and stark naturalism with which he made his name are reshaped within the complex and illusory continuum of a fever dream: Serling spins these tales with a surrealist's knack for exposing truths in unexpected places.

Each *Twilight Zone* tale begins deceptively, grounded in the recognizable, before shoving its hapless protagonist beyond the lip of the uncanny. It's an abyss not at all well marked. Those who tumble down it find themselves in a dark and nebulous dreamscape in which life's reliable features have been compromised, perhaps irretrievably; Serling liked to describe it as "the shadowy area of the almost-but-not-quite." In lieu of a sturdy foothold, doubt, self-division, and anxiety creep in: the passenger becomes a neurotic mess, lonely and dispossessed, and in perpetual terror of the next catastrophe. This is the conditional state of being in the Zone, which is as much a destination as it is a designation—a barometer for the collective psyche in the Age of Duck-and-Cover.

Title Card, *The Twilight Zone* (1959).

Publicity still of Rod Serling (ca. 1959).

On the set of "The Monsters Are Due on Maple Street" (1960) with Jack Weston, Burt Metcalfe, Jason Johnson, and Amzie Strickland.

"Third from the Sun" (1960) with Joe Maross, Fritz Weaver, Lori March, and Denise Alexander.

"Time Enough at Last" (1959) with Burgess Meredith.

The threat of apocalypse saturates *The Twilight Zone*. Even in those episodes not directly concerned with nuclear cataclysm, there persists an air of premonition, a fear of the instant when the lights are permanently put out. Time and again, there's the nagging sense that this is not the way things are meant to be. How did the forces of menace gain control? At what point did the future become so formless and inscrutable?

Faced with prevailing darkness, powerless to hinder it, the populace becomes insecure and self-absorbed. Confusion and fear lurch into violence and hysteria. A power outage gives rise to a frenzied mob intent on rooting out the "others" in their midst ("The Monsters Are Due on Maple Street"). An unidentified flying object compels friends and neighbors to tear at one another in a desperate rush to find a place to hide ("The Shelter"). In these and other parables, the inexorable march toward finality has already begun. "For this is the stillness before the storm, this is the eve of the end," begins Serling's sober narration of "Third from the Sun." William Sturka (Fritz Weaver), a government scientist, has stumbled upon a colossal secret—all-out atomic war, mere days away—that sends him scrambling for an escape route. Even before he reveals what he knows, he finds that his family shares his unshakable feeling of dread. "Everyone I've talked to lately, they've been noticing it—that something's wrong," his daughter (Denise Alexander) says. "That something's in the air. That something's going to happen and everybody's afraid." What was once unthinkable, Sturka confirms, is now unavoidable: "It'll be hell. It'll be holocaust."

But Sturka and his neighbor, a rocket test pilot (Joe Maross), have a contingency plan: they'll hijack an airship and strike out with their broods for a new home, "a place called Earth, the third planet from the sun." Only now do we learn that these doomed beings are not of our world, but another. The dark irony of reversal (a series hallmark) only hardens an inherent pessimism: the last laugh of such a trick ending is on the fleeing aliens who will likely wish they'd sought refuge elsewhere. The volatility of Earth circa 1959 is made even clearer in "Time Enough at Last," when World War III reduces everything to rubble. The only survivor is one Henry Bemis (Burgess Meredith), a loner and a bookworm with the fortuitous habit of sneaking his lunch and some reading material down to the bomb-proof vault of the bank where he clerks. Traipsing through the radioactive ruins, finally free of henpecking wife and unpleasant boss, Bemis comes upon a library, thousands of books spilled out on its stairs.

But as he rejoices, his spectacles slip from his nose and fall to the ground, shattered beyond hope; his future blurred beyond comprehension. Bemis's wail of "It's not fair" is matched with a God's-eye vista of civilization laid flat.

Vacated horizons dominate *The Twilight Zone*: devastated cities, lonely planets, open highways. But bustling urban spaces are just as likely to foster alienation. "Twelve o'clock noon. An ordinary scene. An ordinary city," Serling tells us in his prologue for "Perchance to Dream." Incorporating a piece of footage snipped from *The Crowd* (1928), the camera glides up the facade of an imposing skyscraper and into an open window. With a dissolve, we're inside a psychiatrist's office where Edward Hall (Richard Conte), "the tiredest man in the world," is struggling to comprehend the terrifying visions he's been having, in which he journeys through an amusement park at night: "The kind of place you only see in nightmares," he sputters, having kept himself awake on pills for four days now. "Everything twisted out of shape. But it was real too. Very real." The source of Hall's anxiety is a sultry carnival performer, Maya the Cat Girl (Suzanne Lloyd), whose mysterious attractions have cast a spell over him. In each of his dreams, which unfold in chapters, "like in the adventure serials," she takes him up on a fearsome roller coaster; given his weak heart, Hall fears that his next dream-ride will be his last.

"Perchance to Dream" (1959) with Suzanne Lloyd and Richard Conte.

George T. Clemens's camerawork in "Perchance to Dream"—he lensed most of the series—is darkly oneiric, an evocation of repressed libido and unbridled fear in which a supposed playland becomes a setting of unremitting terror. This dream-like suspension, at once lyrical and unsettling, permeates much of *The Twilight Zone*. Charles Beaumont, who wrote "Perchance," was among a select pool of speculative fiction writers, including Richard Matheson and George Clayton Johnson, whom Serling brought on to the series. (Serling himself wrote two-thirds of the 156 episodes.) Beaumont's "Perchance to Dream" feels like a continuation of Serling's earlier "The Time Element" (*Desilu Playhouse*, 1958). Pete Jenson (William Bendix) is a surly, two-bit horseplayer with the same existential aggravations as Edward Hall: he falls asleep in one place and wakes up in another, in this case Honolulu, December 6, 1941. Remanding himself to a psychiatrist, Gillespie (Martin Balsam), he tries to make sense of his nightly time-traveling woes, how his warnings of the impending Japanese attack on Pearl Harbor are met with derision, how with each return to the past he inches closer to certain death:

> JENSON: When I'm standing by those doors and the planes are coming in, that's where I wake up. But even after I wake up, and I'm laying in bed, thinking about it, I know the dream shouldn't have ended there. It should have gone on beyond that. One of these nights it will go on beyond that.

The flummoxed doctor has little to offer that might alleviate his patient's anxiety; modern medicine, it seems, is hopeless in addressing the psychic ailments of modern man. Falling asleep on Gillespie's couch, Jenson returns to his dream state, but this time his nightmare is brought to fruition. As air raid sirens sound, he cries out, "I told you! I told you! Why wouldn't anybody listen to me!" Only here Serling has a trick up his sleeve, a brain-twister antithetical to a medium wherein everything must be wrapped up with narrative coherence, lest the viewer be too confused to absorb the commercials. From a final shot of Jenson collapsing in his bombed-out hotel room in Honolulu, we're abruptly transported to Gillespie's office. Alone, the psychiatrist stares at his vacant couch, vexed by something he can't quite place. He leaves his office and goes to his local watering hole and orders a drink. On the wall there's a framed photograph that gives him a start. "Who's the guy in the picture?" he asks. "Oh, that's Pete Jenson. Used to tend bar here," the barman says. "He's dead. He was killed at Pearl Harbor."

How's that? Didn't the narrator tell us (twice) that the time of the story is the "now" of 1958? And wasn't Jenson's perspective the dominant one of the story? "The Time Element" arrives at a chiral resolution of unsettling ambiguity: to whom do the events we've seen belong? The sponsor, Westinghouse, wouldn't have it: they made Desi Arnaz come on at the end and deliver a pat explanation. But the viewer response was overwhelming—some six thousand postcards and telegrams demanding more of the same poured into CBS. Thusly encouraged, Serling responded with the pilot for what would become *The Twilight Zone*: "Where Is Everybody?" In this, another roaming nightmare, Mike Ferris (Earl Holliman) wanders through a town that seems to have been abandoned just before his arrival. Automobiles idle at the curb, cigarettes smolder in ashtrays, phones ring in offices, but everywhere Ferris goes, there are no people. Intrigued, then baffled, then paranoid, then outright petrified, he finally crumbles completely when confronted with his own reflection in the mirrored wall of an empty cinema.

Like most of the poor souls sucked into the Zone, Ferris is brought to the precipice through no accord of his own. An astronaut in training, he's been locked inside an isolation chamber for several weeks. In his delirium, he's imagined this ordeal. "We have licked everything but the barrier of loneliness," says a military official at the end as the catatonic Ferris is wheeled away. "Where Is Everybody?" embodies the thematic template of *The Twilight Zone*: the illusory veil between sanity and madness; the surprisingly high fracture rate of the human psyche (and with it a preponderance of mirrors); the fear of ceding self-control to unknowable forces; and, especially, the troubling news that reality is fluid, not fixed. Existential displacement is at the core of the series' noir ethos. Consider, for example, the jolt of self-awakening

"The Dummy" (1962).

that occurs in "The Dummy" when, after much hectoring from the insolent puppet on his knee, a nightclub ventriloquist (Cliff Robertson) comes to the realization that it is *he* who is made of "nothing more than knotty pine and paint." The revelation is capped off with a terrifying chase down a Caligari-esque alley through which the anthropomorphized dummy casts a monstrous shadow.

Expressionistic flourishes are again summoned in "The Four of Us Are Dying," which begins strikingly with discordant jazz music and a blaze of disorienting neon signage. Against such chaos, Arch Hammer (Harry Townes) finds his way to the Hotel

The series pilot: "Where Is Everybody?" (1959) with Earl Holliman.

Real, checks himself into a bare room, and stands before a mirror with a look of curious smugness. Hammer's specialty, as revealed in a remarkable uninterrupted take, is that he can change his features at will. "He's been a salesman, a dispatcher, a truck driver, a con man, a bookie, and a part-time bartender," Serling tells us. "This is a cheap man, a nickel-and-dime man, with a cheapness that goes past the suit and the shirt; a cheapness of mind, a cheapness of taste, a tawdry little shine on the seat of his conscience, and a darkroom squint at a world whose sunlight has never gotten through to him." Intent on gathering money and dames, Hammer shifts through a variety of noir personae—jazz musician, hoodlum, boxer—until he ends up with the wrong face at the wrong time. Gunned down, he dies bleeding on a sidewalk, his death mask in flux.

"The Four Of Us Are Dying" (1960).

With nothing solid against which to measure one's reality, the matter of identity becomes a play of the cards. "Each of us woke up one morning. Here we were in the darkness. No knowledge of who we are. No knowledge of what we will be," observes one of the lost souls in "Five Characters in Search of an Exit." As with Kafka's Gregor Samsa, "who awoke one morning from uneasy dreams," crises of identity are repeatedly tied to cycles of day and night. In "The After Hours," Marsha (Anne Francis) finds herself locked inside a department store past closing. There are only shadows and mannequins. Lifeless eyes follow her frantic movements. Pressing her face to the pebbled glass of a locked door, Marsha cries pitifully for help, and suddenly we're made to see her from a reverse angle, her features smeared, no longer identifiably human. It's the first clue that Marsha isn't who she thinks she is. From the dark, the mannequins cry out: "Climb off it! You know who you are, Marsha! You remember!" One by

"Five Characters in Search of an Exit" (1961).

"Mirror Image" (1960) with Vera Miles and Naomi Stevens.

one, they snap to life, exhorting her to accept what she's apparently forgotten. Come morning, Marsha is found poised on a pedestal in dutiful repose, reverted to her natural state.

In "Mirror Image," Millicent Barnes (Vera Miles), stuck for a stormy night in a bus depot, begins her journey sure of who she is and where she's going. "A girl with a head on her shoulders," Serling tells us, "not given to overdue anxiety or fears, or for that matter even the most temporal flights of fancy." But what was solid and seemingly irrevocable is directly peeled away when Millicent catches a glimpse of herself seated elsewhere in the waiting room. Though she tries to explain away this phenomenon of an apparent double with some talk about "parallel planes" of existence, her destiny is predetermined. Running to catch the bus, Millicent finds her seat already taken by her döppelganger—her anguished expression greeted with the self-satisfied smirk of the "other" who has nullified her existence. Such is the deterministic sway of noir that there's little to gain from applying concerted logic to a moment of crisis. Millicent (like Ferris) ends her sojourn strapped to a gurney—off to the psych ward. The number of nervous breakdowns suffered in the Zone probably amounts to a record of some kind; in this realm, one's sense of being is merely a point of departure. "Next stop, the Twilight Zone," Serling will announce as he ushers yet another cosmically befuddled traveler through one of his dark fables.

The loss of individual autonomy is set forth as a fait accompli. Witness the unfortunate protagonist (Howard Duff) of "A World of Difference" who unexpectedly hears someone yell "Cut!" and discovers that his life is but a movie, complete with a director calling the shots. Existence is what it is, malleable and without shape, and nearly impossible to steer from the inside. "David Gurney has never really thought about the matter of his identity," Serling informs us in "Person or Persons Unknown." "But he's going to be thinking about it a great deal from now on, because that is what

On the set of "A World of Difference" (1960) with Howard Duff.

he's lost." Gurney (Richard Long) awakens one morning to discover that no one knows who he is. Without warning, he's become a stranger to his wife, his friends and colleagues, even his own mother. He simply no longer exists. John Brahm, who directed more *Twilight Zone*s than anyone, stretches the obligatory stinger out to devious effect. Gurney, after being committed to an asylum, escaping, returning home, and fainting upon realizing that he's disappeared from every family photo, finally awakens in his own bed—it was all a bad dream. He begins to excitably recount his ordeal to his wife, who is shown slowly removing the cold cream from her face until she reveals herself to be not his wife at all.

In the absence of certainty, the unsavory aspects of human nature flourish. The series is rife with obsessive-compulsives governed by dark impulses, such as Franklin Gibbs (Everett Sloane) of "The Fever," who becomes unreasonably fixated on a slot machine into which he slides his marriage, his dignity, his life savings. The chain of seduction by which he's hooked into submission neatly follows the classic outline of a noir male led astray by temptation: there's the dowdy, detested wife; the stranger who introduces him to new delights; the struggle to resist what can't be resisted; the sleepless, unfulfilled nights of longing; the somnambulist answering of the inchoate siren's call ("Frank-ling," the slot machine coos with a mouthful of coin); the shredding of all pride; the inevitable rejection; and, finally, the shameful suicide when all reserves are spent. Despite its emphasis on crime and sin, noir propagates an essentially conservative morality: those who transgress are punished and condemned.

The moment of Gibbs's self-reckoning, like most such confrontations in the series, occurs in a mirror, as a wholly subjective encounter. His wife (Vivi Janiss) doesn't see the one-armed bandit that chases him to his death; she sees only her husband screaming pitifully at his own reflection before hurling himself through a window. A similar "I vs. Me" encounter occurs in "Nervous Man in a Four-Dollar Room" when furtive, nail-biting stooge Jackie Rhoades (Joe Mantell) is given that wallop of noir directives: kill a man, or be killed himself. "You always look like somebody's trying to squeeze you through a door," George (William D. Gordon), the despicable hoodlum for whom Rhoades works, sneers as he tosses over a handgun. "Tonight, I'm gonna let you be a man. Tonight I'm gonna let you show some muscle for a change." After George leaves, Rhoades is seen from an overhead shot, clawing himself in agony, as Jerry Goldsmith's syncopated score (snip-snip-snip, like shears) fills the soundtrack.

"Nervous Man in a Four-Dollar Room" (1960) with Joe Mantell.

So begins the shredding of Rhoades's soul, a battle of wills between his mousy, pushover self ("Why am I scared? Why am I all the time scared?") and his more confident, conscientious other ("I know you, Jackie Rhoades. You ain't no killer."), who appears in the mirror over the bureau. A crummy rented room is again the setting for a bout of self-loathing in "Last Night of a Jockey." Grady (Mickey Rooney) is a jockey banned from the sport for gambling on his own races; he's a disgrace, "a rotten apple bruised and yellowed by dealing in dirt," Serling tells us. Unable to face himself, Grady smashes all the reflective objects in his room, but his nagging inner voice will not leave him alone. Wishing aloud that he were a "bigger" man, Grady collapses into a sleep; hours later, he finds that he's outgrown his bed—like Alice, he's sprouted to an unseemly size. He is now, as wished for, ten feet tall—a grotesque. So when the phone rings and

"Last Night of a Jockey" (1963) with Mickey Rooney.

"Walking Distance" (1959) with
Gig Young.

he's given a second chance in the saddle, Grady can only bellow in frustration: he's a giant trapped inside a dollhouse, a real freak.

Aside from conveying the fluidity of identity, mirrors also signify subtle shifts in the arrangement of past and present. In "Walking Distance," it's a mirror that returns the despairing Martin Sloan (Gig Young) to the time and place of his youth. Sloan is a New York advertising executive who, at thirty-six, is already a burnout. One Sunday, he takes a spontaneous drive upstate. Swerving into a service station, he honks impatiently, his brusqueness soothed when he notices a sign for the nearby town of Homewood. "I used to live in Homewood," he tells the attendant. "Grew up there, matter of fact. Haven't been back in twenty, twenty-five years." And so off he sets, on foot, a journey conveyed via a masterful "through the looking-glass" effect by director Robert Stevens: as Sloan, reflected in the mirror of a cigarette machine, turns and walks away, a dolly movement follows his receding figure; with a cut, the camera then slowly cranes back from a mirror behind the counter of a soda fountain to deposit Sloan in the past.

"My major hang-up is nostalgia," Serling once wrote. "I hunger to go back to knickers and ice cream." Strolling through Homewood, the sun on his face, Sloan finds everything as it was when he was a boy, pastoral and perfect. He encounters his still-alive parents (Frank Overton and Irene Tedrow) and his spritely younger self (Michael Montgomery). But when he declares himself to be Martin Sloan, he's rebuffed as a lunatic. The setting shifts to evening. "A man can think a lot of thoughts and walk a lot of pavements between afternoon and night," Serling says. "And to a man like Martin Sloan, to whom memory has suddenly become reality, a resolve can come just as clearly and inexorably as stars in a summer night." This second act of "Walking Distance," in which Sloan tries to ingratiate himself into the fabric of the past, is visually darker and less stable, a reminder of the futility of such an endeavor.

> FATHER: Martin, you have to leave here. There's no room, there's no place. Do you understand that?
>
> SLOAN: I see that now, but I don't understand. Why not?
>
> FATHER: I guess because we only get one chance. Maybe there's only one summer to every customer. That little boy, the one I know, the one who belongs here, this is his summer, just as it was yours once—don't make him share it.

The sweep of chiaroscuro imagery in the sequence that follows continues to build the tragic pressure of the story: the half-lit faces of father and son as Sloan describes his unhappiness; the stir in Sloan's eyes as he hears the faraway strains of calliope music; the tracking close-up of his running feet as he sets off for the merry-go-round; the abrupt shift to frantic, canted framings as Sloan chases after his younger self ("Let me talk to you! Let me tell you something!"); Sloan's agonized reaction after he inadvertently injures the boy (an injury carried over in his present-day limp); the slow procession of children dismounting and exiting the frame until Sloan stands alone, vignetted by shadows; the matching of Sloan's plaintive face to shots of the riderless carousel horses—this to the accompaniment of Bernard Hermann's melancholic underscore for harp and strings, which unifies the wistfulness and potency of Sloan's unrequited yearning for all that has been lost.

"Walking Distance" (1959).

The carousel climax of "Walking Distance" is perhaps the most celebrated set piece of *The Twilight Zone*. It was recalled, fifty years on, in *Mad Men* (2007–2015), a period drama set in the same late 1950s–early 1960s timeframe. Don Draper (Jon Hamm), like Sloan, works in advertising, a profession dedicated to the manufacture of artificial longing; both men lead unfulfilled, anxious lives. The more disquieted these harried executives become, the more frequently homesickness befalls them. In Draper's case, this is complicated by his self-erased past and the innate character flaws which have fully alienated him from his wife and children by the finale of season one ("The Wheel"). Asked to drum up a campaign for Kodak's new Slide Wheel projector, he delivers a stirring rumination on the nature of nostalgia:

> DRAPER: It's a tinge in your heart far more powerful than memory alone. This device isn't a spaceship, it's a time machine. It goes backwards and forwards. It takes us back to a place where we ache to go again. It's not called the Wheel, it's called the Carousel. It lets us travel the way a child travels, around and around, and back home again, to a place where we know we are loved.

Nostalgia, for Draper, is a bittersweet salve. The images he runs in his presentation are of the family he fears he has lost—a family emblematic of the second life he willed into existence. A nostalgic hold on what was (but is now gone) is perhaps the most salient of noir themes. A source of pain, it breeds alienation, loss of identity—chaos. Draper looks to the past because he lacks truth in the present, as does Sloan. Like shapeless, flapping laundry, they've become stuck on the tension line between ideal and reality.

Ralph Harper, in his psychological analysis of fairy tales, *Nostalgia*

"Nightmare at 20,000 Feet" (1963)
with William Shatner.

(1955), writes: "The soul shuddering draws itself up and offers to the depressed consciousness a psychic experience of presence. In nostalgia one smells and tastes, one responds from the darkest corners of oneself, as a renewed whole, to some reality one loves, a person or a place, or even an idea." Paul Schrader, in his "Notes on Film Noir" (1970), plucks a similar string: "Film noir's techniques emphasize loss, nostalgia, lack of clear priorities, insecurity; then submerge these self-doubts in mannerism and style." The noir protagonist longs for yesterday's comforts as a way of fighting the sickness of the grown-up world. "I just want to rest and stop running," Sloan tells his father. His idealizing of the past is symptomatic of both a displeasure with the present and a fear that the future is all used up. This struggle to find a way back home, to the time before the onset of the nightmare, is the essence of many a noir narrative. But the past can never be reclaimed, not even in *The Twilight Zone*.

NEO
NOIR

DANGER MAN
CBS 1961–1966
THE PRISONER
CBS 1968

> Every government has its secret service branch. America, its CIA; France, Deuxième Bureau; England, MI5. NATO also has its own. A messy job? Well, that's when they usually call on me, or someone like me. Oh, yes, my name is Drake, John Drake.
>
> —JOHN DRAKE

THE VOICE IS FLAT, AMERICAN WITH A LILT OF IRISH; ITS TONE COOL, assured, if perhaps a little insolent. Having spelled out his mandate within the alphabetic runes of the spy trade, John Drake (Patrick McGoohan), an international specialist at "messy jobs," saunters from a modernist glass structure, tosses a smart-looking jacket in the back of an even smarter sports car, and speeds away. A swelling jazz theme punctuates the title card; were it not for the promise of global adventure, this could well be *Peter Gunn* or *Staccato*. *Danger Man* debuted in the UK in 1960, on the cusp of the secret agent craze that would grip the decade; the first James Bond film, *Dr. No*, was still two years away. The series' immediate antecedent is the literary Bond, as introduced by Ian Fleming with *Casino Royale* (1953), a work whose pulp tensions and fatalistic plotting owe much to the noir ethos. Looking back further still, *Danger Man* draws upon the rich legacy of the cloak-and-dagger tale.

The British spy thriller, like its American counterpart, the hardboiled detective story, deals in quests, its heroes setting forth through landscapes of moral and political treachery. Raymond Chandler liked to describe the milieu as "a world run by gangsters." Joseph Conrad, in *The Secret Agent* (1907), his great novel of sabotage and intrigue, characterizes it as "this earth of evil." Conrad's prescient vision of the spiritual disfigurement and senseless calamity that would mark the twentieth century effectively invented the modern espionage story. Through two world wars and up to the

Title sequence of *Danger Man* (1964).

OPPOSITE PAGE: "Not So Jolly Roger" (*Danger Man*, 1966) with Patrick McGoohan.

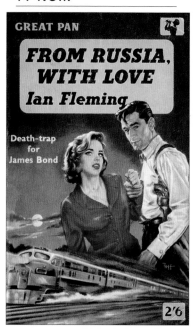

From Russia With Love
(Ian Fleming, Pan, 1957).

Danger Man Annual
(World Distributors, 1965).

brink of a third, his prototype gained picaresque structure in John Buchan's *The Thirty-Nine Steps* (1915); autobiographical legitimacy in Somerset Maugham's *Ashenden* (1922); and a measure of psychological realism in the works of Eric Ambler (*Epitaph for a Spy*, 1937) and Graham Greene (*The Confidential Agent*, 1939). All of these writers, but especially Ambler and Greene, were important to film noir—which, by the advent of the Cold War, occupied much the same thematic and psychic terrain as the spy genre.

It was in this postwar climate that Fleming's decadent rogue rose to popularity in print, followed in due order by the determinedly more understated Drake of television. *Danger Man* was created by writer-producer Ralph Smart. His ITC-produced series *The Invisible Man* (1957–1958), an espionage-themed reworking of the H.G. Wells classic, was the first contemporarily set British program to crack the all-important American market. Commissioned by ITC boss Lew Grade to devise something similar, he responded with a treatment, reportedly fleshed out with input from Fleming, about a well-traveled man of intrigue whose assignments put him on the forefront of the Cold War. There were some early discussions about bringing Bond himself to television, but as legal matters surrounding the novels prevented that, Smart enlisted Ian Stuart Black and Brian Clemens, his writers on *The Invisible Man*, to further develop the character, at that stage known as "Lone Wolf." The result was John Drake, an Irish-American (like McGoohan) security specialist at the beck and call of NATO—a hero of transatlantic appeal.

As *Danger Man* headed to production, its protagonist remained in the hedonistic-warrior mold of 007, only to be steered in a less derivative direction by McGoohan. "Hampering him with phony romance and festooning him with a gun is ridiculous," the actor maintained. "The speed, suspense, and effect are better without this nonsense." McGoohan, who was later to famously turn down the lead in *Dr. No*, urged that Drake be endowed with durable morals, priestly (but practical) views on the opposite sex, a distaste for firearms ("they're noisy and they hurt people," says Drake), and a respect for the sanctity of life. "He is not a thick-ear specialist, a puppet muscle man," the actor explained. "There will be action, plenty of it, but no brutal violence. If a man dies, it is not just another cherry off the tree." McGoohan saw to it that each instance of physical combat be blocked uniquely and with meaning; in *Danger Man*, acts of violence are as consequential as a first kiss.

The boundaries imposed by McGoohan required a shuffling of generic conventions. In lieu of weaponry, Drake is armed with all sorts of gadgetry, from an electric shaver that records conversations to a cigarette lighter that doubles as a camera (gimmicks to be exploited to the hilt in the Bond films). While numerous women—gorgeous, but fatal, down the line—appeal to him, he rejects their overtures with dutiful clearheadedness. He's all business; his manner as pointed as McGoohan's clipped diction. Self-effacing, unpredictable, cunning, Drake chooses each step with professional precision. When danger strikes, he responds fiercely yet fairly. "As Drake wends his knightly way around the world, seeking out villainy," observed Britain's *TV Times* on the series' debut, "his fists will be as virtuous as his cause." Drake, as reconstituted by the fervently Catholic actor who played him, arrived on the air an international detective of keen principle and discernible sangfroid: a chivalric and errant figure, closer in spirit to Chandler's Marlowe than to Fleming's Bond.

Denied the props of gun or girl, Drake cuts a lonely, vulnerable silhouette. Like the noir gumshoe, he operates autonomously, albeit on the grander stage of West versus East, where the outcome of each investigation has global ramifications. As a roving NATO-eye, he's given his cases by a variety of functionaries, intelligence officers, ambassadors and attachés, military brass, politicians—none of whom he knows much about or will ever meet again. Most of these "clients" treat Drake as little more than a hired gun. "Time to Kill," for example, opens in a Paris cafe with Drake being told that he's to execute an enemy agent. "Colonel, I'll take your assignment," he says, "but I won't do your dirty work for you. I'll bring him out alive if I possibly can." Even in these early half-hour installments, before the program expanded, assuming a darker, more complex quality, Drake can be seen exercising a moral righteousness at odds with the goals of his government employers.

Philip Marlowe could be speaking for all eyes and spies when, in *The Big Sleep*, he says, "You don't know what I have to go through or over or under to do your job for you." Drake's assignments are such that he's continually having to untangle the sordid dramas of others—the *Kammerspiele* of hidden guilt that threaten to spill out from behind closed doors to cause unpleasantness of an international variety. In "The Key," Drake, as frequently happens, is called upon to ferret out a traitor: the U.S. embassy in Vienna has a mole. Unless Drake can prove otherwise, the ambassador (Charles Carson) will be taking the rap. Drake homes in on the local CIA man, Logan (Robert Flemyng), who appears to live simply but happily with his much younger foreign-born wife, Maria (Monique Ahrens). Drake takes an immediate liking to Logan, whom he senses is not the "sort of man to sell his country," a sentiment dismissed by the ambassador: "Bah, that's the way they train them."

Distinguishing "Us" from "Them" requires Drake to read people—expressions, gestures, tics. Attuned to role-playing, he begins to suspect that Maria, whose soft features and open body language cast her wifely devotion in ambiguous terms, isn't who she seems. Soon enough, he confirms that Maria has been stealing documents

"To Our Best Friend" (*Danger Man*, 1965).

"Fish on a Hook" (*Danger Man*, 1964).

from Logan's safe and passing them on to her Russian lover-contact, Alex (Charles Gray). Logan, learning of this, and believing Maria's tearful explanation that she "had no choice," turns himself in as the traitor. "You're a good agent," Drake tells him, "and a very poor liar." To rectify Logan's romantic illusions, Drake takes him to the hotel where Maria has gone to meet Alex, and forces him to listen to the conspirators' conversation via a wiretap. "Did the old fellow swallow it?" Alex asks. "You should have heard me," Maria laughs. "What a tragedy. You would have cried." Moments later, as she's led away by the authorities, Maria turns pointedly away from her anguished husband. Over this chilling rejection, Drake intercedes on the soundtrack to voice an uncertainty about his trade that could well be the leitmotif of the series: "Other people's dirty work. Someone's got to do it. Someone's got to, I suppose."

John Drake moves at a bristling pace. Touching down someplace exotic—Lisbon one week, Hong Kong the next, all impeccably conveyed with second-unit background plates—he hits the ground running: there are chases, spectacular bouts of action, double- and triple-dealings, masquerades and charades. Crisis resolved, Drake beats a hasty exit via the nearest train, plane, or boat. In the U.S., CBS aired most of the half-hour *Danger Man*s in the summer of 1961, just as the Berlin Wall was going up; the entire series remained in worldwide syndication until 1964, when it was reactivated in an hour-long form. In this incarnation, Drake works mostly for M9, a make-believe wing of Her Majesty's Secret Service. Even then, his assignments seem to come down from someplace else. "To Our Best Friend" finds him in a row of phone booths receiving his orders from a stranger in a raincoat two doors down; in "Yesterday's Enemies" he's roused in the middle of the night when his television turns itself on and a talking head begins to outline the details of an impending assignment as though it were a BBC News report.

Danger Man's high-gloss production values (it was the most expensive British program of its day) do little to disguise an overriding tone of pessimism and bleakness, an impression fostered, visually, by its stark monochromatic photography. Brutal realism, in contrast to the fantastical air of contemporaneous fare like *The Man From U.N.C.L.E.* (1964–1968), *Get Smart* (1965–1970), or *Mission: Impossible* (1966–1973), is the pitch, which perhaps explains the alterations made to the series for its reintroduction to U.S. audiences as *Secret Agent*. Along with the re-titling, CBS scrapped the British version's enigmatic title sequence, with its interplay of positive-negative imagery, and replaced Edwin Astley's moody harpsichord theme with the surf rock–inspired "Secret Agent Man," sung by Johnny Rivers. Having never seen *Danger Man*, lyricists Steve Barri and P. F. Sloan looked to the 007 franchise for inspiration, yielding a song of dubious compatibility to the low-key work at hand. Yet one stanza stands out, for it curiously foreshadows the enumeration to be foisted upon Number Six in *The Prisoner*, McGoohan's follow-up to *Danger Man*: "They've given you a number / And taken away your name." The expendability of an agent, a salient theme of *Danger Man*, emerges as a central question of *The Prisoner*.

Anonymity—through stealth, deception, official non-existence—is a hallmark of the espionage genre. Conrad, in *The Secret Agent*, describes his Verloc as a "famous and trusty secret agent, so secret that he was never designated otherwise but by the symbol Δ in the late Baron Stott-Wartenheim's official, semi-official, and confidential correspondence." Similarly, the hero of Fritz Lang's *Spione* (1928), one of the first spy films, is known only as No. 326, as if to acknowledge the basis of the espionage trade as but an impersonal system of information management and control. Drake, though allowed to keep his name, is likewise treated as a line in a ledger—and an erasable one at that. While this threat of depersonalization (or deactivation) is a hard fact any noir spy must face—John le Carré explores it thoroughly in his Smiley novels—for Drake it serves only to bolster his fierce individualism. Instructed to retrieve a purloined roll of microfilm or to rescue a scientist with too many secrets in his head, he must balance his orders from on high against his own personal code.

Drake is often dispatched on the vaguest of directives, such as in "Fish on the Hook," when he's put on a plane to Cairo and given thirty-six hours to locate someone known only by a code name. Should he fail, Drake is told, M9's entire Middle Eastern network will collapse. The frontier into which he's thrust is a place of persistent tension and hostility. To successfully integrate himself, he must have at his disposal the skills, languages, and behaviorisms of countless nationalities and cultures—an array of personae. With each adventure, Drake plays a "type"—gun-runner, gambler, layabout, manservant, journalist, and so on. Outside his interactions with his handlers, he's rarely ever himself, nor is he allowed to be: "To everyone he meets he stays a stranger," as another line from "Secret Agent Man" goes. The confusion inherent in this game of existential hide-and-seek is deliriously explored in the oneiric "The Ubiquitous Mr. Lovegrove," in which Drake, racing to the airport, smashes up his car, falls unconscious, and awakens in an alternate reality. Drake's hallucination is that another John Drake has entered the scene and racked up a ghastly gambling debt, an indiscretion resulting in Lovegrove (Eric Barker), a pesky M9 numbers-cruncher, stalking him wherever he goes.

BELOW: Title sequence, *Secret Agent* (1965).

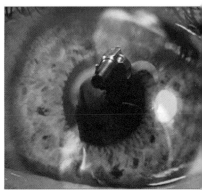

"Yesterday's Enemies" (1964).

"To Our Best Friend" (1965).

"The Man Who Wouldn't Talk" (1965).

"The Ubiquitous Mr. Lovegrove" pays curious homage to T. S. Eliot's "The Love Song of J. Alfred Prufrock" (1915), not only with its iconography of clocks and mirrors, and its fusing of the literal and the symbolic, but via a disorienting visual schema of forced perspective compositions and jagged jump cuts, which emulate the stream-of-consciousness style of Eliot's verse. Most of the story takes place in and around the private casino where Drake is said to have incurred his losses. Concurrent with his bizarre encounters with Lovegrove and other oddballs—a mysterious femme fatale (Adrienne Corri), a randy widow (Patsy Rowlands), a meddlesome doorman (Desmond Llewellyn)—Drake is put to the screws by the club's shifty manager, Alexander (Francis De Wolff). Having deduced that Drake isn't the travel agent he claims to be but rather a *traveling agent*, Alexander figures that Drake will pony up to retain his professional anonymity.

DRAKE: Are you sure you've got the right John Drake?
ALEXANDER: Which John Drake do you think you are?

In the face of this and other challenges to his identity (and sanity), Drake is left to rely upon his values—his integrity. Invariably, this sets him in opposition not only to his own controllers, but to the agents of the "other side." The game of spycraft in which he's engaged is one in which espionage and counter-espionage are on the same level: they exist merely to cancel each other out. The impact of inhabiting such a mire is a cumulative sense of cynicism married to the unsettling self-admission that his is a ridiculous and ultimately circular existence.

Drake traverses a world in which principles of fair play have been subverted by entities (on both sides) whose policies are nebulous, self-serving, or contradictory. Throughout the series, he's lied to by his handlers ("It's Up to the Lady"); his confidences betrayed ("The Outcast"); his investigations hampered ("Yesterday's Enemies"); his instructions clouded ("Judgement Day"). "To Our Best Friend" finds Drake racing to clear his good friend Bill Vincent (Donald Houston), the station chief in Baghdad, of turncoat accusations before M9 sends its assassin to deal with the matter. In "A Room in the Basement," Drake is forced to work off-book when a fellow operative (John Tremball), held hostage in a foreign embassy, is disavowed by the bureaucrats who sent him there. He's again on his own in "The Man Who Wouldn't Talk" when a colleague (Norman Rodway) turns murderously psychopathic after being imprisoned behind the Iron Curtain. A long, harrowing close-up of Drake coming to the realization that his fellow agent has no control over his urges speaks reams about how a life of "dirty work" can corrupt the spirit and disease the mind.

In "Whatever Happened to George Foster?" Drake learns that wealthy industrialist Lord Ammanford (Bernard Lee) has been covertly destabilizing a mineral-rich banana republic for his own greedy ends. Though told by his superiors to let it be ("politics and industry are inseparable," they say), Drake confronts Ammanford, who seconds the warning: "I can ruin you, Drake, physically, professionally, mentally, you name it. And there's nothing you can do in return to harm me. Absolutely nothing." Roused by such arrogance, Drake launches an unsanctioned inquiry into Ammanford's past. What he finds is that Ammanford is in fact one George Foster, former chauffeur, who some years earlier abandoned his wife, changed his name, and fled to Australia, where he married an heiress; jumping classes, he returned to England on the rungs of the ruling elite. His stature is now such that he can orchestrate, and simultaneously profit from, the violent overthrow of a struggling, exploitable nation. "International business," as Ambler points out in *The Mask of Dimitrios* (1939), "may conduct its operations with scraps of paper, but the ink it uses is human blood."

For a moral hero like Drake, such unconscionable pursuit of gain is cause for personal vendetta. Despite being threatened, bribed, beaten, and lied to in his search for the truth, he takes his dossier of findings, marches into Ammanford's home, and extorts the faux aristocrat into correcting his crimes. And the charlatanism he exposes is emblematic of the larger ideological paradoxes put under scrutiny in *Danger Man*. It's purely through chance that Drake, sent to report on a faraway civil war, stumbles upon Ammanford's scheme. The money trail behind the insurgency leads him back to London, to the innocuously named Society for Cultural Relations with South America, a philanthropic organization chaired by Ammanford. Such masking of malevolence behind a respectable facade, a mainstay of noir, is part and parcel of the circuitous and seemingly contradictory policy-making that steers Drake around the globe. Throughout the series, much is made of Britain's declining postcolonial power, as well as its history of manipulative imperialistic and capitalistic interferences.

In "Man on the Beach," Drake is in Jamaica, investigating yet another internal security breach, when he is himself accused of treason, a matter complicated when his sole ally in the region, Sir Allen Grose (David Hutcheson), is inexplicably killed. That Drake has knowingly allowed himself to be framed by the opposition means little to the functionaries prone to pointing fingers; like Jack Bauer of *24*, he's at the mercy of those with little comprehension of how the game is played on the ground. Drake's path to clearing himself and exposing the mole leads to the seaside home of Lady Kilrush (Juliet Harmer), Sir Allen's married lover, who refuses to believe that blood could be spilled in this idyllic corner of the Empire:

LADY KILRUSH: Here, why should anything happen here?

DRAKE: It's a virus. It can turn up anywhere.

LADY KILRUSH: You?

DRAKE: I'm part of the disease.

"The Man on the Beach" (1965).

When Drake finally untangles it all, he's disgusted to learn that his unseen adversary is but a little man, an assistant in the local controller's office. There are no Mabuse-like figures in *Danger Man*—no Blofelds or Goldfingers. Its villains act from avarice, coercion, folly; none embody the archetype of the outsized megalomaniac intent on remaking history. Leave it to the unseen tiers of leadership, the politicians and bankers, to embrace that dangerously narcissistic urge. Drake, meanwhile, deals with their ranks of impressionable minions. In the world of the series, the worst sins against Western democracy are committed by those within Drake's own organization—the imprint, no doubt, of the Cambridge Five, whose infiltration of the British intelligence service on behalf of the Soviet Union was just coming to light in the early 1960s.

Title Sequence, *The Prisoner* (1968).

As *Danger Man* progresses, Drake is steadily pressed with ennui. He feels the Empire crumbling around him; he has no one to trust and nothing concrete to believe in, yet he strives mightily to retain his scruples. The sense that he's staked his life, and the lives of others, on a geopolitical chess match of futile aim builds until, finally, in *The Prisoner*, Drake—or rather his avatar, the anonymous Number Six—calls it quits. It's well known that McGoohan went to his grave insisting that *The Prisoner* was not a sequel to *Danger Man*. While this may be the "official" case, there's no denying the link between Drake's disillusionment and petulance and Number Six's defiance and anti-authoritarianism. Both series toy with orthodoxies. While each trades in the conventions of the spy genre, neither does so without a countervailing irony or deflation. Because Drake is a "man of danger," we expect him to have adventures and get results; what is not anticipated is the unsettling frequency with which his efforts are undermined, hampered, or neutralized. Number Six, while perhaps not Drake, is most certainly a Drake-like figure who has simply had enough of the lies spun by the incorrigibly corrupt forces that pull the strings of government and enterprise.

Each *Prisoner* begins with a replay of its basic premise: maneuvering through London traffic, a nameless government operative makes his way to headquarters and indignantly resigns his post. Returning home, he's rendered unconscious by a yellow smoke plumed through the keyhole. He awakens, disoriented but still apparently in his own living room, lifts his blinds, and gazes through the window. What he's confronted with, rather than the expected cityscape of dreary London, is a picture-perfect vista of the Village. A cutaway reveals that he is himself being viewed, via closed-circuit television, by a cabal of dour, officious men. At once, we're made to realize that *The Prisoner* is about perception and viewing—looking at things, looking through things, and being looked at; in short, the art of spying. A surveilling eye is a constant presence in the Village. There are cameras everywhere, hidden in walls, clocks, radios,

SCENES FROM: "Arrival" (1968).

strung up in lampposts, embedded in the marble statuary that dots the grounds. The loss of privacy is complemented by a dissolution of identity. In the Village, everyone's been stripped of a name and given a number.

The Prisoner is Number Six, an appellation he rebels against almost immediately. Hoping to make sense of his confinement, he learns only that his captors want information—the reason for his resignation. The ceaseless interrogations that he's subjected to are overseen by a succession of Number Twos (the job turns over rather quickly), who, in turn, are answerable to a higher power, the unseen Number One. Such lack of clear leadership and the attendant absence of accountability echoes the infuriating chain of command that Drake faces in *Danger Man*. Number Six, his destiny apparently controlled by the interchangeable Number Twos, is trapped in an abstract nightmare resistant to any known formula:

> NUMBER SIX: I am not a number. I am a free man!
> NUMBER TWO: It's six of one, half a dozen of the other.

Number Six remains steadfast in his refusal to answer the one question ("Why did you resign?") that the Number Twos pose over and over. He will not bow down to authority. Endless attempts are made to break him: he's bribed, tricked, drugged, and prodded. As his ordeal escalates, he becomes stronger rather than weaker, defiant rather than submissive. *The Prisoner* brings the duel of spy versus counterspy to its metaphysical termination.

In the series treatment, devised with George Markstein and David Tomblin, McGoohan writes: "Our hero is a man who held a highly confidential job of the most secret nature. He therefore has knowledge which is invaluable or highly dangerous depending on which side of the fence he falls." The affiliation of Number Six's tormentors is left deliberately vague—red herrings abound. Easy answers, never a part of the noir world, aren't to be found. Number Six is left to wonder, as are we, is it Us or Them? In "Colony Three," an early *Danger Man* segment, Drake is sent to infiltrate a place much like the Village, a top-secret spy camp designed by the opposition to resemble a rural British hamlet; later, in "To Our Best Friend," he deduces that the wife of his friend Bill Vincent is a sleeper-agent who received her training in a "complete replica of an English

On the set of "Free for All" (1968) with Patrick McGoohan.

town." The notion of an idyllic setting harboring something sinister fascinated McGoohan. It was his idea to film *The Prisoner* in Portmeirion, Wales, an actual holiday destination, the idiosyncratic architecture of which doubled for many of the Continental locales in *Danger Man*.

For all its whimsicality, the Village is a place of suffocation and menace, wedged between mountain and sea, and policed by a giant white balloon, Rover, which asphyxiates anyone who gets out of line. When Number Six objects to the conditions of his policed existence, Number Two responds by painting it in utopian terms: "What in fact has been created? An international community. A perfect blueprint for world order. When the sides facing each other suddenly realize they're looking into a mirror, they'll see that this is the pattern for the future." The matter of which side of the looking glass he is trapped behind is of little consequence to Number Six. He thinks only of escaping with his ideals and integrity intact. "I will not make any deals with you," he declares in the series' most famous soliloquy. "I will not be pushed, filed, stamped, indexed, briefed, debriefed, or numbered. My life is my own."

In "Chimes of Big Ben," Number Six manages to escape to London, where he's put through a debriefing by his former superiors. Disinterested in hearing about the Village, they want only to know why their agent resigned in the first place. Already wary, Number Six has his suspicions confirmed when he hears the titular clock strike an incorrect number of times. Frantic, he rips apart the office until it's revealed to be a stage set: he remains trapped in the Village. The frustrating cycle is repeated in "Many Happy Returns" when Number Six emerges from a troubled sleep to find the Village eerily deserted. He builds a raft, loads up on provisions, and sets sail. Weeks later, arriving at his London flat, he's greeted by Mrs. Butterworth (Georgina Cookson), the present occupant, who returns the keys to the Lotus 7 that was once his. Number Six drives his old sports car to his old office and, once more, tells his old superiors about the Village. This time around, they seem to take his word for it, and arrange for him to retrace the route of his escape via helicopter. On approach, a switch is flipped, and Number Six is plummeted back to where he began. Awaiting him at his cottage is Mrs. Butterworth, the new Number Two. It's all an empty spectacle—a recurring noir nightmare posed as a dream of freedom.

The Prisoner revels in its spiraling, dreamlike logic, as in "Schizoid Man," when Number Six awakens to find that key aspects of his already vexing existence have been reversed. Formerly clean-shaven, he now wears a full mustache; his blond hair has turned black. Where he was once right-handed, he's now confoundingly left-handed. And when he slips on his jacket (patterned opposite to what it once was), he sees that it bears the badge of Number Twelve. Outside, the villagers address him as Number Twelve, as does Number Two, who then enlists him in a plot to convince "Number Six" that he's not who he thinks he is. Number Six (Twelve) is made to engage his doppelgänger in a variety of physical and mental duels meant to confuse both men about their identities. Through force of will Number Six gains the upper hand, at which point Number Two sends Rover to intervene. The balloon, however, kills the wrong Number; to prevail, Number Six has to impersonate his impersonator. It's an ending quite similar to that of "The Ubiquitous Mr. Lovegrove," in which Drake gains release from his nightmare state by destroying the mirror in which his "other" is reflected.

Almost everything in *The Prisoner* is turned upside down and inside out: doubling, masquerade, performance, and role reversal are its preoccupations. "Once Upon a Time," the penultimate episode, places Number Six in a room with Number Two (played in this installment by Leo Kern), for a frightful contest of psychological stamina known as Degree Absolute. Number Six triumphs, leaving behind a fallen Number Two. In the finale, "Fall Out," our hero is unmasked as the omniscient Number One—perhaps the most contentious "reveal" in television history. Is this, then, the final destination of the disgruntled and burned-out secret agent: the role of puppet-master and grand oppressor? McGoohan, who never intended *The Prisoner* to be consumed from a literal perspective, said only that he "wanted to have controversy, arguments, fights, discussion, and anger; waving of fists in my face saying, How dare you!'" "Fall Out" concludes in typically ambivalent and circular fashion: Number Six, having (we think) escaped the Village, is seen steering a smart-looking car through the infinity loop of a London traffic circle. One half expects McGoohan's Irish-American lilt to break over the soundtrack and begin the adventure anew.

"Fall Out" (1968).

THE FUGITIVE
ABC 1963–1967

I am escaped with the skin of my teeth.
—Book of Job

I N *THE FUGITIVE*, THE TRIALS OF JOB ARE PUT TO THE SERVICE OF AN ENDURING noir archetype: the man on the run. Our fugitive is Richard Kimble, a doctor sentenced to die for murdering his wife. That Kimble (David Janssen) is innocent is of little consequence to the system that has condemned him. Indeed, it has sent one of its fiercest agents, a police lieutenant named Philip Gerard (Barry Morse), to make sure he meets his appointment with the executioner. And this is how Kimble is introduced: shackled to a scowling lawman and staring glumly out a train window. "Richard Kimble ponders his fate as he looks at the world for the last time and sees only darkness," the Narrator, voiced without sentiment by William Conrad, intones. "But in that darkness, fate moves its huge hand." With an ungodly screech, the train derails, and the future, for Kimble, is again turned inside out. Amid the chaos, he manages a miraculous escape; falsified identification papers and a bottle of hair dye become his tokens through the noir world.

Publicity still for *The Fugitive* with David Janssen as Richard Kimble.

Though Kimble has skirted death, his fate remains questionable. Without sanctuary, he roams the country, rootless and haunted. Like Job, who "shall return no more to his house, neither shall his place know him any more," Kimble is a tragic yet resilient figure, his stamina for loneliness and stigmatization repeatedly tested as he is run through the mill by a force beyond his control. As created by Roy Huggins and overseen by producer Quinn Martin, *The Fugitive* operates as an anthologized collection of morality plays: with each installment, Kimble is deposited in a new locale, where he's forced to exercise his integrity and fortitude to resolve a crisis. But the overriding conceit is that of the noir thriller.

When not evading the law, Kimble is driven by a need for vindication: on the night of his wife's murder, he witnessed a one-armed man fleeing his house. If he can find this elusive figure, he can free himself from his predicament.

To finance his travels, Kimble takes on all sorts of no-questions-asked jobs: custodian, lifeguard, dishwasher, chauffeur, delivery man, fish hatchery worker, merry-go-round operator, sail mender, bartender, lettuce picker, veterinary assistant, and so forth. Kimble's ever-evolving identity, his various aliases and made-up backstories, ensure his survival. Were he to reveal himself, he'd be back on the train to death row. Even the simplest of interactions bears the threat of danger. And the people he meets as he hops from town to town are, by and large, an anxious, conflicted, trouble-brewing bunch, like Lucey Russell (Lois Nettleton), the stranded motorist he stops to aid in "Man on a String." Because Lucey is shortly to be accused of murdering her married lover, Kimble finds himself handed a walk-on role in a bit of local theater he'd do best to avoid. Incidents like these, as the episode's title suggests, situate our fugitive as an unwitting puppet in a never-ending parade of human dysfunction. He's always having to work through someone else's conflicts or extricate himself from them, all the while keeping himself off the radar before someone with a badge finds out who he really is.

Publicity still of Roy Huggins (ca. 1963).

The relationships Kimble forms are fleeting, and nearly always doomed. A lasting romance is out of the question. In "Fear in a Desert City," while tending bar in a lounge in Phoenix, he takes a quiet liking to the resident pianist, Monica Welles (Vera Miles). When he goes out to the parking lot one night, and sees Monica's ex-husband (Brian Keith) slapping her around, he chivalrously intervenes. Soon enough, a pair of menacing cops, friends of the brute, show up at Kimble's boarding house, tell him to pack up his hair dye and his one suit, and shove him on the next bus. Kimble's perennial alienation from society emerges as the signifier of his integrity—his heroism. A pediatrician in his old life, he can't help but exercise an innate need to help others. Like Jean Valjean in *Les Miserables* (1862), he becomes a force of good in a world that remains hostile to his presence. And, like Hugo's fugitive, he has a Javert determined to return him to the gallows.

Gerard, though he only appears in about one-third of the episodes, casts a long shadow. He's the embodiment of the dark currents that continue to shape Kimble's existence. The most fascinating aspect of Morse's portrayal (aside from his unusually expressive eyebrows) is that he manages to turn this methodical bureaucrat into a transcendent presence. His ability to anticipate Kimble's every move is uncanny. "Gerard has a way of sensing things," Kimble concedes in "The End Is But the Beginning." "He's brilliant. He knows me. Maybe better than I know myself." Yet the way in which Gerard figures in Kimble's narrative represents an inversion of heroic values. Prior to *The Fugitive*, the police, the

Publicity still for *The Fugitive* (1964).

Fridays and the Ballingers, were lunchbox heroes, figures of authority whose upholding of the law reflected the solid foundation of American justice. *The Fugitive*, in making its protagonist the victim of judicial miscarriage, turns the tidy moral code of black-and-white television on its head. Kimble, the supposed malefactor, is the hero, while Gerard, the instrument of the law, is the villain.

In his obsessive drive to capture the fugitive, Gerard acts from an unquestioning sense of duty. He remains acutely, if not proudly, indifferent to Kimble's plight. "The law says he killed his wife," he asserts. "I uphold the law." For Gerard, there's no possibility of ambiguity, no alternative outcome, and certainly no acceptance of the accused's improbable defense that a man missing a limb bludgeoned Helen Kimble to death. The good doctor, on the other hand, functions very much in a gray zone, physically and spiritually. There are no absolutes in his world. He's an anonymous and transient figure—a thumb stuck out from the side of a road. His only constant is the necessity of avoiding his pursuer, who looms like a specter. Here we have the essence of *The Fugitive*: the struggle to live while death, clad in a macintosh and a fedora, nips at one's heels. "There is," says the Narrator, "no peace for Richard Kimble."

Despite having no recourse to the law, or even the protection of society, Kimble remains a virtuous and moral individual. This is especially true in those instances where revealing himself to be a doctor, someone adept at emergency medicine, means betraying whatever outward identity he's assumed. In "Nightmare at Northoak," he valiantly rescues a group of schoolchildren from a burning bus, an action that directly leads to his capture by Gerard after his picture is placed in the newspaper. Kimble's selflessness is such that he's willing to risk his vindication, if not his life, to help others—even Gerard, whom he rescues from certain death on more than one occasion. Given the opposite points Kimble faces (life/death, safety/peril, self-interest/compassion), it's no coincidence that crossroads, train yards, bus depots, and highway exchanges are part of the stock geography summoned up in *The Fugitive*. Kimble is forever at an intersection.

The suspended state in which he exists is shaped by repeated incidents of blind chance. There is, for starters, his fleeting encounter with Fred Johnson (Bill Raisch), the one-armed man, who runs directly in the path of his automobile after killing Mrs. Kimble. Had Kimble arrived home a few seconds later or earlier, he'd have no alternate theory—a good thing, perhaps. As it happens, he shows up in time to nearly run the murderer over, a coincidence that proves to be a real curse when no one believes what he says he saw. In the chronology of the series, Kimble's intersection with the one-armed man—framed through the windshield, face half obscured by shadow—marks the point where, in a flash, everything changes. Life for him is never the same. The system, however, proceeds as it always does. Kimble's ensuing trial (shown in flashback) follows a logical pattern whereby the case is processed, analyzed, and judged according to a consensus of objective reason (a jury of twelve) while his subjectively based defense (the evidence of one) is rejected. The system isn't designed for contingencies of the absurd. Kimble may as well have seen a gnome in a polka-dotted jumpsuit dancing on his hood.

The logic that leads to Kimble being sentenced to death is then righted by an act of illogic: the train derailment that enables him to escape Gerard's custody. While seemingly free, he continues to be detoured by the random, the calamitous, and the bizarre with unholy frequency, an arrangement underscored by the seemingly haphazard arrangement of the series, which leaps forward and backward in time with each installment, as if reveling in the unpredictable flux of the noir world. In "The Girl from Little Egypt," Kimble is strolling along the edge of an empty highway in the middle of the night when, from nowhere, a car barrels into him. He awakens in a hospital. Once his domain, it's now a site of entrapment: hospitals mean officials and officials mean police. Even when the presence of the law is subdued, there's the pesky threat of the would-be detective, the vigilant citizen whose suspicions are easily aroused. Kimble is eternally at the mercy of those who, through logical deduction, conclude that his is the face staring back from the "wanted" posters Gerard has plastered all over the country.

Because Kimble consistently finds himself embroiled in the petty dramas of others, he's also ripe for persecution by those who view him as an interloper. Add to that his enigmatic nature, his necessary aloofness, and he's frequently made to serve as the unwitting blank slate upon which another's frustrations are projected, as happens in "The Girl from Little Egypt." Ruth Norton (Pamela Tiffin), the girl who runs him over, couldn't see him through her tears: she'd just learned that her boyfriend, Paul Clements (Ed Nelson), is another woman's husband. Even after she breaks things off, Paul continues to nose around her business. Kimble, through no fault of his own (aside from traveling by thumb), is once more enmeshed in a sordid affair that will only make his life more nervous. When Paul learns that Ruth has taken the injured Kimble in, he becomes jealous, enlisting a cop friend to find out who this "George Browning" really is. From there, it's only a matter of time before the connection is made—cue a hasty scram to the nearest means of long-haul transportation.

ABOVE: "The Girl from Little Egypt" (1963).

The unforeseen—that huge, sweeping hand of fate—is a given in the noir universe. A lawyer nonchalantly notarizes a bill of sale and gets poisoned for it in *D.O.A.* (1950). A musician who resembles an at-large criminal is arrested and his life ruined in *The Wrong Man* (1954). A hitchhiker accepts a ride from a stranger who dies behind the wheel and learns that "fate, or some mysterious force, can put the finger on you or me for no good reason at all" in *Detour* (1945). The classic cycle is littered with men inexplicably targeted for death, doom, or detention. These are the humbled and defeated souls of noir, trapped between individual will and the machinations of an indifferent universe. Of the hardboiled noir writers, David Goodis was perhaps the most adept at delineating, in spare, haunting prose, the cruel nightscape in which the man on the run finds himself, as in this passage from *Nightfall* (1947):

> The policeman shrugged. All the policemen shrugged. The woods shrugged and the sky shrugged. None of them especially cared. It meant nothing to them. It meant nothing to the universe with the exception of this one tiny, moving, breathing thing called Vanning, and what it meant to him was fear and fleeing. And hiding. And fleeing again. And more hiding.

The Goodis character most aligned with Kimble is Vincent Parry of *Dark Passage* (1946). A convicted wife killer like Kimble, Parry escapes custody and sets out to exonerate himself. In the 1947 film of *Dark Passage*, Parry, played by Humphrey Bogart, undergoes plastic surgery in an effort to evade the authorities. Bogart-Parry's change in appearance is dealt with by a first-person camera deployed up to the point when his bandages are removed. Even then, his perspective remains the dominant one, as he's in every scene of the picture. His paranoiac adventure is established as a singular experience, the result being that we crave another reality against which to check the claustrophobic one thrust upon us. In *The Fugitive*, Kimble's subjective stance is set in tense contrast to a traditional third-person narrative—as anchored by the objective Narrator—through which we're made aware of realities other than Kimble's. Scenes in which Kimble is not alone in the frame, or not in the frame at all, nevertheless lend credence to his hunted state by presenting actions and dialogue that endorse his harrowing plight. Far from contradicting his anxiousness, the parallel strains and subplots of the series' anthology-thriller narrative legitimatize it.

Perception and identity are closely tied to the existential conflict at the heart of noir. J.P. Telotte, in *Voices in the Dark: The Narrative Patterns of Film Noir* writes, "Through our seeing, in the movies no less than in our daily lives, we gauge our separation from the world and from those around us who, in contrast, seem to possess a secure and easy sense of identity or to inhabit a comfortable place of their own." The act of looking is given great emphasis in *The Fugitive* through repeated close-ups of Kimble anxiously assessing his surroundings. Because of the ubiquitous flyers and newspaper articles bearing his mugshot, he's acutely self-conscious of how his face may be perceived and judged. As if imploring others to pay him no heed, he makes himself smaller, inconsequential. Janssen's body language—his stooped pose, his reticent manner—reflects the persona of someone content with being unnoticed. The series' signature image of Kimble glancing furtively over his shoulder, ill at ease with himself and the world at large, evokes a distinctly modern alienation.

As in Goodis's fiction, there is throughout *The Fugitive* a profound sense of melancholia and longing. Kimble is estranged not only from society, due to the circumstances of his criminal conviction, but from himself, by virtue of the various identities he must assume if he's to remain alive long enough to clear his name. "The tragic sufferer is more alone than anyone," the theologian and literary critic Ralph Harper tells us in *The Path of Darkness* (1968). "Fate has isolated him, made him an existential solitary, outside the bounds of the ideal and the probable." The fear of revealing his true self, of betraying his anxious gaze, envelops Kimble in a fog of exhausting distress: no matter where or how far he journeys, the more alone he becomes. "A man cannot run forever," the Narrator says in "Never Wave Goodbye." Or, from "Fear in a Desert City," a fuller assessment:

> Now six months a fugitive, this is Richard Kimble with a new identity and, for as long as it is safe, a new name: James Lincoln. He thinks of the day when he might find the man with one arm, but now is now. And this is how it is with him. Another journey, another place. Walk neither too fast nor too slow. Beware the eyes of strangers. Keep moving.

BELOW: "Nightmare at Northoak" (1963).

With each of these pronouncements, we're left to wonder whether there will come a day when the doctor's nerves will finally give out. "I can't run anymore," he says in "The End Is But the Beginning." "I can't even stand up." In "Landscape with Running Figures," he's so fatigued he signs the wrong name (his real one) in the registry of a motel: cue the ringing phone in Gerard's office.

"Nightmare at Northoak," the episode in which Kimble is jailed after performing a heroic deed, begins oneirically, with a deep-staged image of Kimble on a deserted urban block, suitcase in hand, casting a shadow toward the camera. There's no music, just the persistent clip-clap of footsteps—not his. At first, he sees no one, but then, from the mist, the silhouette of Gerard emerges. Kimble ducks down a dark alley and presses himself into the shadows. The footsteps grow nearer. A succession of canted angles brings Kimble through a maze of passageways until he hits a dead end. He begins to claw at an impossibly high wall—a hopeless trap. "Finally, Kimble, finally," Gerard says, drawing his gun. Close-ups of eyes are cross-cut—one set murderous, lighted from below; the other wild with fear. Gerard squeezes the trigger. A loud crack thrusts Kimble into his equally frightful waking nightmare. He's spent the night in a roadside ditch; the sound that's jostled him awake is the sound of a school bus popping its axle and bursting into flame.

Promotional artwork for
The Fugitive (Iran, 1963).

Later, after Kimble has saved the burning children, and landed himself in jail, the chase dream is repeated. This time, he awakens to find Gerard staring him in the face:

GERARD: How you must hate me.

KIMBLE: It's all very easy for you, Gerard, black and white.

GERARD: Yes, it has to be, which gives you the advantage. Any disguise you choose—hero to a whole town.

KIMBLE: Saving kids from a burning bus? That's a disguise? You know, for all the thinking I've done about you, I don't know how your mind works at all. But maybe I do. I'm a fugitive, so nothing I do is decent.

GERARD: All this time, all those places, haven't you been living a lie?

KIMBLE: I had no choice, didn't I? Gerard, when they take me down to that holding cell, and give me my last meal, walk me to the door and strap me in that chair, my words are going to be exactly the same: I didn't kill her.

GERARD: No, of course you didn't. Tucson, Dallas, Los Angeles, Seattle, Atlanta, Miami, Northoak. All those rooms. All those days and nights alone, remembering and imagining, until the difference between reality and fantasy is not quite so clear anymore.

Gerard, until very nearly the end, insists that Kimble has imagined the one-armed man as a way of assuaging his own guilt. Were Kimble not already positioned as the hero, someone above reproach, Gerard's theory of projection would seem to have some credence. Indeed, on those handful of occasions when Kimble does manage to catch up with the one-armed man—glimpsed in the window of a moving bus in "Chase in the Windy City"; obscured by a respirator in "Wife Killer"—his ability to make a conclusive identification is thwarted, as if to suggest that he sees what he needs to see to keep his faith alive.

Given his nightmares of enclosure, it's little wonder that Kimble seeks out the wide-open spaces of the frontier. Huggins, in patterning *The Fugitive* after his earlier "wandering hero" series, *Cheyenne* (1955–1963), saw Kimble as a man of the plains: "I wanted to have a hero who behaved like a Western hero—who was totally free, had no permanent residence or commitments, no responsibilities." The American Dream, the sustaining model for upward mobility in the postwar years, is tossed aside, replaced with what Huggins, in his proposal, described as "a preoccupation with guilt and salvation which has been called the American Theme." Kimble has seen his prosperous haute-bourgeois life, his suburban home and place in the community, sullied by an ugly tabloid crime. Now a fugitive, he's both an outlaw and a hobo of the highways: "One foot on the ground, the other on the first bus out of town," the Narrator tells us. "The tags in his clothes come from stores all over the country," someone remarks after rifling through Kimble's belongings. Affluence and stability have given way to evasiveness and itinerancy. Kimble's familiarity with the country-club world of his old life gets him in trouble more than once, such as in "Where the Action Is," when the owner of a chi-chi resort (Telly Savalas) suspects something to be a little off with his new towel boy, Kimble.

Nearly every episode begins with the Narrator delineating the double life of our hero. "For every acquaintance he makes, a man reveals a different face, a different identity," we're told in "Stranger in the Mirror." "To the people of this Midwestern city, this man is John Evans, itinerant laborer. To those who know him better, he is Dr. Richard Kimble, convicted murderer." In the story that follows, Kimble's narrative precondition is placed in ironic counterpart to the secret life being led by his outwardly affable but inwardly sociopathic employer and host, Tony Burrell (William Shatner), a former cop. Burrell, along with his wife, Carole (Julie Sommars), runs a day camp for boys where Kimble has signed on as a handyman. Kimble's arrival coincides with a rash of gruesome murders that has the community abuzz: policemen found with their heads smashed in, their badges ripped off. Frustrated that he isn't in on the investigation, Burrell regales Carole and Kimble with his theories on the crimes.

Kimble, attuned to the signs of a fractured personality, begins to wonder whether Burrell, whom he's spied sneaking off in the middle of the night, might be the killer. When another murder occurs, Kimble's immediate impulse is flight: he's already a target of inquiry by the local sheriff. But when Carole discovers the missing badges of the slain cops arranged like trophies in her husband's humidor, she appeals to Kimble for help. Reluctantly, Kimble obliges. Confronted with the evidence, Burrell launches into a defensive rant. Kimble, the stranger, is the fiend, he insists. Cycling through the foggy layers of his sins, through the delusions and rationalizations that have led to his steering of the truth into a more acceptable reality, Burrell finally acknowledges the unthinkable. "I fell asleep and I don't remember," he wails. "Does that make me a murderer, a madman who goes around killing?" Burrell's dawning realization of the horrific acts he's committed showcases a state of paranoia turned inward.

Kimble suffers from this as well, and there are numerous times when he questions his own declaration of innocence and wonders whether he might be, as society has dictated (and as Gerard continually reminds him), guilty after all. Intermittent flashbacks sketch out his troubled marriage—the alcoholic tantrums of Helen Kimble (Diane Brewster), the miscarriage that left her infertile, the arguments into the night about whether to adopt a child. It's even intimated that a divorce was on the table when Helen was killed. The result is that Kimble shoulders guilt for her death beyond the guilt ascribed to him by the courts. "But you're innocent," he's assured in "The End Is But the Begin-

Publicity still for *The Fugitive*.

ning," after explaining his story to a sympathetic listener. "Am I really?" Kimble wonders. "I left my wife alone. Some man came along and killed her." Kimble assumes not only the surface aspects of guilt, the furtiveness and restlessness, but the inner turmoil, the angst and shame, as well.

The elusive nature of all certainty, even of one's own actions, bores to the existential crisis that drives so many of noir's troubled, dislocated males. This is illustrated most vividly in "Escape Into Black" when Kimble is stricken with amnesia after barely surviving a gas explosion in a diner. Regaining consciousness in a hospital, he's unable to produce his real name, let alone any of his countless aliases, a state he likens to "being at the bottom of a well." Dr. Towne (Ivan Dixon), the attending psychiatrist, proposes to help Kimble recover his memory by injecting him with sodium pentathol and then asking him a series of leading questions. It's in scenarios like this that the signature Quinn Martin formula, with its demarcated act structure, its periodic intrusions of stentorian narration, its always-reliable movement from conflict to suspense to resolution, takes on an additional layer of inexorability. The closer Kimble gets to remembering his past, the closer he gets to climbing back on death row.

Where in most episodes Kimble is the one who facilitates the solving of the problem of the hour, here it's Towne who takes on that role. "I think your mind is hiding something from you," he prompts. "I think you don't want to remember who you are. You don't want to be that person any longer." Incrementally, the elements of Kimble's former life coalesce until he recalls that he was married once, but is now a widower. "Maybe you were glad she died," Towne offers. "Maybe that's the guilt you carry around on your back." Kimble, in his nebulous state, is ultimately left with the conclusion that he did kill his wife, and boards a train to turn himself in to Gerard. "Well, you see, I've had this accident, and my mind, my mind isn't really working that properly," he mumbles over the phone to the startled lawman in arranging the appointment. Only at the last minute, after a probing consideration of his reflected image in the window of the train triggers his memory of the night fate waved its giant hand, does Kimble regain his composure and leap to safety, niftily repeating his initial hair's-breadth escape from Gerard.

Through four seasons, the success of *The Fugitive* hinged on its ingeniously elastic premise. It was, until its very end, one long, unresolved chase. When it came time to wind down the series, Quinn Martin insisted it be given a definitive conclusion, an unheard-of notion at the time, but one which, in retrospect, situates *The Fugitive* on the vanguard of the novelistic form favored by today's serialized dramas. Aired in two parts, "The Judgment" sums up Kimble's ordeal in the cruelest of ways by revealing that there was, all along, a witness to the death of Helen Kimble. Through flashback, the fateful night of the murder is revisited in crazily tilted frames: Kimble storming away after a row; Helen drunkenly phoning a neighbor, Lloyd Chandler (J.D. Cannon), who arrives to find her in the bedroom; the strange noise that draws Helen downstairs; the one-armed man, Fred Johnson, surprised in the act of robbery, defensively reaching for a blunt object; and, most unsettling of all, the sight of Chandler, paralyzed on the stairs, looking on as Helen is killed and doing nothing about it.

The revelation of Chandler's passivity is made all the more sour when it comes to light that he's a decorated war hero. (Even the one-armed killer, right before fleeing the scene, throws him a withering glance of disgust.) Years on, sulking around his den, surrounded by his collection of firearms, Chandler continues to feel shame over his cowardly inaction. From this point, "The Judgment" pulls strands from the crime melodrama playbook to tie up all loose ends. The trope of the traumatized veteran merges with the blackmail scheme of the lowlife who senses a big payoff: Johnson, threatening to expose Chandler, demands that he cough up an unreasonable sum. Gerard, having finally come to acknowledge Kimble's phantom as a person of interest, twists this information into a trap: Kimble, thinking he's finally caught up with his quarry, practically runs into the lieutenant's arms. That all four men are in interconnected states of stasis (and at each other's throats) is convenient to the chess-like climax.

The unresolved past is brought forcefully into the present in that most iconic of noir settings, an abandoned amusement park. Rather than pay off Johnson, Chandler tries to kill him, and fails. Gerard and Kimble, arriving just as Johnson makes a gun-blazing exit, join the fray. Wounded, Gerard passes his revolver to Kimble, who pursues Johnson to the top of the park's observation

On the set of "The Judgment" (1967). "The day the running stopped."

ABOVE: Janssen awaits his call to shoot his climactic confrontation with the one-armed man (BELOW).

tower. Just as Kimble manages to induce a confession, Gerard, crawling over to Chandler's discarded rifle, snipes Johnson. The look on Kimble's face as he watches his wife's killer tumble to his death is startling in its ambivalence: Kimble has yet to learn Chandler's secret, and Gerard has just killed his alibi. It will be up to Chandler, who's held the key to this nightmare all along, to come forward and testify to what he witnessed. *The Fugitive* ends outside the same courthouse where Kimble was sentenced to die a lifetime ago. Fully exonerated, he walks away with a new love interest (Diane Baker) on his arm—only to pause in his tracks, flight response activated, as a police car passes down the street. But where else could he run?

UNIVERSAL NOIR '64

A S PRESIDENT OF MCA, LEW WASSERMAN HAD A KNACK FOR FINDING
diamonds where others saw coal. His acquisition, in 1958, of Universal-
International's fabled backlot, followed by a reverse-leasing deal through
which MCA effectively swallowed the studio itself for free, remains a master-
stroke of corporate maneuvering, as does his purchase of Paramount's pre-1948
library, which sold handsomely to content-starved broadcasters at a time when
movies were presumed to have little afterlife. Around town, MCA was known
as "The Octopus," and it entered the 1960s as the dominant force in entertainment. When Robert Kennedy, the attorney general, cried monopoly, Wasserman
simply sliced off MCA's talent agency arm and merged Revue Studios, the telefilm factory he'd presciently started in 1950, with Universal's operations. By
1963, MCA-Universal was the leading supplier of programming to the three networks, and it was around this time that Wasserman and his lieutenant, Jennings
Lang, came up with a new product line: "Project 120," a series of original,
feature-length films made for television. Of the three projects initially put into
production, two were remakes of venerable films noirs, *The Killers* (1946) and
Ride the Pink Horse (1947); the third was an adaptation of *The Widow-Makers*
(1946), an unpublished novel by screenwriter Michael Blankfort. Each "Project
120" telefeature was accorded a budget of just under one million dollars, a figure
generous by television standards, but well within "B" picture status by Hollywood's.

The Killers (1964).

To produce and direct *The Killers*, Wasserman
hired Don Siegel, a veteran of pictures like *Crime in the
Streets* (1956) and *The Lineup* (1958). Siegel had been
slated to helm Universal's 1946 treatment of the
property before studio politics intervened; the job went
to Robert Siodmak instead. The inspiration for both
versions is Ernest Hemingway's "The Killers," first published in *Scribner's Magazine* in 1927, a time when true-
life accounts of gangsterism dominated urban headlines.
In Hemingway's story, two men named Max and Al enter
Henry's Lunch-Room early one evening. After tying up
Sam, the cook, and Nick Adams, a neighborhood boy,
and threatening George, the counterman, they announce

their intention: "We're going to kill a Swede." Their target is ex-prizefighter Ole Andreson, a/k/a the Swede, whom they expect will soon be taking his supper; he fails to appear, and the gangsters leave. Nick runs down to Ole's rooming house. Ole refuses to look at Nick or, despite what Nick tells him, to move: "There isn't anything I can do about it," he mumbles from the shadows. Returning to the diner, Nick tells George, "I can't stand to think about him waiting in the room and knowing he's going to get it. It's too damned awful." But all George can offer is the useless advice that Nick "better not think about it."

Written with a terseness that builds with foreboding unease, "The Killers" presaged many of the thematic concerns that would come to be associated with the gangster cycle of the 1930s and film noir of the 1940s. Through a careful yet contradictory assemblage of details—there's great confusion about menus, clocks, signs, and names—Hemingway summons forth a world of obfuscation and instability. Al and Max give no reason as to why they must kill the Swede: it simply must be done. While violent and threatening, they look like "a vaudeville team" in their matching derbies and tight overcoats, and bide their time waiting for the Swede with a constant patter of insults, sarcasm, and bad jokes. Their speech patterns, calculated posturing, and deliberate mannerisms escalate the tension while giving body to the now-familiar prototype of the performative, self-aware heavy. Nick, who we're told "had never had a towel in his mouth before," is left traumatized by these two, but he's even more disturbed by his interlude with Ole, whose passivity in the face of death defies all human instinct.

Refusing to believe that any situation could be so hopeless, Nick urges Ole to "go to the police" or "get out of town" or "fix it up some way," to which Ole replies, "No. I got in wrong." This vague admission of a prior indiscretion—elaborated upon by George's speculative comment, "He must have got mixed up in something in Chicago"—becomes the seedling of both Siodmak's and Siegel's adaptations of "The Killers." Picking up where Hemingway left off, Siodmak and his screenwriters (Anthony Veiller and John Huston) begin with the killers succeeding in their mission, and then rewind to reveal how it all came to be. The yield is a classic double narrative: a present-day inquest led by an insurance investigator, Reardon (Edmond O'Brien), prompts a succession of flashbacks (eleven total) in which it's gradually revealed how the once-proud Swede (Burt Lancaster) was lured into crime by a dangerous woman (Ava Gardner) whose withdrawal of affection left him spiritually crushed.

In addressing the Swede as an enigma to be posthumously pieced together, *The Killers* follows the model of Orson Welles's *Citizen Kane* (1941), wherein differing perspectives of Kane's shadowy past are recalled for the benefit of an investigative journalist. Such intertwining of past and present, a central conceit in noir, is likewise suggested in Hemingway's prevalent theme of arrested time, from the anxious killers who wait in the "now" for a victim stuck in the "then" to

The Killers (film, 1946) with Charles McGraw and William Conrad.

The Killers (*Buick-Electra Playhouse*, 1959) with Dane Clark and Robert Middleton.

The Killers (1964) with Lee Marvin and Clu Gulager.

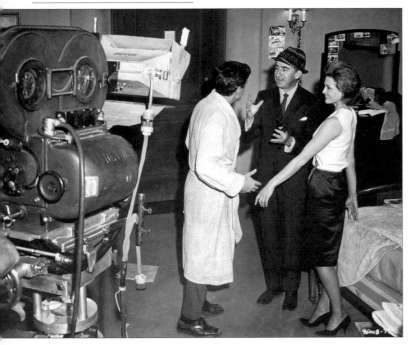

On the set of *The Killers* (1963) with John Cassavetes, Don Siegel, and Angie Dickinson.

the diner clock that runs late to the Swede who refuses to run at all. Reardon, obsessed with getting to the core of the Swede's dark past, enacts the quest of a seeker-hero drawn deeply into the night world by morbid curiosity. Siodmak's rounding out of Hemingway's text with stock types is made complete with a police detective (Sam Levene) who serves as the Swede's unheeded conscience, and with an underworld boss (Albert Dekker) around whom the pivotal set piece of a payroll heist revolves.

Siegel's remake, officially billed as *Ernest Hemingway's The Killers*, retains the basic elements of its predecessor while flip-flopping the narrative impetus. In place of a reputable hero, he promotes the two assassins, renamed Charlie (Lee Marvin) and Lee (Clu Gulager), into the position of investigating a murder they themselves have committed. Streamlining Siodmak's complex flashback structure to conform to the act breaks required of commercial television, but otherwise retracing the original film's threads of greed, double-cross, and sexual treachery, Siegel's version is a model of efficiency entirely befitting the modern corporatized world in which his updated scenario takes place. Charlie and Lee, who conceal their silenced weapons in expensive leather satchels and dress like MCA executives, are in effect traveling businessmen whose product happens to be death. Siegel opens his film with these two marching into a school for the blind and demanding to see one "Jerry Nichols" (John Cassavetes), an instructor there, whom they promptly gun down. Afterwards, on the train ride home, Charlie allows himself a measure of speculation: "If they had a chance, they always ran, but he just stood there and took it." Mystified, he suggests they find out who hired them and why.

The man they've exterminated was Johnny North, a once-celebrated

The Killers (1964) with John Cassavetes and Angie Dickinson.

The Killers (1964) with John Cassavetes and Claude Akins.

The Killers (1964) with John Cassavetes, Robert Phillips, and Norman Fell.

racecar driver. By talking to North's old mechanic, Earl Sylvester (Claude Akins), the killers begin to fathom how the champion "got in wrong." In the first and most substantial of Siegel's three flashbacks, we see how North fell hard for Sheila Farr (Angie Dickinson), a track moll who, as Siegel wrote in his production notes, "gets her kicks—almost a feeling of orgasm—via the speed and danger of racing cars." The sexual spark is palatable from their first shared frame. "Fast enough for you?" North asks, as he takes Sheila for a spin around the track. Her response is a lusty laugh and a hard, suggestive press on North's knee, urging him to accelerate. Dashing off to meet Sheila for a date on the eve of his big race, North pointedly rejects Earl's warning that he's about to hit every curve in the downfall of a man undone by a woman. Only after he smashes up his car and lays immobilized in the hospital, his eyes wrapped in bandages, his career destroyed, does North realize the extent to which his potency has been sapped.

The Killers (1964) with Ronald Reagan.

During his convalescence, North learns from Earl that Sheila is the mistress of gangster Jack Browning (Ronald Reagan); he's but the latest of her dalliances with boxers, bullfighters, and other men of sport. "I feel great. I feel smart. I had to get my eyes boiled before I could see," he cries out. North's boiled eyes become a metaphor for the disorientation induced by the noir femme fatale. Even after his vision returns, he remains oblivious to Sheila's duplicitous nature. Blindness and perception are linked with North throughout the film, from the sightless students who bear witness to his death to the dark sunglasses his executioners wear to the driving goggles he removes upon first meeting Sheila, and which are then symbolically cracked during his smash-up. In contrast to Gardner's femme fatale in the Siodmak film, whose ambiguous nature is cued in compositions that obscure her features, Dickinson's Sheila is framed and key-lighted in ways that enhance her overt sexuality while leaving little to the imagination—and still North remains confounded in her presence.

Some months after the accident, when Sheila tracks North down to the boarding house where he now lives in despondency, their lopsided relationship remains situated in optical terms:

> NORTH: What do you want?
>
> SHEILA: A guy. The same guy I saw the first time I saw you.
>
> NORTH: That guy is dead. That guy was so in love with you he couldn't see straight.

Yet the way North stares at her, lingering in his doorway, pursing her lips, makes it clear that his clarity remains compromised. The tawdriness of the room, the flashing neon outside the window, seem to conspire against him. Sheila, on the other hand, knows exactly what she sees in North: a patsy to be twisted around her finger. Imploring him to be a "winner" again, she convinces North to be the wheelman in a million-dollar mail truck heist that Browning and his crew are planning. From there, North traces a somnambulist route to

Advertisement for *The Killers* (1969). Five years pased before the "made-for-TV" film was allowed on television.

The Killers (1964) with Angie Dickinson and Ronald Reagan.

the tragic end predicted for him by Earl. Betrayed by Sheila, shot by Browning, he ends up in a grave-like ditch, his hand clutched to an oozing wound; in the chronology of the film, it's our last view of him before Charlie and Lee saunter in some years later and finish the job.

The Killers may be North's tragedy, but it is, in the end, the killers' journey. Where Lee, a cackling psychopath of a sidekick, evokes the antics of Hemingway's hoods by gargling with whiskey and spouting off inane non sequiturs, Charlie presents himself as a sharp and sober instrument of death. He's someone for whom the numbers and sums that fail to click into place set off big alarms. "The first thing you told me was never to think about a job," Lee reminds him. Only Charlie can't help but think: the higher-than-usual fee they've received to kill North disturbs his inner mechanism. Somewhere, he reasons, lies a treasure. After coercing additional details of the caper from Browning's henchman Mickey Farmer (Norman Fell), whom they parboil in a steam bath, Charlie and Lee set out to confront Browning, who's reinvented himself as a real estate developer. "You're welcome to see my books," the gangster sniffs when the killers show up at his high-rise office. "Yeah, which set?" Charlie asks, and it's perhaps an inside joke that Siegel, in this scene of corporate respectability masking underworld enterprise, has planted a scale model of Wasserman's Universal City tower on Browning's desk.

Faced with Charlie's silenced gun, Browning eagerly points the killer-detectives in the direction of his lethal paramour (now wife). The brutality that's subsequently unleashed on Sheila, whom Charlie and Lee beat and humiliate before dangling from a window by her heels, seems intended as much to extract the location of the heist loot as it is to punish her for what she did to North, whose fall from grace they've come to regard with sympathy. Upon hearing Sheila describe how she and Browning left North for dead, Charlie cryptically thanks her for solving his riddle. "You didn't need us," he adds. Outside, Charlie and Lee are ambushed by Browning, who snipes them from a rooftop; only Charlie survives. Critically wounded, he makes his way to the Brownings' posh home to find them emptying a wall safe. Sheila, ever the self-preservationist, instinctively distances herself from her husband as Charlie raises his gun; the sideways look of resignation on Browning's face neatly parallels North's stoicism in the face of death.

Upon rebuffing Sheila's offer to split the money ("Lady, I don't have the time," he sighs in the film's most famous line), Charlie commits his final kill before stumbling onto the well-manicured lawn and expiring on a heap of cash. Crime, no surprise, is a zero-sum game, but Siegel's take on this maxim is brazen in its defeatism. His harsh palette, shallow compositions, and garishly surreal process shots only heighten the decay of a world unwelcoming to honor or decency. Unlike the Siodmak film, there are few shadows, only a flat, hostile light that illuminates every drop of spilled blood. The film had just begun production when President Kennedy was shot in the head under the Texas sun. Siegel was in a costume fitting with Dickinson when the news came over the radio: "A loud, piercing scream from Angie cut through the announcer's voice," he recalls in his autobiography. "I rushed to her as she started to topple to the floor. She was crying hysterically."

The delirium of the times informs *The Killers*, not only in the cruelly matter-of-fact violence by which its principals are claimed, but in the livid anarchy of a world gone to hell: the police show up (or so an off-screen siren suggests) only when all the schemers are dead. Given the cultural mood, NBC deemed the film unsuitable for broadcast; detoured to the second-run circuit, it became one of Universal's most profitable releases of the 1960s. In its stead, the breezy, Hitchcockian thriller *See How They Run*, as *The Widow-Makers* was retitled, became the first "Project 120" telefeature to air, followed shortly by another cynically violent Siegel production, *The Hanged Man*. Yet the legacy of *The Killers* endures. One need only look at the philosophy-spouting, skinny-tie-wearing assassins of *Pulp Fiction* (1994) to see its impact on the contours of neo noir—a movement Siegel's color film noir effectively set in motion.

The Hanged Man (1964) is billed as an adaptation of *Ride the Pink Horse*, a novel by Dorothy B. Hughes first brought to the screen in 1947 by Robert Montgomery. Hughes, who also supplied the source material for *The Fallen Sparrow* (1943) and *In a Lonely Place* (1950), specialized in stories of complex, embittered loners ground to the bone by the intensity of their emotions—the poisonous masculinity that defines the noir antihero. She opens *Pink Horse* (1946) in a dusty southwestern town with Sailor, the disillusioned lackey of a corrupt politician, stepping off a bus after a four-day trip from Chicago: "He stood there, helpless anger knotting his nerves. Monotonously cursing the Sen, the dirty, double-crossing, lying, whoring Senator Willis Douglas. It was the Sen's fault he was in this God-forsaken town and no place to rest his feet. He hadn't wanted to come here." What follows, in prose that bleeds the past with the present, is the slow-burning meltdown of a would-be extorter: Sailor, who alone knows the truth about how the Sen murdered his own wife, has decided to sell his silence for five thousand dollars. Though pushed around and strung along by the powerful man he once idolized but now detests, Sailor has little interest in bloodshed: he simply wants to collect what he reckons he's owed and jump the border.

Unable to secure a hotel room, Sailor falls in with Pancho, the half-breed operator of the town's carousel, who gives him a ratty blanket and space on the ground to lay his head. During the day, as he tries to muster up the courage to face the Sen, he's followed around by an indigenous girl, Pila, whose imploring eyes and young-old face fill him with unease. Though he curses Pancho and Pila, along with everyone else in town, it's only among their "dark faces" that Sailor finds sanctuary—at the bottom of a class structure he so desperately

Ride the Pink Horse (film, 1947) with Robert Montgomery.

The Hanged Man (1964) with Robert Culp.

wants to climb. All the while, McIntyre, a homicide detective who came up from the same slums as Sailor, and has likewise followed the mighty Sen to New Mexico, pesters Sailor for answers about what happened in Chicago. Sailor, fixated on the big payoff, made unwell by the torrent of thoughts regarding his former mentor, spins himself up so tightly that there's only one plausible, disastrous outcome to his quest. Hughes's story is one of vindication thwarted. No man, especially one as screwed-up as Sailor, can prevail against a force as elusively powerful and comfortably elite as the Sen.

In Montgomery's film (scripted by Ben Hecht and Charles Lederer), Sailor becomes Gagin, a disaffected war veteran from points unknown, while the Senator becomes Frank Hugo (Fred Clark), the hearing-impaired gangster who killed Gagin's friend, Shorty. Stripped of Sailor's crippling neuroses, Gagin is a dangerous and driven operator—a more blunt version of Montgomery's Philip Marlowe in *Lady in the Lake* (1947). In keeping with the emerging movement of film noir, the story is further changed by the elevation of a femme fatale named Marjorie (Andrea King), and by scenes of Gagin working his way past Hugo's torpedoes toward a confrontation with the man himself. Montgomery retains the centrality of Pancho (Thomas Gomez) and Pila (Wanda Hendrix); in their empathy toward Gagin, they provide the emotional core of the story. On the other hand, Montgomery and his writers whip around the blackmail scheme in Hughes's book so that what was psychological is made literal, in the form of a MacGuffin. Gagin has evidence (a canceled bank draft) of the wartime profiteering by which Hugo made his illicit fortune. The most significant change to Hughes's story is that Gagin has no past history with either Hugo or Bill Retz (Art Smith), the federal agent investigating the gangster, as Sailor does with the Sen and McIntyre. He is, as Pancho aptly puts it, "a man with no place."

The film, like the novel, unfolds during Fiesta, the town's annual "celebration of release from gloom, from the specter of evil." The festivities, rooted in religion and ritual, make a mockery of the aggressive self-absorption by which these big-city visitors function. When Pila (Wanda Hendrix) presents Gagin with a talisman meant to ward off evil, Gagin dismisses her as a simpleton; later, though, when Marjorie lures him into an alley where he's knifed in the back, Gagin relies on Pila to patch him up. Killing the hours until his anticipated payoff, he remains a stranger in a milieu which, while geographically part of America, nevertheless feels to him disorienting and foreign—an otherworldliness Montgomery shapes with high-contrast imagery of Gagin struggling to find his way through the maze-like streets. Gagin's discombobulation is further underscored by references to his war past (a history not shared with Sailor, for whom the Sen pulled strings). Hugo dismisses Gagin's extortive demand, his desire to achieve what everyone else seems to have gained in a booming postwar economy, as the result of his being "gussed up because he got nothing out of the war," and then derides him as "one of these haywire veterans who tried to put the bite on me for thirty grand." It's this latter insult, with its undercurrent of anti-patriotism, that jolts Gagin out of his anguished headspace.

In Siegel's remake, *The Hanged Man*, the Sailor-Gagin character is renamed Harry Pace; he's played by Robert Culp, whose scowling, hangdog face situates him as a bloodhound well practiced at diving into holes without thinking. The teleplay by Jack Laird and Stanford Whitmore shifts the locale from New Mexico to the baroque environs of New Orleans in full-on Mardi Gras mode. The raucousness of the celebration, with its emphasis on masquerade and debauchery, provides an apt backdrop for a story centered on two-faced behavior and moral dissoluteness. Siegel opens the picture cold with Pace being ushered into a rural warehouse where the remains of his friend, Whitey Devlin, victim of a mysterious explosion, have been kept on ice awaiting his arrival. "That's him, all right," Pace mutters before crossing the street to a railroad depot and retrieving a piece of paper from a locker. In-

The Hanged Man (1964) with Robert Culp.

formed that the next train to New Orleans is not for several hours, he hitches a ride with the jovial Uncle Picaud (J. Carrol Naish) and his niece, Celine (Brenda Scott), the French Creole counterparts to Pancho and Pila.

After being deposited in the French Quarter, Pace sets out to avenge Devlin's death by killing Arnie Seeger (Edmond O'Brien), the crooked union boss he figures to be responsible. Gun tactfully hidden behind a pillow, he barges into Seeger's hotel suite only to be stopped short by Seeger's wife, Lois (Vera Miles)—Seeger isn't there—whose alluring presence temporarily quells his rage. Lois explains that Devlin, with whom she'd been adulterously involved, was murdered not for the obvious reason, but because he'd acquired a canceled check incriminating to Seeger. Confirming that Pace is now in possession of this evidence, Lois makes a proposition: rather than exterminate Seeger, why not extort him for a large sum and run away with her? Pace remains unswayed, vowing to "save everybody a lot of trouble" by following through, but Lois softly persists. "Help me," she whispers, brushing herself against Pace, who all too quickly capitulates. At once we're presented with an antihero rather softer than Gagin, who in *Ride the Pink Horse* responds to Marjorie's overtures with a diatribe about the "dead fish where her heart ought to be."

The Hanged Man (1964) with Vera Miles and Robert Culp.

At a nightclub, Pace is confronted by Grebb (Norman Fell), a government agent building a case against Seeger. Grebb tries to talk some sense into Pace, urging him to honor his slain friend by simply handing over the check. "It ain't gonna make him any deader," Pace spits back. Pace's shortsightedness in the matter is made all the more clear in the ensuing cutaway, a scene that wasn't in the

The Hanged Man (1964) with Norman Fell and Robert Culp.

SCENES FROM: *The Hanged Man* (1964)
with Robert Culp and Brenda Scott.

shooting script but which Siegel hastily filmed during post-production: a man, framed through the ribs of a headboard, lies alone in a dark room periodically lit by the pulsating neon sign outside his window. The telephone rings, and it's Lois, affirming to the still-very-much-alive Devlin (Gene Raymond) that the triple-cross scheme he's cooked up is moving along nicely. While the scene itself pays homage to some iconic noir imagery, it also marks the point where *The Hanged Man* diverges from its predecessor by introducing an artificial element of suspense, one that leaves the audience too far ahead of Pace. In tipping his cards so early, Siegel effectively undermines the rest of his picture, while promoting his hero as something of a fool—a concession, perhaps, to the tarot-inspired title.

Lacking any backstory, Pace is defined by his present actions, which are resoundingly ineffectual, if not dim-witted, particularly given our foreknowledge of where this is all going. Beginning with his misidentification of Devlin's charred body, he gets almost everything wrong. He misreads Lois's craving for money as a sexual come-on; he brushes off Grebb's prudent advice in the nightclub (in this he's distracted perhaps by Astrud Gilberto, whose performance of her bossa nova hit "The Girl from Ipanema" is given considerable screen time); and he treats Celine, the smitten Creole girl, horridly despite her earnest concern for his well-being. Moreover, as a blackmailer, his skills are woeful. Upon his return to Seeger's place, he's beaten and humiliated by some bodyguards before being dropped at the big man's feet. "Hey, Lois, come on in here," Seeger brays. "I want you to learn about high finance. In this corner, wearing a fifty-dollar suit and fighting out of his class is the gopher. Look at his hands, honey. They're sweaty. That's always the tip-off. The little man, trying for the big score." Doing his best to sound tough, Pace puts forth his terms: a suitcase of money, or the incriminating check goes to Grebb. With the dominoes lined up in no one's favor but Lois and Devlin's, Siegel ends the sequence with a close-up of Seeger, all snarl and spittle; like Pace, he's too blinded by rage to see the machinations at work around him.

With some time to kill before the payoff, Pace cynically uses the infatuated Celine as a cover in a rendezvous with Lois. When Celine pouts afterwards, Pace admonishes her to wise up to the ways of the world: "There isn't any magic anywhere. Nowhere. You got to see the way it really is with people, everybody scratching just to stay alive." Pace also rejects Celine's warning, derived from a tarot card reading, that his involvement with this crew will result in his death—represented, in her view, by the "hanged man" of the deck. Strikingly, the true symbolism of the card is misused, for in the vernacular of tarot it's not death the hanged man card represents but purgatory. Specifically, the card symbolizes a reflective state of suspension wherein one gains illumination, hence its depiction of a fool strung upside down and staring contemplatively at the ground. In this light, Pace's grasping journey, his interchangeable cravings for vengeance and money, might be viewed as a misguided quest for salvation. Pace has little grounding, a condition of rootlessness affirmed by the "no vacancy" signs he's confronted with upon his arrival in New Orleans. With nowhere to stay (until Celine offers him a bed of hay), he should perhaps have returned to wherever he was before this.

Pace's moment of awakening arrives on Shrove Tuesday, the climax of the carnival, with a fantastic set piece in the alley behind a library where he's hidden the check. Just yards away from the Mardi Gras revelers, he's ambushed by Seeger's bodyguards. Siegel stages the action with great depth, the shadowy figures tousling in the foreground contrasting with the colors and commotion of the festivities in the distance. After much shouting and shooting, Pace kills one of his assailants, but is himself shot. Bleeding, he staggers through the swirling costumes and mammoth floats of the orgiastic parade—his frantic, unsteady manner mistaken as part of the fun. Once more, he finds haven with Celine, and once more he fails to appreciate her unconditional devotion because of the sway Lois holds over him. So it's with irony that Celine, in her naiveté, brings Lois, literally clad in the costume of a spider woman, to the ailing Pace with the hope that she'll make him better again. From this we arrive at the "reveal" already tipped: the unmasking of the harlequin who arrives in Lois's wake, gun in hand and full of threats, as Devlin, seemingly resurrected from the dead, which is precisely how Siegel visualizes Pace's gasping reaction.

The Hanged Man (1964).
An incriminating check is later exchanged for a briefcase of cash.

The realization that he's been but a patsy in a larger scheme serves as Pace's moment of illumination—his release. The ensuing exchange of his check for Seeger's suitcase of cash culminates with the second, and final, death of Devlin and the arrest of Seeger, actions courtesy of the ever-resilient Grebb. While order has seemingly been restored, the sight of Lois glaring at her husband and crying while cradling Devlin, her true love, signals the start of a whole new cycle of retribution. After decades of icy femmes fatales, Lois's apparently genuine display of emotion is startling—seemingly more in tune with the despondency displayed by Sailor in Dorothy B. Hughes's source novel. To wit, Siegel ends his film on a quiet note of Lenten sobriety: the Quarter emptied of its masked revelers, Pace and Grebb share a manly handshake and walk away. Hughes, in contrast, ends her novel more critical of her male antihero, and with greater ambivalence about his future. Sailor, having impulsively killed both the Sen and McIntyre, runs weeping into the desert: "No sound stirred behind him, there was no sound in the night but his running steps, his tears. Somewhere in the night Pancho prayed for him, not knowing he prayed for the damned."

In 1966, Universal relaunched its "Project 120" concept under the banner of "World Premiere." Its inaugural effort, *Fame Is the Name of the Game*, is the story of a reporter (Anthony Franciosa) who investigates the death of a high-priced call girl (Jill St. John). It, too, was based on a film noir, *Chicago Deadline*

(1949). *Fame* marked a new direction for Universal: the made-for-television movie as a pilot for a prospective series. This approach not only enabled the studio to gauge public interest in a particular premise, but also, in the case of a failing, allowed its financial investment to be recouped through ancillary markets. The production of pilots was, and remains, a risky and speculative endeavor, and with "World Premiere," Universal settled upon a successful cost-hedging formula that would yield (the rebooted) *Dragnet*, *Kojak*, *Columbo*, and *The Rockford Files*. Prior to that, its primary testing grounds for potential series were filmed anthologies like *The Bob Hope Chrysler Show* (1963–1967) and *Kraft Suspense Theatre* (a/k/a *Crisis*; 1963–1965). The latter, overseen by Roy Huggins, is of particular interest for the number of noir plots it staged, and for the public firing of the wild card on its staff, producer-director Robert Altman.

Altman, like Siegel, knew his way around noir, and was no stranger to controversy. Under contract to Fox, he'd crafted an hour of anthology television so provocatively carnal and disturbingly violent it prompted a Senate inquiry into network standards and practices. "A Lion Walks Among Us" (*Bus Stop*, 1961) features baby-faced pop singer Fabian as a hepcat drifter who cuts a path of destruction and death through a small town, and then sexually humiliates the district attorney's wife in such a way that prosecution becomes impossible. Altman's casting of the teen idol as an unredeemable sociopath was an audacious stroke; even before the show aired, it generated reams of ink. Remorseless murder was still a novelty on television, and the rawness that Altman brought to the material resulted in the show's sponsors, along with some twenty-five affiliates, withdrawing from the broadcast (thus paving the way, three years later, for NBC's rejection of *The Killers*). Altman, somehow, emerged from the imbroglio unscathed, and was hired over to Universal, where he joined Huggins's unit on *Kraft Suspense Theatre*.

Working under Huggins amplified Altman's frustrations with formulaic convention. "I represented what he hated most in television," Huggins recalled, "and that is the very commercial, highly plotted story, and he hated commercial storytelling with a vengeance." Unable to get any of his *Kraft* scripts approved, Altman publicly berated the show ("as bland as its cheese," he declared to *Variety*), effectively terminating his future with Universal. He was, however, obligated to complete one final production, a pilot for a series about state policemen. The resulting telefeature, titled "Once Upon a Savage Night" for its *Kraft* broadcast (1964), and issued theatrically as *Nightmare in Chicago* (1965), finds Altman exploring the looping narrative mode—open, fragmented, character-driven—for which he became renowned in the following decade. Brazenly, he made the film completely on location in and around Chicago with a skeleton crew, almost entirely at night, and under natural lighting conditions, a feat made possible by an ultra-sensitive color film stock developed by Kodak for the military—which used it to capture the smoke trails of missiles launched at night.

"Once Upon a Savage Night" is based on *Murder on the Turn-pike*, a novella by William P. McGivern serialized in *The Saturday Evening Post* in 1961. A police reporter before turning to the pulp trade, McGivern specialized in "dirty cop" noir: *The Big Heat* (1953), *Rogue Cop* (1954), *Shield for Murder* (1954), and *Hell on Frisco Bay* (1955) were all made from his books. Given his track record, the straightforward, *Dragnet*-style *Murder on the Turnpike* seems an anomaly, perhaps an atonement. His Dan O'Leary is a wholesome state trooper responsible for maintaining order along "a brilliant complex of traffic rotaries, interchanges and expressways which carried almost a quarter of a million persons safely to their homes and offices each and every day of the year." O'Leary so cherishes the pike that his sweetheart, Sheila, who works at a Howard Johnson's along his route, teases him about it. Enter Harry Bogan, a killer on the run from New York, whose breach of the expressway in a stolen vehicle triggers an immediate police response. Charged with keeping an eye on the Howard Johnson's, O'Leary misses his chance to capture Bogan, and feels awfully ashamed about it, especially when the fugitive kidnaps Sheila. "She was gone, helpless in a killer's hands, and it was his fault," McGivern writes. Eager to redeem himself, O'Leary catches up with Bogan, saves his girl, and feels no pity when the killer drives himself over a bridge.

In Altman's adaptation, a collaboration with David Moessinger, McGivern's one-time murderer is made a serial killer winding his way through the Midwest. Myron Ellis (Philip Abbott), or, as he's known in the tabloids, "Georgie Porgie," is a strangler of young women, "all the same—tall, blonde, good-looking, a little on the cheap side," as one police official puts it. Hypersensitive to light, he's compelled to wear sunglasses at all hours—a true creature of the night. Altman opens his film at daybreak in a small Indiana town. Shots of the sun peering over a bleak row of houses give way to a jarring close-up of a woman with bulbous eyes and a lipstick-smeared mouth arriving home and drunkenly calling out for her housemate, Norma. A reverse shot reveals Norma: a dead blonde in a red dress with a black necktie wrapped around her throat and a broken clock at her feet

"Once Upon a Savage Night" (*Kraft Suspense Theater*, 1964) with Philip Abbott (above) and Arlene Kieta (below).

BELOW: Opening scene: "Once Upon a Savage Night" (1964).

"Once Upon a Savage Night" (1964) with Jan Marsh, Arlene Kieta, and Phillip Abbott (above) and Ted Knight and Charles McGraw (below).

frozen at twelve minutes past six—a sight that sends Miss Bulbous Eyes on a hysterical, shrieking flight through the neighborhood. Behind her, Ellis slips out from a closet, retrieves his neckwear, and exits by the front door, his arm instinctively rising to block the first rays of dawn.

That night, upon arriving in Chicago, Ellis charms a blonde (Arlene Kieta) at a stoplight with some seasoned banter, takes her to a burlesque club, and quietly throttles her as the floor show roars on nearby. Altman intercuts the seduction and murder of the woman with the listless gyrations of a stripper—who, as she doffs her pièce de résistance and absorbs the jeers of the crowd, finally sees the grim death mask of the victim left crumpled in a corner. Fleeing, Ellis steals a car and makes his way to the Tri-State Tollway, unaware that his path of escape coincides with the route of a military convoy transporting a nuclear missile. It's this matter of national importance, more than the escalating count of dead blondes in Ellis's wake, which activates the Tri-State Police—the ostensible heroes of Altman's intended pilot. "What's all this have to do with us?" Commissioner Lombardo (Ted Knight) wants to know when informed of the carnage; hastily, someone reminds him of the promise he made to the boys in Washington that their confidential package, code-named "Little John," would pass through his jurisdiction unmolested.

Lombardo, whom Knight plays as a smarmy buffoon, dispatches his lieutenants, Brockman (Charles McGraw) and McVea (Robert Ridgely), to handle the crisis. Resolutely serious, their dialogue minimal, Brockman and McVea establish a field office at the Oasis, an all-night highway diner, and set up a dragnet for Ellis. They're at once stymied by the anonymity of their target: "We haven't got a make on him—we've got nothing," Brockman admits. When Ellis stops by the Oasis and orders a sandwich and a glass of milk (which the waitress forgets), he's just another doughy, middle-aged traveler perched at the counter. Only when Ellis beats a man in the parking lot and hijacks his car do the police learn of his distinguishing characteristic, the omnipresent sunglasses—a device suggested by a single line in McGivern's story: "He worked as a night watchman because the sunshine hurt his weak eyes." Surmising their quarry to be light-phobic, Brockman and McVea order that klieg lights be set up at the tollbooth through which Ellis must invariably pass.

Ellis, however, having already provoked a multi-car pileup on the turnpike, is one step ahead of the beleaguered authorities. After looking on, impassively, at the results of his diversion, he returns to the Oasis and kidnaps a sweet-natured waitress, a brunette named Bernadette (Barbara Turner), the one who forgot his milk. Not as frightened as Ellis expects her to be, Bernadette stares back at him with open, curious eyes.

> ELLIS: You're thinking about those girls, aren't you? Well, that was different. I'm not sorry about any one of them. You may not believe this, but every one of those girls, I asked to marry me. They weren't about to be interested in any one man. They were cheap, Bernadette. Dirty.

While Ellis commandeers a maintenance truck and awaits his chance to slip through the toll plaza, he becomes fixated on the egg that Bernadette cradles in her mittens—an old farmer's trick, she explains, for keeping warm. The presence of the maternal symbol brings "Georgie Porgie" to a point of crisis.

The psychopath, Foster Hirsch notes in *Dark Side of the Screen*, "is the dark underside of the noir victim—far gone before the film opens, he remains trapped in an ongoing nightmare." Ellis, quite plainly, has been driven crazy by the lingering dominance of his mother. Her voice, wicked and slurred, is brought up on the soundtrack over the main titles as Ellis, arriving in Chicago, is shown stalking his next victim on a train. And her cackling, disjointed instructions to "be a very good little boy" while she goes out for a spell are directly correlated to the reflected image of the blonde girl in the train's window. Though this sequence isn't in the source story, McGivern does make repeated use of glass and inward gazing in his descriptions of Bogan: "The rain water blurred his features at rhythmic intervals, then the windshield wiper smoothed them out; it was interesting, this alternate fading and sharpening of his reflection." Ellis, on the other hand, is haunted by what he sees through the looking glass.

The voice of Mother is again invoked when Ellis peers through the wraparound windows of the Oasis and observes Bernadette's boyfriend, Ralph (Douglas E. Alleman), the cook, arranging an illicit liaison with the new waitress Wynette (Charlene Lee), a tawdry bottle-blonde: it seems he's abducted Bernadette for a reason. In an oblique and increasingly hysterical monologue, he reveals how his little sister, Mary Ann, became the fatal victim of his mother's sordid episodes: "She was eleven and a half years old. She didn't know like I did." In Ellis's view, Bernadette, like Mary Ann, is an innocent, and in taking her hostage, he perhaps hopes to save her from the sexual maelstrom that destroyed his sister's life. This situating of Ellis as something more than a senseless predator summons up a similar scene in *Psycho* (1960) when Norman Bates reveals to Marion Crane, over sandwiches and milk, his opinions about "cheap" behavior. Moments after unburdening himself to Bernadette, when the police spring their klieg-light trap, Ellis, still wailing for his lost sister, is rendered as helpless and unaccountable a monster as those in Universal's horror films of the 1930s. Bernadette, left holding his crushed sunglasses, looks on sadly. As the sun begins to rise, Brockman and McVea wave the atomic missile caravan—harbinger of a larger nightmare—on its way.

As lensed by ace cameraman Ellis "Bud" Thackery, "Once Upon a Savage Night" makes spectacular use of Kodak's innovative stock, especially in a tracking shot of Ellis fleeing a pursuing mob through a neon-lit shopping district. Thackery's night-for-night cinematography brings a dreamlike fluidity to the incoherent brutality of the proceedings. Unbound from the backlot, Altman vividly merges his signature overlapping dialogue and pseudo-improvisational style with his urban locale. The desolate highways that wrap Chicago, its all-night diners and sordid nightclubs, become integral parts of the narrative fabric. "I didn't know any other way to shoot it," he explained of his naturalistic approach. The use of color, untainted by studio lights, is particularly striking. Visceral reds and oranges dominate: the dress and shoes of Ellis's first victim; the red mouth of his second; the flames that lick his sunglasses during the highway pileup; the red car he steals to make his getaway, followed later by an orange truck; the tangerine shawl and mittens of the captive Bernadette; and, finally, the red-orange tarp of the missile the police are so intent on protecting. Ellis himself is costumed in a beige raincoat for most of the film, bland and unnoticeable until he disrupts the procedures and rituals (the story takes place around Christmas) of the everyday world.

When "Once Upon a Savage Night" was made, just a few years after *Psycho* broke box-office records, the term "serial killer" hadn't yet been coined; it would enter the vernacular in the 1970s, during the Summer of Sam. But the fears raised by such inexplicable horror were certainly in the zeitgeist. In the winter of 1958, Charles Starkweather and his girlfriend, Carol Ann Fugate, had slain eleven citizens of Nebraska and Wyoming; the following year, Richard Hickock and Perry Edward Smith killed the Clutter family of Holcomb, Kansas—a grisliness soon to be imprinted on the American consciousness with the publication of Truman Capote's *In Cold Blood* (1966). Murder was in the air, and it seemed particularly pungent in the heartland. And then there was Kennedy. In McGivern's novella it's not a missile convoy that the killer-on-the-loose disrupts, but a presidential motorcade. While the change was clearly intended to address the national tragedy of Kennedy's assassination, it's no less salient. At the height of the Cold War, the idea of a lone madman disrupting the buildup of America's arsenal was terrifying enough.

THE LONER
CBS 1965–1966

> In the aftermath of the bloodletting called the Civil War, thousands of rootless, restless, searching men traveled west. Such a man was William Colton. Like the others, he carried a blanket roll, a proficient gun, and a dedication to a new chapter in American history: the opening of the West.
>
> —Opening Narration, *The Loner*

OUR FIRST IMPRESSION OF WILLIAM COLTON IN THIS WESTERN FROM Rod Serling is of a solitary figure on horseback pitted against a barren landscape. It's an image synonymous with the myth of the American West—a myth already in the making, in countless dime novels and roadshow spectacles, before the frontier was fully claimed. The white, conquering male of the West is brave, independent, resilient; but also restless, alienated, and violent. As the myth moved into and through the twentieth century, filtered through countless stories, songs, films, and television shows, its standards of heroism became shaded. Serling's Colton (Lloyd Bridges) is a hero of virtue and honor, but he's also melancholic and disillusioned—an existential gunman. Sick of war, of blood and fighting, he's resigned his commission in the Union cavalry and disappeared west-

Publicity still for *The Loner* with Lloyd Bridges as Jeff Colton (1965).

ward, "to get the cannon smoke out of my eyes, the noise out of my ears, maybe some of the pictures out of my head." That urge to hit the open road, the need to see what lies over the next hill, while in its own right uniquely correlated to American notions of individualism, is also a part of the Western mythos, one that will be key to this loner's journey.

Serling conceived *The Loner* in 1960 just as he was finishing what he thought to be his first and only season of *The Twilight Zone*. The so-called "adult Western" was at the height of its popularity; the anthology drama, Serling's metier, was all but finished. His one-hour pilot script about a nomadic veteran known as "The Loner" combined aspects of both. With *The Twilight Zone* gaining an unexpected reprieve, Serling stuffed his script in a drawer. He was on a speaking tour of south-

Publicity still for *The Loner* (1965).

west Asia in early 1965 when he received a cable-gram: due to a schedule shift, CBS needed a half-hour lead-in to its beloved perennial *Gunsmoke* (1955–1975). Might Serling be able to reformat his "Loner" concept in time for the upcoming season? So quickly was the series rushed into production that CBS apparently neglected to read Serling's pages. Expecting something in the vein of their other new oater that season, *The Wild Wild West* (1965–1969)—"chases, running gun battles, runaway stage coaches," as one network executive put it—they were aghast when Serling delivered a horse of a different feather, if not an entirely different Wild West.

Even by the dark standard of a work like *The Searchers* (1956), Serling's take on the genre is un-remittingly downcast. Though set, like John Ford's picture, in "the aftermath of the bloodletting called the Civil War," its despairing worldview is more in tune with that purveyed by the classic cycle of film noir, itself "a cinematic style forged in the fires of war, exile, and disillusion, a melodramatic reflection for a world gone mad," as Tom Flinn writes in "Three Faces of Film Noir" (1972). Like the displaced veterans of *The Blue Dahlia* (1945) and *Ride the Pink Horse* (1947), Colton is a rootless, damaged male uncertain of his role in a postwar society. Serling, himself a vet-eran of World War II, knew something of this: "I was traumatized into writing by war events, by going through a war in a combat situation and feeling the des-perate need for some sort of therapy—get it out of my gut, write it down." The cure, for Colton, is itinerancy: a trusty steed and an open trail. Wised up to the absurdity of resolving conflict through violence, he seeks what Richard Schickel, in a 1965 essay ("Everything's Coming Up Loners"), described as "a viable pres-ent, some place where he won't be expected to kill people."

In the premiere, "An Echo of Bugles," a barroom spat results in Colton being challenged to a duel by "an itchy kid kind of handy with a gun," Merriman (Tony Hill), wryly named. Once Merriman sobers up, Colton is to meet him on a nearby hill—fifteen paces, turn, draw, fire, a time-honored ritual. In the interim, Colton finds his thoughts returning to the end of the war, to the time he stabbed a Johnny Reb, "a boy of sixteen." An oneiric, temporally fractured flashback begins with Colton leading a charge into a Confederate camp. Events unfold in slow motion: the rush of hollering men and blazing rifles, the visual confusion of smoke and haze. Colton dismounts, the camera tight on his eyes, and joins the fray. The view widens; more carnage. Just as the action returns to normal speed, a boy soldier

(Michael Mortensen) springs at Colton, who retaliates with his saber. We see what Colton sees: a clear, innocent face suddenly drained of life, a close-up held uncomfortably long. The Johnny Reb's death is punctuated with the arrival of a messenger announcing the cessation of hostilities: the Treaty of Appomattox has been signed.

The war may be over, but for Colton it will never really go away. At a field hospital where the dead from both sides are being collected, he's counseled by his superior (John Hoyt): "A man carries his wars around with him like a knapsack. He never lets loose. He tries, but he never lets loose. He gets pictures in his head, and for a soldier they're just as much general issue as his boots." But the picture in Colton's head of "a boy skewered on a sword like a piece of meat" is an untenable one. Despite the offer of a promotion, some medals, he turns in his rank. "The next death that I have a hand in, the next killing, if ever I have to kill again, I want it personal," he says. "I want to be able to choose." A quick zoom in to Colton's clouded expression returns us to the dilemma of the present: the duel on the hill. Already, he must act upon his vow—will he kill or be killed?

Guns go off. Merriman falls, wounded but not dead.

MERRIMAN: You could have gone six inches lower. You could have killed me. You had your chance. What happened?

COLTON: I had my chance once before.

From this moment, Colton's conditional pacifism is to be repeatedly challenged, not only by the harshness of the landscape and its hardened settlers, but by the conventions of the Western itself—the genre's emphasis on violent resolution.

The contradictions at play in *The Loner* are made evident in its narrated prologue. Though Colton carries "a proficient gun," he's averse to gunplay; while sensitive to inequality, to the suffering of others, he's among the ranks of those dedicated to "the opening of the West," a euphemism for the bloody campaign of expansionism wrought by American manifest destiny. Within these apparent inconsistencies, Serling stretches the mythos of the West to accommodate his own concerns about mankind's propensity for destruction. "For civilization to survive," he tells us in one of his *Twilight Zone* voiceovers, "the human race has to remain civilized" ("The Shelter," 1960). But the laws and structures that hold society together in the urban East are largely absent in the vacant West. Colton, a career military officer, a graduate of West Point, straddles these realms uneasily. On the one hand, because the Western demands its heroes be straight shooters—marksmanship being an exemplar of ethical code—Colton goes nowhere without his gun strapped to his side. (Indeed, his very name evokes nineteenth-century gunsmith Samuel Colt.) On the other, as a Serling protagonist, a hero of moral imperative, he prefers mediation through verbal discourse. He's a voice of decency, the standard against which the actions of others are judged.

SCENES FROM: "An Echo of Bugles" (1965).

"One for the Wounded" (1965). As originally filmed (below), a brawl sequence was deemed overly violent and restaged (opposite page).

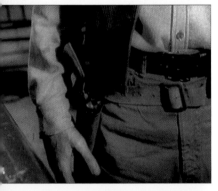

The format of *The Loner* is similar to that of *The Fugitive* and other "wandering hero" programs of the 1960s: with each installment Colton must resolve a communal crisis through moral means. Afterwards, he presses on, unhindered, a solitary figure once again. Serling, in a filmed presentation to potential advertisers, described his loner "as an onlooker to the battle of life and death. He sees in that sudden clarity that comes after protracted combat something of the value of human life and something of the tragedy of death." Like many of Serling's heroes, Colton is an emblem of righteousness—a man unafraid to stand up to jackals and tyrants. By surviving the war, he's gained not only insight, but fortitude, courage, and a heightened sense of moral outrage. These traits, essential to the Western hero, are particularly evident in "Widow on an Evening Stage" and its companion piece, "The Homecoming of Lemuel Stove," both of which deal with racially motivated mob violence. Serling's take on mankind's innate capacity for cruelty and hatred is clear-cut: the setting may be the wild and lawless Old West, but the place is America, in the uneasy years between "I Have a Dream" and a shot ringing out in the Memphis sky.

Colton roams a postbellum frontier conspicuously depopulated of husbands and fathers, not only by the recent war, but by the way of the gun that continues to hold sway. Having survived the horrors of war, Colton has, in the parlance of the era, "seen the elephant," a term summoned up by Yank and Reb soldiers alike to describe what defied description. At the time of the Civil War, with psychiatry and neurology not yet in practice, medicine had no way of dealing with what is now known as post-traumatic stress disorder. Severe cases were diagnosed as "nostalgia," a longing to return to how things were—to the time before the elephant. Even during World War II, the military was at a loss for how to deal with psychoneurotic casualties; the inner scars of war were just as likely to be treated with drugs and electroshock treatment than a regimen of psychotherapy.

Let There Be Light (1945), a documentary John Huston made for the Department of Defense during the war, opens with a group of shell-shocked veterans filing dutifully off a troop ship and into a bus that will take them to an army hospital for treatment. "Here is the human salvage, the final result of all that metal and fire can do to violate mortal flesh," the narrator (Walter Huston) intones. "Some wear the badges of their pain: the crutches, the bandages, the splints. Others show no outward signs, yet they, too, are wounded." Since the film was withheld from public release for thirty-five years, it would be a stretch to suggest that Serling ever saw it. Yet throughout *The Loner*, he invokes similar language to illustrate the debilitating emotional trauma suffered in combat. In "One of the Wounded," the titular figure is a Yankee officer, Col. Phelps (Paul

Richards), left catatonic by the war. "He was delivered to me this way, Mr. Colton," Mrs. Phelps (Anne Baxter) says of her immobile husband. "Dropped off a westbound stage like a consignment of yard goods paid for by the pound. Not a mark on him, not a mark! Not a saber wound or a bullet hole or a scar from a minié ball. Just this, this lump."

The war has walled the Colonel in, drained him of life. Because of this, Mrs. Phelps has to manage the family homestead on her own, with occasional help from itinerant hands like Colton. There are intimations that previous hire-ons have tried to have their way with her; she keeps her room locked, she warns Colton. Paranoid and distressed, she, too, has been marred by the war—collateral damage. She remains confounded by her husband's unresponsiveness. Colton tries to enlighten her: "Do you know how much hell a man has to go through to take away his speech and his strength? More hell, more misery, and more anguish than you ever knew existed." Throughout these exchanges, the ailing warrior remains silent, his pained eyes appraising Colton. By his bearing, we can presume Phelps to be a professional soldier, a figure of standing, like Colton. Yet his debilitated state undermines any notion of glory achieved in battle.

For the most part, the patriotic fare turned out by Hollywood in the 1940s and 1950s refrained from exposing the shock of combat, the dissociation, the difficulty in restarting civilian life. Only in the 1960s did a different view of America's triumph begin to emerge, one shaped by psychologism—a reappraisal of sacrifices made and tolls taken. The vanguard of this realistic approach on television was *Combat!* (1962–1967), especially its first season as overseen by Robert Altman. The World War II of *Combat!* is a grim endeavor, a succession of personal crises suffered through by complex and troubled individuals. "I'm afraid twenty-four hours a day," its hero, Sgt. Saunders (Vic Morrow), says. *Combat!*'s promotion of anguish over triumph is carried over in *The Loner*'s unblinking depiction of the internal damage inflicted upon the soldier. Serling, in his 1960 series pitch, described his hero as "in a retreat from a postwar society psychologically inept at recognizing what are the special needs of returning soldiers." Though he sets *The Loner* nearly a century before World War II, he may just as well be addressing the issues of those returned from Iwo Jima or the Ardennes—issues soon to be introduced to a new generation by the escalating situation in Vietnam circa 1965. *The Loner* would seem to be about three wars.

"One for the Wounded" (*Aired Version*, 1965).

Bridging past, present, and future in this way, *The Loner* is preoccupied with how war and bloodshed remain under the skin. "Two thousand miles from here to Appomattox and four years since the first Bull Run, but none of it, none of it, is more than a moment away, or farther than across the room," Colton tells Phelps's wife in "One of the Wounded." In "The Trial in Paradise," the war is revisited within a decrepit, shadow-laden barn. This is where Colton confronts three physically broken veterans: Hibbard (Robert Lansing), who is blind;

"The Trial in Paradise" (1966).

Allerdyce (Joe Mantell), who has lost an arm; and Manet (Edward Binns), who is without a leg. The trio have kidnapped their former commander, Maj. Dichter (Curt Conway), whom they intend to execute for his displays of cowardice and ineptitude at the Battle of Antietam. As Hibbard tells Colton, who was there too, "You must remember that a line of one hundred men and horses went down like summer wheat that afternoon while Major Dichter sat on his bed composing commendations to himself." That Dichter has since become a frail and self-loathing shell of a man does little to deter his disfigured accusers from their course of vengeance.

Before any killing occurs, Colton insists that things be talked through: a mock trial. Allerdyce opens the testimony: "I'd like to be able to describe the pain of it," he says, "the agony, the torture, when a man suddenly looks across ten feet of earth and he sees his own right hand, the fingers still moving, as if pleading with you to come and get it." Manet describes the hatred he's harbored for Dichter since the war: "I wanted you tied between two horses and each set off in opposite directions. For the first time in my life I wanted to hear a scream that would make me happy." The accused seems happy to oblige. "You want your leg back? An arm? A pair of eyes?" Dichter offers. "I want you to take mine. I want you to kill me." Dichter's daughter (Deanna Lund), corralled as a character witness, attests to how the past continues to haunt her father. "He has nightmares. Sometimes I hear him walking around in his room at night," she says. "Crying for what he is, and for what he wishes he were. Crying for what he's done, and for what he never did. Just crying."

Yet the need for equalization, the ancient notion of tit for tat, persists. When Hibbard proposes "a rope or a bullet" as punishment, Colton counters with a less sanguineous solution:

> COLTON: Don't you know that there's a worse way? A longer way. A way with far more pain and far less hope. Sentence this man to living with guilt, sentence him to a nightmare that he can't wake up from, pick out that afternoon of hell and make him relive it, not just for today or tomorrow but for all the todays and all the tomorrows. That's the price of butchery, Mr. Hibbard. That's the penalty. But if you hang him, or you put a bullet through him, or you whip him to death, then you're the butchers.

In pushing for damnation over execution, Colton exiles Dichter to a place in which he's already well rooted. The trial itself is a farce, an exercise lacking judicial legitimacy. If Dichter's embittered accusers truly wanted to kill him, they'd have done the deed already. What they want are answers, some light shed on why men lose eyes, arms, legs, and lives. Dichter, as Colton argues, "couldn't

On the set of "The Homecoming of Lemuel Stove" (1965) with Brock Peters and Lloyd Bridges.

help being what he was any more than the three of you could help losing what you did." Being stuck in the past, as everyone is in this story, is an unusual narrative method for a Western; the genre tends to focus on progress, frontiers, horizons—openings.

The grip of the past is integral to the plotting of *The Loner*. Its half-hour format and lack of continuing characters aside from Colton require that each episode begins with a conflict already in place—a strategy contingent upon a complex layering of the past over the present. In many instances, Colton's arrival in a community does little to alter an overriding determinism. He's merely the catalyst and observer, as in "Escort for a Dead Man," which finds him summoned to a petered-out mining town to give assistance to a soldier, Andrew Drake (Corey Allen), who briefly served under him. Unable to face combat, Drake had faked his own death and disappeared. "War's never over for a deserter," he now says to Colton. "There's no peace in that kind of living." Drake wants to turn himself over to a court martial, where he'll likely be executed, but first he needs Colton's help evading the trio of thieves whom he swindled and who are now gunning for him.

As directed by Norman Foster, who also made such films noirs as *Kiss the Blood Off My Hands* (1948) and *Woman on the Run* (1950), "Escort for a Dead Man" is rife with noir iconography, from the entrapping shadows of the forsaken hotel where much of the story takes place to the characterization of Drake as a walking corpse. "He came in here late last night with his hat down and his collar up," Cora (Sheree North), the hotelkeeper, tells Colton, immediately linking her guest to any number of noir's doomed fugitives. "They've got the town bottled up," Drake says of the gunmen outside his hotel. "They're waiting for me." As its title implies, "Escort for a Dead Man" is a work at one with noir's fatalistic bent. There's little Drake can do to evade his fate, a point sealed when Cora betrays Drake (and Colton, his would-be escort) to the killers for a handful of gold coins. During the ensuing gun battle, Drake repeatedly yells to Colton, "I told you there's no way out of here!"

The inescapability of the past is once more paramount in "The Vespers," when Colton seeks out an old acquaintance, Booker (Jack Lord). Both men fought at the Battle of Shiloh, one of the grisliest conflicts of the war, albeit on opposite sides. Booker, we learn, followed up his military service with a stint as a hired gun, a line at which he excelled. Having foresworn violence, he's now a preacher and a pacifist. But some unsettled business remains: a gang of outlaws whose numbers Booker thinned by two. "They always find him, always," Booker's pregnant wife, Alice (Joan Freeman), laments. Colton urges Booker to reacquaint himself with that "nice warm feeling you get when you know that your gun's in your holster." Booker holds steadfast to his covenant:

> BOOKER: I promised my God I would never again fire in anger. I would never again take a human life. I cannot turn my back on that promise, not if I want to call myself a man of God. Even when I shake inside with hate, even when I know that a gun, any gun, is an extension of my arm, a part of myself—and that I have a talent for killing that is so special and so perfect. Even then, with the knowledge that there are evil men who have no excuse for staying alive, I cannot break my pact with God.

"To the West of Eden" (1966) with Lloyd Bridges and Ina Balin.

When the gunmen arrive, Booker remains at his pulpit; he has a sermon to deliver, never mind the bullets ricocheting through his church. Only when Alice is wounded does the reverend, eyes ablaze, pick up a gun and demonstrate his suppressed virtuosity. "God forgive me," he says. That violence begets violence is an axiom as old as the Good Book. Serling's addendum is that even the righteous aren't immune to its urge. He pushes the theme even further in "The Kingdom of McComb," in which some Quakers try to hire Colton to deal with the land baron who's been harassing them: "We want thee to kill McComb." The cycle of tit for tat has no end. Serling's West is one long valley of darkness.

At its far end we find the gloomy boarding-house

setting of "The Oath." Colton arrives here one night during a violent storm, to be greeted by a dying gunslinger, Billy Ford (Joby Baker). His insides poisoned from an inflamed appendix, Ford cowers in a darkened corner, unsteadily waving his shooter at the Mexicans who run the place. Upstairs, an unfriendly, alcoholic surgeon (Barry Sullivan) paces back and forth in his room, like Ahab aboard the *Pequod*. The customary plotting of such a scenario would tell us that Colton need only bring the two together—crisis solved. Up the stairs Colton marches, only to learn that the surgeon has lost one of his hands: he can no longer cut men open. He lives only to drink and seethe. The moment at which he was ushered into the nightmare world shapes everything: "A spooky horse, an overturned wagon, a railroad track—and the very foreseeable result of a locomotive wheel pitted against flesh and bone."

"The Oath" (1965) with Barry Sullivan and Lloyd Bridges.

Having been rendered useless, the surgeon has little interest in alleviating anyone else's misery. "I might tell him how lucky he is," he says to Colton of Ford. "When the appendix ruptures the pain goes away and the dying is quite quick and relatively painless—as opposed to my own, which is tedious, extended, and full of agony." With some persuasion, the surgeon finally agrees to come out of his room and guide Colton himself through the procedure. Instruments are cleaned. The patient is laid out. Through the night, Colton operates. And Ford dies anyway. Given the absence of an underlying sin (i.e. murder) that would mark Ford's death as an instance of poetic justice, it's a bitter resolution, as well as an affront to generic convention. The hero has failed; death has prevailed. To this, Serling supplies a coda of unnerving fatalism, set the following morning, in which another young gunslinger rides up to the house, pumps up his chest, and demands to see Ford: they have a score to settle. Either way, Billy Ford's days were up.

Serling's teleplay for "The Oath" draws heavily from the second half of his one-hour pilot script for *The Loner*: Billy Ford is Merriman, Colton's challenger in "An Echo for Bugles," renamed but wounded nonetheless. In both works, and in several other installments, Serling's preoccupation with the hazy division between justice and vengeance amounts to a critique of the Western hero's propensity for bloodshed. *The Loner*'s ultimate statement is that violence is inseparable from notions of American masculinity. Without his gun, a man is nothing. In "The House Rules at Mrs. Wayne's," Colton pays visit to a widow, Martha Wayne (Nancy Gates), whose husband, killed while defending her honor, was returned to her "draped over a horse like a sack of meat." Intent on shielding her son, Jamie (Lindy Davis), from such business, Martha lays out her house rules: "Don't tell him about the war, or Indians, or the things you've done," she instructs Colton. "Don't paint any pictures for him. Don't plant any seeds in his head." To this she adds: no guns around Jamie.

But Jamie already has a fair idea of how guns figure in this world. Aware that his father was killed by a local rancher, Gibson, Jamie suggests that Colton do something about it. Soon enough Colton and Jamie cross paths with Gibson (Lee Philips), who proves himself a real psychopath by forcing Jamie to look on as he viciously humiliates Colton in a saloon. Colton's passivity in the matter disgusts Jamie. Crying, he insists, "Get your gun and pay him back." When Colton demurs, Jamie delivers him a thorough tongue-lashing back at the house ("You're a coward, Mr. Colton! That's what you are!"). Martha looks on aghast, until she finds her own voice:

> COLTON: Where'd you put my gun?
> MARTHA: What do you need it for? To satisfy a little boy, you'll go off killing?
> COLTON: Martha, you've done a good job with that lad: You've taught him decency and respect, and you'll never lack for his love. But you've done one disservice to his father's good name.
> MARTHA: And that's what?
> COLTON: You forgot that elusive requirement for manhood, that thing a man calls honor.
> MARTHA: To wear a gun and to use it, is that what you call honor?
> COLTON: To know right and to know wrong, and to stand alongside one and face the other—that's what I call honor. There's one thing worse than a violent dying, Martha, and that's to be afraid of it. Now may I have my gun?

The gun, of course, is gone: Jamie's already on his way back to the saloon with it. "You won't use it, so I have to," he proclaims when Colton catches up with him. Gibson steps out, amused. Colton snatches the gun from Jamie. Gibson's hand moves to his holster. A classic showdown on a dusty street. Colton can either draw or perish. As in "An Echo of Bugles," he compromises, maiming rather than slaying his adversary. Though Jamie finally seems impressed with him, Colton makes a point of diminishing his triumph. "It's too bad I had to do what I did," he says. "Maybe someday there'll be a new breed of man—your breed. They won't wear guns. They won't have to. But it'll take some time and it'll take some doing. And it can only come after my breed is out of the way."

THE INVADERS
ABC 1967–1968

Who are the invaders? You could have been riding in the bus with one of them this morning and never suspected it. The postman might be one of them. Your dentist, too. Or your barber. You might be having lunch with one today. And it's just possible you may kiss one of them tonight.

—ABC press release, 1967

DAVID VINCENT, THE LONER HERO OF *THE INVADERS*, IS PRESENTED TO US right at the moment of his entry to the noir world. It's a scene drenched in menacing iconography: from the pitch blackness, a pair of headlamps emerge to reveal a misty, lost highway while a narrator solemnly intones, "How does a nightmare begin?" For Vincent (Roy Thinnes), it begins with an ill-advised turn off the main road in pursuit of an all-night diner. Arriving at an establishment long since deserted, he shuts off his engine and allows his eyes to roll shut. Whirring sounds and flashing lights rouse him from his nap: he awakens with a front-row view of a flying saucer descending from the sky. Like any sensible citizen, he runs to the police, only to be met with derision. Persisting with his claims, he's cast to the margins: no one wants to hear his theories about space invaders. Vincent clamors on, determined to prove that what he's witnessed is the first flash of the end of days—a full-on colonization of Earth. His quest is inexorably complicated by the deceptiveness of the invaders, who have disguised themselves in human form and infested every layer of society. They are, for the most part, indistinguishable from the regular citizenry—a fully assimilated enemy.

"The Ivy Curtain" (1967) with Roy Thinnes as David Vincent.

Vincent learns this straightaway in "Beachhead," the pilot for the series, when a sweet motel clerk (Diane Baker) to whom he turns for help reveals herself to be one of Them. "Don't fight us," she suggests. "It's going to happen; you can't stop it." Having presumed he was in human company, Vincent can only shrink in horror and run for the door. Thereafter, he

"Nightmare" (1967).

compulsively scrutinizes everyone he meets for signifiers of alienness, namely a mutated pinkie, but also a lack of heartbeat or pulse (and a correspondingly cold demeanor), only to discover that such characteristics are not shared by all aliens. While singular in purpose, they're as diverse a "people" as the humans they intend to destroy. To create space for their own kind, the aliens (whose own planet, we're told, is a dying one) come up with all manner of calamitous, *Lebensraum*-minded schemes, from speeding along climate change ("Storm") to breeding hordes of flesh-eating butterflies ("Nightmare"), all of which Vincent, in the absence of any official response, is impelled to thwart on his own. And when he does manage to corner or kill an alien, it dematerializes in a flash, leaving nothing behind. His is a confounding crusade.

Larry Cohen, who created *The Invaders*, and then passed his concept, along with a folder of story ideas, over to Quinn Martin, knew his way around the lonely noirscape. His first series, *Branded* (1965–1966), follows the itinerant adventures of a cavalry officer, Jason McCord (Chuck Connors), unjustly accused of cowardice and drummed out of the service. Each installment begins with a replay of McCord's cashiering: a stripping of his decorations and his saber, and a disgraced boot out of the fort. This ritualistic repeating of a public humiliation reinforces the notion that McCord, regardless of where he goes or what he does, is defined by his past, and asserts *Branded* as a Western of considerable pessimism. Cohen's next project was *Blue Light* (1966), about an American spy (Robert Goulet) who goes undercover in Nazi Germany; forced to conceal his true allegiance from his friends and family, he's shunned as a traitor. After that came *Coronet Blue* (1967), featuring an amnesiac (Frank Converse) who has no idea who he is or where he came from, only that some strange men seem to want him dead. In Cohen's outline for the series (which never finished its full run), the character is revealed to be a sleeper agent planted by a vague enemy, a trope explored more fully in *The Invaders*—in which Cohen's preoccupation with men stripped of identity and place in society finds a natural extension.

Because of the ridicule he invites with his doomsday message, Vincent is neither one of Them nor one of Us, but rather an outcast, a branded figure. In this he follows the legacy of innumerable noir protagonists whose complacency is upended without warning. "It's funny how a man's life can change so fast," Vincent says in "Beachhead." "After I saw that saucer, it seems as though I've been cut off from everything piece by piece." His fatalistic observation echoes the words uttered by Al Roberts in *Detour* (1945): "From then on, something else stepped in and shunted me off to a different destination than the one I'd picked for myself." It's perhaps no coincidence that an all-night diner, that bastion of noir geography, figures centrally in the destinies of both men. This is where each first steps into the shoes of noir's "wrong man," a type characterized by Foster Hirsch in *The Dark Side of the Screen* as "a plaything of malevolent noir fate" for whom "a single misstep can precipitate disaster." Roberts, however, for all his complaints about the finger of fate, is an unreliable storyteller. The journey he relates is less determined by "something else" than it is by his own masochistic curiosity. Vincent, too, exhibits this trait, though his tale is at least legitimized by the observations of the neutral yet authoritative Narrator (Bill Woodson).

Prior to the night when "David Vincent, architect, returning home from a business trip" took his own detour from the main road, the future entailed all the securities and comforts an ambitious professional might expect. In veering from the prescribed path—in following one sign ("Bud's Diner–Open 24 Hours") but failing to see a second, more critical marking ("Road Closed")—he moves toward a different and far less certain destiny. While chance is inarguably party to this (how else to explain his encountering a flying saucer in the middle of nowhere?), the fact that Vincent steers himself to the gate of his nightmare-calling is critical to the presentation of him as a hero. Joseph Campbell says as much in *The Hero With a Thousand Faces*: "A blunder—apparently the merest chance—reveals an unsuspected world, and the individual is drawn into a relationship with forces that are not rightly understood." From the moment he makes an ill-advised turn, Vincent's center of gravity shifts to zones unknown. "Once having traversed the threshold," Campbell writes, "the hero moves in a dream landscape of curiously fluid, ambiguous forms, where he must survive a succession of trials."

Vincent's crossing from his old life to his new calling is handled in oneiric terms. Such constructions are crucial to the noir story's emphasis on the subjective experience. Memories, dreams, and fantasies linger on in the ordinary world, shaping events, attitudes, and perceptions, but also smudging the boundary between the real and the unreal. Vincent's close encounter outside a diner "at a few minutes past four on a lost Tuesday morning" is similarly ambiguous. The question of whether he's merely experiencing the hypnogogic vision of "a man too long without sleep to continue his journey" is left open-ended: his nightmare begins but never ends. Joseph Sergeant, who directed "Beachhead," initiates the landing of the saucer by pulling back to reveal with Olympian clarity the desolate clearing in which Vincent has parked. With a snap cut, Vincent is shown in close-up, his eyes fluttering in indication of REM sleep, the stage of unconsciousness in which dreams occur. A red, pulsating glow begins to play across his face, cueing a tighter framing movement. The light steadily intensifies until, as Anthony Wilson describes in his teleplay, Vincent's "eyes are abruptly jarred open—he is suddenly, glaringly awake as if some sixth sense had reached into his brain and wrenched him from his sleeping state." Vincent's anxious gaze holds for a long beat before giving way to the vision that will unalterably change his life.

"Beachhead" (1967).

Later, when Vincent drags his business partner (James Daly) and a local detective (J.D. Cannon) to the clearing, he looks quite the fool, and not for the last time. The sign for "Bud's Diner" now reads "Kelly's Diner." The young honeymooning couple who have pitched a tent in the field where Vincent insists a spaceship landed claim not to have seen or heard anything unusual. His story debunked, Vincent becomes belligerent. "It was here! Right here!" he shouts to a jury of stony, judgmental faces. Back in the office, madly turning out pencil sketches of the UFO imprinted in his head, he remains agitated. The elements of his trauma, and the paranoia it has sown, are clicked into place with a telling comment from his partner, Landers, who likens Vincent's ramblings about aliens to how, after his service in Korea, Vincent "kept talking about what 'they' were doing." Vincent, we gather, has been fixated on rooting out the enemy, any enemy, for some time.

That night Vincent returns, alone, to the clearing and provokes a fight with the campers; innocuous and fair-haired earlier in the day, they are by dark of night menacing and glow-eyed—precisely the enemy invaders Vincent suspected them to be. Knocked unconscious by their fleeing trailer, Vincent awakens in a hospital, and immediately accuses the staff of being un-human; unsurprisingly, his next room is in the psych ward. From here on, he sees everything as a conspiracy against him. He finishes "Beachhead," and begins his quest, shorn of home (burned by the aliens); partner (murdered by the aliens); and livelihood (tarnished by tabloid reporters). With nothing left, he reconscripts himself into service as David Vincent, hunter of aliens. "How does a nightmare end? Perhaps, for David Vincent, it will never end," the Narrator offers. Vincent, by all accounts, is locked in this dream-state.

"Beachhead" (1967) with Roy Thinnes and Diane Baker.

Cohen was especially taken with the picaresque thrillers of Alfred Hitchcock, specifically the trope of a hero wrapped up in events so fantastic they defy belief. From "Beachhead" on, there are numerous instances of Vincent leading the authorities to a site of alien wrongdoing only to find that it's been stripped clean of their presence, as happens to Roger Thornhill in *North By Northwest* (1959) when he brings the police back to the villain's lair (so he says) and is looked on as a nutjob. For Vincent, such patterns of disconcertment, the embarrassment of having his claims invalidated by evidence to the contrary, only deepen his stigmatization. He's repeatedly having to defend his version of reality against what everyone else sees, or wants to see. The absurdity, posed so frequently in the noir thriller, of appearing insane while speaking the truth acquires a frustrating nightmare logic. This same paradigm is also at work in a pair of Cold War "B" pictures, William Cameron Menzies's *Invaders from Mars* (1953) and Don Siegel's *Invasion of the Body Snatchers* (1956), both of which, in their metaphorical linking of communist menace to otherworldly threat, influenced *The Invaders*.

In Menzies's film, child astronomy buff David MacClean (Jimmy Hunt) springs from bed at four o'clock one morning to gaze at the stars, only to witness a spaceship landing in a nearby field. His father goes to investigate, returning, hours later, as a soulless simulacrum, robotic and hostile. Mom follows suit, along with most everybody in town. The security of childhood is replaced with terror and dread, an uncertainty Menzies visualizes with all sorts of Germanic camera tricks. In the face of such a nightmare, David, like his namesake in *The Invaders*, quickly gathers that no one is to be trusted. Much the same happens in Siegel's picture, except here the tone is more realistic, grounded in the recognizable before shifting to horror. The befuddled hero is no child prone to fanciful flights, but rather a man of science. Dr. Miles Bennell (Kevin McCarthy) arrives home from a business trip to find his community in the grip of a "strange neurosis, evidently contagious, an epidemic of mass hysteria." He discovers that pods from outer space are the cause: his friends and neighbors are being transformed into hollow strangers in their sleep, their human forms preserved as hosts for parasitic alien beings. The film climaxes with Bennell, sole holdout, being chased by the Pod People to a freeway, where he shouts out to the passing drivers, "They're after you! They're after all of us!" before turning to the camera and warning all of America, "They're here already! You're next!"

Lest the audience mistake the make-believe, *Body Snatchers* (like *Mars*) is given a framing whereby the events are once removed, a construction *The Invaders* pointedly avoids. Siegel begins and ends his story with Bennell in custody, raving as one would when confronted with total annihilation. His pleas of "I'm not crazy!" and "Listen to me before it's too late!" neatly foreshadow the warnings that come tumbling out of Vincent in *The Invaders*. The fear of death, delivered on the nightmare platter of illogic, activates the intensest of responses: here's the thing to be fought at all costs—the reason to remain alert and vigilant. In all three works, alienness is signified by an absence of core emotions, a deadening of sentiment and life-spark. Though they've dispensed with heart and soul, these alien "others" retain the facility of mind to deceive and manipulate. Theirs is a devious plan of consensual domination: to resist them is to resist the majority, so why not give in and join the party? In *Body Snatchers*, Bennell faces tremendous pressure to stop running and fall in with the swelling ranks of

Poster for *Invasion of the Body Snatchers* (film, 1956).

Detail, *The Invaders* comic No. 2 (1967).

LEFT: *Invaders from Mars* (1953).

FROM TOP TO BOTTOM:
"Vikor" (1967).
"The Innocent" (1967).
"Summit Meeting" (1967).

Pod People, whose persuasive tactics center around the advantages to be had in a world no longer sullied by displays of emotion.

Yet to reject conformity is to embrace one's own humanness, messy as it may be. Or, as Siegel put it: "To not be a pod is to look for challenges and even welcome unhappiness—to affirm your existence." This same dialectic courses through much of *The Invaders*; the struggle between conformity and alienation being crucial to the placement of the noir hero at odds with the social fabric. In seeking to uproot a well-entrenched menace, Vincent makes himself quite the pariah. Roy Thinnes, with his thrice-broken nose (bar fights), imbues his alien hunter with churlish impatience. Alan A. Armer, who produced the series (and, before that, *The Fugitive*), has said that Thinnes "tended to play the role as if the world were against him." But it's precisely this paranoiac, persecuted persona—a high-strung response to the highest of stakes—that's required of the show's premise. Driven as he is by the urgency of needing to be believed before it's all too late, Vincent can come off as boorish, callous, edgy (he seems to subsist on cigarettes and coffee), pugnacious, overzealous, passionate—a fanatic. "I have a job to do, stopping them. It's all I live for, you understand?" he barks in "The Believers."

Vincent's view of self is largely determined by the ticking clock he faces, and thus runs in defiance of the way society at large, trundling along obliviously, perceives him, hence the derogative descriptions his persona summons: "He's a mental case. He's been treated for delusions and fantasies. Tells the police wild stories about things that simply don't exist." ("Vikor"); "This isn't the first time he's had people running around in circles because of his paranoid delusions—he specializes in false alarms." ("Quantity: Unknown") In "Summit Meeting," when warned about his surly, accusatory behavior, Vincent snaps back, "Well, it's kept me alive for the last two years!" In choosing to sacrifice his future so that everyone else may have one, Vincent pays a terrible price. "You know, I've given up my life to fight them—my girl, my business, my plans," he says in "The Innocent." Yet Vincent rarely harbors doubts about his mission or thoughts of surrendering, not even when, in another bit of foul play borrowed from *North by Northwest*, the aliens pour a bottle of rye down his throat and hand him his car keys.

Later in "The Innocent," courtesy of the aliens' ability to induce hallucinatory states in humans, Vincent is seemingly reunited with his former sweetheart, Helen (Katherine Justice), who tries to sell him on how glorious life will be once the aliens complete their conquest. "They can teach us how not to let emotions get in the way of what we want," she says. "That's what happened to us, isn't it? We didn't think clearly. We were so in love that everything was an emotional crisis." Vincent, who has been to this point begrudgingly impressed with Helen's tour of idyll alien-America, now frowns. "It's all wrong, it's all wrong!" he cries out as the illusion evaporates and he finds himself back in the present surrounded by stony-faced aliens. Stunts like these only affirm Vincent's favoring of resistance over capitulation. He refuses to allow his humanity to be compromised. "You're so used to emotion you wouldn't know what to do without it," an alien agent (Diana Hyland) scolds him in "Summit Meeting." "You love but you also hate. You're happy but you're miserable. You love peace, but you make war. You despise us. I'm sorry, David; your way is no better." Yet emotions, unwieldy or contrary as they may be, are what define and defend the human spirit. By this, *The Invaders* pushes beyond mere anti-communist parable to take a stand against dehumanization.

Everywhere Vincent goes he encounters people who've already succumbed to the corruptive influence of the aliens. The lure of material gain, peppered with an intimidating nudge, all but guarantees a steady flow of human collaborationists. In "The Ivy Curtain," the aliens enlist an aging charter pilot to ferry batches of arriving invaders to an indoctrination center. Though Barney Cahill (Jack Warden) suspects something to be off about the arrangement, the bankroll slipped in his pocket—more money than he's ever seen—is more than enough to gain his cooperation. His morals are further compromised by his much younger wife, Stacy (Susan Oliver), who demands all the things beyond her husband's reach. "He has no guts. He had them all shot out in World War Two," she complains to Vincent. Figuring that her share of Barney's increased fortune might suffer were Barney to answer Vincent's queries, Stacy rats the both of them out to the aliens. "I needed the money!" she howls when she learns that Barney will die because of her betrayal. In the end, the Narrator informs us, Vincent leaves town "grimly aware that human behavior can sometimes seem as alien as creatures from another world."

In "Vikor," the aliens find an ideal human collaborator in the form of a dysphoric industrialist to whom they promise "wealth and power beyond your wildest dreams." George Vikor (Jack Lord), a veteran, crippled in Korea, hobbles about pining for that intangible something that will make him feel whole again. Meanwhile, his wife, Sherri (Diana Hyland), has turned alcoholic due to his emotional neglect. Rather than address his marriage, Vikor spends all hours at his factory churning out the regeneration chambers the aliens use to fabricate their humanness. When Vincent learns of this, he insinuates himself into Sherri's confidence and urges her to confront Vikor about the "foreign investors" he seems so intent on pleasing:

> SHERRI: Why, George, why are you doing this awful thing?
> VIKOR: For you. I want you to have everything.
> SHERRI: I had everything, remember?
> VIKOR: Don't you understand, Sherri? They'll be running this planet, and we'll be right on top with them. We'll have everything we ever wanted.

"Vikor" (1967) with Jack Lord.

"Condition: Red" (1967) with Jason Evers and Antoinette Bower.

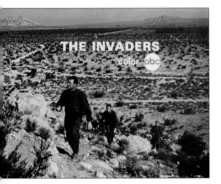

Network interstitial for *The Invaders* (1967).

VINCENT: Excellent terms. All you have to do is sell out the human race.
VIKOR: Yeah, our precious human race. Liars, phonies, hypocrites. When I came back from Korea, I was the big war hero. Medals, interviews, all kinds of fancy promises—until I really needed help. All I asked for was a small loan to start a crummy sheet metal shop. That's when I got my lesson in humanity. They told me a guy with a wooden leg and a plate in his head was a lousy financial risk. Sorry, chum, business is business. The only place you can borrow money on a Medal of Valor is in a hockshop. Their promises are as phony as they are.

As Vincent is quick to point out, Vikor's embittered justification of treason rings as hollow as the trust he places in the aliens. Swelled with self-deception, Vikor remains blind to this until Nexus (Alfred Ryder), his alien partner, outlines the necessity of dispatching Sherri, who has learned too much. When Vikor hesitates, Nexus appeals directly to his feelings of inadequacy: "A slave population of billions, but you won't be a slave. You'll be a master. You're a very sensible man, Mr. Vikor. How can you possibly give up so much for so little?" Hearing it like that, Vikor scurries away, leaving his wife at the mercy of the aliens.

Domestic discord is also at play in "Condition: Red," in which Dan Keller (Jason Evers), a NORAD officer, wakes up in the middle of the night to find his spouse, Laurie (Antoinette Bower), missing, triggering all sorts of marital anxieties. The truth is even worse: she's an alien, and her nocturnal disappearances are due to her pilfering secrets from his briefcase and delivering them to a mysterious house in the woods. Scenes of Laurie riding to her rendezvous point astride a white stallion vividly encapsulate the sexual sway she holds over her human mate. When Keller questions her whereabouts, she leads him up to the bedroom, knocks him under with a strange crown-like contraption, and sucks more secrets from his head. "The Betrayed" navigates an equally sordid family dynamic: patriarch Simon Carver (Ed Begley) is an oilman with a secret past; his severe wife Evelyn (Nancy Wickwire) is secretly an alien; and his daughter, Susan (Laura Devon), from his first marriage, is not-so-secretly in love with Vincent. Having heard of strange happenings out by the Carver derricks, Vincent has hired on under false pretenses; he, too, has a secret. Things boil over when Vincent uncovers an object of value to the aliens. Evelyn, leveraging her knowledge of Simon's shady dealings, pressures Susan to get it back; unwilling to expose her father to scandal, Susan starts taking orders from the aliens—a spiral of treachery that sparks several deaths, including her own.

The deadly, duplicitous female is essential to the plotting of *The Invaders*. Unlike the spider women of the classic cycle, who tend to behave autonomously, and purely for self-gain, the "specimens" on display here, whether human or alien, act the part because they've been instructed (or coerced) to do so. They're controlled agents, much like the lady-communists in *I Led 3 Lives*. In "The Mutation" we learn early on, before Vincent, that Vikki (Suzanne Pleshette), a stripper in a seedy border-town cantina, is an alien assigned to lure Vincent to his death. When Vincent hires Vikki to lead him out to the spot in the desert where she saw "this thing, like lights flashing, fire everywhere," it's an arrangement that generates some trepidation on our part. Perhaps because Vikki, on account of her profession, appears to have a heartbeat, Vincent relaxes his customary guard; were he not so eager to photograph the alien wreckage she's described, our hero might (we hope) exercise more caution. Vikki enacts her role of femme fatale with calculation—hence her half-open bathrobe and erotic yet unobtainable persona upon their first meeting. Once she's hooked Vincent into taking a long drive out to where her friends with ray guns lay in wait, she re-costumes herself in a masculine dress shirt, work jeans, and a hair-covering bandana, all the better to keep her prey sufficiently glued to his seat.

"The Mutation" (1967) with Suzanne Pleshette.

Yet Vikki is unique among aliens in that she's capable of empathy, a mutation that not only moves her to reverse course and protect Vincent from certain death but to express an attraction for him. "Before I met you, I was ashamed of caring because there was no one to care for, but now there is, and I want to stay with you," she admits. When Vincent rejects her, Vikki calls in the alien assassins, only to change her mind again. Vikki's shifting moods, her human-like emotionalism, control the events of the plot; Vincent, unable to decipher her true nature, is kept guessing until the very end. Only when Vikki perishes trying to save him does he learn the price of his caution. Though a source of great tension in this and other episodes, Vincent's incessant sussing out of the fatale from the femme is critical to his survival. But it also demonstrates how *The Invaders* upends generic convention to sustain its undercurrent of paranoia. Our traditional expectation of such fare is that the hero be paired with an attractive opposite for at least part of his quest, a design toyed with in the series through the implicit suggestion that every female Vincent encounters has probably been put in his path to confuse, impede, and likely kill him.

"The Mutation" (1967) with Roy Thinnes.

Elyse Reynolds (Carol Lynley) of "The Believers" is introduced to Vincent in the secret alien prison where both of them are being kept. (Elyse because of her expertise in human psychology; Vincent because he remains a thorn in their side.) Right away, Elyse, who's smart and has big, bright eyes (and passes the pulse test), insinuates herself into Vincent's confidence by helping him escape the place. Though he's initially skeptical of her allegiance, Vincent finally warms to Elyse when she delivers a tearful, highly emotive description of how her brother was abducted by the aliens. Because she's proved herself sufficiently human, Elyse is allowed in Vincent's small circle of like-minded alien-baiters— all of whom promptly becomes targets of alien assassins. Having already fallen for Elyse, Vincent is crushed to learn that she's a turncoat; her excuse that she was forced to betray him only underscores the extortive grasp of the aliens he's sworn to defeat. Throughout the series, the reliability of those whom Vincent interacts with is kept deliberately vague. He's forever having to set traps for

"Quantity: Unknown" (1967) with Jack Weston.

"The Ivy Curtain" (1967).

"Moonshot" (1967) with John Ericson.

people to determine whether they're on his side or with the aliens. Vincent's inability to trust anyone he meets, and by extension the viewer's immediate distrust of every character aside from Vincent, are at the core of *The Invaders*.

The femmes fatale of *The Invaders* enact the bidding of an invasive force which in itself represents a "feminine" threat, a notion reinforced first by the aliens' protruding pinkies—an attempt by Cohen to telegraph their secretiveness and otherness via, in his words, "a symbol of effeminacy"—and secondly by the aliens' narrative embodiment of the female-as-destroyer, a uniquely noir trope. Scheming, mysterious, wily, the aliens can be seen as seeking to undermine, or emasculate, the patriarchal engine of the U.S. at a time of great vulnerability, from the war in Vietnam to civil unrest at home to the escalation of the space race. Numerous scenarios deal with the aliens' infiltration of the military-industrial complex, such as "Moonshot," which revolves around a much-heralded lunar launch. Here, in an episode predating Apollo 11 by two years, we have a team of astronauts on target for fulfilling Kennedy's mandate of landing a man on the moon and returning him safely to Earth; instead they're killed off by the aliens.

Enter the alternate crew, led by national hero Hardy Smith (John Ericson), who, as Vincent uncovers, is really an alien sleeper agent—his human counterpart, the real Hardy Smith, having been killed in Vietnam a few years prior and replaced with a lookalike. The image of Smith staring blankly in a mirror while artificially inducing the heartbeat required of him to pass a pre-flight physical is chilling in its innocuousness (he could just as well be brushing his teeth), and plays directly upon the endemic "enemy amongst us" dread of the Cold War era. Vincent's paranoid but correct assumption that Hardy Smith is not Hardy Smith illustrates that aspect of *The Invaders* most readily exploited in the promotion of the show to viewers. "Face it, they're here among us now, in your city, maybe on your block," a network press release warned. "They're invaders, alien beings from another planet, but they look just like us!"

As Armer, the series producer, explained, "people like to be scared out of their wits, but they're no longer frightened by three-headed monsters, so we've made the invaders look just like the folks next door." If the aim of such marketing was to unsettle the audience, to make it aware of its own vulnerability, the program's depiction of the alien invaders as a secret society operating from within certainly seals the point. "If we are going to poison their minds, sow seeds of hate and destruction, we must be convincing," a class of alien subversives soon to be infiltrating America are instructed in "The Ivy Curtain." The aliens' greatest asset is that they're already among the populace. Only Vincent, operating on the peripheries, is uniquely situated to recognize the alienness of others. And for that he's labeled a lunatic. *The Invaders* puts us dead center on the slippery existential terrain of the noir nightmare.

KOLCHAK: THE NIGHT STALKER
ABC 1972–1975

They broke me down, broke my story down, telling me how it hadn't happened the way I claimed.

—Carl Kolchak

I N *KOLCHAK*, A HORROR-NOIR HYBRID, THE MYTH OF THESEUS AND THE MINOTAUR is given a paranoiac spin. Carl Kolchak (Darren McGavin), our hero, is both a monster-slayer and an investigative journalist, two lines of work he's compacted into one. Kolchak is forever on the scent of the big scoop that might return him to New York, where he was once a star reporter. Exiled to the provinces, and having been fired from rags in Las Vegas and Seattle, he hangs his two-dollar hat at the Chicago outpost of the International News Service. It's here, from a desk that rattles whenever the "L" thunders by, that he types up his encounters with things that go bump in the night. Handed over to his editor, Tony Vincenzo (Simon Oakland), the irritable, close-minded type, Kolchak's outlandish accounts induce yelling and ridicule, along with repeated suggestions that he seek "professional help". "I expect you to report!" Vincenzo hollers. "Not to come up with fairy tales!" Myths and legends figure significantly in Kolchak's adventures, for the monsters he encounters embody an ageless and pervasive fear of the dark.

As we learn in *The Night Stalker* (1972), the television movie that spawned the series, Kolchak has quite the knack for exposing what lurks in shadow, in this instance a centuries-old vampire on the loose in Las Vegas. When young women, all engaged in graveyard-shift casino jobs, begin appearing in the morgue drained of their blood, Kolchak wonders whether the culprit might be "some nutcase who's seen too many vampire movies." After witnessing the fanged, pale-faced, cape-clad suspect, Janos Skorzeny (Barry Atwater), survive two dozen gunshots while tossing scores of policemen around like pillows, he revises his theory: "I hate to say this, but it looks as if we have a real, live vampire on our hands." Although Kolchak is correct, the authorities treat him with hostility, even as

Publicity still for *Kolchak* with Darren McGavin as Carl Kolchak.

ABOVE:
The Night Stalker (1972).

RIGHT: "The Vampire" (1974).

they remain stumped. "Despite the helicopters, the highway patrol, the Jeep posse; despite the blocking of every major road and highway; despite the mass coverage of Las Vegas by every available man in both police and sheriff departments," he tells us, "Janos Skorzeny was still at large." So Kolchak, armed with a wooden stake and a sturdy mallet, takes it upon himself to track and slay the vampire.

After filing the story he's sure will propel him back to the big leagues of newspapering, Kolchak tells his showgirl girlfriend, Gail (Carol Lynley), to pack up for New York: "Kolchak's coming back in style!" Skipping off to City Hall, where he expects to be congratulated, he's instead put through the wringer. Earlier, the local FBI man, Bernie Jenks (Ralph Meeker), a friend, had tried to warn Kolchak about stepping on too many official toes: "You're not the only one who likes to play detective." And now Kolchak, having succeeded where the authorities have failed, is to bear their wrath—a murder one charge. Paine (Kent Smith), the district attorney, and Butcher (Claude Akins), the sheriff, lead the inquisition. With Kolchak's story replaced with one of their own, all that remains is for Kolchak himself to be silenced. "If you open your mouth," Butcher warns, "we'll find you, bring you back, and put you away forever."

Given the option of jail or exile, Kolchak reaches for the phone to notify Gail. "She's not there," rumbles Jenks while Paine fills in the rest: "She's an undesirable element, Kolchak, and we don't want undesirable elements in Las

Vegas." From this cryptic line we cut to a tight shot of Kolchak behind the wheel of his car, a shot that gradually widens to reveal the diminishing skyline of the Strip in the distance. In voiceover, Kolchak tells us how he went broke placing notices for Gail all around the country but never saw her again. He finishes the film as he started it, alone in a dingy room, telling his incredible tale to his portable tape recorder. It's a bitter pattern of triumph capped with defeat to be repeated through a sequel, *The Night Strangler* (1973), and twenty episodes of the subsequent series, officially titled *Kolchak: The Night Stalker*. Though Kolchak always vanquishes the monster, he can never overcome an inherently rotten establishment. Like Theseus, he's fated to walk the labyrinth, only the thread meant to lead him out has instead been hung around his neck.

The Night Strangler (1973).

Airing in the spring of 1972, *The Night Stalker* was seen by a record audience of seventy-five million. Its pitting of a truth-seeking, wisecracking Everyman against the dual adversaries of fantastical evil and ruthless authority has ensured its cult status four decades on. While the vampire itself is pure Lugosi-kitsch, the world it terrorizes is recognizably contemporary and shamefully corrupt. This grounding of the outré within a shell of realism, while an integral part of Richard Matheson's teleplay, was already imbedded in the source material, *The Kolchak Papers*, a then-unpublished manuscript by Jeff Rice, a reporter for a Las Vegas daily. Rice guised his novella as a work of nonfiction submitted by "an irascible second-rate journalist named Carl Kolchak"—a first-person account transcribed "just the way he first set it down in his notes and on tape." In the prologue, he writes of his initial impression of Kolchak, post-disgrace, now working the lower circles of Hollywood flackdom, at a press event in August of 1970:

> He was seedy, gross, aggressive, slightly drunk, and a general hindrance to all of us. But he was also extremely persuasive in his later attempts to get me up to his shabby one-room apartment on the pretext of letting me in on "one of the biggest crime stories of the decade." . . . I felt then that there was something unbalanced about Mr. Kolchak.

Though Rice assures the reader that he's verified Kolchak's account as best he can, along with "cleaning up Kolchak's language, much of which consisted of four-letter words," already there's a suggestion that Kolchak isn't the most reliable of storytellers—an accusation he faces repeatedly in the series. Kolchak himself touches on his familiarity with tall tales in *The Kolchak Papers* when he mentions how his Romanian grandfather filled his ear with all manner of fiendish bedtime stories that "kept me up half the night afterwards."

Rice's double epigraph for the book, memorably paraphrased in Matheson's teleplay, outlines the sociological and psychic terrain Kolchak occupies:

> Socially, a journalist fits in somewhere between a whore and a bartender. But spiritually he stands beside Galileo. He knows the world is round.
>
> —Sherman Reilly Duffy, *Chicago Daily Journal*

Socially, I fit in just fine between the whore and the bartender—both are close friends. And I knew the world was round. I then discovered flat, and that there are things dark and terrible waiting just over the edge to reach out and snatch life from the unlucky wanderer.

—Carl Kolchak, *Las Vegas Daily News*

In his own wanderings, Kolchak treads the uneasy seam between "flat" and "round" with surprising sure-footedness. While he occasionally loses his direction, he never relinquishes his bearing—his nose for news. Confronted with the inexplicable, he persists, even if it requires him to steer his investigation into the parallel plane of the supernatural.

Aside from the vampire of the first telefeature, and the 144-year-old serial killer of the second, Kolchak's travels through the labyrinth bring him face-to-face with Jack the Ripper, a zombie, an invisible alien, a vampiric prostitute, a werewolf, a flaming specter, a satanic senatorial candidate, a shape-shifter, a swamp creature, an energy eater, a rakshasa, an android, a killer ape, a witch, a headless motorcyclist, a succubus, a mummy, a medieval knight, Helen of Troy (as a ghoul), and a primeval lizard. With each quest, Kolchak's ability to function within the seemingly contradictory conceits of both "round" and "flat" enables him to serve as a superior investigator. Yet his own accounting of each triumph, the story with which he hopes to restore his professional reputation, is invariably squashed, discredited, or debunked. As the mystery writer and critic Stuart M. Kaminsky has noted, "Though Kolchak told the truth, he had to live with the pain of never being believed." Because Kolchak's findings refute the prevailing world view, he's cast to the margins, isolated and made to look the paranoid, a condition largely brought on by the institutional denial of his claims.

In an era marred by political scandal and economic recession, Kolchak's adversarial encounters with authority lent him considerable appeal. "I saw a man who is a man with a dream like many others in this country today," McGavin said of his character. "A man beaten by the stock market, kicked down by his situation, fired from a job, dropped down below his point of acceptance in life and scrambling to get back up. To me, he was like the heroes of the 1930s." A striver and a hustler, Kolchak isn't above supplementing his formidable reportage with subterfuge, lies, impersonations, break-ins ("Where there's a window, there's a way"), even bribes, so long as it gets him closer to the heart of the story. More than once, he flashes his INS credentials as if he were a government agent. Only through a little shape-shifting of his own is Kolchak able to sidestep the threshold guardians intent on impeding his progress through the labyrinth.

Hewing to the narrative formula of investigative noir, while at the same time drawing from the dark pool of horror, the series puts forth a dominant night setting filled with bestial forces ever ready to prey on mankind. *The Night Strangler* opens with an off-duty go-go dancer strolling apprehensively through a shadowed alley. "Is someone there?" she calls out, her final words. It's usually an awful incident like this that brings Kolchak, alerted by his police scanner, clattering to the scene, portable tape recorder slung over one shoulder, rinky-dink camera on the other. Immediately, he's greeted with derision and sneers: "Somebody throw a net over Kolchak!" a cop

A publicity still for *Kolchak* (1974).

will shout out. "I think he's about ready for the rubber room!" ("They Have Been, They Are, They Will Be . . .") From the start, there's a cloud of conspiracy over whatever grisly violence has transpired; Kolchak, sensing that facts are being withheld—from him, if not the public—starts digging. It's a construction redolent of private-eye fiction: the uncooperative police stumble along ineffectually while Kolchak, working outside the sanction of the law and unconstrained by its limited perspective, solves the mystery.

Most of the monsters Kolchak confronts have their corresponding archetypes in film noir. The femme fatale becomes the alluring fashion-model witch of "The Trevi Collection"; the corrupt politician becomes the soul-selling senator of "The Devil's Platform"; the revenge-minded criminal becomes the returned-from-the-dead avenger of "The Zombie," and so on. But the monsters of horror are also paradoxical creations, at once feared and denied. As Van Helsing points out in *Dracula* (1898), "The strength of the vampire is that people will not believe him." Kolchak, however, keeps an open reporter's mind. By following each lead to its logical end, no matter how illogical it may seem, he adheres to the exigencies of journalism, which are much the same as detection: the story, or case, is finished when the hidden truth is revealed. So whether the clues point to, say, a bone-sucking extraterrestrial ("They Have Been, They Are, They Will Be . . ."), or a resurrected Aztec deity ("Legacy of Terror"), he pursues the story accordingly. By fitting the pieces of the puzzle together into a cohesive narrative, he arrives at both the scoop and the solution.

Yet because the truths he uncovers make mockery of the official stance on things, Kolchak earns the everlasting resentment of those in power. In "The Zombie," he characterizes his relationship with the local constabulary as "long and bloody, like the Crusades, only without the chivalry." In fact, Kolchak does

"They Have Been, They Are, They Will Be . . ." (1974).

ABOVE: *The Night Strangler* (1973).

Publicity still for *Kolchak* (1974).

have a touch of chivalry; he essentially fancies himself a knight errant, a valorous dispatcher of evil, although underlying motivations remain nebulous. The question of whether he represents the interests of the public so as to promote his own becomes a frequent topic in his heated censorship battles with Vincenzo, as in this one from *The Night Stalker*:

> VINCENZO: You know darn well why we're soft-pedaling this thing.
>
> KOLCHAK: No, tell me why? Could it be because we have been told to?
>
> VINCENZO: Kolchak, you are an idiot. Worse, you're irresponsible. All these murders mean to you is a byline.
>
> KOLCHAK: Well, what the hell difference does it matter what it means to me? The point is that we are suppressing news. We are withholding information.

His protestations aside, Kolchak's ambition to reclaim lost glories by delivering the truth draws him deeply into the night. Though not entirely fearless, he's dogged enough to go down holes others avoid, as in *The Night Strangler* when his pursuit of the monster takes him through a forgotten city beneath the real one, a place out of time. Wandering the dark avenues of this dreamworld, our hero casts a steadfast if lonely shadow.

The prewar era that McGavin cites as shaping Kolchak's values also marks the heyday of the horror picture—namely, the iconic monsters unleashed by Universal-International in the 1930s, but also the starkly atmospheric noir-horror melodramas produced by Val Newton's unit at RKO in the 1940s. With their common root in Weimar cinema, the horror film and film noir have intertwined like the gnarled branches of an old tree. Typically set in dreamlike realms of eternal night, both forms traffic in stories of transgression, entrapment, and dread. Equally strident is their obeisance to a deterministic construction, as in *The Wolf Man* (1941), when hapless Larry Talbot (Lon Chaney, Jr.), recent victim of a strange animal bite, is informed, "Even a man who is pure in heart and says his prayers by night may become a wolf when the wolf bane blooms and the autumn moon is bright." Just as noir is fascinated with the expression of repressed urges, horror thrives on the tension between id and super-ego, a conflict played out in scenarios of uncontrollable human-inhuman transmutation, something Kolchak contends with regularly.

The tropes of horror, drawn as they are from fireside scare stories passed down through the ages, coalesce to provide what J.P. Telotte, in *Dreams of Darkness* (1985), describes as a "labyrinthine, indeterminate, and dark perspective on the modern world and its rule of reason." In playing upon our deep-welled but

"The Spanish Moss Murders" (1974).

seldom-exercised urge for a splash of total chaos, the horror story wickedly allows us to entertain, if only temporarily, a host of dark desires that centuries of religious and rational rule have sought to suppress. Simultaneously, we cross fingers that somebody heroic will come along (with a silver bullet or special stake) and put everything back in order. The pleasures derived from such stories stem from their intensification of the tension between forbidden desire and socially mandated behavior. Most of the monsters of horror are but manifestations of the irrational urges tucked away in the darkest recesses of the human psyche—like the bogeyman summoned into existence in "The Spanish Moss Murders" by a patient in a sleep disorder clinic. By recasting these unseemly terrors in modern contexts, fictions like *Kolchak* remind us of the forces that lay in waiting outside rational dominion.

In the horror-noir, the real world (round) and the other side (flat) overlap, often insidiously, and rarely with warning. Kolchak, unlike the rationalists with whom he clashes, has his feet in both realms. He spends a good portion of each quest waiting, watching, and lurking in the same shadows that obscure the creeping actions of the monsters he pursues. He's also explicitly linked to his quarries, as in "The Werewolf" when the captain of an ocean liner beset with lycanthrope troubles threatens to put Kolchak in irons for asking too many questions—never mind the man-beast ripping passengers apart by the light of the full moon. From *The Night Stalker* on, the authorities are as concerned with halting Kolchak's unofficial investigations as they are with stopping the creatures gobbling up their citizenry. Kolchak, in his pursuit of truth, is apparently the bigger threat, a point underscored by the transference of nomenclature from the original telefeature, in which the vampire is the "night stalker," to the official title of the subsequent series, which casts Kolchak himself as the one who stalks the night.

"Mr. R.I.N.G." (1975) with Darren McGavin and Craig Baxley.

"Mr. R.I.N.G." (1975) with Darren McGavin and Simon Oakland.

In "Mr. R.I.N.G.," as Kolchak tries to untangle a conspiracy involving the military-industrial complex, we're shown how the series twists a newspaper-noir plot à la *All the President's Men* (1976) around its monster-of-the-week core. A teaser takes us inside a secret research facility wherein renowned scientist Avery Walker is tinkering with his latest creation, an android; when Walker turns his back to fiddle with some knobs, the android (Craig Baxley) craftily rises up from its slab, kills Walker, and beats a hasty exit. Official line on the incident: Heart attack claims Nobel Prize winner. Kolchak, assigned to write the obituary, a task he feels beneath his talents, begins to suspect a bigger story when his perfunctory questions about Walker's work elicit slammed doors, zipped lips, and vague threats. Meanwhile, the escaped android, enacting the plight of noir's convict-on-the-lam, only with the limited social capacity of someone encountering the outside world for the first time, causes considerable havoc.

Like most of Kolchak's adventures, "Mr. R.I.N.G." follows a diaristic approach to narrative by unfolding in recollection, as a narrated flashback—drawing on a fluidity of past and present essential to investigative noir. Through voiceover, as relayed to his ever-present tape recorder, Kolchak shapes his passage through the labyrinth. This is his story, his exclusive: we're hearing and seeing it as he re-tells it. "Mr. R.I.N.G.," from a teleplay by L. Ford Neale and John Huff, begins forebodingly, with Kolchak, wearier than usual, staggering into his office and reaching for his recorder:

> KOLCHAK: I don't know when exactly I was in this office last. In some ways it seems like I never left—but no, no, that's not right. For at least a few days I was away, far away, in the hands of men with no faces and no names. They broke me down, broke my story down, telling me how it hadn't happened the way I claimed. At least I think that's what they did—between injections.

Even before Kolchak's journey begins, we know that our intrepid reporter will rouse some very dangerous parties; that his quest will not end well; and that he's been drugged. His tale, in essence one long, lucidly reconstituted memory, proceeds with a taste of defeat already in play.

By committing his adventures to audiotape, Kolchak documents events that are soon to be "watered down, torn apart, and reassembled—in a word, falsified," as he says at the beginning of *The Night Stalker*. Alongside his urgency to get his story told before the authorities peddle theirs, Kolchak's method of narration is redolent of his frustrated, diminished state: alone, he talks to his recorder. Nicholas Christopher, in *Somewhere in the Night: Film Noir and the American City* (1998), writes of how "the mass-produced electronic gadgets of the postwar era made urban man an information gatherer, a spiritual and mental nomad in his own home. The theme of the wanderer, the loner, the nightbird, the urban American isolated with and by his machines as the member (or piece) of an ever-fragmenting society, is very much a noir theme." Just as Kolchak's roving reportage situates him as a figure apart, his attempts to publicly articulate his experiences, his theories and observations, elicit ridicule. Telling the truth in any fashion only isolates him further.

Because Kolchak narrates even those parts of the plot not involving him, we're presented with a fantastical tale that's largely self-corroborated—un-fact-checked, as it were. So it's no surprise that Kolchak's version of things runs counter to that of the authorities, who tend to operate as a pack, and who unilaterally dismiss his stories as the fictions of a lunatic, as in the blistering appraisal administered him by a police captain (John Dehner) in "The Knightly Murders":

> POLICE CAPTAIN: You are a man who has resorted to lies and chicanery to the point of being pathological. I believe that you suffer from autosuggestion, and in an obsessive desire to win approval expressed through the need for a big story, you convince yourself that what you want to be true is true. In short, I believe your brain has turned to onion dip.

In lieu of any empirical evidence—his camera is always destroyed or taken away—Kolchak's tape-recorded accounts stand as the only proof of what he's experienced. These are the truths about the night, according to Kolchak. And so he emerges, as Rice intended, as a storyteller of compromised credibility.

While Kolchak situates his passage through the labyrinth with a subjective perspective, the monsters he encounters are emblematic of the horrors faced by society at large. In this, the series conjoins ancient fears of the night with modern concerns of urban lawlessness: its weekly "villains" are but mythological iterations of the ones appearing on procedurals like *Kojak*. In "The Knightly Murders," the pompous police official, unwilling to accept Kolchak's wild theories about a rash of unexplainable murders, tries to ascribe them to "the epithetic, atomized personality [who] sooner or later erupts." As it stands, his observation is not without currency. Yet the recurring motif of the series is that the police are utterly incapable of dealing with crime as it is, let alone crime erupting from a realm beyond their myopic consideration.

Even the city's "other" government, the illicit underpinning of organized crime, supposed rulers of Chicago after dark, is impelled to relinquish its sovereignty. "The Zombie," from a teleplay by David Chase, opens with a gang of wiseguys sorting the "take," only to be interrupted by a horrendous force pounding against their hideout. Fearing a raid, they react with panic. The doors burst open. The bloodbath ensues with quick, murky flourishes—mayhem through montage. When the smoke settles, the Outfit is reduced in number. But by what, exactly? Many of the series' inciting murders are staged this way, as if the mysterious shadows of the night have assembled into a kinetic force of unknowable malevolence.

In teasingly delaying our view of the monster, the series adheres to a practice as indebted to the suspense paradigm of horror as it is to the economics of weekly television production. Everything builds to Kolchak's arrival at the center of the labyrinth, to the moment of confrontation—the slaying. The delirious climax to "The Zombie" takes place in a junkyard, a bizarre terrain of discarded automobiles piled to the moon, where a murdered numbers runner (Earl Faison), now among the walking dead, has settled in for a nap. Kolchak, having lessoned up on voodoo lore, knows he has only a handful of seconds to pour some salt in the zombie's mouth and sew its lips shut before all hell breaks loose. Halfway through the operation, when the zombie's eyes pop open, Kolchak flees, only to regain his nerve and cannily lure the monster into a fatal trap. Evil terminated, he slumps to the ground and reaches for his camera—smashed, of course. Once more, he lacks the proof with which to substantiate an adventure beyond belief.

"The Zombie" (1974).

"The Ripper" (1974).

Traditional hero myths hold that after the climactic ordeal of the vanquishing, the hero is rewarded with a treasure hard to attain. Kolchak, in never being allowed to publish his stories, is never rewarded, and thus must repeat both his journey through the labyrinth and the grand slaying. No wonder, as he explains in "The Ripper," that he favors sneakers because "I run a lot." In mythology, the treasure is given feminine attributes, such as the hand of a princess; Kolchak, having lost his would-be wife in *The Night Stalker*, is denied that reward as well. Though he saves the community, he remains on its fringes. Not once does he get to put his story over the wire. What he's left with, then, is his own solitary existence and his portable tape recorder, his only willing listener. In the end, he's made to confront the most abject of fears: the loneliness of his own voice.

HARRY O
ABC 1973–1976

> What we have here is a show of the 1970s using a character of the 1940s.
> —David Janssen

WHEN DAVID JANSSEN AWOKE ON THE MORNING OF FEBRUARY 13, 1980, complaining of chest pains, his wife, Dani, phoned for an ambulance. By the time the paramedics arrived, it was too late: "*Fugitive* star, 48, dies of massive heart attack," said the evening papers. Invariably, the fact that Janssen smoked and drank like a sailor on shore leave found its way into every obituary. What often got overlooked was that Janssen was a workhorse, an actor never on break. He spent the day before he died shooting a TV film. For four years, he devoted his entire waking life to *The Fugitive*. Barry Morse, his co-star on that show, described him as "the hardest-working actor there probably has ever been in the whole history of television." *Harry O*, in which he plays an aging, wincing private-eye with a bullet lodged near his spine, a part created for him by producer Howard Rodman, was his final series role. And for it, Janssen laid the bone-weary but persevering tally of his own life right on the counter, like a bar tab covered with too many cigarette burns and glass rings.

Circular marks are important in *Harry O*, beginning with the one in the title, an indicator of neutrality, but also the symbol of a cavity. As a detective, Orwell effects closure through discovery—clues, keys, secrets. He digs until the mystery

Publicity still for *Harry O* (1975) with David Janssen.

ends. But he's also driven by something more elusive, what Rodman, in his treatment for the series, described as "an unfulfilled inchoate hunger." The centrality of a larger quest is made clear in *Such Dust as Dreams Are Made On* (1973), the first of two pilot films Rodman made with director Jerry Thorpe. It opens with a nighttime shot of Orwell's raftered, unseaworthy boat, *The Answer,* the stenciled name of which is put forth like a title card. From this framing of the boat's stern, as the camera pulls back through a window and slowly pans around a modest beach shack, what seemed to be an objective establishing shot becomes a gaze of subjectivity: this is somebody's point of view. Not Orwell's—he's passed out, facedown, on the bed—but rather that of the lurking figure, features obscured, who takes a chair beside the unconscious detective.

Such Dust as Dreams Are Made On (1973) with David Janssen and Martin Sheen.

Such Dust as Dreams Are Made On (1973) with Janssen and Sal Mineo.

Such Dust as Dreams Are Made On (1973) with Kathy Lloyd and Sheen.

When the alarm clock that's been ticking with growing urgency since the fade in goes off, Orwell is finally made aware of the gun aimed at him by the stranger in his room. Yet he stays as is, flat and half-awake:

STRANGER: I called the police to find you.

ORWELL: I'm in the phone book.

STRANGER: Well, they said they retired you four years ago on a line-of-duty disability pension. You got a bullet in you.

ORWELL: What do you want?

STRANGER: My name is Harlan Garrison. Doesn't that mean anything to you? Well, about four years ago, on Friday, January eighteenth, around one-twenty a.m., you and another cop got a call on a burglary in progress at a drugstore. When you got there, there were two guys with guns. You got shot, and your partner was killed. I'm the guy that shot you.

ORWELL: What do you want?

Though Garrison (Martin Sheen), bankroll in hand, offers to pay for an operation to have the bullet taken out of Orwell, there's more to his visit than an exchange of cash for absolution. Three weeks back from Vietnam and already in a jam, he needs the services of a private-eye: "I want to hire you to help me find the guy I was in the drugstore with that night. He's trying to kill me." Orwell remains noncommittal, immobile; mostly, he wants to go back to sleep. Garrison persists. The war, he says, cleansed him of his taste for heroin, his criminal urges: "Who I am now and who I was when I shot you are two completely different guys." One wonders whether Orwell feels the same disparity between then and now. Surely he didn't live like this, alone, in near-squalor, prior to that night Garrison put a bullet in him.

When Orwell at last makes a play for Garrison's gun, he ends on his back like an overturned turtle. By the first commercial, he's yet to stand on his feet. Soon enough, we'll learn that this detective doesn't even have a working automobile: he gets around Southern California on public transportation, which makes for some interesting detecting. Like much of 1970s neo noir, from *Chinatown* (1974) to *The Long Goodbye* (1975), *Such Dust as Dreams Are Made On* seems intent on demythifying its central archetype, or at least paring it to the root. Its very title returns us to the start of the classic cycle, to Humphrey Bogart's famous line at the close of *The Maltese Falcon* (1941)—"The stuff that dreams are made of . . ."—while also alluding to Prospero's summation of the human experience in Shakespeare's *The Tempest*: "We are such stuff / As dreams are made on / And our little life / Is rounded with a sleep." Along these contours, Rodman sets forth a detective-hero suspended between death and life, hence Thorpe's oneiric staging of the introductory sequence as if it were an existential wake-up call.

Orwell takes the case; the money he leaves on the floor. Garrison's old partner, Walter Scheerer (Sal Mineo), he learns, has graduated to underworld big shot, a wholesaler of heroin. Their falling out was over a girl, Marilyn Bedestrom (Kathy Lloyd), who now runs with Scheerer. Garrison feels responsible for having turned her toward a life of indecency; his motivations in hiring Orwell are numerous. Already, there's a full plate of classic themes: guilt, betrayal, vengeance, addiction, the inescapable past. In drawing from 1940s film noir, *Such Dust as Dreams Are Made On* contrasts the present as a washed-out, fallen world, one in which relations are murky, distances severe. One of the few moments of genuine human contact occurs when Orwell gruffly tosses a can of beer over to Garrison—his way of affirming their client-detective relationship, uneasy as it may be. Later, when Orwell tracks Scheerer down to an all-night diner, the setting evokes the nocturnal desolation of Edward Hopper's "Nighthawks." But where the detectives and gangsters of yore overlapped on some levels, Orwell, with his neckwear of yesteryear, takes his place opposite an uncouth, disheveled kingpin who noisily licks his fingers over a greasy platter of ribs before rolling over to a nearby payphone to loudly conduct a long-distance drug deal.

When Scheerer goes off to the washroom, leaving Orwell alone by the window, the old-school neon sign in the background restores a sense of nostalgic repose—one abruptly splintered by the drive-by goons who spray the space with gunfire. Orwell, hobbled by the bullet he carries in his back, looks helplessly on as Scheerer gets away. And in the end, with Scheerer killed and Garrison handcuffed (results reversed in the expanded, late-night-movie version), the serving of justice offers but tentative closure. The past remains an open wound. Orwell will continue to work toward unraveling the riddle scribbled on his boat. Each quest becomes his way of challenging the "sleep" or, more genre-appropriate, the "big sleep." *Variety*, in reviewing *Such Dust*, nailed its intent as "an approximation of the mood and motivations of the Dashiell Hammett–Raymond Chandler school of private-eyes"—before going on to note how "Janssen's semi-sullen interpretation of the lead did not look too much like a character viewers could get too fond of." On this point, the backers, ABC and Warner Bros., concurred. Orwell, for all his vulnerability, comes off as prickly, embittered, unsmiling—too hardboiled, as they saw it. To women especially, our wheel-less hero isn't entirely decent: he begins the first day of his investigation by gaming a lady friend (Mariana Hill) for bus fare and ends it by entering a bar, eyeballing a pick-up (Margot Kidder), and growling, "You have a car, don't you?"

Smile, Jenny, You're Dead (1974) with John Henderson, Martin Gabel, and David Janssen.

Orwell's inaccessibility can also be attributed to a constrictive narrative structure that favors his perspective at the expense of an inner life—the glimpses of compassion we demand of our heroes, even the surly ones. In developing a second pilot, *Smile, Jenny, You're Dead* (1974), Rodman and Thorpe sought to address such concerns with the addition of a first-person voiceover, and a repositioning of their womanizing detective as a man capable of romance: in between rescuing a fashion model (Andrea Marcovicci) from a deranged stalker (Zalman King), our hero falls in love, and Rodman's teleplay takes further steps to establish Orwell as an appealing series lead. The film opens with him discovering scruffy, homeless Liberty Cole (Jodie Foster) camping out in *The Answer*. Hearing that the waif's mother (Ellen Weston) is in jail for stealing some tins from a grocery, Orwell finagles her release. Liberty's beaming endorsement ("You're all right") seems tailored to demonstrate the detective's fittingness as prime-time material.

"For the Love of Money" (1975) with Janssen and Anthony Zerbe.

"Elegy for a Cop" (1975) with David Janssen.

Though both pilots were filmed in Los Angeles, ABC, in commissioning a series, insisted that *Harry O* be set elsewhere, like its current hit, *The Streets of San Francisco* (1972–1977). Harry Orwell became a retired San Diego cop with a bullet in his back. After the first thirteen episodes were in the can, Warners, citing cost overruns, intervened: Orwell was returned to LA, specifically Malibu. In both locales, he's paired with the genre mainstay of a police lieutenant who's both nemesis and ally. In the San Diego segments, Orwell knocks heads with Manny Quinlan (Henry Darrow); for the rest of the series, he parries with K.C. Trench (Anthony Zerbe). That neither approves of Orwell's methodology, nor he of theirs, is central to private-eye noir. Though a former cop himself, Orwell has released himself from the left-brain, ratiocinative approach of the police, and operates on an altogether different plane of intuition, as he makes clear in "Elegy for a Cop":

> TRENCH: I have mixed feelings about you, Orwell. I suppose in some ways you're a good detective, but a really good detective is an organization man; you never share your information.
>
> ORWELL: I don't have information. If I want information, I go to you. What I have is hunches.
>
> TRENCH: But I don't trust hunches.
>
> ORWELL: Well, then, what do you want me to share them with you for?
>
> TRENCH: That's why I always have mixed feelings about you, Orwell.

Oftentimes, Orwell's take on a case is to crack open a beer, plant himself in a beach chair, and think. His mind is constantly circulating, churning, but not in the analytical manner of Trench or Quinlan, who deal only in parts, evidence, hard facts. Orwell considers the whole "O," along with the areas beyond the perimeter: it's how he's able to piece it all together in advance of the police.

Orwell's stake in each mystery is made clear through the subjectivity he imposes as narrator. His voiceovers, delivered in Janssen's signature four-pack-a-day rasp, are introspective and lyrical, his words and thoughts playing off one another to provide something more than cursory exposition. From "The Admiral's Lady," as Orwell strolls along his beloved beach:

ORWELL: It was one of those afternoons. The crossword puzzle annoyed me. I didn't feel like working on the boat, and the fog was getting ready. I could feel it coming in my back. The seagull's scream didn't tell me anything. I had no premonition. I had no picture in my mind of Andrea Tannehill fighting for her life in the water—not then, and not hours later, when it actually happened.

By introducing us to events he's not yet witnessed but will soon be forced to unravel, Orwell situates himself as both storyteller and investigator. *Smile, Jenny, You're Dead* opens similarly, with Orwell speaking of characters whose troubles will shortly be his:

ORWELL: Days happen. Today I get up, my back hurts, I run my mile—I don't know anybody named Jennifer. I live in my world, Jennifer lives with her colonel. If you said Harry O to her, she'd say, who?

Through voiceover, we're eased from Orwell's hermetic world where "days happen" to the public world where anything can happen. Orwell's looping narration works in tandem with the unusual visual design established by Thorpe of master shots resized in camera through zooms and pans; cluttered foregrounds offsetting deep-staged backgrounds; and extreme wide-lens compositions coupled with a use of forced perspective, typically from an angle where a wall or other solid object should be. Scene and act breaks tend to involve a smudge of color slowly reconstituted to reveal a faraway Orwell, who is then brought from the rear of the frame to the forefront through a languidly paced camera movement. Idioms like these mirror Orwell's immersion in a mysterious world in which the truth itself is constantly shifting.

In "Gertrude," the series premiere, Thorpe culminates his zoom-and-pan introduction with a forced-perspective placement in which a telephone is given a disproportionally privileged foreground position while, in the distance, Orwell tinkers away on *The Answer*. Orwell's distaste for telephones, or any alarming intrusion, is a recurring motif. It's made clear in *Such Dust as Dreams Are Made On* when he's awakened by an alarm clock he never set, and repeated in *Smile, Jenny, You're Dead* when he tells us how, as soon as he gets his boat put back together, "I'm going out in the ocean where they don't have telephones. Telephones bug me." In "Gertrude," the dominating telephone continues to ring, unheeded, as Orwell begins his narration:

ORWELL: Now where I wanted to be was in Idaho Falls, Idaho, because that's where the circus was playing that day. I would have got in my car and gone

"Gertrude" (1974) with David Janssen and Julie Sommars.

there—it was only nine hundred and seventy miles—but the car was in Roy Bardello's garage for a new muffler and the starter motor rebuilt.

Rambling on about his automotive troubles, Orwell shuffles into his shack for another beer, returns outside, and finally approaches the ringing instrument in the foreground. "I figured I'd answer the phone if it rang eighteen times," he concludes. And so he does.

The caller, Gertrude Blainey (Julie Sommars), wants Orwell to locate her brother, Harold (Les Lemmon), a sailor gone AWOL. Harold, Orwell learns, got himself mixed up with a gang of diamond smugglers and, from there, into all kinds of trouble with the Navy. Overwhelmed, he absconded with the stones and went into hiding—hence the unpleasant men, military and criminal, who keep pestering Gertrude. Orwell, because he behaves oppositely from the frantic actions of everyone else, finds Harold first. "Now a professional knows what he is doing and moves in a straight line. So you just go after him in a straight line," he explains over a sequence of skittish Harold sneaking up on Gertrude's house. "But your ordinary amateur criminal is usually some sort of an eccentric. Probably doesn't know himself what he's going to do next. If you try to follow him, you're going to lose his trail, so what you have to do is keep one step ahead of him and let him catch up to you." Just as Orwell finishes his narration, a circular camera pan delivers poor, dim Harold into the room where Orwell patiently waits.

Orwell consistently succeeds through the simplest of measures. Earlier in "Gertrude," aware that he's being tailed by a government agent, he boards a public bus. "A bus moves with a different rhythm than somebody's car," he tells us. "When I was on the force, I had to tail a guy on a bus once. It was the worst forty-five minutes I ever spent." Exploiting his knowledge of the transport schedule, Orwell steps off one bus and onto another, leaving his pursuer behind. As with the trapping of Harold, it's emblematic of how he triumphs by remaining in harmony with the subtle patterns that his adversaries tend to ignore. In both scenes, Orwell's voiceover points us to the sly, passive control he wields. Yet as narrator he's not entirely forthcoming. Only at the end of "Gertrude" do we learn that he's known all along that his client, despite her performative displays of dizzy innocence, her anti-femme-fatale-ness, is wholly complicit in Harold's escapade; indeed, she's already booked their South American getaway.

Robert E. Thompson, who produced the San Diego episodes, has said of Orwell: "He could almost be described as an existentialist. He knows the world is not perfect—God is not always in his heaven—justice does not always triumph—but he has to act as though those were true." Given his past, Orwell is particularly attuned to the minute-by-minute collisions of logic and illogic that determine the course of things. Put differently, he's keen to the unreliability of the universe—the notion that one has little control over flying bullets (or falling beams). In dropping out, in leaving the chaos of the city for the peace of the beach, he's carved out a small corner of serenity—a safe, logical haven. Yet as we see in an episode like "Shadows at Noon," he continues to accept the illogical as an equal facet of existence. Robert Dozier's teleplay begins customarily, with Orwell on the beach giving voice to his elliptical thoughts:

> ORWELL: How do I know what I'm going to want for dinner tomorrow? How do I know I'm going to want dinner tomorrow? How do I know there's going to be a tomorrow? When you live alone, your thinking gets funny. Next time I'll make a list.

From this acknowledgment of his solitary bachelor state, Orwell jumps to his policy on home security: "Locking the house isn't one of my favorite things either. There's nothing funny about that; logic requires it. I don't have a key." Bag of groceries in hand, Orwell arrives at his front step only to find a locked door. He does the logical thing: he knocks. Marilyn Sidwell (Diane Ewing), frazzled and sopping wet, answers:

> MARILYN: Yes?
>
> ORWELL: Are you the lady of the house?
>
> MARILYN: What do you want?

Presenting himself as a delivery man, Orwell gains entry to his home. It's a refreshing take on the classic noir trope of the ordinary segueing to the absurd with little forewarning. But it's also revealing of Orwell's nature, his willingness to allow things to take their course.

Marilyn is anxious, on the run from something (or someone), and bleeding: she has a sea-urchin spine stuck in her foot. While Orwell does his best to patch up the wound, the poison pushes Marilyn into a fever. Orwell, despite having promised not to phone a doctor, does so anyway. With Marilyn sedated, the doctor informs Orwell that his houseguest appears to have escaped from nearby Los Robles Sanitarium. We're reminded of how *Kiss Me Deadly* (1955) similarly begins with a private eye coming to the rescue of a fleeing mental patient. Likewise, a view of Marilyn's wet dress hanging on a line in Orwell's kitchen invokes *Vertigo* (1958), another story in which a semi-retired detective is compelled to undress and save a damaged woman. As in both of these films, Orwell's involvement with Marilyn will entail themes of identity, madness, and criminal misdeed.

"Shadows at Noon" (1974) with David Janssen and Diane Ewing.

When the whitecoats arrive to return her to Los Robles, Marilyn says to Orwell: "I don't belong in a mental institution. I'm there only because it suits other people's needs. I'm as sane as you are, Mr. Orwell." Marilyn's words trouble the detective. "Being as sane as I am may not be the highest recommendation in the world," he tells us as she's driven away, "but another one of my least favorite things is betraying a trust. I wasn't particularly proud of myself." Director Paul Wendkos punctuates this self-assessment by settling his camera on the stern of *The Answer*. Orwell starts his archaeology. From Lt. Quinlan, he learns that Marilyn "went to pieces two years ago when her father died" and that she was committed to Los Robles by her sister and brother-in-law, the Rankins (Marla Adams and Guy Stockwell), who now control the family fortune. Denied permission to visit Marilyn, Orwell arranges with her psychiatrist, Dr. Mirakian (Michael Strong), to have himself temporarily committed.

Only, once inside, he finds that none of the hospital staff will acknowledge his undercover status. To them, he's just another nutcase, a judgment fattened by Orwell's claim, met with rolled eyes, that he's "really a private detective." The noir realm is rife with those deemed insane for telling the truth. A phone call to Mirakian, placed at Orwell's insistence, seals the diagnosis: "Yes, I'm familiar with Harry Orwell," the psychiatrist says. "He was committed under the name of Howard Rogers. That duality should speak for itself—he's apt to be violent." Having told no one (aside from the lying doctor) of his infiltration, Orwell is left to take his place among the inmates. Whiling away his time on janitorial duty, he tries to figure out how to gain access to the Disturbed Ward, where Marilyn is housed. "Well, that's very simple," someone says. "You cause a disturbance." Asylum logic becomes the subject of Orwell's voiceovers:

> ORWELL: If you were ever drafted, you might begin to understand how it felt. A little bit unreal, like walking underwater. The hard part was maintaining your own sense of balance. You were sane and they weren't. Or was it the other way around? After a while it's not easy to tell the difference. There was really only one way to be sure: if you had a key in your pocket and could go home at night, you were sane.

Orwell's narration, originating from inside a psychiatric clinic, calls into question the very nature of a profession predicated on unlocking figurative doors. To involve oneself in the troubles of others, to search for answers that raise more questions, is already, some would argue, a sign of lapsed sanity. Yet from Hammett and Chandler onward it's been expected of the detective-hero that by his quest, his moral imperative, he'll keep a lid on the lunacy that threatens to undermine societal order.

Except in the first pilot, in which Orwell's perspective dominates, *Harry O* follows the standard formula of intercutting scenes of the detective-hero with scenes of the villain(s). Michael Eaton, in his monograph on *Chinatown*, describes this stratagem as "the orchestration of knowledge." So it goes that in "Shadows at Noon," concurrent with Orwell's ordeal, we're given a primer on how the supposedly sane world outside Los Robles functions. For starters, we learn how the Rankins, in cahoots with Mirakian, fatally poisoned Marilyn's father, and then exacerbated Marilyn's already fragile state by killing her beloved dog, Pluto, and replacing it with a near-lookalike. Marilyn's seemingly deranged complaints that Pluto was no longer Pluto guaranteed her institutionalization.

The loony logic of it all is frightening, a reminder of how consensus determines one's place in society. Mirakian, moreover, is not Mirakian at all, but rather a disgraced quack from back East who killed the real Mirakian and stole his identity; once the Rankins learned of his dark secret, they blackmailed him into assisting in their lunatic scheme. Mirakian is really Howard Rogers—or, rather, Harry Orwell is now Howard Rogers, fugitive doctor.

Finally, inadvertently, Orwell commits the disturbance that gets him sent to the Disturbed Ward. Shot up with sodium pentothal, he awakens in an existential haze, thinking he really is Howard Rogers. Marilyn is now the one who comes to his rescue. Reminded of who he is and why he's ventured here, Orwell stages an escape. His passage with Marilyn through a web of unnaturally shadowed corridors and stairwells gives the episode its literal title; once they're outside, the chiaroscuro scheme dissolves to sunshine and primaries—the day world at noon. Afterwards, the Rankins rounded up and Mirakian dead by suicide, Orwell and Marilyn share a promising walk along the shore. But as Wendkos's camera completes a long, backward zoom, we're shown the same ominous wagon that carted Marilyn away at the beginning. "Paranoid schizophrenia," Orwell quietly explains. "People get better, they get worse." Los Robles, it seems, is where Marilyn belongs. Orwell himself ends where he began, alone on the shore, lost in thought.

TV Prevue (1975). Promotional artwork for *Harry O*.

With thirteen *Harry Os* in the can, ABC and Warners decided a reassessment was in order beyond a relocation to Los Angeles. Orwell's convertible, forever in repair, was returned to him—the idea being that squealing tires made for good television in this age of jiggling angels and bionic heroes. To the "no more buses" ultimatum was added "no more bullet in Orwell's back." (Janssen, having permanently injured his knee in college, then aggravated it further through his years on *The Fugitive*, couldn't help but move with an unsteady gait.) To sever Orwell's ties with San Diego, scenarios were devised wherein the detective travels up the coast on a case ("For the Love of Money") and ends up staying after learning that his cottage has been bulldozed to make way for condominiums ("Sound of Trumpets"). Further closure came with "Elegy for a Cop," from a teleplay by Rodman, in which, because of the red ink incurred, entire sequences from *Such Dust as Dreams Are Made On* were repurposed for a new story. Walter Scheerer, the junkie-thief who killed Orwell's partner, became the drug-dealing boyfriend of Lt. Quinlan's drug-addled niece, Marilyn. When Quinlan sets off for Los Angeles to bring her home, he's gunned down by Scheerer: he expires on a sidewalk, in broad daylight, before a small crowd of nervous onlookers.

In having Orwell avenge Quinlan's death by repeating, through an alternate chain of events, but involving the same crazy, violent world of drugs, his original

Advertisement for Excedrin with David Janssen (1975).

"Street Games" (1975).

"Street Games" (1975) with Maureen McCormick.

"Exercise in Fatality" (1975).

chase of Scheerer, Rodman effectively bends the universe of *Harry O* back on itself. As metaphor, the killing of Quinlan also equates to the squelching of Rodman's original vision. It's an in-joke (a dark one) given additional heft when Orwell pays tribute to his slain friend by requesting of his barkeep that a bottle of tequila labeled with Quinlan's name be kept on a top shelf, near the light.

BARKEEP: What'll I do when the bottle runs out?

ORWELL: Nothing. Nobody lives forever.

That the dream is by nature impermanent, if not exceptionally volatile, is particularly evident in how heroin, that bête noire of 1970s crime drama, shapes the noir ethos of *Harry O*—beginning with the bullet in Orwell's back, put there by a junkie. In *Such Dust as Dreams Are Made On*, we're given an extended lesson, delivered by a police chemist for Orwell's benefit, of how heroin is manufactured— a demonstration appended throughout the series by scenes of sweaty, despondent users (teenaged girls, mostly) clamoring for the drug. "She's coming down hard," Orwell is told in "Street Games" as he's led to the back room of a seedy bar where the object of his quest, a sixteen-year-old runaway (Maureen McCormick), writhes on a cot, begging for a fix. Orwell spends considerable time returning these fallen souls to their broken or unwelcoming homes. Much like Lew Archer, he's a fierce advocate of the aggregated family, "I drifted down on the short hairs and the long hairs, the potheads and the acid heads, draft dodgers and dollar chasers, swingers and walking wounded, idiot saints, hard cases, foolish virgins," writes Ross Macdonald in his Lew Archer novel *The Instant Enemy* (1968): Orwell, like Archer, casts an empathetic rather than judgmental eye on the counter culture, as we're shown in "Exercise in Fatality" during his relentless scouring of the city's lower depths for a pregnant junkie (Nora Heflin) booted out by her hot-headed cop father (Ralph Meeker). The series' depiction of youth drug culture is a pessimistic one in which salvation offers little comfort. One addict, anticipating the horror of withdrawal, cries out to Orwell: "Have you ever been in hell, mister? Have you ever had your whole mind and body hurt you so bad you wanna die?"

Drugs circulate through noir in a vicious collision of greed, oppression, and self-debasement. Implicit in this theme is a strong critique of American enterprise during the time of economic turndown with which *Harry O* coincided. In "Anatomy of a Frame," when Lt. Trench is accused of murdering a junkie-informant, Orwell's efforts to clear him lead to a wealthy dentist who doubles as a drug lord, a linking of the upper class with the criminal class entirely compatible with the social structures of noir. Those who enrich themselves through illicit gain hold influence and power, the ability to govern others, giving rise to a system of indentured servitude. Orwell learns this plainly in "Ruby" when he exposes a network of disaffected ghetto kids coerced into serving as couriers in a vast heroin-trafficking ring. The rapacious dehumanization trickles down to infect the very core of society, the family unit. "Look at you, you're an animal,"

Quinlan says to his strung-out niece in "Elegy for a Cop." "You don't care what happens, you don't have any love, you don't have any feeling for your family."

As *Harry O* presents it, the scourge of the needle becomes a metaphor for a generational rejection of authority—heroin as rebellion. Narratively, it also enables a continuation of the hostile-witness paradigm so critical to private-eye noir, as in Orwell's attempt, in "Elegy for a Cop," to elicit some information from Marilyn, now suffering withdrawal in a prison hospital:

ORWELL: How are you?

MARILYN: Go die somewhere.

ORWELL: I want Walter Scheerer.

MARILYN: I hope you get cancer.

Though the scene is repeated from *Such Dust as Dreams Are Made On*, its context remains undiminished. In entering the dark tunnel of withdrawal, Marilyn faces that moment of life that most approximates death. To be forced off the drug is to become the voyeur of one's own destruction. Heroin is repeatedly equated with death, the big sleep, not only in how it knocks the user under, but in how each fix could well be the last. To be on the needle is to exist in stasis, to straddle, within the same intake, the dream and the dust. So it's with irony that Orwell's own liminal state, his forcible retirement, his removal from a normal life to one on the margins, comes courtesy of a junkie. Part of what makes *Harry O* such a fascinating work of noir is that there's no ultimate answer for our detective. His existence is as roundabout as his name. Days happen. The sleep awaits.

"One for the Road" (1975).

CLOSING SCENES: TV NOIR IN CONTEXT

CHAOS AND ORDER

T HE SCENE IN *DOUBLE INDEMNITY* (1944) of Mr. Dietrichson splayed across the train tracks, discarded like a broken umbrella, is one of the seminal images in classical film noir. Having enacted the "perfect murder," the conspirators scramble away under cover of darkness: there are alibis to secure, some insurance papers to fill out. The noir night is the time of chaos. It's the period of instigation, crimes committed, corpses produced. Which isn't to say that such disruptions are unfamiliar to the day, but that the chaos of such behavior is best kept in the shadows. "Night in Gotham City. Only the faintest rays of moonlight break through the steamy darkness," reads the writer's bible for *Batman: The Animated Series* (1992–1994). "Shadows are black, twisted, and frightening. The thick night air carries many sounds: breaking glass, sputtering neon, harsh, bitter voices, and police sirens. Always police sirens. Most of Gotham's daytime inhabitants have long since fled to the suburbs or into security-gated apartments. This is not a safe place after dark." As the creators of this and many other works of noir see it, night, city, and chaos go together in an unholy trinity. The savior, typically, is a figure representative of or associated with, the law—sometimes in a cape, mostly not. The noir story thrives on an uneasy equilibrium between chaos and order.

The Great Train Robbery (film, 1903) with Justus D. Barnes.

Crime Story (1986–1988) opens its serialized storyline with a shot of an unmarked police sedan outside a neon-lit diner in Chicago. The radio crackles: a gang of masked robbers have taken over a nightclub. The men who roar off to address the chaos are tough, no-nonsense types; on the ride over, each makes sure his revolver is at full barrel. Already, there is the promise of more violence. The boys at the morgue will be busy for the next week. Guns and the men who carry them have been ingrained on American screens since the dawn of the movies, a time close enough to the taming of the Wild West that its rule of the bullet naturally carried over into early crime pictures like *The Great Train Robbery* (1903) and *The Musketeers of Pig Alley* (1912). Prohibition brought the gunslinger to the city, a place of illicit pleasures

"Pilot" (*Crime Story*, 1987) with Sam Keahna.

OPPOSITE: *Scarface* (film, 1932) with Paul Muni and Ann Dvorak.

Little Caesar (film, 1931) with Edward G. Robinson.

In the studio with *Gang Busters* (radio, ca. 1937).

and unhealthy appetites. For those of a certain inclination, untold riches were there for the taking, a promise at the center of the gangster cycle—with its kingpins of vice hustling their way to the top of the heap—that gripped the public imagination in the 1920s and 30s. Films like *Little Caesar* (1931) and *Scarface* (1932), or the radio anthology *Gang Busters* (1935–1957), offered rags-to-riches-to-coffin fables of brazen, colorful men who grabbed what they could before the arm of the law brought them down a size.

In the midst of the Depression, the audience's money was on the (Robin) hoods. Economic inequality had made definitively clear how much there was to go around, so why not cheer on those with the initiative to stake their share? John Dillinger, for all the banks he emptied, was a bona fide folk hero. His exploits answered a need for chaos enacted on the public's behalf, even if in the end the public came in droves to view his bullet-ridden body. Yet there persisted a sinister edge to such mythologies that went beyond a fantasy redistribution of wealth. Ernest Hemingway's "The Killers," written for *Scribner's* in 1927, introduces a pair of big-city hitmen, Al and Max, who march into a small-town diner and demand to see the Swede, a man they intend to extinguish. The killers never actually kill, nor is their mission given reason; their presence alone—their speech and mannerisms, the directness of their gaze—disturbs the social order. They enter and exit as harbingers of the dark forces laying in wait just outside everyday life.

Hemingway wrote "The Killers" before the movies talked, before radio had discovered drama, before television began telecasting; the heavies who have crossed our fictions since owe some debt to Al and Max. In Robert Siodmak's 1946 adaptation, the killers follow through with the killing, as do the duo in the live television production of 1959. With Don Siegel's full-color version, made for NBC in 1963 but released theatrically, they're promoted as our heroes. They not only pull off the hit, but turn around and try to make sense of it. Siegel was only a few days into production when President Kennedy was assassinated, a tragedy immortalized in a few grisly frames of amateur film. For many, this act of chaos marked the beginning of a different, less shiny America—for what kind of country allowed its leader to be shot, followed, days later, by the alleged shooter himself being shot on live television? And these were average men, Oswald and Ruby, not necessarily photogenic, but camera-ready nonetheless. Grim television became the norm: Vietnam, Kent State, RFK and MLK, Watergate, and yet another doomed chief executive (this one confessing involvement in an affair straight out of a "B" thriller). America's newscasts seemed to be coming from that point where the sidewalk ended.

Real life has always been at the center of a noir vision of America. James M. Cain came at the idea for *Double Indemnity* while covering (he was a journalist then) the 1927 slaying of Albert Snyder by his wife, Ruth, and her lover, Judd Gray. From the details of this tabloid-made case, Cain found the grist for a novella "about a married woman who falls in love with another man, kills her husband, fraudulently attempts to collect insurance, attempts to kill her lover and gets killed by him for selfish motives." Even before it appeared in serial form in *Liberty* magazine (1936), *Double Indemnity* was generating controversy around Hollywood, where it had been banned by the Hays Office on moral grounds. In constructing a passable screenplay from a property condemned as "a blueprint for murder," Billy Wilder and his co-scenarist Raymond Chandler had many hoops to jump through. The film that emerged is perhaps the quintessential account of a noir loser brought to his doom by a secret thirst for chaos.

Aroused to murder, Walter Neff (Huff in the book) is as swayed by the maddening scent of honeysuckle he associates with Phyllis Dietrichson and her tawdry ankle bracelet, as he is by the chance to finally game the system, as represented by his fatherly colleague, claims investigator Barton Keyes. So it goes that Walter and Phyllis produce a body, that of the harried Mr. Dietrichson, who should have looked before he

The Killers (film, 1964).

Double Indemnity (film, 1944) with Barbara Stanwyck and Fred MacMurray.

TOP: "Soft Eyes" (*The Wire*, 2006) with Jamie Hector.

CENTER: "The Prodigal Son" *Miami Vice* (1985) with Philip Michael Thompson.

BOTTOM: "The Price Is Murder" (*Peter Gunn*, 1959) with Robert Carricart and Lola Albright.

signed. Gangsters were expected to pull the death-trigger; a Glendale housewife and a wisecracking insurance salesman, less so. Hemingway's cold-hearted killers needn't be professionals in whose coat pockets snub-nosed pistols awaited a chance to croak. They could be middle-class citizens with whom a large swath of the audience might identify, up till the point where the banter and innuendo turned to talk of garroting someone's husband. *Double Indemnity* brushed the fantasy of chaos with the realness of desire; or, as Cain put it, "there's no mystery . . . they do it for sex or money or both."

Cain wrote *Double Indemnity* as Huff's first-person confession: "I'm going to put it through, straight down the line, and there won't be any slips." Variants of this line appear throughout the film, as if to underscore the ironic outcome of a cause-and-effect chain as sure as the path of a bullet. "I'm a croupier in that game," Huff says of the insurance trade. "I know all their tricks, I lie awake nights thinking up tricks, so I'll be ready for them when they come at me." Walt White of *Breaking Bad* (2008–2013) likewise falls into the trap of thinking he has all the angles covered. Diagnosed with terminal cancer, with few funds to cover his medical expenses, and even less to leave behind to his family, he draws on an unused doctorate in chemistry to covertly refashion himself as Heisenberg—the Mr. Big of the meth trade. His "perfect crime" goes just as miserably awry as the one in *Double Indemnity* (a work the series actively invokes), resulting in chaos all around. In place of the sexualized femme fatale, Walt responds to the tempting allure of the easy fix; by "breaking bad," he'll make himself a man again, just as Neff tries to address his frustrations of bachelorhood and the daily grind by agreeing to murder.

It's not uncommon for chaos to be a byproduct on the route toward personal order. In Cornell Woolrich's *The Black Angel*, the young newlywed Alberta Murray is torn out of her complacency when her husband is convicted of killing a showgirl. Believing him innocent, Alberta sets out to find the true culprit, an endeavor to right a wrong through which she imparts much destruction. She ends her quest thoroughly corrupted by the night world, and no longer in love with the husband whose exoneration she has miraculously achieved. Such blurring of chaos and order is critical to the noir sensibility, especially in the positioning of an antihero as a figure of empathy. Richard Kimble of *The Fugitive* is a fugitive because the law has determined that he murdered his wife. Kimble is innocent, but justice is as single-minded as it is blind, and so he runs. Society seeks to restore moral order (and true justice) by returning Kimble to death row; Kimble can only return order to his own life by locating the elusive one-armed man he saw fleeing the scene of the crime.

Ostracized, left to roam the margins, Kimble experiences suffering and loneliness in ways the gangsters of the 1930s never had to endure. It was the noir movement of the intervening years, with its psychological underpinning, that helped make society's outcasts relatable—neurotic and insecure, like most of us. This is the wicked trick that noir plays on its audience: it asks us to identify with people who do, or are said to have done, horrible, despicable things. We find ourselves rooting for folks who, in the end, may not be worth rooting for at all. Wilder had intended on ending *Double Indemnity* with a scene of Neff being led into the gas chamber, but this proved unnecessary. Keyes's admonishments to the gun-shot Neff are enough. His gentle lighting of Neff's last cigarette tells us that the flame of American justice is emphatic and fair, but not easily extinguished. Keyes is a tenacious investigator, as is Philip Gerard, the policeman sent after Kimble. Hank Schrader, the DEA-agent brother-in-law of Walt White, may mask his flaws and insecurities with an oversized sense of bravado, but he, too, is a force of the law to be reckoned with. His dogged pursuit of the legendary Heisenberg is such that his quarry is left with very little wiggle room.

As set out by the postwar semidocumentary police cycle, the law in noir works through tedium—the methodology of fingerprints, ballistic analysis, surveillance, diagrams on chalkboards, endless strategy. The interrogation room, with its high-beam key light bearing down on the uncooperative suspect, is an especially important location. To truly bring about justice, the law has to engage the criminal. In the prewar era, the law was a boisterous presence. For every Prohibition-era fable charting the upward rise of an unusually charismatic criminal, there were righteous responses like *G-Men* (1935) espousing the necessity of agents of the law "equipped to shoot to kill with the least possible waste of bullets." The moral, as it were, of such police-centered works is that lawlessness and disorder must be greeted with blunt force. Not only investigative tenacity, but ample gunpower is required to address the terror perpetrated by the bold-faced names of the crime blotter. Through curled fist and sawed-off shotgun, through threats of death or life in prison, the law prevails. Such an approach is made amply clear in the famous opening to *Gang Busters*—a blaze of sirens, whistles, screeching tires, chain-gang irons, and thundering tommy guns so boisterous it yielded its own term in slang: "to come on like gangbusters."

In The Black Alibi, another Woolrich novel adapted for early television (in 1946), a series of gruesome killings are initially blamed on an escaped jaguar. But the revealed truth is truer to the nature of the night: the culprit is a deranged man who dresses up in a scalped pelt and tears at his victims with animalistic frenzy. Insanity runs rampant through noir. Its fictions, in literature, film, and television, are wholly founded on the axiom that people go off their head without warning, and typically without reason. They stab their wives; they rob their employers; they plot heinous acts of brutality, deceit, and conspiracy. The serial killer in "Once Upon a Savage Night" (Kraft Suspense Theatre, 1964) has a thing for strangling blonde girls he deems to be "cheap." He has no control over what he does. The police who set up a dragnet to

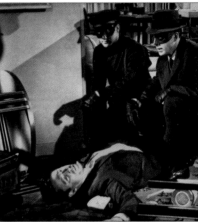

TOP: *Rocky King, Inside Detective* (1949) with Roscoe Karns.

CENTER: "Ace in the Hole" (*The Green Hornet*, 1967) with Van Williams and Bruce Lee.

BOTTOM: "The Hunger Artist" (*CSI: Crime Scene Investigation*, 2002) with Paul Guilfoyle, William Petersen, and Tricia Helfer.

"The Long Bright Dark" (*True Detective*, 2014).

CLOCKWISE, BELOW:

"Escape Artist" (*Danger*, 1952) with Cloris Leachman and John Conte.

"The Dresden Doll" (*77 Sunset Strip*, 1960) with Myrna Fahey and Roger Smith.

"The Carnival Ends at Midnight" (*Run for Your Life*, 1966) with Ben Gazzara, Anne Helm, and Peter Lawford.

catch him are only able to deal with symptoms of the chaos he enacts; his psychological malfeasance is beyond their scope. The law for the most part deals only in impact, in the after-effects. So it goes that the splayed-out corpse is the prototypical instigating image of the crime story.

Walt White of *Breaking Bad* commits his first murder out of self-preservation, but by the seventh or eighth, it's clear that the power to take a life has gone to his head. The criminal urge, by general consensus, represents an upending of the natural order. But there's very often a fantastical dream logic at work in how crime is punished, as in how Lincoln Burrows of *Prison Break* (2005–2009; 2017) finds himself in line for execution because of a conspiracy dreamed up by others, or how, in an

FROM TOP RIGHT:
"John Omar Pinson" (*Gang Busters*, 1954) with Sam Edwards.

"The Man Who Killed Hitler" (*Hands of Murder*, 1949) with Bruno Wick.

"Chapter Two" (*Mindhunter*, 2017).

Publicity Still for *Prison Break* (2006) with Dominic Purcell.

episode of *The Defenders* (1961–1965), a murderer on death row imagines himself in the role of jailer, condemning his accuser to the electric chair. For the audience, criminal displays can be rather exciting—a glimpse of forbidden darkness. We expect to be titillated, and yet, conversely, we also demand a confirmation of the prevailing morality. The rule of law, after all, dictates a sober response to insanity. Acts of murder, transgression, and deviance cannot, in the end, go unpunished. And so there are agents of order who restore a status quo (minus a criminal) to a world fond of chaos. A noir story is ultimately a chronicle of crime and punishment—or, in broader terms, one of disruption and restitution.

Behind the scenes on *Dragnet* (ca. 1950). Jack Webb and Barton Yarborough with LAPD Sgt. Vance Brasher.

LIGHT AND SHADOW

> Where there is no light, one cannot see, and when one cannot see, his imagination starts to run wild. He begins to suspect that something is about to happen. In the dark, there is mystery.
>
> —JOHN ALTON, *Painting with Light* (1949)

Rendezvous in Black (William Irish a/k/a Cornell Woolrich, Presses de la Cité, 1957).

"The Patsy" (*Tightrope*, 1959).

RIGHT: Publicity still for *Hawaiian Eye* (1960).

THE IMAGINATIVE CLASHES of light and dark that distinguish *He Walked by Night* (1949), *The Big Combo* (1955), and other works photographed by John Alton mark the stylistic apotheosis of classical noir. His evocative treatment of fog, mist, and smoke; his use of a strong backlight to create depth within the frame; and his casting of artificial shadows on actual locations fused the expressive storytelling of the silent era with the postwar desire for urban realism. Though the cultural confluences that gave rise to such an approach have abated, the aesthetic lingers on. Stream an episode of *CSI: Crime Scene Investigation* (2000–2015) or *The X Files* or *True Detective* (2014–) or *Stranger Things* (2016–) and you'll encounter the Alton-esque image of a silhouetted figure probing a darkened space with a flashlight that sends a crazily tilting beam around the frame. The intent of sensibility is hard to miss, even if the contextual potency has lapsed. Our awareness of a "noir style" and the meaning we infer from it relies on connotations passed down through the decades. Long shadowy fingers snatch at the heels of a murderer; a lattice-patterned ceiling threatens to collapse on a hapless victim of fate; a face is crossed with oblique lines at a moment of moral indecision—these and other representations of duress paint the contours of a night world somewhere between dream and reality.

"It is the associations that film noir repeatedly elects to make that are telling," explain Alain Silver and Elizabeth Ward in *Film Noir: The Encyclopedia*, first published in 1979. "The dark streets become emblems of alienation; the character's unrelenting gaze becomes obsessive; the whole environment becomes deterministic, hostile, chaotic." Noir visualizes its stories in such a way as to draw together outer and inner states of being. Light and form, setting and composition, are as important to characterization as dialogue and performance. ("Slums, bars, gambling joints, where the filament

Double Indemnity (1944) with Barbara Stanwyck, Fred MacMurray, and Edward G. Robinson.

of a lamp is the only bright spot, and other dimly lit places are good," notes Alton.) While the noir style is an amalgam of many ideas and idioms, its regard for atmospheric suggestiveness has roots in techniques developed in Germany at Ufa between the wars. Robert Wiene, Fritz Lang, F.W. Murnau, and others working in the expressionist vein exerted a fierce control over light, geometry, and environment to create the requisite tone owed a script likely to be concerned with psychological and societal disharmony.

"The tortured characters of the German silent cinema are part of an alien malevolent world, permeated by fate," Andrew Tudor writes in *Image and Influence* (1976)."They are constrained by the unknown; powerful forces wash over them; their world is dislocated within itself." One of the more iconic images from Weimar cinema is the shot of the somnambulist Cesare (Conrad Veidt) creeping along a wall in *The Cabinet of Dr. Caligari*. (See next page, top left) The shadow he casts is made from the absence of light, but is indistinguishable from the shadows painted on the flats, as if to suggest the unavoidability of one's "other," or shadow self, springing to life. This shot has been replicated countless times in all kinds of genres. The figure below is from *The Invaders*. David Vincent (Roy Thinnes), like Cesare, is placed at a lower-thirds focal point, poised for flight but hindered by an unmovable obstacle.

RIGHT, TOP TO BOTTOM:

"The Case of the Lady in Hiding" (*Treasury Men in Action*, 1955).

"The Carpella Collection" (*Run for Your Life*, 1967).

The Hanged Man (1964).

"The Fix" (*77 Sunset Strip*, 1960).

"Are You Now or Have You Ever Been?" (*Angel*, 2000).

LEFT: "The Experiment" (*The Invaders*, 1967).

The Cabinet of Dr. Caligari (1920).

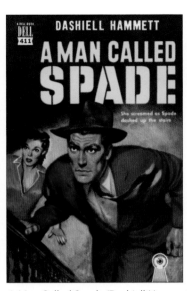

A Man Called Spade (Dashiell Hammett, Dell, 1950).

BELOW: "A Hole in the City" (*Naked City*, 1961).

ABOVE: Publicity still for *Kolchak* (ca. 1974).

BELOW: Publicity still for *M Squad* (ca. 1957).

ABOVE: "Heat" (*Dark Angel*, 2000).

BELOW: "Paradise Lost" (*Man Against Crime*, 1952).

RIGHT: "Sing a Song of Murder" (*Peter Gunn*, 1960).

ABOVE: *Nighthawks* (Edward Hopper, 1942).

LEFT: Advertisement for *CSI: Crime Scene Investigation* (2000).

Cesare may have a limp body in his hands, but Vincent, too, carries the burden of wanting to avoid detection. The balance of negative space to illuminated area is the same, as is the directive influence of the lines and arcs that jut through each image to create a mood of tension and furtiveness. Neither of these men is moving along a sure path; the night threatens to swallow them both.

Just as a creative use of Germanic shadow play deprives the noir world of definition and certainty, glass and other reflective surfaces imbue ambiguity and spatial tension. Synonymous with duality and doubling, fragmented ego, deception, claustrophobia, or the questionable nature of existence itself, mirrors are perhaps the most ubiquitous of noir's symbolic devices. Along with doorways, windows, and corridors, they're commonly employed to create a frame within the frame, visually dividing a character from others. Similarly, bars and light patterns, structural grids, and other bisecting elements of urban geography serve to border and isolate the human figure. Noir's regard for the urban setting as an entrapping maze complements a narrative thematically keyed to passages and thresholds. Caught up in an uncertain world, its characters are constantly in motion, scrambling up ladders and down stairs, opening doors with caution, taking refuge in dark corners or seeking a measure of order in the daylight, all the while interacting with an inherently unpredictable and hostile matrix.

FROM TOP:

"Northwest Passage" (*Twin Peaks*, 1990).

Publicity still for *The Shield* (2004).

"The Tragic Success of Alfred Tiloff" (*Naked City*, 1961).

"The Dummy" (*The Twilight Zone*, 1962).

THE INVESTIGATIVE JOURNEY

There is nothing so deceptive as the distance of a light upon a pitch-dark night, and sometimes the glimmer seemed to be far away upon the horizon and sometimes it might have been within a few yards of us.

—Sir Arthur Conan Doyle, *The Hound of the Baskervilles* (1902)

M OST NOIR STORIES INVOLVE some sort of investigative journey—the seeking of truths, the solving of a mystery, the completion of a puzzle. The noir investigator is typically a private eye or a plainclothes policeman, but not always so: there are insurance investigators, investigative reporters, snoops and spies, fixers and hired guns, masked detectives, phantasmic detectives, serial-killing detectives, alien-hunting detectives, and so on. Paladin of *Have Gun– Will Travel* (1957–1963)—the title comes from his calling card—is a troubleshooting detective in cowboy clothes who embodies the knightly, chivalric essence of an archetype transferable to almost any genre. David Janssen, who played detectives in *Richard Diamond* and *Harry O*, likened the modern sleuth to the Western gunslinger: "The hero is invincible; he gets the girl and never marries her; the convertible car has replaced the horse." Nearly all of the heroes (or antiheroes) discussed in this book undertake, at one time or another, a quest of detection.

BELOW: On the set of *Have Gun– Will Travel* with Richard Boone and director Ida Lupino (ca. 1960).

As a literary creation, the investigator originated with Edgar Allan Poe in *The Murders in the Rue Morgue* (1841). His C. Augustin Dupin is an independently wealthy, uncannily observant Parisian who lives by night and regards the police as dim-witted competitors. The Dupin stories reflect a taste for the macabre and a particular fascination with scientific methodology, elements that Sir Arthur Conan Doyle would capitalize on a few decades later with his Sherlock Holmes tales. Holmes, like Dupin, solves his crimes through forensic analysis and intellectual prowess. Confronted with a corpus delicti, he gathers testimony, assembles evidence, and formulates a hypothesis to determine the likely culprit. Extrapolated upon by the likes of Agatha Christie and Dorothy L. Sayers, the classic (and mostly British) whodunit reigned until the 1920s—when Dashiell Hammett, an American, and a former Pinkerton detective, thoroughly upended it with a new type of mystery, hardboiled and of the streets. Hammett, as Raymond

The Maltese Falcon (film, 1941) with Humphrey Bogart, Peter Lorre, Mary Astor, and Sydney Greenstreet.

CLOCKWISE BELOW, FROM LEFT:

Philip Marlowe (1959).

Advertisement for *Murder, My Sweet* (1944).

Advertisement for *The Outsider* (1968).

Kiss Me, Deadly (Mickey Spillane, Signet, 1953).

Time cover, "The Corpse in the Living Room" (1959).

Advertisement for *Martin Kane, Private Eye* (1949).

CLOCKWISE FROM TOP LEFT:

Richard Diamond, Private Detective (1960) with David Janssen.

Mickey Spillane's Mike Hammer (1957) with Darren McGavin.

Staccato (1959) with John Cassavetes.

77 Sunset Strip (1958) with Efrem Zimbalist, Jr.

Publicity still for *The Adventures of Sam Spade* (radio, ca. 1946) with Howard Duff.

Chandler, his heir apparent, liked to say, "took murder out of the Venetian vase and dropped it in the alley."

The detective stories in which Hammett's Sam Spade and Chandler's Philip Marlowe figure take place in an urban environment immune to the ratiocinative scrutiny of high-minded sleuths, but ripe for navigation via instinct, wiles, and guts. Spade's self-appointed task, if not pleasure, is to catalyze the undoing of criminal schemes. He's an amoral, ruthless hero, albeit one who functions by a code. As played by Humphrey Bogart in John Huston's adaptation of *The Maltese Falcon* (1941), Spade launched the private-eye strain of film noir, followed in short order by *Murder, My Sweet* (1944), with Dick Powell as Marlowe. Edward Dymtryk, who directed that picture, remarked on the distinction between the two: "After all, what is Marlowe? He's no Sam Spade. He's an eagle scout among the tough guys. He's a moral, ethical man, with a strong sense of responsibility." Through fire and water, Marlowe traverses a corruptive terrain, for which Chandler fitted him with resilient armor. "He must be a complete man and a common man and yet an unusual man," he writes in "The Simple Art of Murder" (1944). "He must be, to use a rather weathered phrase, a man of honor, by instinct, by inevitability, without thought of it, and certainly without saying it. He must be the best man in his world and a good enough man for any world."

The noir investigator inhabits an uncontrollable and constantly shifting milieu to which he (sometimes she) must adjust or perish. "The hard-boiled detective sets out to investigate a crime but invariably finds that he must go

LEFT: *The Big Sleep* (film, 1946) with Humphrey Bogart.

COLUMN ONE:

Danger Man (1965) with Patrick McGoohan.

Batman: The Animated Series (1993).

Wiseguy (1988) with Ken Wahl.

COLUMN TWO:

Kolchak (1974) with Darren McGavin.

The Invaders (1967) with Roy Thinnes.

The X-Files (1995) with David Duchovny.

beyond the solution to some kind of personal choice or action," writes John G. Cawelti in *Adventure, Mystery, and Romance* (1976). "While the classical writer typically treats the actual apprehension of the criminal as a less significant matter than the explanation of the crime, the hard-boiled story usually ends with a confrontation between detective and criminal." The inherent appeal of investigative noir is that the detective-hero is generally put before us as an emblem of identification—the ideal of American masculine virtue and justice emphatically served. John Paterson, paraphrasing Chandler, offers this formulation in "A Cosmic View of the Private Eye" (1953):

> He is Everyman's romantic conception of himself: the glorification of toughness, irreverence, and a sense of decency almost too confused to show itself. He is the common man become suddenly, magically aggressive, become purified by righteous and legitimate anger—and become, at last, devastatingly effective.

FAR LEFT: *The Man Called X* (1956) with Barry Sullivan and Byron Keith.

LEFT: *Casey, Crime Photographer* (radio, 1945) with Staats Cotsworth.

BELOW LEFT: *Casey, Crime Photographer* (1951) with Richard Carlyle.

BELOW: *Casey, Crime Photographer* (1951) with Maria Riva and Darren McGavin.

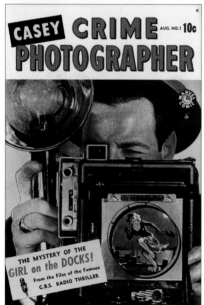

ABOVE: *Casey, Crime Photographer* (Marvel Comics, 1949).

This expectation of violence as the means of resolving a case is carried to a lurid extreme in the pulp fiction of Mickey Spillane, whose *I, the Jury* (1947) and *Kiss Me Deadly* (1952) made him one of the bestselling authors of the twentieth century. Shrewd but not bright, Spillane's Mike Hammer is a blunt, reactionary avenger—a thick-ear specialist. Hammett's and Chandler's heroes, on the other hand, regard sadism with distaste. Fisticuffs and shoot-outs are an unfortunate by-product of their profession. Most of the seeker-heroes of television noir are cast in the Hammett-Chandler mode. Yet because the genre, as exercised in episodic television, demands a punctuation of impact, their cases are invariably wrapped up with bursts of Spillane-like violence.

The telefilm boom of the 1950s swelled the ranks of television detectives: Richard Diamond, Peter Gunn, Stuart Bailey, Johnny Staccato, even, briefly, Marlowe, Hammer, and Hammett's *Thin Man*. In a 1959 cover story, *Time* magazine acknowledged the phenomenon with a sterling assessment of television's most prominent urban hero:

His work habits are abominable. He is busiest when the sky over the city is a grey suspicion of dawn, the hour when streetwalkers quit, grifters count their take, and busted junkies begin to jitter with the inside sweats. He is a loner, but his world is filled with friends. He knows the cop with the abused arches, the complaisant heiress, the slick saloon proprietor, the sick comic, the sullen stoolie who talks in the guarded whisper of cell block and exercise yard. He is furiously honest, but he can spot a rigged wheel with a sharper's skill. He is hard-muscled, handsome, handy with a snub-nosed .38, and his hide is as tough as the bluing on a pistol barrel. Decent, disillusioned and altogether incredible, he is a soap opera Superman. He is television's Private Eye.

LEFT: Publicity still for *Veronica Mars* (2006) with Kristen Bell.

BELOW: *Man with a Camera* (1958) with Charles Bronson.

In the dark city of the noir mystery, a landscape charged with fear and change, motives are never clear, and truths are stashed away for reasons as dark and inscrutable as the night. Of that night, Paterson writes, "He who would master it must bring with him qualities other than those of the intellect." Or, as Hammett's Continental Op says in *The Dain Curse* (1929), "Nobody thinks clearly, no matter what they pretend. Thinking's a dizzy business, a matter of catching as many of those foggy glimpses as you can and fitting them together the best you can." What links all detectives is the winding, labyrinthine nature of a narrative stitched together with glimmers of clues, drawing the detective deeper toward an unknown end somewhere in the night world.

THE NOIR SETTING

Promotional Booklet, *Naked City* (ca. 1965).

Set Design, *Batman: The Animated Series* (1992).

THE DARK AMERICAN CITY so central to our conception of noir is very often a setting of unholy vigor and much dread: dark and violent, full of motion, exhaust, and noise; a place of bustle, but also very lonely, and frequently destructive to the unsuspecting. Such depictions first gained prominence in the pulp fiction of the 1920s and 30s. It was during this era that the demographic balance of the U.S. shifted from rural to urban; to many, the nation's might as a rising world power was to be found in its epicenters of commerce, culture, and population. The big city held the pulse of America; here was where the future was being made, especially in New York, where the buildings seemed to grow taller by the day—a marvel embodied by the magnificent shot of a camera gliding endlessly up the facade of a skyscraper at the start of *The Crowd* (1928). That same year, Dashiell Hammett, a former Pinkerton detective, began typing out his determinedly streetwise private eye adventure, *The Maltese Falcon*:

> Where Bush Street roofed Stockton before slipping downhill to China-town, Spade paid his fare and left the taxicab. San Francisco's night-fog, thin, clammy, and penetrant, blurred the street. A few yards from where Spade had dismissed the taxicab a small group of men stood looking up an alley. Two women stood with a man on the other side of Bush Street, looking at the alley. There were faces at windows.

In introducing a new kind of detective, Hammett wasn't just claiming a genre away from the pipe-smoking, he was mapping the other side of urban America, in terms that were bleak, ominous, and camera-ready. (That line about the fog is practically a screen direction.) These are streets ripe for chaos, streets in which guns go off and men crumble and heads crane to catch a glimpse of the stiff being loaded into the back of a wagon. These are streets, as Raymond Chandler so evocatively put it, saturated with "the smell of fear." This other cityscape was not of promise, but of grit and dread.

Hammett and Chandler, along with others of the hardboiled school—W.R. Burnett, Cornell Woolrich, James M. Cain, Dorothy B. Hughes, David Goodis (and later, Jim Thompson and Mickey Spillane)—saw the new American city as the realization of all that was sour and awful about modern society. The city was dangerous and corruptive, blighted with crime, deviance and other symptoms of moral decay, and ruled over by a penthouse-class of faceless, corporate gangsters. For all its sweaty, kinetic density, the thriving American city was alienating and ultimately hostile to the individual, to the little man trying to scrape together the monthly rent, an impression rounded out by realist

LEFT: The Cabinet of Dr. Caligari (film, 1920).

painters and photographers like Edward Hopper, Reginald Marsh, and Arthur Fellig (a/k/a Weegee the Famous). The mean streets of America became the nexus of the noir story. Through its portals passed the heroes and the antiheroes: the depressed, the driven, the sleepless, the confined, the frightened, the insane, the vindictive, the despondent. In many works, the architecture appears anthropomorphized, as if the city, though built of glass and steel and asphalt, has the will to entice, ensnare, and destruct.

The Naked City (film, 1948).

Such unrestful notions of city life are found as well in F.W. Murnau's late-silent masterpiece *Sunrise* (1927), perhaps the definitive fusion of Weimar-styled angst with Hollywood spectacle: the film positions the mythic American city as the wellspring of the darkest human impulses. But it was the bookends of expressionist German cinema, *The Cabinet of Dr. Caligari* (1920) and *M* (1931), which would have the profoundest impact on subsequent treatments of the city. In each, a deranged character is steered through an urban matrix reflective of an inescapable psychological state. But where Robert Weine saw his city in cleanly angular, art-directed lines, Fritz Lang made his into a spiraling rat's nest. The dim, stifling passages through which Franz Beckert, the child murderer of *M*, is hunted belong to a city in which "the air has been replaced by theatrical light," as David Thomson writes in *The Big Screen: The Story of the Movies* (2012). He goes on to describe Lang's fiercely designed city as "a mortuary in which human figures make their frantic dance." The morbid, suffocating atmosphere achieves its keenest expression in the chalk-letter "M" (for *Mörder*) anonymously scrawled on Beckert's coat; the city is encouraging of his sickness, yet inhospitable to his kind. He becomes a figure of sympathy, if only because he can't find a way out of the maze and into some light.

"Pilot" (*Breaking Bad*, 2008).

Through early studio-bound film noir and into the similarly constrained live era of television, the city continues to isolate, mislead, and distract. Blueprinted in an era of economic failure and widespread chaos, and built to its heights under the shadow of the Bomb, the noirified metropolis is very much alive, but already bearing the wisp of death. Its beating heart seems to invite disaster. A corresponding sense of imminent destruction informs much of postwar noir. Nightfall and neon (a sun gone away), endless rain (nuclear fallout), and an interminable sense of waiting (for something awful to happen), are an intrinsic part of its iconography:

> A dark street in the early morning hours, splashed with a sudden downpour. Lamps form haloes in the murk. In a walk-up room, filled with the intermittent flashing of a neon sign from across the room, a man is waiting to murder or be murdered.

This passage from *Hollywood in the Forties* (1968), by Charles Higham and Joel Greenberg, opens a chapter titled "Black Cinema," the first English-language analysis of film noir. Such visions of urban America, they tell us, "were made by

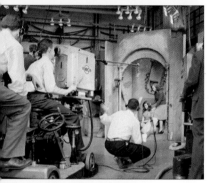

hard-bitten men who knew city life inside out: they have the flavor of a neat Scotch on-the-rocks." The importance of topography to the image-makers of noir is evident in the titular placement of setting in many film and television noirs: the correlations of time and city, specific addresses and landmarks, references to urban practices and rituals. Most chronicles of law and order begin with some establishment of locale. A police car, sirens blazing, tears down a Chicago avenue in *M Squad*. "This is Los Angeles," Friday tells us at the start of *Dragnet*. The title sequence for *Staccato* sends its private eye dashing through an eerily barren New York, his gaze tense, his body braced for violence. At a distance, the Manhattan of *Naked City* (1958–1963) appears as a shimmering beacon of order and promise. But from within its canyons a different perspective emerges, one in which the intoxicating allure of the city is complicit in all manner of broken hopes and dreams, spilled blood and despairing cries: "There are eight millions stories in the Naked City; this has been one of them." In these and other crime stories, the investigator-hero is situated as an indispensable fixture in the identity of the city, as if his removal or retirement would trigger a collapse of the social order.

The open-eyed semidocumentary approach came about as the result of the newsreels, namely producer Louis de Rochemont's *March of Time* serials, by which the carnage and misery unfolding overseas during World War II was conveyed to the civilian populace. Postwar, Rochemont spearheaded a drive toward greater realism in the urban crime thriller. As the materially artificial but highly atmospheric cityscapes of *This Gun for Hire* (1942) and *Murder, My Sweet* (1944) gave way to naturalism—a need to bring the camera to the real mean streets—a vision of America emerged that was truer to the grunge and grime of the human carnival. For Hollywood, this meant parlaying the technological advances in mobile film equipment into a trend toward the "story based on actual case files." Television, meanwhile, remained tethered to the studio by virtue of its live feed: it rendered the outside world allusively, via off-camera street noises, painted skyline backdrops, and abstractly rendered sets meant to suggest constricted urban spaces. Until the

ABOVE: *This Gun for Hire* (film, 1942).

TOP TO BOTTOM:
M (film, 1931).
Mysteries of Chinatown (1950).
Black Alibi (1946).
Publicity still for *Peter Gunn* (1959).

COLUMN ONE, TOP TO BOTTOM:

Promotional artwork for
Crime Story (1987).

"The Shop of the Four Winds"
(*Staccato*, 1959).

"In the Dark" (*Angel*, 1999).

"Where Is Everybody?"
(*The Twilight Zone*, 1959).

COLUMN TWO, TOP TO BOTTOM:

The Night Stalker (1972).

Title Sequence (*Kojak*, 1973).

"The Man with Frank's Face"
(*M Squad*, 1960).

"Prodigal Son" (*Miami Vice*, 1985).

"Brother's Keeper"
(*Prison Break*, 2005).

"Lullaby" (*Angel*, 2001).

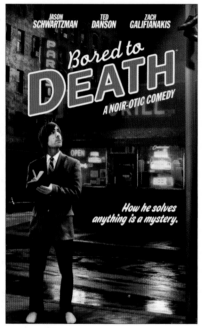

Advertisement for *Bored to Death* (2009).

1950s, when the industry moved to film, television remained an almost entirely interior-bound arena.

It seems fitting that the odd exception should be the archetypically titled *City at Midnight* (1949), a live anthology which took its cameras into the streets of New York to find the natural setting for the stories it wanted to tell. "The sense of realism and actuality, which represents television at its best, is enormously enhanced," wrote critic Jack Gould. "To see real rain falling on the actors or to hear the throaty whistle of a tugboat in the upper bay is a highly welcome departure from the usual synthetic effects concocted in the studio." Relying on street lamps and other industrial fixtures for illumination, *City at Midnight* fully exploited the sensitivity of the Image-Orthicon to stage on-location broadcasts of city-centric originals like "Dock Hands" and "52nd Street." In the former, the Brooklyn wharf, in all its cacophonous seediness, becomes the backdrop for the travails of a stevedore lured into crime by a pack of waterfront thieves; in "52nd Street," which tells of a promising jazz musician from the sticks led astray by a siren in a mink coat, a handful of actors were thrust into the Three Deuces nightclub at its most decadent hour. The boisterous smoke-filled venue, with its integrated sea of ecstatic faces nodding in time to blaring bebop, provided the ideal backing for a story themed on temptation and downfall.

"In the long run," *Variety* remarked of *City at Midnight*, "this show might mean to television what Louis de Rochemont's *House on 92nd Street* meant to the film industry—the opening of a broad, new production vista." In 1945, Rochemont and his director, Henry Hathaway, had produced a spy thriller in the style of a documentary. The film was released just six weeks after the annihilation of Hiroshima and Nagasaki; in the interim, Rochemont rejigged it so that the MacGuffin—the object the FBI wants back—became an atomic secret. It is perhaps the first fictive depiction of a world the total end of which was no longer a fantastical notion but a distinct possibility. Nuclear anxiety, and with it the Red Scare and blacklisting, pushed mid-century noir toward a greater cognizance of real-life concerns, just as the catastrophe of 9/11 would influence the story directions of *24* (2001–2010; 2014) and *Mr. Robot* (2015–). As if to confirm its credibility as the "true" account, the docu-noir boasted its connection to actual places, actual events and people. *Dark of Night* (1953), the only other live series to regularly lug its beastly cameras out into the streets, ripped its stories straight from the headlines.

For fact-based filmed series like *I Led 3 Lives*, shooting the real city, with its precarious intersections and throngs of strange faces, was not only a matter of establishing sober intent, but an opportunity to gain natural ambience with a very low budget. "We shot the hell out of Hollywood," Jon Epstein, the story editor on the series, explained. "I think we were the first company to really shoot on the streets—it was cheaper." *I Led 3 Lives* paints the city as an engulfing threat by which psychological awareness is intensified. Herbert Philbrick, a bundle of nerves because he juggles the roles of citizen, spy, and communist, is haunted by the fear of discovery. Moving through crowds with caution, glancing over his shoulder at every turn, flinching at the gazes of others, he narrates his thoughts in dissociative second person: "Play it like any other day, Philbrick. Act casual. Say something to the newsboy the way you always do." Even the most innocuous of encounters, like a man taking the neighboring seat at a luncheonette, sends him into a tailspin of paranoia. For Philbrick, the entire city is a trap.

The apprehensiveness of the Cold War informs the relationship between environment and individual in many television noirs of the 1950s and 60s. In Rod Serling's *The Twilight Zone*, terrors real and imagined are schematized with nightmare logic. In other shows, the fear is less overt, but still prevalent. Richard Kimble of *The Fugitive* dashes across the country in flight from a death sentence; scenes of him creeping through a train yard or sticking his thumb out from the side of a lonely highway affirm him as a figure with a target on his back. The insular world of the studio-bound *Peter Gunn*, where it's always nighttime, and often raining, seems to suggest a post-apocalyptic landscape. Here, the human diorama is played out under a poisoned, perpetually darkened sky. There are elements of this as well in the spookily deserted backlot streets of *Staccato* and *77 Sunset Strip*, which suggest nothing less than a complete urban evacuation. In these shows, a cutaway to a stock shot of the real New York, the real Los Angeles, offers not only an anchoring of locale, but a relief from the suffocation.

The move to location work begun with *I Led 3 Lives* and other early telefilm programs, like Bernard Girard's docu-noir anthology *Rebound*, continued with *Naked City*, which presents New York naturalistically and plausibly: the city's problems are its characters' problems. The police procedural in particular thrives on such symbiosis. The use of the real city, with its smog and traffic and lived-in architecture, becomes a badge of credibility, as well as the means of delving into extant social conditions which, in turn, bolster the authenticity of the drama. The unblinking vista of the docu-noir, with its focal point the burned-out urban center, is borrowed for all types of genres from the 1960s onward. In *The Rockford Files* (1974–1980) and *Harry O*, zoom-lens effects, sun flares, and other optical aberrations correlate the decaying landscape to the mindsets of the past-their-prime heroes. As these transitional noirs give way to the full-blown neo-noir look of *Miami Vice* (1984–1990) and *Crime Story*, the real world becomes, briefly, the foundation for additional layers of art direction and stylization. Thereafter, TV noir reverts to a realistic style, most especially in the probing, hand-held camerawork of *Homicide: Life on the Street* (1984–1990); *The Wire* (2002–2008); and *The Shield* (2002–2008). What unites much of the noir on television, regardless of how it tells its story, is a consistent regard for the city as character.

But the hinterlands of America are a source of anxiety and noir atmosphere

TOP TO BOTTOM:

"Northwest Passage" (*Twin Peaks*, 1990).

"The Matt Bass Scheme" (*The Untouchables*, 1961).

"Home Again" (*The X-Files*, 2015).

as well. The perceived freedoms of the open West provide little sanctuary for the on-the-run antiheroes of not only *The Fugitive*, but *The Loner* and *The Invaders*. The small, insular communities through which these ramblers pass are just as likely to sprout danger as the large city. The frontier is also a source of terror in *Breaking Bad*, which in its third season introduces a pair of assassins, "The Cousins," who sneak across the border to kill Walt White, über-baron of the meth trade. Framed in extreme wide angles that reveal much of the seemingly serene, blue-skied terrain, these stoic killers, dragging with them a giant ax (token of their rural origins), make their way to Albuquerque, where Walt remains oblivious to their deathly mission from the shelter of his tract home. A fastidious type, Walt clings to order, even when turning out batches of artisanal crank, and so it's with irony that his bid for familial stability yields so much disorder and destruction.

Twin Peaks (1990–1991; 2017), the very title of which suggests a natural geographic order, thrives on this concept of imbalance. A serialized noir in which events assume a cumulative force, its title sequence opens with a montage that establishes its Pacific Northwestern setting as an idyll of order. Images of the river that leads through town and provides the source of power for its lumber mill suggest this to be a place where things move simply and predictably. As trees are felled, sawed, and floated off to the outside world, we wonder whether this community is not a last redoubt from the spitefully unpredictable city. But as Angelo Badalamenti's theme music fades away, the happily chirping bird that was our first image of this far-off town is forgotten, for the flow of water that provides Twin Peaks with its rhythmic orderliness has quietly flushed out the corpse of the homecoming queen. Defiled and butchered, Laura Palmer lies wrapped in plastic, victim of a gruesome sex crime. From there, series creators David Lynch and Mark Frost turn the very nature of the noir investigation inside out, while still paying tribute to a veritable roll call of classic noir titles.

Agent Cooper, a detective from the big city, arrives. Inspired by the sway of the mystical Douglas firs that are the hallmark (and mark of industry) of Twin Peaks, he tosses aside the FBI rulebook and opens himself to clues that defy reason, or even diagnosed patterns of human deviance. As his methodology turns to the metaphysical, a seeming contradiction of the realism that some would place at the core of noir, *Twin Peaks* illustrates the ease with which the style and narrative of noir can be fused with the conventions, if not the extravagances, of other genres by introducing a woodsy setting, a tradition of hybridization continued with *The X-Files*. In it, the rural regions of America yield all sorts of bizarre occurrences that would seem to defy normal—which is to say, scientific—FBI methods of investigation. Agents Mulder and Scully venture through the deep, dark forests of a pastoral nation only hinted at in the classic cycles of film and television noir. Nonetheless, the series's quintessential image involves them plunging into the night, flashlight in hand—an endeavor at the center of any noir story.

BIBLIOGRAPHY

General Bibliography

Alloway, Lawrence. *Violent America: The Movies 1946–1964.* New York: The Museum of Modern Art, 1971.

Anderson, Christopher. *Hollywood TV: The Studio System in the Fifties.* Austin: University of Texas Press, 1994.

Appel, Alfred. *Nabokov's Dark Cinema.* New York: Oxford University Press, 1974.

Appel, Alfred. "Fritz Lang's American Nightmare," *Film Comment*, November 1974.

Atkinson, Michael. *Ghosts in the Machine: The Dark Heart of Pop Cinema.* New York: Limelight Editions, 1999.

Biesen, Sheri Chinen. *Blackout: World War II and the Origins of Film Noir.* Baltimore: Johns Hopkins University Press, 2005.

Boddy, William. *Fifties Television: The Industry and Its Critics.* Urbana, IL: University of Illinois Press, 1990.

Borde, Raymond and Etienne Chaumeton. *A Panorama of American Film Noir 1941–1953.* Trans. by Paul Hammond. San Francisco: City Lights Books, 2002. [First published as *Panorama du film noir americain*, Paris: Les Éditions de Minuit, 1955.]

Butler, Jeremy G. *Television Style.* New York: Routledge, 2010.

Cameron, Ian. *A Pictorial History of Crime Films.* London: Hamlyn, 1975.

Cameron, Ian, ed. *The Book of Film Noir.* New York: Continuum, 1993.

Campbell, Joseph. *The Hero with a Thousand Faces* [2nd ed.]. Princeton, NJ: Princeton University Press, 1968.

Cawelti, John G. *Adventure, Mystery, and Romance: Formula Stories as Art and Popular Culture.* Chicago: University of Chicago Press, 1976.

Chandler, Raymond. "The Simple Art of Murder," *The Saturday Review*, 15 April 1950.

Chandler, Raymond. "Writers in Hollywood," *The Atlantic*, November 1945.

Christopher, Nicholas. *Somewhere in the Night: Film Noir and the American City.* Emeryville, CA: Shoemaker & Hoard, 2006.

Cochran, David. *American Noir: Underground Writers and Filmmakers of the Postwar Era.* Washington, D.C.: Smithsonian Institution Press, 2000.

Conrad, Mark, ed. *The Philosophy of Film Noir.* Lexington, KY: The University Press of Kentucky, 2007.

Copjec, Joan, ed. *Shades of Noir: A Reader.* New York: Verso, 1993.

Davis, Mike. *City of Quartz: Excavating the Future in Los Angeles.* New York: Verso, 1990.

DeForest, Tim. *Storytelling in the Pulps, Comics, and Radio: How Technology Changed America.* Jefferson, NC: McFarland, 2004.

Dickos, Andrew. *Street with No Name: A History of the Classic American Film Noir.* Lexington, KY: The University Press of Kentucky, 2002.

Dimendberg, Edward. *Film Noir and the Spaces of Modernity.* Cambridge, MA: Harvard University Press, 2004.

Dixon, Wheeler Winston. *Film Noir and the Cinema of Paranoia.* New Brunswick, NJ: Rutgers University Press, 2009.

Eisner, Lotte. *The Haunted Screen: Expressionism in the German Cinema and the Influence of Max Reinhardt.* Berkeley: University of California Press, 1969.

Gerani, Gary with Paul H. Schulman. *Fantastic Television.* New York: Harmony Books, 1977.

Goldenson, Leonard H. with Marvin J. Wolf. *Beating the Odds: The Untold Story Behind the Rise of ABC: The Stars, Struggles, and Egos That Transformed Network Television By the Man Who Made It Happen.* New York: Scribner, 1991.

Gorman, Ed, Bill Pronzini, and Martin H. Greenberg, eds. *American Pulp.* New York: Carroll & Graf, 1997.

Gorman, Ed, Lee Server, and Martin H. Greenberg, eds. *The Big Book of Noir.* New York: Carroll, 1998.

Hardy, Phil. *The Overlook Film Encyclopedia: The Gangster Film.* Woodstock, NY: Overlook Press, 1999.

Harper, Ralph. *The World of the Thriller.* Cleveland: The Press of Case Western Reserve University, 1969.

Harper, Ralph. *The Path of Darkness.* Cleveland: The Press of Case Western Reserve University, 1968.

Heimann, Jim. *Sins of the City: The Real Los Angeles Noir.* San Francisco: Chronicle Books, 1999.

Higham, Charles and Joel Greenberg. *Hollywood in the Forties.* New York: A. S. Barnes, 1968.

Hiney, Tom and Frank MacShane, eds. *The Raymond Chandler Papers: Selected Letters and Non-Fiction, 1909–1959.* New York: Atlantic Monthly Press, 2000.

Hirsch, Foster. *The Dark Side of the Screen: Film Noir.* New York: Da Capo Press, 1986.

Hirsch, Foster. *Detours and Lost Highways: A Map of Neo-Noir.* New York: Limelight Editions, 1999.

Horsley, Lee. *The Noir Thriller.* London: Palgrave Macmillan, 2001.

Inciardi, James A. and Juliet L. Dee. "From the Keystone Cops to *Miami Vice*: Images of Policing in American Popular Culture." *Journal of Popular Culture*, Fall 1987.

Jameson, Richard T. "Son of Noir," *Film Comment*, November–December 1974.

Jensen, Paul. "Film Noir and the Writer: Raymond Chandler," *Film Comment*, November–December 1974.

——. "Raymond Chandler: The World You Live In," *Film Comment*, November–December 1974.

Johnson, Kevin. *The Dark Page: Books That Inspired American Film Noir, 1940–1949.* Introduction by Paul Schrader. New Castle, DE: Oak Knoll Press, 2007.

Kaminsky, Stuart. "*Little Caesar* and Its Role in the Gangster Film Genre," *Journal of Popular Film*, Summer 1972.

Keaney, Michael F. *Film Noir Guide: 745 Films of the Classic Era, 1940–1959.* Jefferson, NC: McFarland, 2003.

Kracauer, Siegfried. *From Caligari to Hitler: A Psychological History of the German Film.* Princeton, NJ: Princeton University Press, 1947.

Krutnik, Frank. *In a Lonely Street: Film, Genre, Masculinity.* New York: Routledge, 1991.

Krutnik, Frank, Steve Neale, Brian Neve, and Peter Stanfield, eds. *"Un-American" Hollywood: Politics and Film in the Blacklist Era.* New Brunswick, NJ: Rutgers University Press, 2007.

Lafferty, William. "A Reappraisal of the Semi-Documentary in Hollywood, 1945–1948." *The Velvet Light Trap*, June 1983.

Longworth, James L., Jr. *TV Creators: Conversations with America's Top Producers of Television Drama* [two vols.]. Syracuse, NY: Syracuse University Press, 2000 and 2002.

Marc, David and Robert J. Thompson. *Prime Time, Prime Movers*. Boston: Little, Brown, 1992.

Marling, William. *The American Roman Noir: Hammett, Cain, and Chandler*. Athens, GA: University of Georgia Press,1995.

Martin, Richard. *Mean Streets and Raging Bulls: The Legacy of Film Noir in Contemporary American Cinema*. Lanham, MD: Scarecrow Press, 1997.

Muller, Eddie. *Dark City: The Lost World of Film Noir*. New York: St. Martin's, 1998.

Naremore, James. *More Than Night: Film Noir in its Contexts*. Berkeley, CA: University of California Press, 1998.

O'Brien, Geoffrey. *Hardboiled America: Lurid Paperbacks and the Masters of Noir*. New York: Da Capo, 1997.

Osgerby, Bill and Anna Gough-Yates, eds. *Action TV: Tough Guys, Smooth Operators, and Foxy Chicks*. London: Routledge, 2001.

Osteen, Mark. "The Big Secret: Film Noir and Nuclear Fear," *Journal of Popular Film and Television*, Summer 1994.

Palmer, R. Barton. *Hollywood's Dark Cinema: The American Film Noir*. New York: Twayne, 1994.

Paterson, John. "A Cosmic View of the Private Eye," *Saturday Review*, 22 August 1953.

Phillips, Gene D. *Creatures of Darkness: Raymond Chandler, Detective Fiction, and Film Noir*. Lexington, KY: University Press of Kentucky, 2000.

Place, J. A. and L. S. Peterson, "Some Visual Motifs of Film Noir," *Film Comment*, January–February 1974.

Rabinowitz, Paula. *Black & White & Noir: America's Pulp Modernism*. New York: Columbia University Press, 2002.

Schrader, Paul. "Notes on Film Noir," *Film Comment*, Spring 1972.

Server, Lee. *Encyclopedia of Pulp Fiction Writers*. New York: Facts on File, 2002.

Server, Lee. *Danger Is My Business: An Illustrated History of the Fabulous Pulp Magazines*. San Francisco: Chronicle Books, 1993.

Server, Lee. *Over My Dead Body: The Sensational Age of the American Paperback*. San Francisco: Chronicle Books, 1994.

Shadoian, Jack. *Dreams and Dead Ends: The American Gangster Film*. New York: Oxford University Press, 2003.

Shales, Tom. "Video Noir: TV's Long Shadow," *Washington Post*, 16 July 1978.

Silver, Alain and James Ursini. *Film Noir: An Encyclopedic Reference to the American Style*. Woodstock, NY: Overlook Press, 1992. [Revised and republished as *Film Noir: The Encyclopedia*, 2010.]

Silver, Alain and James Ursini. Paul Duncan, ed. *Film Noir*. Cologne: Taschen, 2004.

Silver, Alain and James Ursini. *The Noir Style*. Additional Material by Robert Porfirio and Linda Brookover. Woodstock, NY: Overlook Press, 1999.

Silver, Alain and James Ursini. *L.A. Noir: The City as Character*. Santa Monica, CA: Santa Monica Press, 2005.

Silver, Alain and James Ursini. *Film Noir Reader*. New York: Limelight Editions, 1996. As well as *Film Noir Reader 2*, 1999; *Film Noir Reader 3*, 2001; *Film Noir Reader 4*, 2004.

Silver, Alain and James Ursini. *The Noir Style*. Woodstock, NY: Overlook Press, 1999.

Slocum, David J., ed. *Violence and American Cinema*. New York: Routledge, 2001.

Stempel, Tom. *Storytellers to the Nation: A History of American Television Writing*. New York: Continuum, 1992.

Stephens, Michael L. *Film Noir: A Comprehensive, Illustrated Reference to Movies, Terms, and Persons*. Jefferson, NC: McFarland, 1995.

Telotte, J. P. *Voices in the Dark: The Narrative Patterns of Film Noir*. Urbana, IL: University of Illinois Press, 1989.

Thomson, David. *The Big Screen: The Story of the Movies*. New York: Farrar, Straus and Giroux, 2012.

Tuska, John. *Dark Cinema: American Film Noir in Cultural Perspective*. Westport, CT: Greenwood Press, 1984.

Tuska, John. *In Manors and Alleys: A Casebook on the American Detective Film*. Westport, CT: Greenwood Press, 1988.

Ward, Elizabeth and Alain Silver. *Raymond Chandler's Los Angeles: A Photographic Odyssey Accompanied by Passages from Chandler's Greatest Works*. Woodstock, NY: Overlook Press, 1987.

Willett, Ralph. *The Naked City: Urban Crime Fiction in the USA*. Manchester: Manchester University Press, 1996.

Introduction

Bargainnier, Earl F. "Melodrama as Formula," *Journal of Popular Culture*, Winter 1975.

"Casey, Press Photographer: Adventures of Dashing News Cameraman Make Exciting Listening," *Tune In*, February 1945.

"Cast Selected for WCBW-CBS Television Adaptation of *Crime Photographer*," CBS press release, 19 September 1945.

Chandler, Raymond. *The Big Sleep*. New York: Avon, 1942.

Clemenko, Harold B. "Detective Story," *TV Guide*, 14 November 1952.

"Coaxial Cable, Linking East and Midwest Video Outlets, Will Be Opened Tonight," *New York Times*, 11 January 1949.

Cooper, Wyllis. "Television Production As Viewed by a Motion Picture Producer," *Journal of the Society of Motion Picture Engineers*, August 1944.

"*Crime Photographer*, Long a Popular CBS Radio Feature, Comes to TV," CBS press release, 12 April 1951.

"Dead on Arrival," *Time*, 25 January 1954.

Dunning, John. *On the Air: The Encyclopedia of Old-Time Radio*. New York: Oxford University Press, 1998.

Dupuy, Judy. "Rev. of *Sorry, Wrong Number*," *Televiser*, March–April 1946.

Gomery, Douglas. "Finding TV's Pioneering Audiences," *Journal of Popular Film & Television*, Fall 2001.

Gould, Jack. "Crime, Mystery Shows Top Hooper Survey," *New York Times*, 18 August 1947.

Hammett, Dashiell. *The Maltese Falcon*. New York: Knopf, 1957.

Hand, Richard J. *Terror on the Air!: Horror Radio in America, 1931–1952*. Jefferson, NC: McFarland, 2006.

Haycraft, Howard. "The Burgeoning Whodunit," *New York Times*, 6 October 1946.

Hutchens, John K. "Report on Television's Way with a Melodrama," *New York Times*, 7 December 1941.

Huxley, Aldous. *The Perennial Philosophy*. London: Chatto & Windus, 1946.

"Image Orthicon Unveiled by RCA; Sock Reaction to Light Potentialities," *Variety*, 31 October 1945.

Kaufman, William I., ed. *The Best Television Plays of the Year*. New York: Merlin Press, 1950.

Kaufman, William I., ed. *The Best Television Plays 1950–1951*. New York: Merlin Press, 1952.

"*Lady in the Lake*: the Camera Becomes the Hero in a Robert Montgomery Picture," *Life*, 13 January 1947.

Landry, Bob. "*Mummy Case*, Television's Equivalent of *Great Train Robbery*, Shown in NY," *Variety*, 18 May 1938.

——. "Television's Future—and When," *Variety*, 4 January 1939.

Lindley, Denver. "Before Your Very Eyes," *Collier's*, 18 March 1939.

"Murder Most Foul," *Life*, 28 April 1952.

Nachman, Gerald. *Raised on Radio*. Berkeley and Los Angeles: University of California Press, 1998.

Neale, Steve. "Melo Talk: On the Meaning and Use of the Term Melodrama," *Velvet Light Trap*, Fall 1993.

Porter, Russell B. "Play Is Broadcast by Voice and Acting in Radio-Television," *New York Times*, 12 September 1928.

Reich-Baxter, John. "Getting Suspense into Video Drama," *Televiser*, June 1950.

Ritchie, Michael. *Please Stand By: A Prehistory of Television*. New York: Overlook Press, 1995.

Schickel, Richard. "Rerunning Film Noir," *The Wilson Quarterly*, Summer 2007.

Schindler, Raymond C. "TV Detectives Make Me Laugh," *Los Angeles Times*, 1 November 1953.

Skutch, Ira, ed. *Five Directors: The Golden Years of Radio*. Lanham, MD: Scarecrow Press, 1998.

Steffens, Mildred. "Television Drama," *Telescreen*, April 1946.

"Television Camera with the Eyes of a Cat!," RCA advertisement, *Televiser*, October 1950.

"Television: The Infant Grows Up," *Time*, 24 May 1948.

"TV's Westward Swing: Seventy Percent of Net Shows To Come from Hollywood," *The Billboard*, 17 June 1957.

Udelson, Joseph H. *The Great Television Race: A History of the American Television Industry, 1925–1941*. Tuscaloosa, AL: University of Alabama Press, 1982.

Van Horne, Harriet. "Views Coming Up: The Television Boys Are Pawing the Ground, Waiting to Spend Millions of Dollars to Entertain You Right at Home," *Collier's*, 13 October 1945.

"Who's Doing It in the Whodunits: *Dragnet* Tops in Reality But Private Eyes Are Still Open for Business," *TV Guide*, 18 September 1953.

The Black Angel (1945) and Other Early Noir Melodrama

Allan, Doug. *How to Write for Television*. New York: E. P. Dutton & Company, 1946.

Coe, Fred and Wyliss Cooper. *Lights Out*, teleplays. WNBT, 1945. NBC Collection, The Library of Congress, Washington, D.C.

Coe, Fred. *Bedelia*, teleplay. WNBT, 1945. NBC Collection, The Library of Congress, Washington, D.C.

Colling, Ernest. *The Black Angel*, teleplays. WNBT, 1945. NBC Collection, The Library of Congress, Washington, D.C. *Note*: All that remains of this series are fragments of the narration pre-recorded by Mary Patton on 27 January and 8 February, 1945; these are also held at the Library of Congress. *The Black Angel* was telecast in four parts: "Heartbreak," 28 January 1945; "Dr. Death," 11 February 1945; "Playboy," 18 February 1945; "The Last Name," 25 February 1945.

Colling, Ernest. *The Black Alibi*, teleplays. WNBT, 1946. NBC Collection, The Library of Congress, Washington, D.C.

Gates, Philippa. "The Maritorious Melodrama: Film Noir with a Female Detective," *Journal of Film and Video*, Fall 2009.

Hamilton, Patrick. *Angel Street*, teleplay. WNBT, 1945. NBC Collection, The Library of Congress, Washington, D.C.

Haycraft, Edward. "Evolution of the Whodunit in the Years of World War II," *New York Times*, 12 August 1945.

Hubbell, Richard. *Television Programming and Production*. New York: Murray Hill Books, 1945.

Koehler, Joe. Revs. of *Angel Street*, *The Billboard*, 26 January, 1946; *Dark Hammock*, *The Billboard*, 12 January 1946; "Dr. Death" (*The Black Angel*), *The Billboard*, 17 February 1945.

NBC Activity Report, 1945. NBC Collection, The Library of Congress, Washington, D.C. (Includes results of the first-ever television viewer survey regarding a dramatic program, conducted on January 28, 1945.)

Nevins, Francis M. Jr. *Cornell Woolrich: First You Dream, Then You Die*. New York: The Mysterious Press, 1988.

Orr, Mary and Denham, Reginald. *Dark Hammock*, teleplay. WNBT, 1946. NBC Collection, The Library of Congress, Washington, D.C.

Orr, Mary and Denham, Reginald. *Dark Hammock: A Play in Three Acts*. New York: Dramatists Play Service, 1946.

Patton, Mary (as told to Jena Phelps). "Acting on Television Is Tough—and Exciting," *Telescreen*, April 1946.

Phelps, Donald. "Cinema Gris: Woolrich-Neill's *Black Angel*." *Film Comment*, January–February 2000.

"Production's the Thing at NBC," *Televiser*, July–August 1946.

"Programming: WNBT [NBC], New York," *Television*, April 1945.

Reich, John, "Stage Plays for Television," *Televiser*, January–February 1946.

Rice, Robert. "Onward and Upward with the Arts: Diary of a Viewer," *The New Yorker*, 30 August 1947.

Royal, John F. *Television Production Problems*. New York: McGraw-Hill, 1948.

Skutch, Ira. *I Remember Television: A Memoir*. Metuchen, NJ: The Directors Guild of America and The Scarecrow Press, 1989.

Stanley, Fred. "Hollywood Crime and Romance," *New York Times*, 19 November 1944.

Woolrich, Cornell. *The Black Angel*. New York: Doubleday, Doran & Company, 1943.

Woolrich, Cornell. *Blues of a Lifetime: The Autobiography of Cornell Woolrich*. Mark T. Bassett, ed. Bowling Green, OH: The Popular Press, 1991.

Woolrich, Cornell. *The Bride Wore Black*. New York: Simon & Schuster, 1940.

Zolotow, Maurice. "Report on Television," *Coronet*, April 1945.

The Anthologies

"Balestrero's Nightmare: Life Story of Musician Falsely Accused of Theft Is Hit on TV," *Life*, 1 February 1954.

Barnouw, Eric. *The Golden Web: A History of Broadcasting in the United States, vol. 2, 1933–1953.* New York: Oxford University Press, 1968.

Barnouw, Eric. *The Image Empire: A History of Broadcasting in the United States, vol. 3, from 1953.* New York: Oxford University Press, 1970.

Baughman, James L. *Same Time, Same Station: Creating American Television, 1948–1961.* Baltimore: Johns Hopkins University Press, 2007.

Bernstein, Walter. *Inside Out: A Memoir of the Blacklist.* New York: Knopf, 1996.

Bretz, Rudy. *Techniques of Television Production.* New York: McGraw-Hill, 1953.

"CBS-TV Dramatic Program Requirements," CBS memorandum, ca. 1950. Print Archives, Paley Center for Media.

Chayefsky, Paddy. *Television Plays.* New York: Simon & Schuster, 1955.

Crosby, John. "Critic Mourns Passing of Five-Year-Old *Suspense*," *New York Herald Tribune*, 20 August 1954.

"Director Participation: Sidney Lumet Kisses, Fights, Dies, Running Two Top TV Shows a Week," *Life*, 8 June 1953.

"*Faceless Man* in Web-Sponsor Hassle," *The Billboard*, 7 April 1951.

Frankenheimer, John. *John Frankenheimer: A Conversation with Charles Champlin.* Burbank, CA: Riverwood Press, 1995.

Franklin M. Heller Papers, Billy Rose Theatre Collection, NYPL, New York. Note: Heller produced such live anthologies as *The Trap*, *The Web*, and *Danger*.

Gould, Jack. "Half-Act Drama," *New York Times*, 10 February, 1952.

Gould, Lewis L., ed. *Watching Television Come of Age: The New York Times Reviews by Jack Gould.* Austin: University of Texas Press, 2002.

"*The Hands of Murder*, A New Mystery Series," *New York Times*, 30 September 1949.

Harrington, Evans. "Knife in the Dark," *Saturday Evening Post*, 4 September 1954.

Highsmith, Patricia. *Plotting and Writing Suspense Fiction.* Boston: The Writer, 1966.

Kisseloff, Jeff. *The Box: An Oral History of Television, 1920–1961.* New York: Viking Penguin, 1995.

Krampner, John. "The Minds Behind TV's Most Fabled Anthology Take a Look Back," *Emmy*, June 1997.

Levine, R. M. "Live from New York, It's *Playhouse 90*—In the Beginning was Martin Manulis." *American Film*, December 1981.

Millstein, Gilbert. "Patterns of a Television Playwright," *New York Times Magazine*, 2 December 1956.

Miner, Worthington. *Worthington Miner: A Directors Guild of America Oral History.* Metuchen, NJ: Scarecrow Press, 1985.

Newcomb, Horace. *TV: The Most Popular Art.* New York: Anchor, 1974.

"A Place to Experiment," *Time*, 13 February 1950.

Raines, Halsey. "On Location in Gotham," *New York Times*, 15 April 1956.

Serling, Rod. *Four Television Plays.* New York: Simon & Schuster, 1957.

Smith, Cecil. "Paddy Made TV's 'Small Moment' An Art Form," *Los Angeles Times*, 5 August 1981.

Stasheff, Edward and Rudy Bretz. *The Television Program: Its Writing, Direction, and Production.* New York: A. A. Wynn. 1951.

Steele, L. T. "Report on Television," *American Mercury*, May 1948.

Stoetzel, George J. "White Is Black in Television," *New York Times*, 2 January 1949.

Stoetzel, George J. "Lighting Is Improved: Better Pictures Produced with Less Power," *New York Times*, 24 April 1949.

Stuart, William L. *Night Cry.* New York: The Dial Press, 1948.

"*Suspense*—Within Limits," *TV Guide*, 21 May 1954.

"Terror on TV," *Life*, 12 December 1949.

"What They Pay in Television," *New York Times*, 14 May 1950.

"What TV Is Doing to America," *U.S. News and World Report*, 2 September 1955.

Wilk, Max. *The Golden Age of Television: Notes from the Survivors.* New York: Delacorte Press, 1976.

Woolrich, Cornell. *The Black Path of Fear.* New York: Doubleday, Doran, 1944.

The Detectives

"Able *Kane*." *TV Guide*, 07 May 1954.

Bellamy, Ralph. *When the Smoke Hit the Fan.* New York: Doubleday, 1979.

"Bill Gargan as *Martin Kane*." *TV Guide*, 17 September 1949.

"Blueprint for *Man Against Crime*." Memorandum by R. J. Reynolds Tobacco to William Esty Agency, 1949. Tobacco Control Archives, Archives and Special Collections, UCSF.

"Dead on Arrival." *Time*, 25 January 1954.

"*Detective Story*: New Police Drama Is Super-Realistic Reporting," *Life*, 2 May 1949.

Frost, Barbara. "Ralph Bellamy Against Crime." *TV Guide*, 5 June 1951.

Gargan, William. *Why Me?* New York: Doubleday, 1969.

Gent, George. "Amiable Private Eye." *New York Times*, 30 August 1953.

Gould, Jack. "Rev. of *Martin Kane*," *New York Times*, 11 September 1949.

Inglis, Ruth A. "Lee Tracy in TV Action." *The American Mercury*, December 1953.

"The *Kane* Quartet." *Newsweek*, 27 March 1950.

"Lee Tracy vs. *Martin Kane*." *TV Guide*, 14 August 1953.

Marceau, William. "*Plainclothes Man*," *TV Digest*, 2 February 1952.

"Mr. Detective: Qualifications For a Successful Man Against Crime," *Radio-TV Mirror*, October 1951.

"Only One Murder." *Time*, 3 November 1952.

"Nominee for Alabama Atty. Gen. Murdered," *Los Angeles Times*, 19 June 1956.

Pennock, Pamela. "Televising Sin: Efforts to Restrict the Televised Advertising of Cigarettes and Alcohol in the United States, 1950s to 1980s," *Historical Journal of Film, Radio, and Television*, September 2005.

Pollay, Richard W. "Chronological Notes on the History of Cigarette Advertising." Working paper, 1987. History of Advertising Archives, University of British Columbia.

"Private Eye with Muscles," *TV Guide*, 15 May 1953.

"The Private Life of a Private Eye," *TV Guide*, 13 February 1952.

Weinstein, David. *The Forgotten Network: DuMont and the Birth of American Television*. Philadelphia: Temple University Press, 2004.

"William Gargan to Star in Adventure Series on Both WOR-Mutual and NBC Video," *New York Times*, 29 July 1949.

Hollywood Noir: The Rise of the Telefilm

"Agency Tours *Ford* Show to Sell Video," *The Billboard*, 4 March 1950.

"Big Advertisers Get Sales Pitch on *Gangbusters*," *The Billboard*, 10 July 1954.

Boddy, William. "The Studios Move into Prime Time: Hollywood and the Television Industry in the 1950s," *Cinema Journal*, Summer 1985.

Brady, Thomas F. "Television Had Another 'First' Last Week," *New York Times*, 31 August 1947.

———. "Hollywood Agenda: Looking Ahead," *New York Times*, 19 October 1947.

———. "Hollywood Gets on Television's Bandwagon," *New York Times*, 2 May 1948.

———. "Film Studio Lists Stories for Video," *New York Times*, 19 October 1948.

———. "Television Deal and Other Items," *New York Times*, 24 October 1948.

Bricken, Jules. "Success or Flop Hinges on One Thing—The Script." *The Billboard*, 14 June 1952.

"California as a Program Source," *Television*, April 1951.

"Consolidated Sells Hollywood as Sub for Ozzie," *The Billboard*, 6 June 1953.

Coughlan, Robert. "Now It Is Trouble That Is Supercolossal in Hollywood," *Life*, 13 August 1951.

"Crosby Sets High-Gear Production," *The Billboard*, 15 March 1952.

"Fairbanks Plans Sales Push for New Film Process," *The Billboard*, 20 August 1949.

Fairbanks, Jerry. "Film's Role in Video," *New York Times*, 13 June 1948.

Fairbanks, Jerry. "Everyone Wants a Cut, But TV Pic Isn't Big Enough," *The Billboard*, 14 June 1952.

"Filmed TV," *Newsweek*, 12 February 1952.

"Flight to the West," *Time*, 6 March 1950.

Girard, Benard. "Wise Planning Can Mean Both Quality and Economy," *The Billboard*, 15 June 1952.

Gould, Jack. "Satan's Waitin' Seen on Film," *New York Times*, 2 July 1950.

———. "A Plea for Live Video," *New York Times*, 7 December 1952.

Griswold, Wesley. "Why TV Is Going Movie-Mad," *Popular Science*, February 1955.

Heath, Arch B. and J. Raymond Hutchinson. "Making Motion Pictures for Television," *Televiser*, Spring 1945.

Hill, Gladwin. "Hollywood Is Wary of TV," *New York Times*, 24 April 1949.

———. "Showing Hollywood a Trick," *New York Times*, 25 June 1950.

"Hollywood Is Humming," *Time*, 20 October 1951.

"Hollywood TV Films," *Life*, 16 November 1953.

"Jerry Fairbanks to Produce Motion Pictures for NBC Television Outlet," *New York Times*, 14 January 1948.

Jerry Fairbanks Production Records, ca. 1940–1970, Performing Arts Special Collections, UCLA, Los Angeles.

Lafferty, William. "'No Attempt at Artiness, Profundity, or Significance': *Fireside Theatre* and the Rise of Filmed Television Programming," *Cinema Journal*, Fall 1987.

Lohan, Sidney. "Regarding a Tale of Woe from Hollywood," *New York Times*, 24 October 1948.

Lyons, Arthur. *Death on the Cheap: The Lost B Movies of Film Noir*. New York: Da Capo Press, 2000.

Kitses, Jim. *Gun Crazy* (BFI Film Classics). London: British Film Institute, 1996.

Mayer, Martin. "ABC: Portrait of a Network," *Show*, October 1961.

McCarthy, Todd and Charles Flynn, eds. *Kings of the Bs: Working Within the Hollywood System*. New York: E. P. Dutton, 1975.

McKaye, Milton. "The Big Brawl: Hollywood vs. Television," *Saturday Evening Post*, 26 January 1952.

"Plenty TV Pix If P&G-Levoy Venture Clicks," *The Billboard*, 9 July 1949.

Rand, Abby. "2500 Films—How Will They Change TV?," *Television*, July 1956.

Rubin, Stanley. "A Very Personal History of the First Sponsored Series on National Television," *The Journal of e-Media Studies*, 2008.

Schallert, Edwin. "Television Enters Big-Money Class," *Los Angeles Times*, 24 October 1948.

Scheuer, Philip K. "Link to Connect Movies and Television Forged," *Los Angeles Times*, 22 February 1948.

"Screen Gems This Week Bought *Edge of the Law*," *The Billboard*, 16 August 1952.

Taylor, John Russell. *Hitch: The Life and Times of Alfred Hitchcock*. New York: Da Capo Press, 1996.

"Ten Writers on Ford Pix at Screen Gems," *The Billboard*, 21 November 1953.

Woolrich, Cornell. "Three O'Clock," *Detective Fiction Weekly*, 1 October 1938.

Dragnet

Crosby, John. "*Dragnet* on Television." *New York Herald Tribune*, 6 February, 1952.

"Detective Story," *Newsweek*, 14 January 1952.

Domanick, Joe. *To Protect and to Serve: The LAPD's Century of War in the City of Dreams*. New York: Pocket Books, 1994.

"*Dragnet*," *TV Guide*, 15 February 1952.

Eells, George. "For *Dragnet*'s Jack Webb Crime Pays Off," *Look*, 8 September 1953.

"He Taught TV a Lesson," *TV Guide*, 24 July 1954.

Hewes, Henry. "Radio: Realistic 'Cops and Robbers' Saga," *New York Times*, 3 June 1951.

"How to Live on TV," *Newsweek*, 27 May 1957.

Hubler, Richard G. "Jack Webb: The Man Who Makes *Dragnet*," *Coronet*, September 1953.

"Jack, Be Nimble!," *Time*, 15 March 1954.

Jack Webb Collection of Scripts for Radio and Television, 1949–1975. Arts Library Special Collections, UCLA, Los Angeles.

Lewis, Richard Warren. "Happiness Is a Return to the Old Days," *TV Guide*, 19 October 1968.

"Life of Crime," *Time*, 22 September 1952.

Luciano, Patrick and Gary Corville. "Behind Badge 714:

The Story of Jack Webb and *Dragnet*," *Filmfax*, August–September and October–November 1993.

"The Mystery of Sgt. Friday's Partners," *TV Guide*, 12 December 1952.

Ovington, Reg. "Crime Without Guns," *Sunday Pictorial Review*, 28 June 1953.

Palmer, Barton R. "*Dragnet*, Film Noir, and Postwar Realism." In *The Philosophy of TV Noir*, Steven M. Sanders and Aeon J. Skoble, eds. Lexington, KY: The University Press of Kentucky, 2008.

"*Real, Rapid, Rugged: Dragnet* Catches Thirty-Eight Million Viewers," *TV Guide*, 10 April 1953.

"Real Thriller," *Time*, 15 May 1950.

Tregaskis, Richard. "The Cops' Favorite Make-Believe Cop," *Saturday Evening Post*, 26 September 1953.

"TV's Most Misunderstood Man," *TV Guide*, 23 March 1957.

Webb, Jack (as told to Dean Jennings). "The Facts About Me," *Saturday Evening*, 5, 12, and 19 September 1959.

Webb, Jack. *The Badge*. Englewood Cliffs, NJ: Prentice-Hall, 1958.

"Why Jack Webb Wants to Give Up *Dragnet*," *TV Guide*, 11 December 1953.

I Led 3 Lives

"Actor, Writer, Traveler: Now He's a TV Hero Who Fights Communism," *TV Guide*, 4 December 1953.

Doherty, Thomas Patrick. *Cold War, Cool Medium: Television, McCarthyism, and American Culture*. New York: Columbia University Press, 2003.

Jamison, Barbara Berch, "Actor with Eight Jobs: Richard Carlson Divides Time Among the Things He Likes to Do Best," *New York Times*, 9 May 1954.

Kackman, Michael. "Citizen, Communist, Counterspy: *I Led 3 Lives* and Television's Masculine Agent of History," *Cinema Journal*, vol. 38, no. 1, 1998.

"Nine Years Under Cover," *Time*, 11 February 1952.

Philbrick, Herbert, A. *I Led 3 Lives*. New York: McGraw-Hill, 1952.

Platt, David. "TV Series Saluting Stoolie Recalls Jack London's Classic on Scabs," *Daily Worker*, 9 September 1953.

"*3 Lives* Scores Victory in Syndicated Adventures," *The Billboard*, 31 July 1954.

Ziv Television Programs. Materials prepared for the annual award given by the Freedoms Foundation at Valley Forge, 1953, including correspondence from Elmer L. Lindseth, president, and Ralph M. Besse, executive vice president, The Cleveland Electric Illuminating Company. The Paley Center for Media.

M Squad

Johnson, Bob. "Assorted Blasts from an Angry Man," *TV Guide*. 3 October 1957.

Kirk, Christina. "Interview with Lee Marvin," *New York Sunday News*, 16 April 1966.

"Man in a Strait Jacket," *TV Guide*. 7 February 1959.

Page, Don. "*M Squad*'s Fiction, But It's Believable to Viewers," *Los Angeles Times*, 7 December 1958.

Slocum, William J. "The Scourge of Chicago's Hoodlums," *Coronet*, April 1949.

Stern, Michael. "The Toughest Cop in America," *Argosy*, April 1955.

Thomey, Ted. *The Glorious Decade*. New York: Ace Books, 1971.

Zec, Donald. *Marvin: The Story of Lee Marvin*. New York: St. Martin's Press, 1980.

Richard Diamond and Peter Gunn

Bender, Harold. "Diamond in a Beautiful Setting," *Pictorial TView*, 1 June 1958.

"David Janssen, Returning as Richard Diamond, Is Happy to Turn in His Saddle and Six-Gun," CBS press release, 26 January 1959.

Edwards, Blake. "The TV Scene: Taste of Public Runs in Cycles," *Los Angeles Times*, 3 November 1958.

"The Genius, the Movie Idol and the Private Eye," *TV Guide*, 12 September 1959.

"Have Gun, Will Unravel," *TV Guide*, 3 January 1959.

Hyams, Joe. "Writer Is Image of His Detectives," *Los Angeles Times*, 30 November 1959.

Lidz, Franz. "The Private Eye by Twilight," *New York Times*, 7 April 2002.

Luhr, William and Peter Lehman. "The Case of the Missing Lead Pipe Cinch: Blake Edwards' *Gunn* Within the Context of His Genre Films," *Wide Angle*, Spring 1976.

"Man with the Golden Touch," *TV Guide*, 13 February 1960.

Misurell, Ed. "A Private Eye Goes Western," *Pictorial TView*, 19 April 1959.

"The Nine Lives of a Private Eye!," *Parade*, 20 August 1950.

Page, Don. "Marlowe, King of All Sleuths, Comes to TV," *Los Angeles Times*, 4 October 1959.

"Private Eye Roughs Up Fifteen-Percenters," *Variety*, 14 January 1958.

Tepper, Ron. "*Peter Gunn* Background Music Lifts Composer Out of Realm of Unknown," *Los Angeles Times*, 15 March 1959.

Sunset Strip

Adams, Val. "Sleuthing Music in Hawaii—Private Eye Show to Be Treat for Ear," *New York Times*, 26 April 1959.

"The Address Is 77 Sunset Strip," *TV Guide*, 11 January 1964.

Baughman, James Lewis. "ABC and the Destruction of American Television, 1953–1961," *Business and Economic History: Second Series*, vol. 12, 1983.

Brady, Frank. *Hefner*. New York: Macmillan, 1974.

Huggins, Roy. *The Double Take*. New York: William Morrow & Co, 1946 [New York: Pocket Books, 1948]

Huggins, Roy. "Now You See It." *The Saturday Evening Post*, 25 May 1946.

Huggins, Roy. "Appointment with Fear," *The Saturday Evening Post*, 28 September 1946.

Huggins, Roy. "Death and the Skylark," *Esquire*, December 1952.

Mayer, Martin. "ABC: Portrait of a Network," *Show: The Magazine of the Arts*, October 1961.

McMurphy, Jean. "Efrem Zimbalist—a Private Eye with Culture," *Los Angeles Times*, 29 March 1959.

Scheuer, Philip. "Tone Private 'Op' in *I Love Trouble*," *Los Angeles Times*, 17 December 1947.

Shanley, John P. "Zimbalist—Private Eye with Musical Ear," *New York Times*, 15 March 1959.

——. "Maverick's Creator—a Cynical Approach," *New York Times*, 5 April 1959.

Stoddard, Sylvia. "77 *Sunset Strip*," *Television Chronicles*, January 1998.

Staccato

Cassavetes, John. "... And the Pursuit of Happiness," *Films and Filming*, February 1961.

Cassavetes, John. "This Film Called *Shadows*," *The Observer* (*Weekend Review*), 14 August 1960.

Cassavetes, John. "What's Wrong with Hollywood," *Film Culture*, April 1959.

"The Chip's Off His Shoulder," *TV Guide*, 28 November 1959.

Fine, Marshall. *Accidental Genius: How John Cassavetes Invented the American Independent Film*. New York: Hyperion, 2005.

Hoberman, J. "Beat Street: Meet Johnny Staccato, John Cassavetes' Hipster TV Detective," *Film Comment*, March–April 2005.

Lindbloom, Roland. "This TV Deception Draws No Gripes," *Newark Evening News*, 8 November 1959.

Linderman, Lawrence. "The Playboy Interview: John Cassavetes," *Playboy*, July 1971.

Humphrey, Hal. "*Staccato* Is Out of *Peter Gunn*," *Mirror News*, 10 September 1959.

Nathan, David. "I Welcome the New Johnny Staccato," *London Daily Herald*, 10 October 1960.

"No Torn Shirts for Him," *TV Guide*, 5 October 1957.

Salmaggi, Bob. "John Cassavetes: A Change of Heart," *New York Herald Tribune*, 2 August 1959.

Smith, Cecil. "Actor Directs No-Script Film," *Los Angeles Times*, 31 January 1960.

Smith, Cecil. "Actor Directs No-Script Film," *Los Angeles Times*, 31 January 1960.

Torre, Maria. "*Staccato* Blast Fired at Timidity of Sponsors," *New York Herald Tribune*, 8 December 1959.

The Twilight Zone

Albarella, Tony, ed. *As Timeless as Infinity: The Complete Twilight Zone Scripts of Rod Serling, vols. 1–10*. Colorado Springs, CO: Gauntlet Press, 2004–2011.

"Anatomy of a Script," *TV Guide*, 5 November 1960.

"Billion-Dollar Whipping Boy," *Television Age*, 4 November 1957.

Engel, Joel. *Serling: The Dreams and Nightmares of Life in the Twilight Zone*. Chicago: Contemporary, 1989.

"Fading into the *Twilight Zone*," *TV Guide*, 30 June 1962.

Harper, Ralph. *Nostalgia: An Existential Exploration of Longing and Fulfillment in the Modern Age*. Cleveland:, The Press of Western Reserve University, 1966.

Herndon, Ben, "Douglas Heyes: Behind the Scenes at *The Twilight Zone*," *Rod Serling's The Twilight Zone*, August 1982.

Herndon, Ben. "Great Shows: *The Twilight Zone*," *Emmy Magazine*, October 1982.

Keller, Allan. "Rod Serling: No One Tells Me What to Write," *New York World Telegram and Sun*, 26 December 1959.

Mandell, Paul. "'Walking Distance' from *The Twilight Zone*," *American Cinematographer*, June 1988.

Parker, James Edward. "Rod Serling's *The Twilight Zone*: A Critical Examination of Religious and Moralistic Themes and Motifs Presented in the Film Noir Style," diss., Ohio University, 1987.

"Rod Serling: Creator, Writer, Host," CBS press release, 13 September 1961.

Sander, Gordon F. *Serling: The Rise and Twilight of Television's Last Angry Man*. New York: Dutton, 1992.

Schumer, Arlen. *Visions from The Twilight Zone*. San Francisco: Chronicle Books, 1991.

Serling, Rod. "Seeking Far Horizons," *TV Guide*, 7 November 1959.

Serling, Rod. *Stories from The Twilight Zone*. New York: Bantam, 1960.

Serling, Rod. *More Stories from The Twilight Zone*. New York: Bantam, 1961.

Serling, Rod. "Rod Serling Tells Why Live Drama Is Dying," *New York Herald Tribune*, 8 August 1960.

Stanyard, Stewart T. *Dimensions Behind The Twilight Zone*. Toronto: ECW Press, 2007.

Wolfe, Peter. *In the Zone: The Twilight World of Rod Serling*. Bowling Green, OH: Bowling Green State University Popular Press, 1997.

Zicree, Mark Scott. *The Twilight Zone Companion, Second Edition*. Hollywood, CA: Silman-James, 1989.

Danger Man and The Prisoner

Asimov, Isaac. "Hitch Your Wagon to a Rock," *TV Guide*, 31 August 1968.

Barthel, Joan. "An Enigma Comes to American TV," *TV Guide*, 25 May 1968.

Carrazé, Alain and Hélène Oswald. *The Prisoner*. London: WH Allen & Co., 1990.

Chapman, James. *Saints & Avengers: British Adventure Series of the 1960s*. London: I. B. Tauris, 2002.

"*Danger Man*," ITC Pressbook, 1960.

"*Danger Man*, New Action Series, Bows on CBS Television," CBS press release, 9 February 1961.

Gardella, Kay. "The British Are Coming Warns CBS' *Secret Agent*," *New York Daily News*, 14 April 1965.

McGoohan, Patrick. "The LA Tapes," *Number Six*, Spring 1985.

Miller, Jeffrey S. *Something Completely Different: British Television and American Television*. Minneapolis, MN: University of Minnesota Press, 2000.

Musel, Robert. "James Bond Is No Hero to Him: The Incorruptible Patrick McGoohan," *TV Guide*, 14 May 1966.

Peel, John. *Number Six: The Prisoner Book*. Los Angeles: Schuster & Schuster, 1988.

Rogers, Dave. *The Prisoner and Danger Man*. London: Boxtree Limited, 1989.

"The Romantic Appeal of Patrick McGoohan," ITC press release, 1960.

Sakol, Jeannie. "Patrick McGoohan: Ferocious Goody Two-Shoes," *Cosmopolitan*, December 1969.

White, Matthew and Jaffer Ali. *The Official Prisoner Companion*. New York: Warner Books, 1998.

The Fugitive

Braxton, Greg. "Huggins' Brainchild on Big Screen: *Fugitive* Busts Out," *Los Angeles Times*, 6 August 1993.

Coyle, Paul Robert. "Great Shows: *The Fugitive*," *Emmy Magazine*, November–December 1982.

Dern, Marian. "Ever Want to Run Away from It All?," *TV Guide*, 22 February 1964.

"The Fuge," *Newsweek*, 26 April 1965.

Goodis, David. *Nightfall*. New York: Vintage Books, 1947.

Gordon, Stanley. "TV's Longest Chase," *Look*, 18 May 1965.

Hano, Arnold. "David's Dropping: Success Has Left *Fugitive*

Janssen Tired, Tense and Physically Ailing," *TV Guide*, 6 March 1965.

Kirk, Christina. "David Janssen: TV's *Fugitive*," *Coronet*, December 1965.

Morse, Barry. *Remember with Advantages: Chasing The Fugitive and Other Stories from an Actor's Life*. Jefferson, NC: McFarland & Co., 2006.

Nachman, Gerald. "David Janssen, TV's *Fugitive*, Finds a Safe Haven in the Role," *New York Post*, 20 August 1965.

Robertson, Ed. *The Fugitive Recaptured*. Los Angeles: Pomegranate Press, 1993.

Smith, Cecil. "A Show of Survival Manages to Survive," *New Haven Register*, 26 April 1964.

Whitney, Dwight. "He Never Did Much Running," *TV Guide*, 2 November 1963.

——. "He's the Long Arm of the Law—Who Always Ends Up a Little Short," *TV Guide*, 12 September 1964.

——. "The End of a Long Run," *TV Guide*, 19 August 1967.

Universal Noir

"A New Kind of King," *Time*, 1 January, 1965.

"Alone at Last: *Johnny North*," *TV Guide*, 2 May 1964.

Altman, Robert. David Thompson, ed. *Altman on Altman*. New York: Faber and Faber, 2006.

Adams, Val. "Movie Nights," *New York Times*, 28 January 1964.

Gardner, Paul. "New Film of *Ride the Pink Horse*," *New York Times*, 19 November 1964.

Goodwin, Fritz. "Bestriding the Entertainment World Like a Colossus," *TV Guide*, 25 July 1964 and 1 August 1964.

Hampton, Howard. "*The Killers*," *Film Comment*, March–April 1996.

Harding, Henry. "MCA vs USA," *TV Guide*, July 28, 1962.

Hemingway, Ernest. *The Nick Adams Stories*. New York: Scribner, 1972.

Hughes, Dorothy B. *Ride the Pink Horse*. New York: Duell, Sloan, and Pearce, 1946.

Hunter, Marjorie. "ABC Head Backs *Bus Stop* Episode, Tells Senators He Feared to Discourage Talent," *New York Times*, 25 January 1962.

Kaminsky, Stuart. *Don Siegel: Director*. New York: Curtis Books, 1974.

"*Killers* Done to Death," *Time*, 30 November 1959.

McGivern, William P. "Murder on the Turnpike," *Saturday Evening Post*, 7, 14, and 21 January 1961. Republished in *The Killer on the Turnpike and Other Stories*, New York: Pocket Books, 1961.

"Meanwhile Back in Hollywood, Efficiency Takes Over," *Life*, 20 December 1963.

"Mystery of Kraft TV *Suspense*: Bland as Cheese or Strong as Garlic?," *Variety*, 10 September 1963.

O'Brien, Daniel. *Robert Altman: Hollywood Survivor*. New York: Continuum, 1995.

Schumach, Murray. "Script Stressed by TV Executive," *Los Angeles Times*, 7 July 1961.

Siegel, Don. *A Siegel Film: An Autobiography*. Boston: Faber & Faber, 1993.

Smith, Cecil. "Colorful Uses of Film in the Night," *Los Angeles Times*, 2 April 1964.

——. "Making Movies to Fit the Tube," *Los Angeles Times*, 15 November 1964.

"Their Names Are on the Dotted Line," *TV Guide*, 13 April 1963.

"Twenty-Five Stations Yank Fabian *Bus Stop* Seg; ABC Blasted," *Variety*, 6 December 1961.

"Turnpike TV," *New York Times*, 15 September 1963.

Zuckoff, Mitchell. *Robert Altman: The Oral Biography*. New York: Knopf, 2009.

The Loner

Albarella, Tony. "Cowboy with a Conscience: *The Loner*," *Filmfax*, December 2000 and January 2001.

Frank, Stanley. "TV's Most Provocative Show," *Saturday Evening Post*, 13 February 1960.

Goodwin, F. "*The Loner*, Or: How They Put a Skin Diver on a Horse," *TV Guide*, 20 November 1965.

Lardner John. "The Air: The Hybrid West," *The New Yorker*, 18 Jan and 25 Jan 1958.

Let There Be Light. John Huston, dir., U.S. Army Pictorial Services, 1946.

Johnson, Robert. "A Headache in Three Acts: That's Rod Serling's Opinion of Writing for TV," *TV Guide*, 11 May 1957.

Lardner, John. "The Air: The Hybrid West," *The New Yorker*, 18 January 1958.

McVeigh, Stephen. *The American Western*. Edinburgh: Edinburgh University Press, 2007.

Metress, Christopher. "Submitted for their Approval: Rod Serling and the Lynching of Emmett Till," *The Mississippi Quarterly*, Winter 2008.

Quinn, Robert S. "A Study of Selected Teleplays of Rod Serling," diss., Univ. of Wisconsin, Madison, 1966.

Schickel, Richard. "Everything's Coming Up Loners," *Life*, 12 November 1965.

The Invaders

Armer, Alan. "Producer's Platform: Meet *The Invaders*," ABC press release, 14 December 1966.

Bowie, Stephen. "*The Invaders*: The Nightmare Has Already Begun." *Outré*, Fall 2000 and Spring 2001.

Etter, Jonathan. *Quinn Martin, Producer: A Behind-the-Scenes History of QM Productions and Its Founder*. Jefferson, NC: McFarland, 2003

"Fair Warning! *The Invaders* Are Infiltrating Our Planet," ABC press release, 30 December 1966.

Gerani, Gary. "*The Invaders*," *Starlog*, 16 September 1987.

Grant, Barry Keith. *Invasion of the Body Snatchers* (BFI Film Classics). London: Palgrave Macmillan, 2010.

Humphrey, Hal. "Larry's a Young Man in a Hurry," *Los Angeles Times*, 12 April 1965.

Reed, Rex. "Beware! *The Invaders* Are Coming!," *New York Times*, 19 March 1967.

"Strange Site Seeker," ABC press release, 3 February 1967.

Wilson, Anthony. "Beachhead," teleplay (final shooting draft). QM Productions, 25 February 1966.

Kolchak

"Darren McGavin: Interview," *New York Daily News*, 1 December 1974.

Dawidziak, Mark. *The Night Stalker Companion*. Beverly Hills, CA: The Pomegranate Press, 1997.

Diehl, Digby. "Old Take-Me-or-Leave-Me McGavin," *TV Guide*, 18 Jan 1969.

Kaminsky, Stuart M. (with Jeffrey H. Mahan). *American Television Genres*. Chicago: Nelson-Hall. 1985.

Rice, Jeff. *The Night Stalker* [*The Kolchak Papers*]. New York: Pocket Books, 1973.

Rice, Jeff. *The Night Strangler*. New York: Pocket Books, 1974.

Roegger, Berthe. "*Kolchak: The Night Stalker*," *Fangoria*, December 1979.

Smith, Cecil. "Dan Curtis Becomes New Pied Piper of Monster Tales," *Los Angeles Times*, 14 January 1973.

——. "K-K-K-Kolchak Is C-C-C-Coming Back in *The Night Stalker*," *Los Angeles Times*, 11 August 1974.

Stump, Al. "Orchestrated by Hoot Owls and Funnier Than a Hyena's Laugh," *TV Guide*, 15 December 1973

Telotte, J.P. *Dreams of Darkness: Fantasy and the Films of Val Lewton*. Urbana, IL:University of Illinois Press, 1985.

Harry O

Adler, Dick. "TV Cost Crisis: Should Producers Share the Blame?," *Los Angeles Times*, 14 November 1974.

Buck, Jerry. "One More Chance for *Harry O*," *The Courier-Journal & Times* [Associated Press], 3 February 1974.

Gardella, Kay. "Janssen Takes Second Stab at Pilot Film on ABC," *New York Daily News*, 31 January 1974.

Haber, Joyce. "A Series Game of Musical Shares," *Los Angeles Times*, 5 November 1974.

Knight, Bob. "WB Manages Rare Feat: Turning *Harry O* Around," *Variety*, 26 March 1975.

Robertson, Ed. "*Harry O*," *Television Chronicles*, July 1997.

Rodman, Howard. "So Long, Harry Orwell," *Panorama*, May 1980.

Rodman, Howard. Prefatory Notes and Outlines for *Such Dust as Dreams Are Made On*, 1972–1973. *Howard Rodman Papers, 1942–1977*, Wisconsin Historical Society, Madison, WI.

Smith, Cecil. "*Harry O* Says Farewell to San Diego, Hello to Santa Monica," *Los Angeles Times*, 8 December 1974

Stump, Al. "Whoops!: David Janssen Is Everything a Hero Should Be and More: He's a Klutz," *TV Guide*, 11 January 1975.

Thompson, Robert E. "Characters' Relationships More Important Than Whodunit Aspects in *Harry O*," ABC press release, 7 August 1974.

Thorburn, David. "Is TV Acting a Distinctive Art Form?" *New York Times*, 14 August 1977.

"Writers on Writing: Individualism and the Craft," *Fade In*, Winter 1979.

Zito, Stephen. "New Grub Street—West: Television Writers vs. the System," *American Film*, June 1977.

ACKNOWLEDGMENTS

Many of the chapters for TV Noir grew directly out of research I conducted for various exhibition projects during my time at the Paley Center for Media (formerly known as the Museum of Television & Radio). Aside from reflecting a deep-rooted fascination with film noir, this book is the distillation of fifteen-plus years spent as a curator, historian, and caretaker of television, both old and new. For that opportunity, as singular as it was unexpected, I'd like to thank Ron Simon for his mentorship and encouragement. I'd also like to acknowledge the valuable contributions of David Bushman with respect to the following chapters: *Dragnet, 77 Sunset Strip, The Loner, Harry O,* and *The Invaders.* And no book on television, or pop culture in general, is complete without the assistance of Jane Klain, the Paley's invaluable librarian.

In addition, I am especially grateful to Tracy Carns and the folks at The Overlook Press for their patience as *TV Noir* developed and evolved over nearly ten years. Thank you also to Bernard Schleifer for a superb design, Liz Driesbach for her terrific jacket, and Michael Mah and Paul Sugarman for their invaluable contributions. A shout-out is also owed to Paul Lucas of Janklow & Nesbit for shepherding this project up a very steep hill, and to his former colleague Svetlana Katz for initially bringing it to market. Special thanks as well to Mike Mashon and Karen Fishman at the Moving Image Section of the Library of Congress, and to the staff members of the Library of Performing Arts/New York Public Library at Lincoln Center and the UCLA Film & Television Archive. And, finally, a huge tip of the hat to Lauren Wilson for her editorial insight, copyediting expertise, and enduring support.

Excepting those images from my private collection, the illustrations in *TV Noir* are courtesy of Photofest Inc., and for that I am deeply indebted to Ron and Howard Mandelbaum for allowing me to spend many deliriously happy days digging through their magnificent archive. Additional images were sourced from Eddie Brandt's Saturday Matinee and Jerry Ohlinger's Movie Material Store. All images in this book are the respective copyright of CBS Corporation, Disney-ABC Television Group, Fox Entertainment Group, NBCUniversal, Netflix, Sony Pictures Entertainment, Time Warner, Viacom, and related subsidiaries. Any omissions will be credited in a future edition.

INDEX

INDEX

INDEX